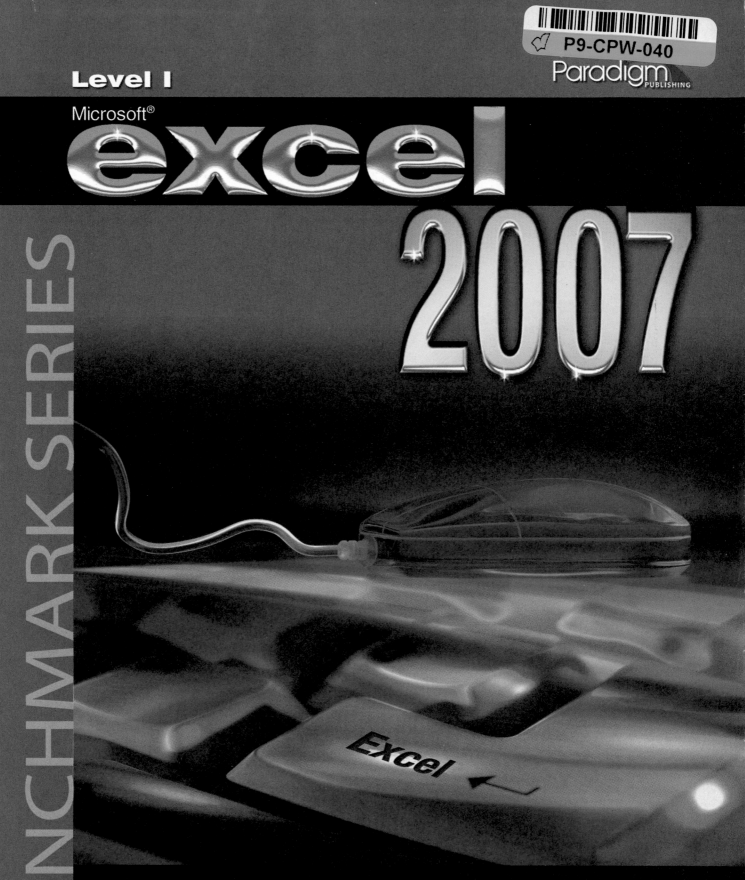

Level I

Microsoft®

excel
2007

BENCHMARK SERIES

Nita Rutkosky
Pierce College at Puyallup
Puyallup, Washington

Audrey Rutkosky Roggenkamp
Pierce College at Puyallup
Puyallup, Washington

Paradigm PUBLISHING

Managing Editor	Sonja Brown
Production Editor	Donna Mears
Cover and Text Designer	Leslie Anderson
Copy Editor	Susan Capecchi
Desktop Production	John Valo, Desktop Solutions
Proofreader	Laura Nelson
Indexer	Nancy Fulton

Acknowledgments: The authors and editors wish to thank Pamela J. Silvers, Chairperson, Business Computer Technologies, Asheville-Buncombe Technical Community College, Asheville, North Carolina, for testing the instruction and exercises for accuracy.

Care has been taken to verify the accuracy of information presented in this book. However, the authors, editors, and publisher cannot accept responsibility for Web, e-mail, newsgroup, or chat room subject matter or content, or for consequences from application of the information in this book, and make no warranty, expressed or implied, with respect to its content.

Photo Credits: Introduction page 1 (clockwise from top), Lexmark International, Inc., courtesy of Dell Inc., all rights Hewlett-Packard Company, Logitech, Micron Technology, Inc.; Excel Level 1 pages 1, 3, 4 © Corbis; photos in Student Resources CD, courtesy of Kelly Rutkosky and Michael Rutkosky.

Trademarks: Microsoft is a trademark or registered trademark of Microsoft Corporation in the United States and/or other countries. Some of the product names and company names included in this book have been used for identification purposes only and may be trademarks or registered trade names of their respective manufacturers and sellers. The authors, editors, and publisher disclaim any affiliation, association, or connection with, or sponsorship or endorsement by, such owners.

We have made every effort to trace the ownership of all copyrighted material and to secure permission from copyright holders. In the event of any question arising as to the use of any material, we will be pleased to make the necessary corrections in future printings. Thanks are due to the aforementioned authors, publishers, and agents for permission to use the materials indicated.

ISBN 978-0-76382-990-2 (Text)
ISBN 978-0-76383-005-2 (Text + CD)

© 2008 by Paradigm Publishing, Inc.
875 Montreal Way
St. Paul, MN 55102
E-mail: educate@emcp.com
Web site: www.emcp.com

Printed in the United States of America

16 15 14 13 12 11 10 09   3 4 5 6 7 8 9 10

CONTENTS

Unit 2 Enhancing the Display of Workbooks — 155

Chapter 5 Moving Data within and between Workbooks — 157

Chapter 6 Maintaining Workbooks — 199

Benchmark Microsoft Excel 2007 is designed for students who want to learn how to use this powerful spreadsheet program to manipulate numerical data in resolving issues related to finances or other numbers-based information. No prior knowledge of spreadsheets is required. After successfully completing a course using this textbook, students will be able to

- Create and edit spreadsheets of varying complexity
- Format cells, columns, and rows as well as entire workbooks in a uniform, attractive style
- Analyze numerical data and project outcomes to make informed decisions
- Plan, research, create, revise, and publish worksheets and workbooks to meet specific communication needs
- Given a workplace scenario requiring a numbers-based solution, assess the information requirements and then prepare the materials that achieve the goal efficiently and effectively

In addition to mastering Excel skills, students will learn the essential features and functions of computer hardware, the Windows XP operating system, and Internet Explorer 7.0. Upon completing the text, they can expect to be proficient in using Excel to organize, analyze, and present information.

Achieving Proficiency in Excel 2007

Since its inception several Office versions ago, the Benchmark Series has served as a standard of excellence in software instruction. Elements of the book function individually and collectively to create an inviting, comprehensive learning environment that produces successful computer users. On this and following pages, take a visual tour of the structure and features that comprise the highly popular Benchmark model.

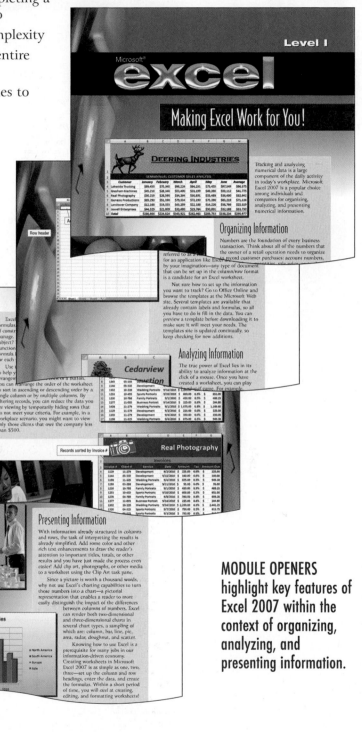

MODULE OPENERS highlight key features of Excel 2007 within the context of organizing, analyzing, and presenting information.

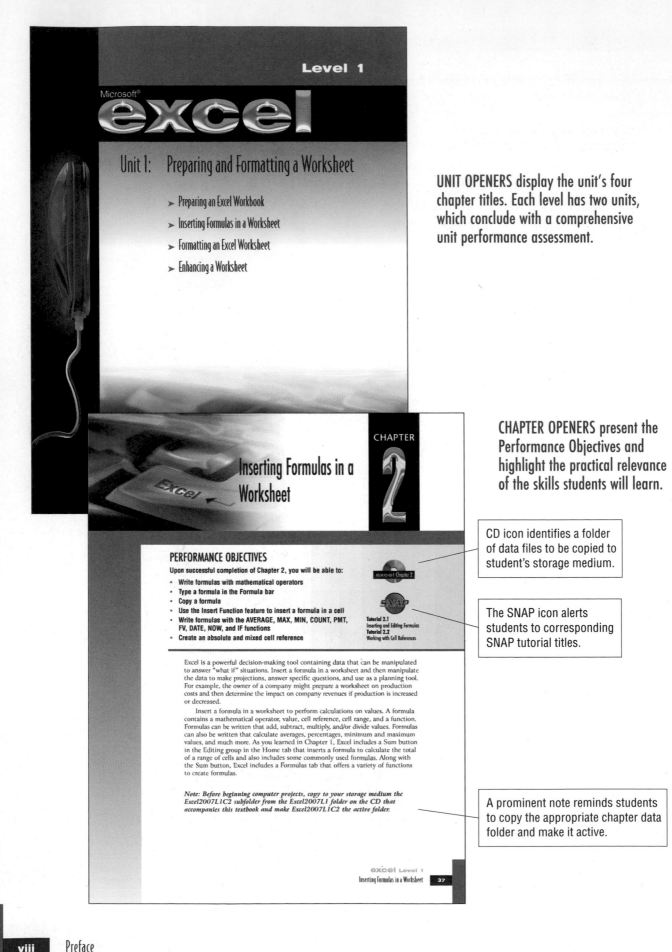

Level 1

Microsoft®
excel

Unit 1: Preparing and Formatting a Worksheet

➤ Preparing an Excel Workbook
➤ Inserting Formulas in a Worksheet
➤ Formatting an Excel Worksheet
➤ Enhancing a Worksheet

UNIT OPENERS display the unit's four chapter titles. Each level has two units, which conclude with a comprehensive unit performance assessment.

CHAPTER **2**

Inserting Formulas in a Worksheet

CHAPTER OPENERS present the Performance Objectives and highlight the practical relevance of the skills students will learn.

PERFORMANCE OBJECTIVES

Upon successful completion of Chapter 2, you will be able to:

• **Write formulas with mathematical operators**
• **Type a formula in the Formula bar**
• **Copy a formula**
• **Use the Insert Function feature to insert a formula in a cell**
• **Write formulas with the AVERAGE, MAX, MIN, COUNT, PMT, FV, DATE, NOW, and IF functions**
• **Create an absolute and mixed cell reference**

excel Chapter 2

SNAP
Tutorial 2.1
Inserting and Editing Formulas
Tutorial 2.2
Working with Cell References

CD icon identifies a folder of data files to be copied to student's storage medium.

The SNAP icon alerts students to corresponding SNAP tutorial titles.

Excel is a powerful decision-making tool containing data that can be manipulated to answer "what if" situations. Insert a formula in a worksheet and then manipulate the data to make projections, answer specific questions, and use as a planning tool. For example, the owner of a company might prepare a worksheet on production costs and then determine the impact on company revenues if production is increased or decreased.

Insert a formula in a worksheet to perform calculations on values. A formula contains a mathematical operator, value, cell reference, cell range, and a function. Formulas can be written that add, subtract, multiply, and/or divide values. Formulas can also be written that calculate averages, percentages, minimum and maximum values, and much more. As you learned in Chapter 1, Excel includes a Sum button in the Editing group in the Home tab that inserts a formula to calculate the total of a range of cells and also includes some commonly used formulas. Along with the Sum button, Excel includes a Formulas tab that offers a variety of functions to create formulas.

Note: Before beginning computer projects, copy to your storage medium the Excel2007L1C2 subfolder from the Excel2007L1 folder on the CD that accompanies this textbook and make Excel2007L1C2 the active folder.

A prominent note reminds students to copy the appropriate chapter data folder and make it active.

excel Level 1
Inserting Formulas in a Worksheet **37**

New! PROJECT APPROACH: Builds Skill Mastery within Realistic Context

Instruction and practice are organized into multipart projects that focus on related program features. A project overview identifies the tasks to accomplish and the key features to use in completing the work.

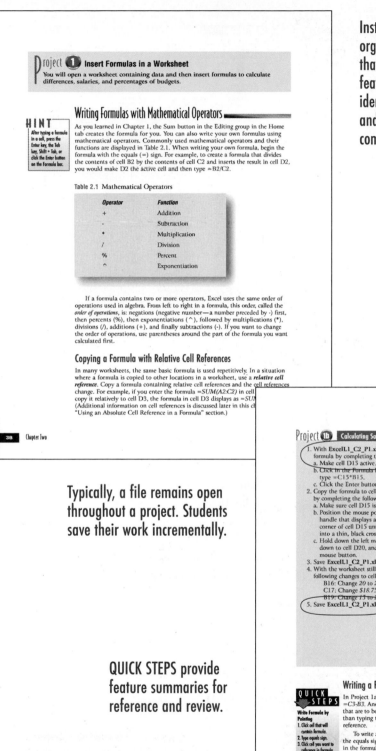

Typically, a file remains open throughout a project. Students save their work incrementally.

QUICK STEPS provide feature summaries for reference and review.

Following each project part, the text presents instruction on the features and skills necessary to accomplish the next task.

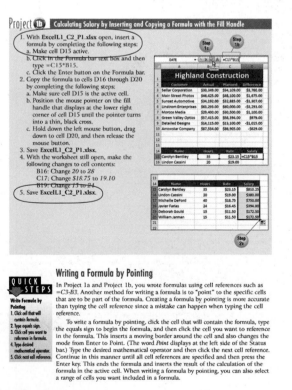

Each project exercise guides students step by step to the desired outcome. Screen captures illustrate what the screen should look like at key points.

Text in magenta identifies material to type.

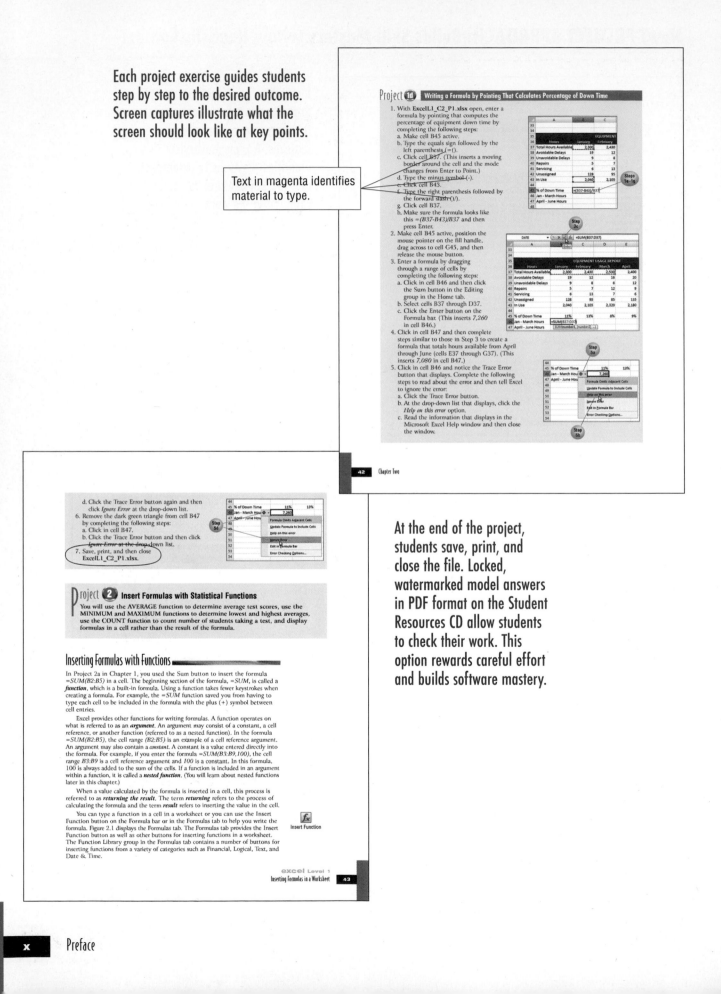

At the end of the project, students save, print, and close the file. Locked, watermarked model answers in PDF format on the Student Resources CD allow students to check their work. This option rewards careful effort and builds software mastery.

Inserting Formulas with Functions

In Project 2a in Chapter 1, you used the Sum button to insert the formula =SUM(B2:B5) in a cell. The beginning section of the formula, =SUM, is called a *function*, which is a built-in formula. Using a function takes fewer keystrokes when creating a formula. For example, the =SUM function saved you from having to type each cell to be included in the formula with the plus (+) symbol between cell entries.

Excel provides other functions for writing formulas. A function operates on what is referred to as an *argument*. An argument may consist of a constant, a cell reference, or another function (referred to as a nested function). In the formula =SUM(B2:B5), the cell range (B2:B5) is an example of a cell reference argument. An argument may also contain a *constant*. A constant is a value entered directly into the formula. For example, if you enter the formula =SUM(B3:B9,100), the cell range B3:B9 is a cell reference argument and 100 is a constant. In this formula, 100 is always added to the sum of the cells. If a function is included in an argument within a function, it is called a *nested function*. (You will learn about nested functions later in this chapter.)

When a value calculated by the formula is inserted in a cell, this process is referred to as *returning the result*. The term *returning* refers to the process of calculating the formula and the term *result* refers to inserting the value in the cell.

You can type a function in a cell in a worksheet or you can use the Insert Function button on the Formula bar or in the Formulas tab to help you write the formula. Figure 2.1 displays the Formulas tab. The Formulas tab provides the Insert Function button as well as other buttons for inserting functions in a worksheet. The Function Library group in the Formulas tab contains a number of buttons for inserting functions from a variety of categories such as Financial, Logical, Text, and Date & Time.

Insert Function

CHAPTER REVIEW ACTIVITIES: A Hierarchy of Learning Assessments

CHAPTER summary

- Change column width using the mouse on column boundaries or with options at the Column Width dialog box.
- To automatically adjust a column to accommodate the longest entry in the column, double-click the column header boundary on the right.
- Change row height using the mouse on row boundaries or with options at the Row Height dialog box.
- Insert a row in a worksheet with the Insert button in the Cells group in the Home tab or with options at the Insert dialog box.
- Insert a column in a worksheet with the Insert button in the Cells group or with options at the Insert dialog box.
- Delete a specific cell by clicking the Delete button arrow and then clicking *Delete Cells* at the drop-down list. At the Delete dialog box, specify if you want to delete just the cell or an entire row or column.
- Delete a selected row(s) or column(s) by clicking the Delete button in the Cells group.
- Delete cell contents by pressing the De____ the Editing group and then clicking Cl____
- Apply font formatting with buttons in ____
- Use the Mini toolbar to apply font for____
- Apply alignment formatting with but____ Home tab.
- Preview a worksheet by clicking the O____ clicking *Print Preview*.
- Change the size of the worksheet displ____ Preview tab or with the Zoom slider b____ Status bar.
- Use the Themes button in the Themes ____ theme to cells in a worksheet that app____ effects. Use the other buttons in the T____
- Format numbers in cells with the Acc____ Comma Style, Increase Decimal, and D____ group in the home tab. You can also a____ the Format Cells dialog box with the N____
- Apply formatting to cells in a workshe____ box. This dialog box includes the follo____ Alignment, Font, Border, and Patterns____
- Press F4 or Ctrl + Y to repeat the last ____
- Use the Format Painter button in the C____ formatting to different locations in a w____
- Hide selected columns or rows in a wo____ the Cells group in the Home tab, point ____ *Hide Columns* or *Hide Rows*.

CHAPTER SUMMARY captures the purpose and execution of key features.

- To make a hidden column visible, select the column to the left and right, click the Format button in the Cells group, point to *Hide & Unhide*, and then click *Unhide Columns*.
- To make a hidden row visible, select the row above and below, click the Format button in the Cells group, point to *Hide & Unhide*, and then click *Unhide Rows*.

COMMANDS review

FEATURE	RIBBON TAB, GROUP	BUTTON	KEYBOARD SHORTCUT
Format	Home, Cells	Format	
Insert cells, rows, columns	Home, Cells	Insert	
Delete cells, rows, columns	Home, Cells	Delete	
Clear cell or cell contents	Home, Editing		
Font	Home, Font		
Font size	Home, Font		
Increase Font Size	Home, Font		
Decrease Font Size	Home, Font		
Bold	Home, Font		
Italic	Home, Font		
Underline	Home, Font		
Borders	Home, Font		
Fill Color	Home, Font		
Font Color	Home, Font		
Top Align	Home, Alignment		
Middle Align	Home, Alignment		
Bottom Align	Home, Alignment		
Orientation	Home, Alignment		
Align Text Left	Home, Alignment		

COMMANDS REVIEW summarizes visually the major features and alternative methods of access.

FEATURE	RIBBON TAB, GROUP	BUTTON	KEYBOARD SHORTCUT
Center	Home, Alignment		
Align Text Right	Home, Alignment		
Decrease Indent	Home, Alignment		Ctrl + Alt + Shift + Tab
Increase Indent	Home, Alignment		Ctrl + Alt + Tab
Wrap Text	Home, Alignment		
Merge & Center	Home, Alignment		
Print Preview		Print, Print Preview	Ctrl + F2
Themes	Page Layout, Themes		
Number Format	Home, Number	General	
Accounting Number Format	Home, Number	$	
Percent Style	Home, Number	%	Ctrl + Shift + %
Increase Decimal	Home, Number		
Decrease Decimal	Home, Number		
Format Painter	Home, Clipboard		
Repeat			F4 or Ctrl + Y

CONCEPTS check

Test Your Knowledge

Completion: In the space provided at the right, indicate the correct term, symbol, or command.

1. To automatically adjust a column width to accommodate the longest entry in the cell, do this with the mouse on the column boundary.

2. By default, a column is inserted in this direction from the column containing the active cell.

3. To delete a row, select the row and then click the Delete button in this group in the Home tab.

CONCEPTS CHECK questions assess knowledge recall.

____, you can clear

____ or selected cells.

____ a cell.

____ nter data within

____ ned fashion

____ e Home tab to

____ atus bar, to

____ s $50.25, Excel
____ mber.

____ as 25%, Excel
____ mber.

____ the Alignment
____ dialog box with

15. You can repeat the last action performed with the command Ctrl + Y or pressing this function key.

16. The Format Painter button is located in this group in the Home tab.

17. To hide a column, select the column, click this button in the Cells group in the Home tab, point to *Hide & Unhide*, and then click *Hide Columns*.

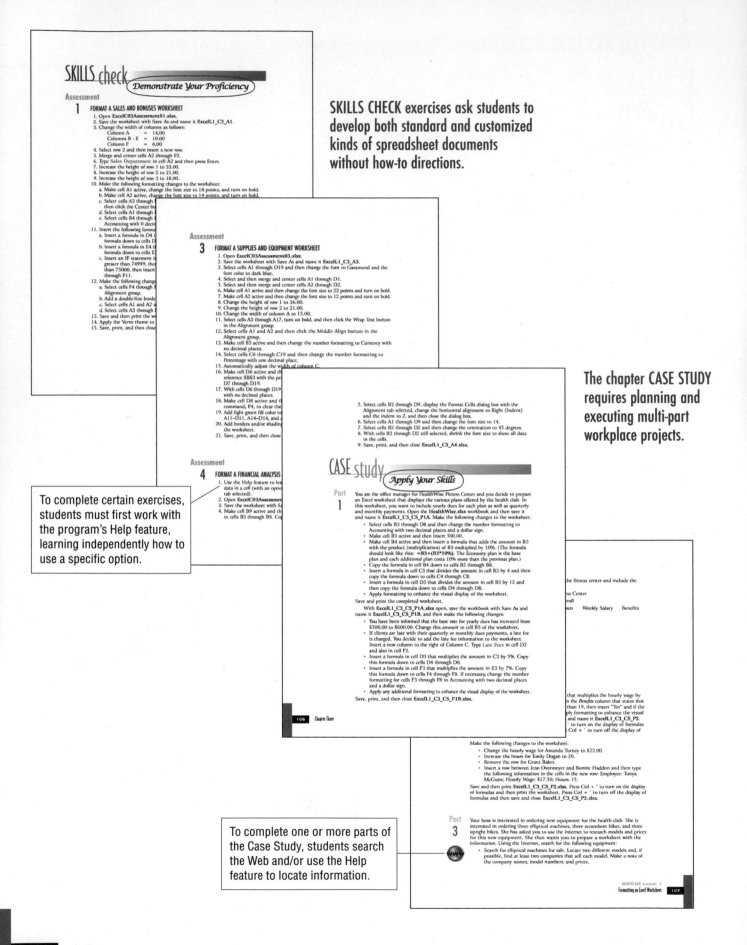

SKILLS check
Demonstrate Your Proficiency

Assessment

1 FORMAT A SALES AND BONUSES WORKSHEET

1. Open ExcelC03Assessment01.xlsx.
2. Save the worksheet with Save As and name it ExcelL1_C3_A1.
3. Change the width of columns as follows:

   Column A = 14.00
   Column B - E = 10.00
   Column F = 6.00
4. Select row 2 and then insert a new row.
5. Merge and center cells A2 through F2.
6. Type Sales Department in cell A2 and then press Enter.
7. Increase the height of row 1 to 33.00.
8. Increase the height of row 2 to 21.00.
9. Increase the height of row 3 to 18.00.
10. Make the following formatting changes to the worksheet:
    a. Make cell A1 active, change the font size to 18 points, and turn on bold.
    b. Make cell A2 active, change the font size to 14 points, and turn on bold.
    c. Select cells A3 through [...] then click the Center bu[...]
    d. Select cells A1 through [...]
    e. Select cells B4 through [...] Accounting with 0 deci[...]
11. Insert the following formu[...]
    a. Insert a formula in D4 t[...] formula down to cells D[...]
    b. Insert a formula in E4 t[...] formula down to cells E[...]
    c. Insert an IF statement i[...] greater than 74999, the[...] than 75000, then inser[...] through F11.
12. Make the following chang[...]
    a. Select cells F4 through [...] Alignment group.
    b. Add a double-line bord[...]
    c. Select cells A1 and A2 a[...]
    d. Select cells A3 through [...]
13. Save and then print the w[...]
14. Apply the Verve theme to [...]
15. Save, print, and then close [...]

Assessment

3 FORMAT A SUPPLIES AND EQUIPMENT WORKSHEET

1. Open ExcelC03Assessment03.xlsx.
2. Save the worksheet with Save As and name it ExcelL1_C3_A3.
3. Select cells A1 through D19 and then change the font to Garamond and the font color to dark blue.
4. Select and then merge and center cells A1 through D1.
5. Select and then merge and center cells A2 through D2.
6. Make cell A1 active and then change the font size to 22 points and turn on bold.
7. Make cell A2 active and then change the font size to 12 points and turn on bold.
8. Change the height of row 1 to 36.00.
9. Change the height of row 2 to 21.00.
10. Change the width of column A to 15.00.
11. Select cells A3 through A17, turn on bold, and then click the Wrap Text button in the Alignment group.
12. Select cells A1 and A2 and then click the Middle Align button in the Alignment group.
13. Make cell B3 active and then change the number formatting to Currency with no decimal places.
14. Select cells C6 through C19 and then change the number formatting to Percentage with one decimal place.
15. Automatically adjust the width of column C.
16. Make cell D6 active and th[...] reference $B$3 with the pe[...] D7 through D19.
17. With cells D6 through D19 [...] with no decimal places.
18. Make cell D8 active and t[...] command, F4, to clear the [...]
19. Add light green fill color to[...] A11-D11, A14-D14, and [...]
20. Add borders and/or shading[...] the worksheet.
21. Save, print, and then close [...]

Assessment

4 FORMAT A FINANCIAL ANALYSIS [...]

1. Use the Help feature to lea[...] data in a cell (with an optio[...] tab selected).
2. Open ExcelC03Assessmen[...]
3. Save the worksheet with S[...]
4. Make cell B9 active and the[...] in cells B3 through B8. Co[...]

SKILLS CHECK exercises ask students to
develop both standard and customized
kinds of spreadsheet documents
without how-to directions.

To complete certain exercises,
students must first work with
the program's Help feature,
learning independently how to
use a specific option.

5. Select cells B3 through D9, display the Format Cells dialog box with the Alignment tab selected, change the horizontal alignment to Right (Indent) and the indent to 2, and then close the dialog box.
6. Select cells A1 through D9 and then change the font size to 14.
7. Select cells B2 through D2 and then change the orientation to 45 degrees.
8. With cells B2 through D2 still selected, shrink the font size to show all data in the cells.
9. Save, print, and then close ExcelL1_C3_A4.xlsx.

CASE study
Apply Your Skills

Part 1

You are the office manager for HealthWise Fitness Center and you decide to prepare an Excel worksheet that displays the various plans offered by the health club. In this worksheet, you want to include yearly dues for each plan as well as quarterly and monthly payments. Open the **HealthWise.xlsx** workbook and then save it and name it **ExcelL1_C3_CS_P1A**. Make the following changes to the worksheet:

- Select cells B3 through D8 and then change the number formatting to Accounting with two decimal places and a dollar sign.
- Make cell B3 active and then insert 500.00.
- Make cell B4 active and then insert a formula that adds the amount in B3 with the product (multiplication) of B3 multiplied by 10%. (The formula should look like this: =B3+(B3*10%). The Economy plan is the base plan and each additional plan costs 10% more than the previous plan.)
- Copy the formula in cell B4 down to cells B5 through B8.
- Insert a formula in cell C3 that divides the amount in cell B3 by 4 and then copy the formula down to cells C4 through C8.
- Insert a formula in cell D3 that divides the amount in cell B3 by 12 and then copy the formula down to cells D4 through D8.
- Apply formatting to enhance the visual display of the worksheet.

Save and print the completed worksheet.

With **ExcelL1_C3_P1A.xlsx** open, save the workbook with Save As and name it **ExcelL1_C3_CS_P1B**, and then make the following changes:

- You have been informed that the base rate for yearly dues has increased from $500.00 to $600.00. Change this amount in cell B3 of the worksheet.
- If clients are late with their quarterly or monthly dues payments, a late fee is charged. You decide to add the late fee information to the worksheet. Insert a new column to the right of Column C. Type Late Fees in cell D2 and also in cell F2.
- Insert a formula in cell D3 that multiplies the amount in C3 by 5%. Copy this formula down to cells D4 through D8.
- Insert a formula in cell F3 that multiplies the amount in E3 by 7%. Copy this formula down to cells F4 through F8. If necessary, change the number formatting for cells F3 through F8 to Accounting with two decimal places and a dollar sign.
- Apply any additional formatting to enhance the visual display of the worksheet.

Save, print, and then close **ExcelL1_C3_CS_P1B.xlsx**.

The chapter CASE STUDY
requires planning and
executing multi-part
workplace projects.

[...] the fitness center and include the

[...]ss Center
[...]roll

[...]urs   Weekly Salary   Benefits

[...] that multiplies the hourly wage by
[...]n the *Benefits* column that states that
[...]than 19, then insert "Yes" and if the
[...]ply formatting to enhance the visual
[...] and name it ExcelL1_C3_CS_P2.
[...]` to turn on the display of formulas
[...] Ctrl + ` to turn off the display of

Make the following changes to the worksheet:

- Change the hourly wage for Amanda Turney to $22.00.
- Increase the hours for Emily Dugan to 20.
- Remove the row for Grant Baker.
- Insert a row between Jean Overmeyer and Bonnie Haddon and then type the following information in the cells in the new row: Employee: Tonya McGuire; Hourly Wage: $17.50; Hours: 15.

Save and then print **ExcelL1_C3_CS_P2.xlsx**. Press Ctrl + ` to turn on the display of formulas and then print the worksheet. Press Ctrl + ` to turn off the display of formulas and then save and close **ExcelL1_C3_CS_P2.xlsx**.

Part 3

Your boss is interested in ordering new equipment for the health club. She is interested in ordering three elliptical machines, three recumbent bikes, and three upright bikes. She has asked you to use the Internet to research models and prices for this new equipment. She then wants you to prepare a worksheet with the information. Using the Internet, search for the following equipment:

- Search for elliptical machines for sale. Locate two different models and, if possible, find at least two companies that each sell each model. Make a note of the company names, model numbers, and prices.

To complete one or more parts of
the Case Study, students search
the Web and/or use the Help
feature to locate information.

UNIT PERFORMANCE ASSESSMENT: Cross-Disciplinary, Comprehensive Evaluation

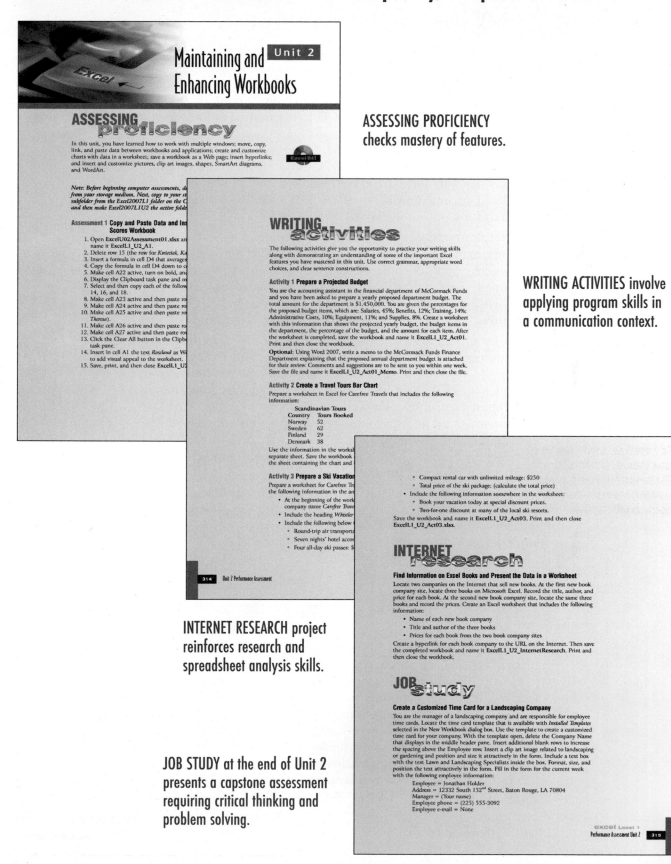

ASSESSING PROFICIENCY
checks mastery of features.

WRITING ACTIVITIES involve
applying program skills in
a communication context.

INTERNET RESEARCH project
reinforces research and
spreadsheet analysis skills.

JOB STUDY at the end of Unit 2
presents a capstone assessment
requiring critical thinking and
problem solving.

Student Courseware

Student Resources CD Each Benchmark Series textbook is packaged with a Student Resources CD containing the data files required for completing the projects and assessments. A CD icon and folder name displayed on the opening page of chapters reminds students to copy a folder of files from the CD to the desired storage medium before beginning the project exercises. Directions for copying folders are printed on the inside back cover. The Student Resources CD also contains the model answers in PDF format for the project exercises within chapters. Files are locked and watermarked, but students can compare their completed documents with the PDF files, either on screen or in hard copy (printed) format.

Internet Resource Center Additional learning tools and reference materials are available at the book-specific Web site at www.emcp.net/BenchmarkExcel07XP. Students can access the same resources that are on the Student Resources CD along with study aids, Web links, and tips for using computers effectively in academic and workplace settings.

SNAP Training and Assessment SNAP is a Web-based program that provides hands-on instruction, practice, and testing for learning Microsoft Office 2007 and Windows. SNAP course work simulates operations of Office 2007. The program is comprised of a Web-based learning management system, multimedia tutorials, performance skill items, a concept test bank, and online grade book and course planning tools. A CD-based set of tutorials teaching the basics of Office and Windows is also available for additional practice not requiring Internet access.

Class Connections Available for both WebCT and Blackboard e-learning platforms, Paradigm's Class Connection provides self-quizzes and study aids and facilitates communication among students and instructors via e-mail and e-discussion.

Instructor Resources

Curriculum Planner and Resources Instructor support for the Benchmark Series has been expanded to include a *Curriculum Planner and Resources* binder with CD. This all-in-one print resource includes planning resources such as Lesson Blueprints and sample course syllabi; presentation resources such as teaching hints and handouts; and assessment resources including an overview of assessment venues, model answers for intrachapter projects, and annotated model answers for end-of-chapter and end-of-unit assessments. Contents of the *Curriculum Planner and Resources* binder are also available on the Instructor's CD and on the password-protected Instructor's section of the Internet Resource Center for this title at www.emcp.com.

Computerized Test Generator Instructors can use ExamView test generating software and the provided bank of multiple-choice items to create customized Web-based or print tests.

System Requirements

This text is designed for the student to complete projects and assessments on a computer running a standard installation of Microsoft Office 2007, Professional Edition, and the Microsoft Windows XP operating system with Service Pack 2 or later. To effectively run this suite and operating system, your computer should be outfitted with the following:

- 500 MHz processor or higher; 256 MB RAM or higher
- DVD drive
- 2 GB of available hard-disk space
- CD-ROM drive
- 800 by 600 minimum monitor resolution; 1024 by 768 recommended
  Note: Screen captures in this book were created using 1024 by 768 resolution; screens with higher resolution may look different.
- Computer mouse or compatible pointing device

About the Authors

Nita Rutkosky began teaching business education courses at Pierce College in Puyallup, Washington, in 1978. Since then she has taught a variety of software applications to students in postsecondary Information Technology certificate and degree programs. In addition to co-authoring texts in the *Benchmark Office 2007 Series*, she has co-authored *Signature Word 2007, Marquee Office 2007,* and *Using Computers in the Medical Office: Microsoft Word, Excel, and PowerPoint 2003.* Other textbooks she has written for Paradigm Publishing include books on previous versions of Microsoft Office along with WordPerfect, desktop publishing, keyboarding, and voice recognition.

Audrey Rutkosky Roggenkamp has been teaching courses in the Business Information Technology department at Pierce College in Puyallup including keyboarding, skill building, and Microsoft Office programs. In addition to titles in the *Benchmark Office 2007 Series*, she has co-authored *Using Computers in the Medical Office, Marquee Office 2007,* and *Signature Word 2007.*

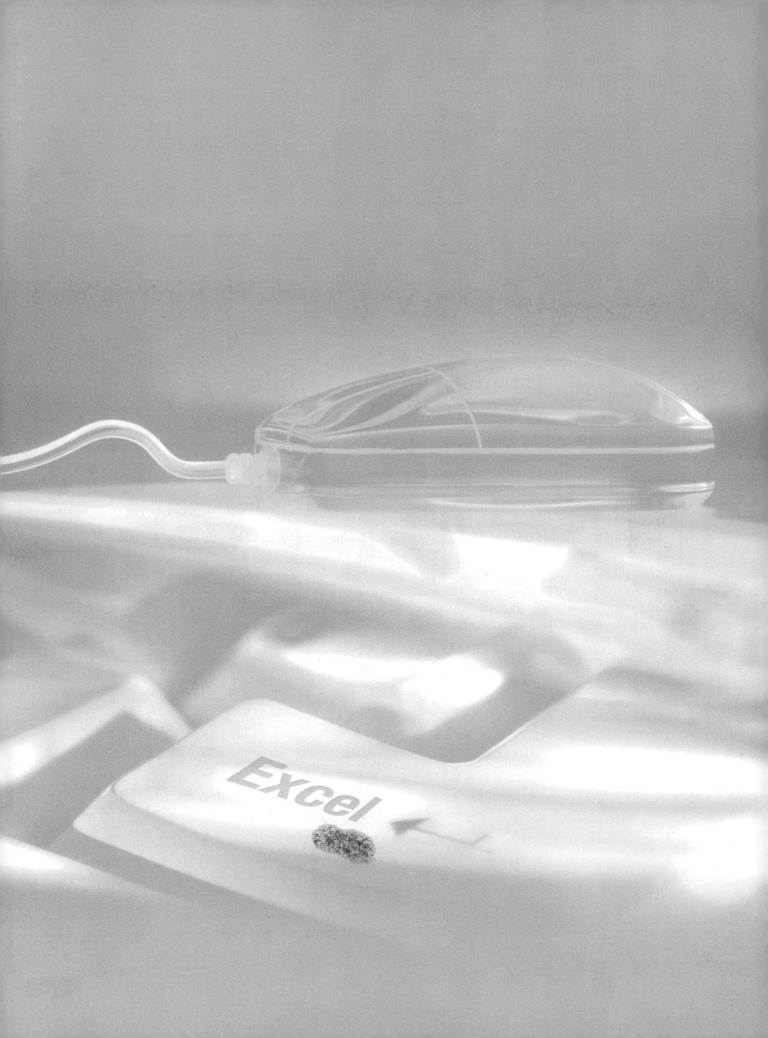

Getting Started in Office 2007

In this textbook, you will learn to operate several computer application programs that combine to make an application "suite." This suite of programs is called Microsoft Office 2007. The programs you will learn to operate are the software, which includes instructions telling the computer what to do. Some of the application programs in the suite include a word processing program named Word, a spreadsheet program named Excel, a database program named Access, and a presentation program named PowerPoint.

Identifying Computer Hardware

The computer equipment you will use to operate the suite of programs is referred to as hardware. You will need access to a microcomputer system that should consist of the CPU, monitor, keyboard, printer, drives, and mouse. If you are not sure what equipment you will be operating, check with your instructor. The computer system shown in Figure G.1 consists of six components. Each component is discussed separately in the material that follows.

Figure G.1 Microcomputer System

CPU

CPU stands for Central Processing Unit and it is the intelligence of the computer. All the processing occurs in the CPU. Silicon chips, which contain miniaturized circuitry, are placed on boards that are plugged into slots within the CPU. Whenever an instruction is given to the computer, that instruction is processed through circuitry in the CPU.

Monitor

The monitor is a piece of equipment that looks like a television screen. It displays the information of a program and the text being input at the keyboard. The quality of display for monitors varies depending on the type of monitor and the level of resolution. Monitors can also vary in size—generally from 14-inch size up to 21-inch size or larger.

Keyboard

The keyboard is used to input information into the computer. Keyboards for microcomputers vary in the number and location of the keys. Microcomputers have the alphabetic and numeric keys in the same location as the keys on a typewriter. The symbol keys, however, may be placed in a variety of locations, depending on the manufacturer. In addition to letters, numbers, and symbols, most microcomputer keyboards contain function keys, arrow keys, and a numeric keypad. Figure G.2 shows an enhanced keyboard.

Figure G.2 Keyboard

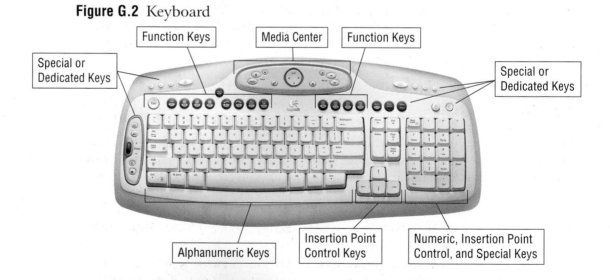

The 12 keys at the top of the keyboard, labeled with the letter F followed by a number, are called *function keys*. Use these keys to perform functions within each of the suite programs. To the right of the regular keys is a group of *special* or *dedicated keys*. These keys are labeled with specific functions that will be performed when you press the key. Below the special keys are arrow keys. Use these keys to move the insertion point in the document screen.

A keyboard generally includes three mode indicator lights. When you select certain modes, a light appears on the keyboard. For example, if you press the Caps Lock key, which disables the lowercase alphabet, a light appears next to Caps Lock. Similarly, pressing the Num Lock key will disable the special functions on the numeric keypad, which is located at the right side of the keyboard.

Disk Drives

Depending on the computer system you are using, Microsoft Office 2007 is installed on a hard drive or as part of a network system. Whether you are using Office on a hard drive or network system, you will need to have available a DVD or CD drive and a USB drive or other storage medium. You will insert the CD (compact disc) that accompanies this textbook in the DVD or CD drive and then copy folders from the CD to your storage medium. You will also save documents you complete at the computer to folders on your storage medium.

Printer

A document you create in Word is considered soft copy. If you want a hard copy of a document, you need to print it. To print documents you will need to access a printer, which will probably be either a laser printer or an ink-jet printer. A laser printer uses a laser beam combined with heat and pressure to print documents, while an ink-jet printer prints a document by spraying a fine mist of ink on the page.

Mouse

Many functions in the suite of programs are designed to operate more efficiently with a mouse. A mouse is an input device that sits on a flat surface next to the computer. You can operate a mouse with the left or the right hand. Moving the mouse on the flat surface causes a corresponding mouse pointer to move on the screen. Figure G.1 shows an illustration of a mouse.

Using the Mouse

The programs in the Microsoft Office suite can be operated using a keyboard or they can be operated with the keyboard and a mouse. The mouse may have two or three buttons on top, which are tapped to execute specific functions and commands. To use the mouse, rest it on a flat surface or a mouse pad. Put your hand over it with your palm resting on top of the mouse and your wrist resting on the table surface. As you move the mouse on the flat surface, a corresponding pointer moves on the screen.

When using the mouse, you should understand four terms—point, click, double-click, and drag. When operating the mouse, you may need to point to a specific command, button, or icon. Point means to position the mouse pointer on the desired item. With the mouse pointer positioned on the desired item, you may need to click a button on the mouse. Click means quickly tapping a button on the mouse once. To complete two steps at one time, such as choosing and then executing a function, double-click a mouse button. Double-click means to tap the left mouse button twice in quick succession. The term drag means to press and hold the left mouse button, move the mouse pointer to a specific location, and then release the button.

Using the Mouse Pointer

The mouse pointer will change appearance depending on the function being performed or where the pointer is positioned. The mouse pointer may appear as one of the following images:

- The mouse pointer appears as an I-beam (called the I-beam pointer) in the document screen and can be used to move the insertion point or select text.

- The mouse pointer appears as an arrow pointing up and to the left (called the arrow pointer) when it is moved to the Title bar, Quick Access toolbar, ribbon, or an option in a dialog box. For example, to open a new document with the mouse, position the I-beam pointer on the Office button located in the upper left corner of the screen until the pointer turns into an arrow pointer and then click the left mouse button. At the drop-down list that displays, make a selection by positioning the arrow pointer on the desired option and then clicking the left mouse button.

- The mouse pointer becomes a double-headed arrow (either pointing left and right, pointing up and down, or pointing diagonally) when performing certain functions such as changing the size of an object.

- In certain situations, such as moving an object or image, the mouse pointer becomes a four-headed arrow. The four-headed arrow means that you can move the object left, right, up, or down.

- When a request is being processed or when a program is being loaded, the mouse pointer may appear with an hourglass beside it. The hourglass image means "please wait." When the process is completed, the hourglass image is removed.

- The mouse pointer displays as a hand with a pointing index finger in certain functions such as Help and indicates that more information is available about the item.

Choosing Commands

Once a program is open, you can use several methods in the program to choose commands. A command is an instruction that tells the program to do something. You can choose a command using the mouse or the keyboard. When a program such as Word or PowerPoint is open, the ribbon contains buttons for completing tasks and contains tabs you click to display additional buttons. To choose a button on the Quick Access toolbar or in the ribbon, position the tip of the mouse arrow pointer on a button and then click the left mouse button.

The Office suite provides access keys you can press to use a command in a program. Press the Alt key on the keyboard to display KeyTips that identify the access key you need to press to execute a command. For example, press the Alt key in a Word document and KeyTips display as shown in Figure G.3. Continue pressing access keys until you execute the desired command. For example, if you want to begin spell checking a document, you would press the Alt key, press the R key on the keyboard to display the Review tab, and then press the letter S on the keyboard.

Figure G.3 Word KeyTips

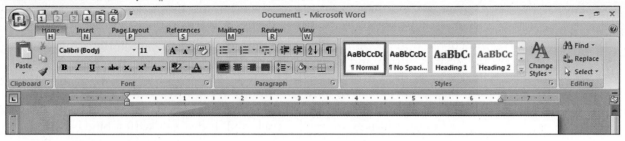

Choosing Commands from Drop-Down Lists

To choose a command from a drop-down list with the mouse, position the mouse pointer on the desired option and then click the left mouse button. To make a selection from a drop-down list with the keyboard, type the underlined letter in the desired option.

Some options at a drop-down list may be gray-shaded (dimmed), indicating that the option is currently unavailable. If an option at a drop-down list displays preceded by a check mark, that indicates that the option is currently active. If an option at a drop-down list displays followed by an ellipsis (…), a dialog box will display when that option is chosen.

Choosing Options from a Dialog Box

A dialog box contains options for applying formatting to a file or data within a file. Some dialog boxes display with tabs along the top providing additional options. For example, the Font dialog box shown in Figure G.4 contains two tabs—the Font tab and the Character Spacing tab. The tab that displays in the front is the

Figure G.4 Word Font Dialog Box

Dialog box tabs

| Font | Character Spacing |

Font:

+Body

+Body
+Headings
Agency FB
Aharoni
Albertus Extra Bold

Font style:

Regular

Regular
Italic
Bold
Bold Italic

Size:

11

8
9
10
11
12

Font color: Automatic

Underline style: (none)

Underline color: Automatic

Effects

Check boxes

☐ Strikethrough
☐ Double strikethrough
☐ Superscript
☐ Subscript

☐ Shadow
☐ Outline
☐ Emboss
☐ Engrave

☐ Small caps
☐ All caps
☐ Hidden

Preview

+Body

This is the body theme font. The current document theme defines which font will be used.

Default...   OK   Cancel

active tab. To make a tab active using the mouse, position the arrow pointer on the desired tab and then click the left mouse button. If you are using the keyboard, press Ctrl + Tab or press Alt + the underlined letter on the desired tab.

To choose options from a dialog box with the mouse, position the arrow pointer on the desired option and then click the left mouse button. If you are using the keyboard, press the Tab key to move the insertion point forward from option to option. Press Shift + Tab to move the insertion point backward from option to option. You can also hold down the Alt key and then press the underlined letter of the desired option. When an option is selected, it displays with a blue background or surrounded by a dashed box called a marquee. A dialog box contains one or more of the following elements: text boxes, list boxes, check boxes, option buttons, spin boxes, and command buttons.

Text Boxes

Some options in a dialog box require you to enter text. For example, the boxes below the *Find what* and *Replace with* options at the Excel Find and Replace dialog box shown in Figure G.5 are text boxes. In a text box, you type text or edit existing text. Edit text in a text box in the same manner as normal text. Use the Left and Right Arrow keys on the keyboard to move the insertion point without deleting text and use the Delete key or Backspace key to delete text.

Figure G.5 Excel Find and Replace Dialog Box

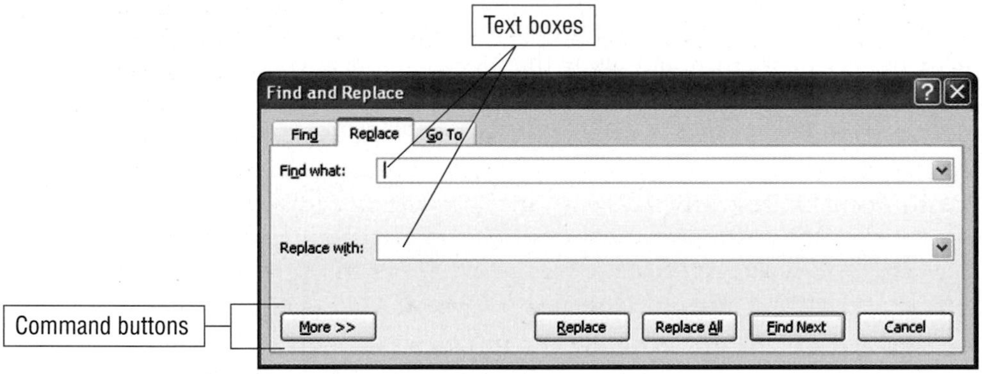

List Boxes

Some dialog boxes such as the Word Open dialog box shown in Figure G.6 may contain a list box. The list of files below the *Look in* option is contained in a list box. To make a selection from a list box with the mouse, move the arrow pointer to the desired option and then click the left mouse button.

Figure G.6 Word Open Dialog Box

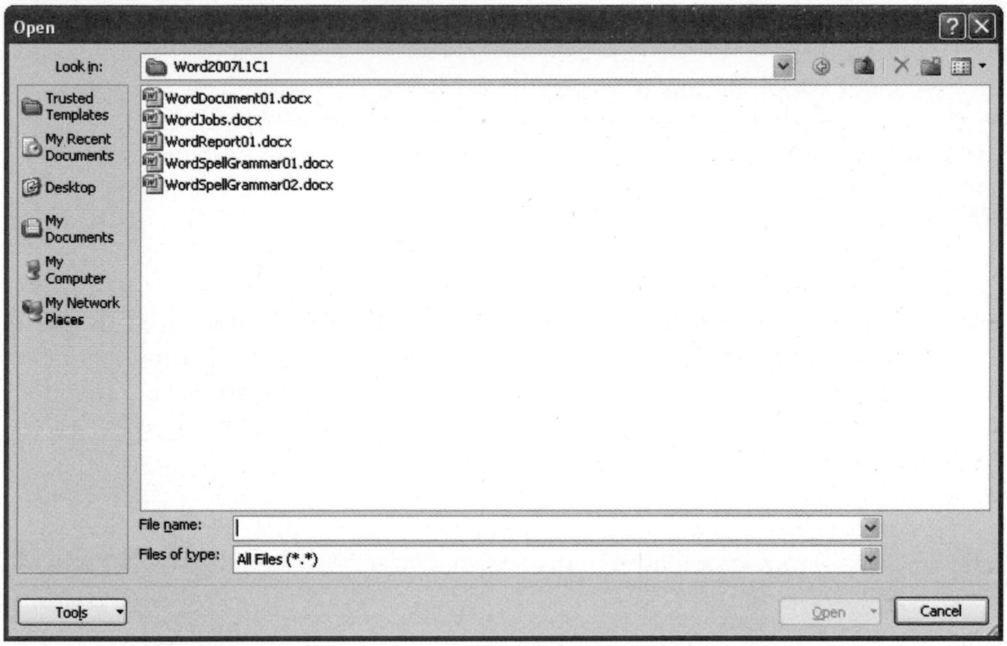

Some list boxes may contain a scroll bar. This scroll bar will display at the right side of the list box (a vertical scroll bar) or at the bottom of the list box (a horizontal scroll bar). You can use a vertical scroll bar or a horizontal scroll bar to move through the list if the list is longer than the box. To move down through a list on a vertical scroll bar, position the arrow pointer on the down-pointing arrow and hold down the left mouse button. To scroll up through the list in a vertical scroll bar, position the arrow pointer on the up-pointing arrow and hold down the left mouse button. You can also move the arrow pointer above the scroll box and click the left mouse button to scroll up the list or move the arrow pointer below the scroll box and click the left mouse button to move down the list. To move through a list with a horizontal scroll bar, click the left-pointing arrow to scroll to the left of the list or click the right-pointing arrow to scroll to the right of the list.

To make a selection from a list using the keyboard, move the insertion point into the box by holding down the Alt key and pressing the underlined letter of the desired option. Press the Up and/or Down Arrow keys on the keyboard to move through the list.

In some dialog boxes where enough room is not available for a list box, lists of options are inserted in a drop-down list box. Options that contain a drop-down list box display with a down-pointing arrow. For example, the *Underline style* option at the Word Font dialog box shown in Figure G.4 contains a drop-down list. To display the list, click the down-pointing arrow to the right of the *Underline style* option box. If you are using the keyboard, press Alt + U.

Check Boxes

Some dialog boxes contain options preceded by a box. A check mark may or may not appear in the box. The Word Font dialog box shown in Figure G.4 displays a variety of check boxes within the *Effects* section. If a check mark appears in the box, the option is active (turned on). If the check box does not contain a check mark, the option is inactive (turned off). Any number of check boxes can be active. For example, in the Word Font dialog box, you can insert a check mark in any or all of the boxes in the *Effects* section and these options will be active.

To make a check box active or inactive with the mouse, position the tip of the arrow pointer in the check box and then click the left mouse button. If you are using the keyboard, press Alt + the underlined letter of the desired option.

Option Buttons

The Word Print dialog box shown in Figure G.7 contains options in the *Print range* section preceded by option buttons. Only one option button can be selected at any time. When an option button is selected, a green circle displays in the button. To select an option button with the mouse, position the tip of the arrow pointer inside the option button and then click the left mouse button. To make a selection with the keyboard, hold down the Alt key and then press the underlined letter of the desired option.

Figure G.7 Word Print Dialog Box

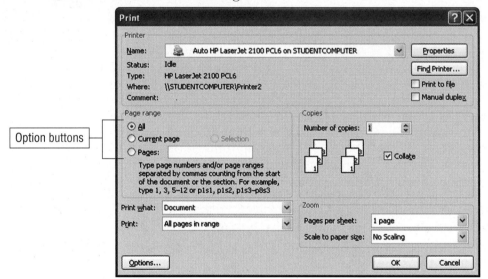

Spin Boxes

Some options in a dialog box contain measurements or numbers you can increase or decrease. These options are generally located in a spin box. For example, the Word Paragraph dialog box shown in Figure G.8 contains spin boxes located after the *Left, Right, Before,* and *After* options. To increase a number in a spin box, position the tip of the arrow pointer on the up-pointing arrow to the right of the desired option and then click the left mouse button. To decrease the number, click the down-pointing arrow. If you are using the keyboard, press Alt + the underlined letter of the desired option and then press the Up Arrow key to increase the number or the Down Arrow key to decrease the number.

Figure G.8 Word Paragraph Dialog Box

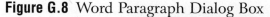

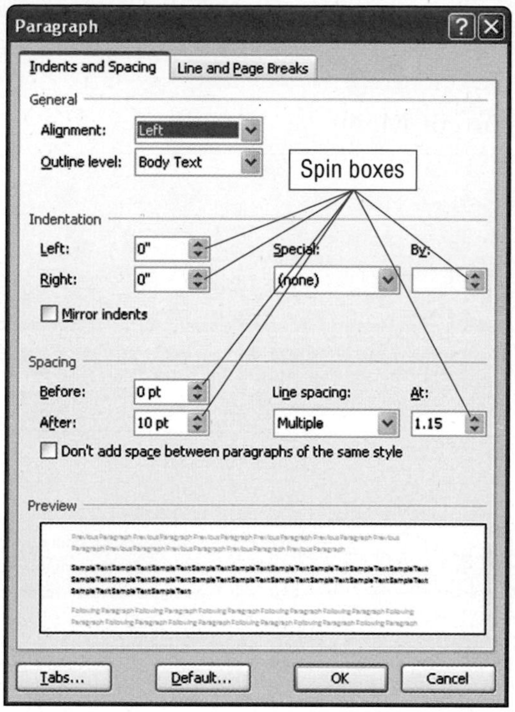

Command Buttons

In the Excel Find and Replace dialog box shown in Figure G.5, the boxes along the bottom of the dialog box are called command buttons. Use a command button to execute or cancel a command. Some command buttons display with an ellipsis (...). A command button that displays with an ellipsis will open another dialog box. To choose a command button with the mouse, position the arrow pointer on the desired button and then click the left mouse button. To choose a command button with the keyboard, press the Tab key until the desired command button contains the marquee and then press the Enter key.

Choosing Commands with Keyboard Shortcuts

Applications in the Office suite offer a variety of keyboard shortcuts you can use to executive specific commands. Keyboard shortcuts generally require two or more keys. For example, the keyboard shortcut to display the Open dialog box in an application is Ctrl + O. To use this keyboard shortcut, hold down the Ctrl key, type the letter O on the keyboard, and then release the Ctrl key. For a list of keyboard shortcuts, refer to the Help files.

Choosing Commands with Shortcut Menus

The software programs in the suite include menus that contain commands related to the item with which you are working. A shortcut menu appears in the file in the location where you are working. To display a shortcut menu, click the right mouse button or press Shift + F10. For example, if the insertion point is positioned in a paragraph of text in a Word document, clicking the right mouse button or pressing Shift + F10 will cause the shortcut menu shown in Figure G.9 to display in the document screen.

Figure G.9 Word Shortcut Menu

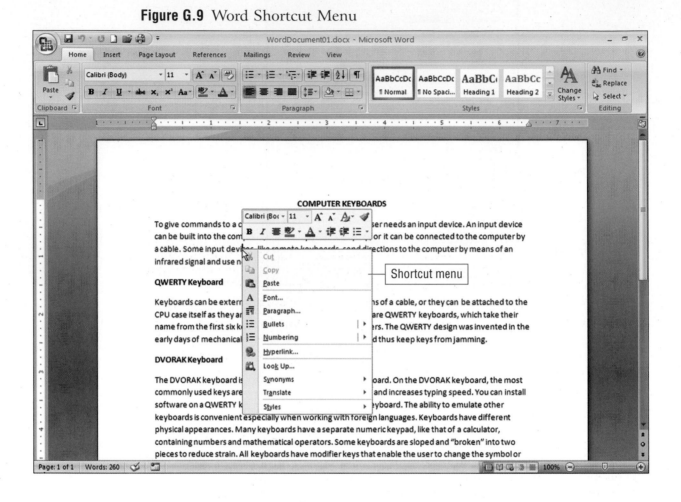

To select an option from a shortcut menu with the mouse, click the desired option. If you are using the keyboard, press the Up or Down Arrow key until the desired option is selected and then press the Enter key. To close a shortcut menu without choosing an option, click anywhere outside the shortcut menu or press the Esc key.

Working with Multiple Programs

As you learn the various programs in the Microsoft Office suite, you will notice how executing commands in each is very similar. For example, the steps to save, close, and print are virtually the same whether you are working in Word, Excel, or PowerPoint. This consistency between programs greatly enhances a user's ability to transfer knowledge learned in one program to another within the suite. Another appeal of Microsoft Office is the ability to have more than one program open at the same time. For example, you can open Word, create a document, and then open Excel, create a spreadsheet, and copy the spreadsheet into Word.

When you open a program, the name of the program displays in the Taskbar. If you open a file within the program, the file name follows the program name on the button on the Taskbar. If you open another program, the program name displays on a button positioned to the right of the first program button. Figure G.10 shows the Taskbar with Word, Excel, and PowerPoint open. To move from one program to another, click the button on the Taskbar representing the desired program file.

Figure G.10 Taskbar with Word, Excel, and PowerPoint Open

Completing Computer Projects

Some computer projects in this textbook require that you open an existing file. Project files are saved on the Student CD that accompanies this textbook. The files you need for each chapter are saved in individual folders. Before beginning a chapter, copy the necessary folder from the CD to your storage medium. After completing projects in a chapter, delete the chapter folder before copying the next chapter folder. (Check with your instructor before deleting a folder.)

The Student CD also contains model answers in PDF format for the project exercises within (but not at the end of) each chapter so you can check your work. To access the PDF files, you will need to have Adobe Acrobat Reader installed on your computer's hard drive. A free download of Adobe Reader is available at Adobe Systems' Web site at www.adobe.com.

Copying a Folder

As you begin working in a chapter, copy the chapter folder from the CD to your storage medium using the My Computer window by completing the following steps:

1. Insert the CD that accompanies this textbook in the CD drive.
2. Insert your storage medium in the appropriate drive.
3. At the Windows XP desktop, open the My Computer window by clicking the Start button and then clicking *My Computer* at the Start menu.
4. Double-click the CD drive in the contents pane (probably displays as *Office2007_Bench* or *Word2007, Excel 2007*, etc. followed by the drive letter).
5. Double-click the *StudentDataFiles* folder in the contents pane.
6. Double-click the desired folder name in the contents pane. (For example, if you are copying a folder for a Word Level 1 chapter, double-click the *Word2007L1* folder.)
7. Click once on the desired chapter subfolder name to select it.
8. Click the <u>Copy this folder</u> hyperlink in the *File and Folder Tasks* section of the task pane.
9. At the Copy Items dialog box, click the drive where your storage medium is located and then click the Copy button.
10. After the folder is copied to your storage medium, close the My Computer window by clicking the Close button (white X on red background) that displays in the upper right corner of the window.

Deleting a Folder

Before copying a chapter folder onto your storage medium, you may need to delete any previous chapter folders. Do this in the My Computer window by completing the following steps:

1. Insert your storage medium in the appropriate drive.
2. At the Windows XP desktop, open the My Computer window by clicking the Start button and then clicking *My Computer* at the Start menu.
3. Double-click the drive where you storage medium is located in the contents pane.
4. Click the chapter folder in the list box.
5. Click the <u>Delete this folder</u> hyperlink in the *File and Folder Tasks* section of the task pane.
6. At the message asking if you want to remove the folder and all its contents, click the Yes button.
7. If a message displays asking if you want to delete a read-only file, click the Yes to All button.
8. Close the My Computer window by clicking the Close button (white X on red background) that displays in the upper right corner of the window.

Viewing or Printing the Project Model Answers

If you want to access the PDF model answer files, first make sure that Adobe Acrobat Reader is installed on your hard drive. Double-click the folder, double-click the desired chapter subfolder name, and double-click the appropriate file name to open the file. You can view and/or print the file to compare it with your own completed exercise file.

Customizing the Quick Access Toolbar

The four applications in the Office 2007 suite—Word, Excel, PowerPoint, and Access—each contain a Quick Access toolbar that displays at the top of the screen. By default, this toolbar contains three buttons: Save, Undo, and Redo. Before beginning chapters in this textbook, customize the Quick Access toolbar by adding three additional buttons: New, Open, and Quick Print. To add these three buttons to the Word Quick Access toolbar, complete the following steps:

1. Open Word.
2. Click the Customize Quick Access Toolbar button that displays at the right side of the toolbar.
3. At the drop-down list, click *New*. (This adds the New button to the toolbar.)
4. Click the Customize Quick Access Toolbar button and then click *Open* at the drop-down list. (This adds the Open button to the toolbar.)
5. Click the Customize Quick Access Toolbar button and then click *Quick Print* at the drop-down list. (This adds the Quick Print button to the toolbar.)

Complete the same steps for Excel, Access, and PowerPoint. You will only need to add the buttons once to the Quick Access toolbar. These buttons will remain on the toolbar even when you exit and then reopen the application.

Using Windows XP

A computer requires an operating system to provide necessary instructions on a multitude of processes including loading programs, managing data, directing the flow of information to peripheral equipment, and displaying information. Windows XP Professional is an operating system that provides functions of this type (along with much more) in a graphical environment. Windows is referred to as a ***graphical user interface*** (GUI— pronounced *gooey*) that provides a visual display of information with features such as icons (pictures) and buttons. In this introduction, you will learn the basic features of Windows XP:

- Use desktop icons and the Taskbar to launch programs and open files or folders
- Organize and manage data, including copying, moving, creating, and deleting files and folders
- Customize the desktop by changing the theme, background, colors, and settings, and adding a screen saver
- Use the Help and Support Center features
- Customize monitor settings

Historically, Microsoft has produced two editions of Windows—one edition for individual users (on desktop and laptop computers) and another edition for servers (on computers that provide service over networks). Windows XP is an upgrade and a merging of these two Windows editions and is available in two versions. The Windows XP Home Edition is designed for home use and Windows XP Professional is designed for small office and workstation use. Whether you are using Windows XP Home Edition or Windows XP Professional, you will be able to complete the steps in the projects in this introduction.

Before using one of the software programs in the Microsoft Office suite, you will need to start the Windows XP operating system. To do this, turn on the computer. Depending on your computer equipment configuration, you may also need to turn on the monitor and printer. If you are using a computer that is part of a network system or if your computer is set up for multiple users, a screen will display showing the user accounts defined for your computer system. At this screen, click your user account name and, if necessary, type your password and then press the Enter key. The Windows XP operating system will start and, after a few moments, the desktop will display as shown in Figure W.1. (Your desktop may vary from what you see in Figure W.1.)

Figure W.1 Windows XP Desktop

icon

Taskbar

Exploring the Desktop

When Windows XP is loaded, the main portion of the screen is called the ***desktop***. Think of the desktop in Windows as the top of a desk in an office. A business person places necessary tools—such as pencils, pens, paper, files, calculator—on the desktop to perform functions. Like the tools that are located on a desk, the desktop contains tools for operating the computer. These tools are logically grouped and placed in dialog boxes or panels that you can display using icons on the desktop. The desktop contains a variety of features for using your computer and software programs installed on the computer. The features available on the desktop are represented by icons and buttons.

Using Icons

Icons are visual symbols that represent programs, files, or folders. Figure W.1 identifies the *Recycle Bin* icon located on the Windows XP desktop. The Windows XP desktop on your computer may contain additional icons. Programs that have been installed on your computer may be represented by an icon on the desktop. Also, icons may display on your desktop representing files or folders. Double-click an icon and the program, file, or folder it represents opens on the desktop.

Using the Taskbar

The bar that displays at the bottom of the desktop (see Figure W.1) is called the Taskbar. The Taskbar, shown in Figure W.2, contains the Start button, a section that displays task buttons representing open programs, and the notification area.

Figure W.2 Windows XP Taskbar

Start button   Task button area   Notification area

Click the Start button, located at the left side of the Taskbar, and the Start menu displays as shown in Figure W.3 (your Start menu may vary). You can also display the Start menu by pressing the Windows key on your keyboard or by pressing Ctrl + Esc. The left column of the Start menu contains *pinned programs*, which are programs that always appear in that particular location on the Start menu, and links to the most recently and frequently used programs. The right column contains links to folders, the Control Panel, online help, and the search feature.

Figure W.3 Start Menu

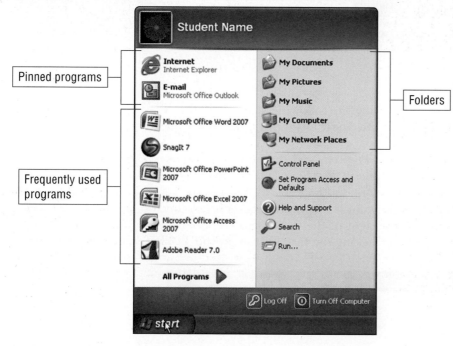

Pinned programs

Frequently used programs

Folders

To choose an option from the Start menu, drag the arrow pointer to the desired option (referred to as *pointing*) and then click the left mouse button. Pointing to options at the Start menu that are followed by a right-pointing arrow will cause a side menu to display with additional options. When a program is open, a task button representing the program appears on the Taskbar. If multiple programs are open, each program will appear as a task button on the Taskbar (a few specialized tools may not).

Project ① Opening Programs and Switching between Programs

1. Open Windows XP. (To do this, turn on the computer and, if necessary, turn on the monitor and/or printer. If you are using a computer that is part of a network system or if your computer is set up for multiple users, you may need to click your user account name and, if necessary, type your password and then press the Enter key. Check with your instructor to determine if you need to complete any additional steps.)
2. When the Windows XP desktop displays, open Microsoft Word by completing the following steps:
   a. Position the arrow pointer on the Start button on the Taskbar and then click the left mouse button.
   b. At the Start menu, point to *All Programs* (a side menu displays) and then point to *Microsoft Office* (another side menu displays).
   c. Drag the arrow pointer to *Microsoft Office Word 2007* in the side menu and then click the left mouse button.
   d. When the Microsoft Word program is open, notice that a task button representing Word displays on the Taskbar.

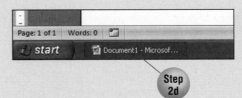

Step 2d

3. Open Microsoft Excel by completing the following steps:
   a. Position the arrow pointer on the Start button on the Taskbar and then click the left mouse button.
   b. At the Start menu, point to *All Programs* and then point to *Microsoft Office*.
   c. Drag the arrow pointer to *Microsoft Office Excel 2007* in the side menu and then click the left mouse button.
   d. When the Microsoft Excel program is open, notice that a task button representing Excel displays on the Taskbar to the right of the task button representing Word.
4. Switch to the Word program by clicking the task button on the Taskbar representing Word.

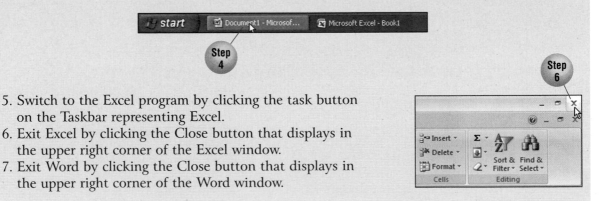

Step 4

Step 6

5. Switch to the Excel program by clicking the task button on the Taskbar representing Excel.
6. Exit Excel by clicking the Close button that displays in the upper right corner of the Excel window.
7. Exit Word by clicking the Close button that displays in the upper right corner of the Word window.

Exploring the Notification Area

The notification area is located at the right side of the Taskbar and contains the system clock along with small icons representing specialized programs that run in the background. Position the arrow pointer over the current time in the notification area of the Taskbar and today's date displays in a small yellow box above the time. Double-click the current time displayed on the Taskbar and the Date and Time Properties dialog box displays as shown in Figure W.4.

Figure W.4 Date and Time Properties Box

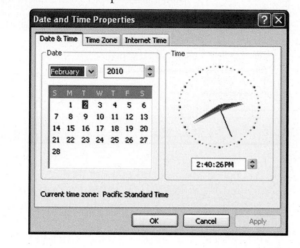

Change the date with options in the *Date* section of the dialog box. For example, to change the month, click the down-pointing arrow at the right side of the option box containing the current month and then click the desired month at the drop-down list. Change the year by clicking the up- or down-pointing arrow at the right side of the option box containing the current year until the desired year displays. To change the day, click the desired day in the monthly calendar that displays in the dialog box. To change the time, double-click either the hour, minute, or seconds and then type the appropriate time or use the up- and down-pointing arrows to adjust the time.

Some programs, when installed, will add an icon to the notification area of the Taskbar. Display the name of the icon by positioning the mouse pointer on the icon and, after approximately one second, the icon label displays in a small yellow box. Some icons may display information in the yellow box rather than the icon label. If more icons have been inserted in the notification area than can be viewed at one time, a left-pointing arrow button displays at the left side of the notification area. Click this left-pointing arrow button and the remaining icons display.

Setting Taskbar Properties

By default, the Taskbar is locked in its current position and size. You can change this default setting, along with other default settings, with options at the Taskbar and Start Menu Properties dialog box, shown in Figure W.5. To display this dialog box, position the arrow pointer on any empty spot on the Taskbar and then click the right mouse button. At the shortcut menu that displays, click *Properties*.

Figure W.5 Taskbar and Start Menu Properties Box

Each property is controlled by a check box. Property options containing a check mark are active. Click the option to remove the check mark and make the option inactive. If an option is inactive, clicking the option will insert a check mark in the check box and turn on the option (make it active).

Project ② Changing Taskbar Properties

1. Make sure Windows XP is open and the desktop displays.
2. Hide the Taskbar and remove the display of the clock by completing the following steps:
   a. Position the arrow pointer on any empty area on the Taskbar and then click the right mouse button.
   b. At the shortcut menu that displays, click *Properties*.
   c. At the Taskbar and Start Menu Properties dialog box, click *Auto-hide the taskbar*. (This inserts a check mark in the check box.)
   d. Click *Show the clock*. (This removes the check mark from the check box.)
   e. Click the Apply button.
   f. Click OK to close the dialog box.

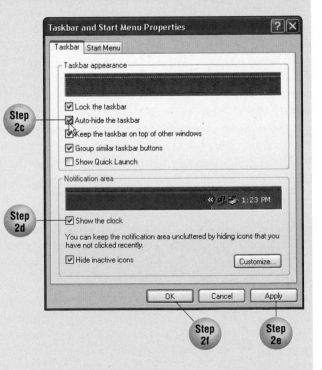

3. Display the Taskbar by positioning the mouse pointer at the bottom of the screen. When the Taskbar displays, notice that the time no longer displays at the right side of the Taskbar.
4. Return to the default settings for the Taskbar by completing the following steps:
   a. With the Taskbar displayed (if it does not display, position the mouse pointer at the bottom of the desktop), position the arrow pointer on any empty area on the Taskbar and then click the right mouse button.
   b. At the shortcut menu that displays, click *Properties*.
   c. At the Taskbar and Start Menu Properties dialog box, click *Auto-hide the taskbar*. (This removes the check mark from the check box.)
   d. Click *Show the clock*. (This inserts a check mark in the check box.)
   e. Click the Apply button.
   f. Click OK to close the dialog box.

Turning Off the Computer

When you are finished working with your computer, you can choose to shut down the computer completely, shut down and then restart the computer, put the computer on standby, or tell the computer to hibernate. Do not turn off your computer until your screen goes blank. Important data is stored in memory while Windows XP is running and this data needs to be written to the hard drive before turning off the computer.

To shut down your computer, click the Start button on the Taskbar and then click *Turn Off Computer* at the Start menu. At the Turn off computer window, shown in Figure W.6, click the *Stand By* option and the computer switches to a low power state causing some devices such as the monitor and hard drives to turn off. With these devices off, the computer uses less power. Stand By is particularly useful for saving battery power for portable computers. Tell the computer to "hibernate" by holding down the Shift key while clicking the *Stand By* option. In hibernate mode, the computer saves everything in memory, turns off the monitor and hard drive, and then turns off the computer. Click the *Turn Off* option if you want to shut down Windows XP and turn off all power to the computer. Click the *Restart* option if you want to restart the computer and restore the desktop exactly as you left it. You can generally restore your desktop from either standby or hibernate by pressing once on the computer's power button. Usually, bringing a computer out of hibernation takes a little longer than bringing a computer out of standby.

Figure W.6 Turn Off Computer Window

Managing Files and Folders

As you begin working with programs in Windows XP, you will create files in which data (information) is saved. A file might contain a Word document, an Excel workbook, or a PowerPoint presentation. As you begin creating files, consider creating folders into which those files will be stored. You can complete file management tasks such as creating a folder and copying and moving files and folders at the My Computer window. To display the My Computer window shown in Figure W.7, click the Start button on the Taskbar and then click My Computer. The various components of the My Computer window are identified in Figure W.7.

Figure W.7 My Computer Window

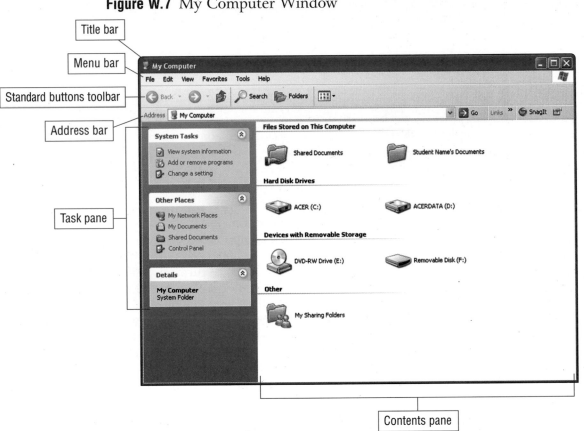

Copying, Moving, and Deleting Files/Folders

File and folder management activities might include copying and moving files or folders from one folder or drive to another, or deleting files or folders. The My Computer window offers a variety of methods for copying, moving, and deleting files/folders. You can use options in the task pane, drop-down menu options, or shortcut menu options. This section will provide you with the steps for copying, moving, and deleting files/folders using options in the task pane.

To copy a file/folder to another folder or drive, first display the file in the contents pane by identifying the location of the file. If the file is located in the My Documents folder, click the <u>My Documents</u> hyperlink in the *Other Places* section of the task pane. If the file is located on the hard drive, double-click the desired drive in the contents pane; if the file is located on a USB drive, DVD, or CD, double-click the desired drive letter. Next, click the folder or file name in the contents pane that you want to copy. This changes the options in the task pane to include management options such as renaming, moving, copying, and deleting folders or files. Click the <u>Copy this folder</u> (or <u>Copy this file</u>) hyperlink in the task pane and the Copy Items dialog box displays as shown in Figure W.8. At the Copy Items dialog box, click the desired folder or drive and then click the Copy button.

Figure W.8 Copy Items Dialog Box

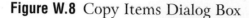

To move adjacent files/folders, click the first file or folder, hold down the Shift key, and then click the last file or folder. This selects and highlights all files/folders from the first file/folder you clicked to the last file/folder you clicked. With the adjacent files/folders selected, click the <u>Move the selected items</u> hyperlink in the File and Folder Tasks section of the task pane and then specify the desired location at the Move Items dialog box. To select nonadjacent files/folders, click the first file/folder to select it, hold down the Ctrl key, and then click any other files/folders you want to move or copy.

You can easily remove (delete) a file or folder from the My Computer window. To delete a file or folder, click the file or folder in the contents pane, and then click the <u>Delete this folder</u> (or <u>Delete this file</u>) hyperlink in the task pane. At the dialog box asking you to confirm the deletion, click Yes. A deleted file or folder is sent to the Recycle Bin. You will learn more about the Recycle Bin in the next section.

In Project 3, you will insert the CD that accompanies this book into the DVD or CD drive. When the CD is inserted, the drive may automatically activate and a dialog box may display on the screen telling you that the disk or device contains more than one type of content and asking what you want Windows to do. If this dialog box displays, click Cancel to remove the dialog box.

1. At the Windows XP desktop, insert the CD that accompanies this textbook into the appropriate drive. If a dialog box displays telling you that the disk or device contains more than one type of content and asking what you want Windows to do, click Cancel.
2. At the Windows XP desktop, open the My Computer window by clicking the Start button on the Taskbar and then clicking *My Computer* at the Start menu.
3. Copy a file from the CD that accompanies this textbook to the drive containing your storage medium by completing the following steps:
   a. Insert your storage medium in the appropriate drive.
   b. In the contents pane, double-click the drive containing the CD (probably displays as *Office2007_Bench* followed by a drive letter). (Make sure you double-click the mouse button because you want the contents of the CD to display in the contents pane.)
   c. Double-click the *StudentDataFiles* folder.
   d. Double-click the *WindowsXP* folder in the contents pane.
   e. Click ***WordDocument01.docx*** in the contents pane to select it.
   f. Click the Copy this file hyperlink located in the *File and Folder Tasks* section of the task pane.

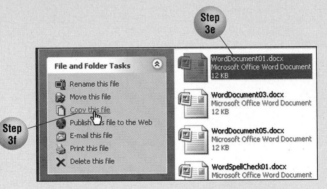

   g. At the Copy Items dialog box, click in the list box the drive containing your storage medium.
   h. Click the Copy button.

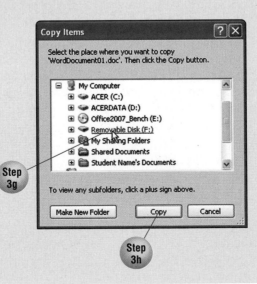

4. Delete **WordDocument01.docx** from your storage medium by completing the following steps:
   a. Click the <u>My Computer</u> hyperlink located in the *Other Places* section of the task pane.
   b. Double-click in the contents pane the drive containing your storage medium.
   c. Click ***WordDocument01.docx***.
   d. Click the <u>Delete this file</u> hyperlink in the *File and Folder Tasks* section of the task pane.

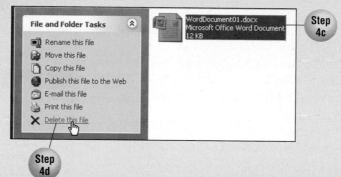

   e. At the message asking you to confirm the deletion, click Yes.
5. Copy the WindowsXP folder from the CD drive to the drive containing your storage medium by completing the following steps:
   a. Click the My Computer hyperlink in the *Other Places* section of the task pane.
   b. In the contents pane, double-click the drive containing the CD (probably displays as *Office2007_Bench* followed by a drive letter).
   c. Double-click the *StudentDataFiles* folder.
   d. Click the *WindowsXP* folder in the contents pane to select it.
   e. Click the <u>Copy this folder</u> hyperlink in the *File and Folder Tasks* section of the task pane.
   f. At the Copy Items dialog box, click the drive containing your storage medium.
   g. Click the Copy button.
6. Close the window by clicking the Close button (contains a white *X* on a red background) located in the upper right corner of the window. (You can also close the window by clicking File on the Menu bar and then clicking *Close* at the drop-down list.)

Selecting Files/Folders

You can move, copy, or delete more than one file or folder at the same time. Before moving, copying, or deleting files/folders, select the desired files or folders. Selecting files/folders is easier when you change the display in the contents pane to List or Details. To change the display, open the My Computer window and then click the Views button on the Standard Buttons toolbar. At the drop-down list that displays, click the *List* option or the *Details* option.

To move adjacent files/folders, click the first file or folder, hold down the Shift key, and click the last file or folder. This selects and highlights all files/folders from the first file/folder you clicked to the last file/folder you clicked. With the adjacent files/folders selected, click the <u>Move the selected items</u> hyperlink in the *File and Folder Tasks* section of the task pane and then specify the desired location at the Move Items dialog box. To select nonadjacent files/folders, click the first file/folder to select it, hold down the Ctrl key, and then click any other files/folders you want to move or copy.

Project ④ Copying and Deleting Files

1. At the Windows XP desktop, open the My Computer window by clicking the Start button and then clicking *My Computer* at the Start menu.
2. Copy files from the CD that accompanies this textbook to the drive containing your storage medium by completing the following steps:
   a. Make sure the CD that accompanies this textbook and your storage medium are inserted in the appropriate drives.
   b. Double-click the CD drive in the contents pane (probably displays as *Office2007_Bench* followed by the drive letter).
   c. Double-click the *StudentDataFiles* folder in the contents pane.
   d. Double-click the *WindowsXP* folder in the contents pane.
   e. Change the display to Details by clicking the Views button on the Standard Buttons toolbar and then clicking *Details* at the drop-down list.

   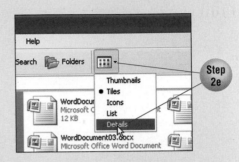

   f. Position the arrow pointer on **WordDocument01.docx** in the contents pane and then click the left mouse button.
   g. Hold down the Shift key, click *WordDocument05.docx*, and then release the Shift key. (This selects **WordDocument01.docx**, **WordDocument02.docx**, **WordDocument03.docx**, **WordDocument04.docx**, and **WordDocument05.docx**.)

   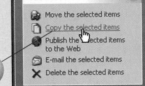
   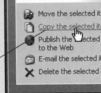

   h. Click the <u>Copy the selected items</u> hyperlink in the *File and Folder Tasks* section of the task pane.
   i. At the Copy Items dialog box, click the drive containing your storage medium and then click the Copy button.
3. Display the files and folder saved on your storage medium by completing the following steps:
   a. Click the <u>My Computer</u> hyperlink in the *Other Places* section of the task pane.
   b. Double-click the drive containing your storage medium.
4. Delete the files from your storage medium that you just copied by completing the following steps:
   a. Change the view by clicking the Views button on the Standard Buttons toolbar and then clicking *List* at the drop-down list.
   b. Click *WordDocument01.docx* in the contents pane.
   c. Hold down the Shift key, click *WordDocument05.docx*, and then release the Shift key. (This selects **WordDocument01.docx**, **WordDocument02.docx**, **WordDocument03.docx**, **WordDocument04.docx**, and **WordDocument05.docx**.)
   d. Click the <u>Delete the selected items</u> hyperlink in the *File and Folder Tasks* section of the task pane.

   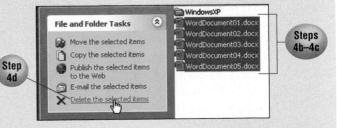

   e. At the message asking you to confirm the deletion, click Yes.
5. Close the window by clicking the Close button (white *X* on red background) that displays in the upper right corner of the window.

Manipulating and Creating Folders

As you begin working with and creating a number of files, consider creating folders in which you can logically group the files. To create a folder, display the My Computer window and then display in the contents pane the drive where you want to create the folder. Click File on the Menu bar, point to *New*, and then click *Folder* at the side menu. This inserts a folder icon in the contents pane and names the folder *New Folder*. Type the desired name for the new folder and then press Enter.

Project 5 — Creating a New Folder

1. At the Windows XP desktop, open the My Computer window.
2. Create a new folder by completing the following steps:
   a. Double-click in the contents pane the drive that contains your storage medium.
   b. Double-click the *WindowsXP* folder in the contents pane. (This opens the folder.)
   c. Click File on the Menu bar, point to *New*, and then click *Folder*.
   d. Type **SpellCheckFiles** and then press Enter. (This changes the name from *New Folder* to *SpellCheckFiles*.)
3. Copy **WordSpellCheck01.docx**, **WordSpellCheck02.docx**, and **WordSpellCheck03.docx** into the SpellCheckFiles folder you just created by completing the following steps:
   a. Click the Views button on the Standard Buttons toolbar and then click *List* at the drop-down list.
   b. Click once on the file named *WordSpellCheck01.docx* located in the contents pane.
   c. Hold down the Shift key, click once on the file named *WordSpellCheck03.docx*, and then release the Shift key. (This selects **WordSpellCheck01.docx**, **WordSpellCheck02.docx**, and **WordSpellCheck03.docx**.)
   d. Click the Copy the selected items hyperlink in the *File and Folder Tasks* section of the task pane.
   e. At the Copy Items dialog box, click in the list box the drive containing your storage medium.
   f. Click *WindowsXP* in the list box.
   g. Click *SpellCheckFiles* in the list box.
   h. Click the Copy button.
4. Display the files you just copied by double-clicking the *SpellCheckFiles* folder in the contents pane.

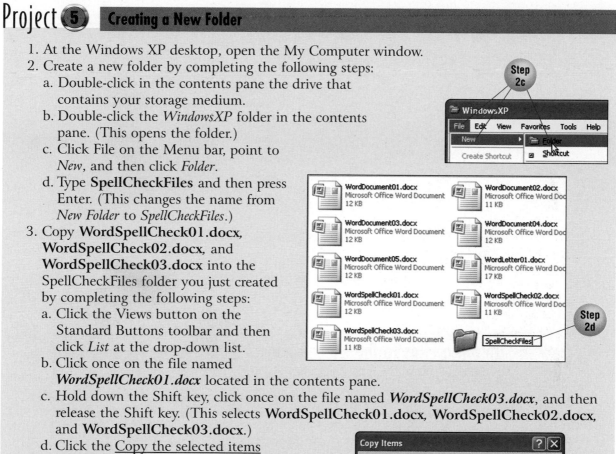

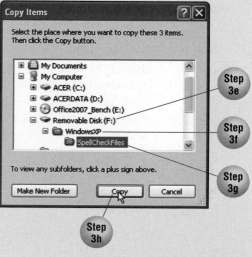

5. Delete the SpellCheckFiles folder and its contents by completing the following steps:
   a. Click the Up button on the Standard Buttons toolbar. (This displays the contents of the WindowsXP folder which is up one folder from the SpellCheckFiles folders.)
   b. Click the *SpellCheckFiles* folder in the contents pane to select it.
   c. Click the <u>Delete this folder</u> hyperlink in the *File and Folder Tasks* section of the task pane.
   d. At the message asking you to confirm the deletion, click Yes.
6. Close the window by clicking the Close button located in the upper right corner of the window.

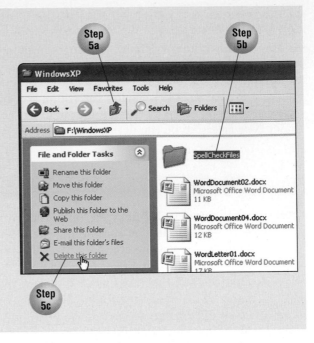

Using the Recycle Bin

Deleting the wrong file can be a disaster but Windows XP helps protect your work with the Recycle Bin. The Recycle Bin acts just like an office wastepaper basket; you can "throw away" (delete) unwanted files, but you can "reach in" to the Recycle Bin and take out (restore) a file if you threw it away by accident.

Deleting Files to the Recycle Bin

A file/folder or selected files/folders deleted from the hard drive are sent automatically to the Recycle Bin. Files/folders deleted from a disk are deleted permanently. (Recovery programs are available, however, that will help you recover deleted text. If you accidentally delete a file/folder from a disk, do not do anything more with the disk until you can run a recovery program.)

One method for deleting files is to display the My Computer window and then display in the contents pane the file(s) and/or folder(s) you want deleted. Click the file or folder or select multiple files or folders and then click the appropriate delete option in the task pane. At the message asking you to confirm the deletion, click Yes. Another method for deleting a file is to drag the file to the *Recycle Bin* icon on the desktop. Drag a file icon to the Recycle Bin until the *Recycle Bin* icon is selected (displays with a blue background) and then release the mouse button. This drops the file you are dragging into the Recycle Bin.

Recovering Files from the Recycle Bin

You can easily restore a deleted file from the Recycle Bin. To restore a file, double-click the *Recycle Bin* icon on the desktop. This opens the Recycle Bin window shown in Figure W.9. (The contents of the Recycle Bin will vary.) To restore a file, click the file you want restored, and then click the <u>Restore this item</u> hyperlink in the *Recycle Bin Tasks* section of the task pane. This removes the file from the Recycle Bin and returns it to its original location. You can also restore a file by positioning the arrow pointer on the file, clicking the right mouse button, and then clicking *Restore* at the shortcut menu.

Figure W.9 Recycle Bin Window

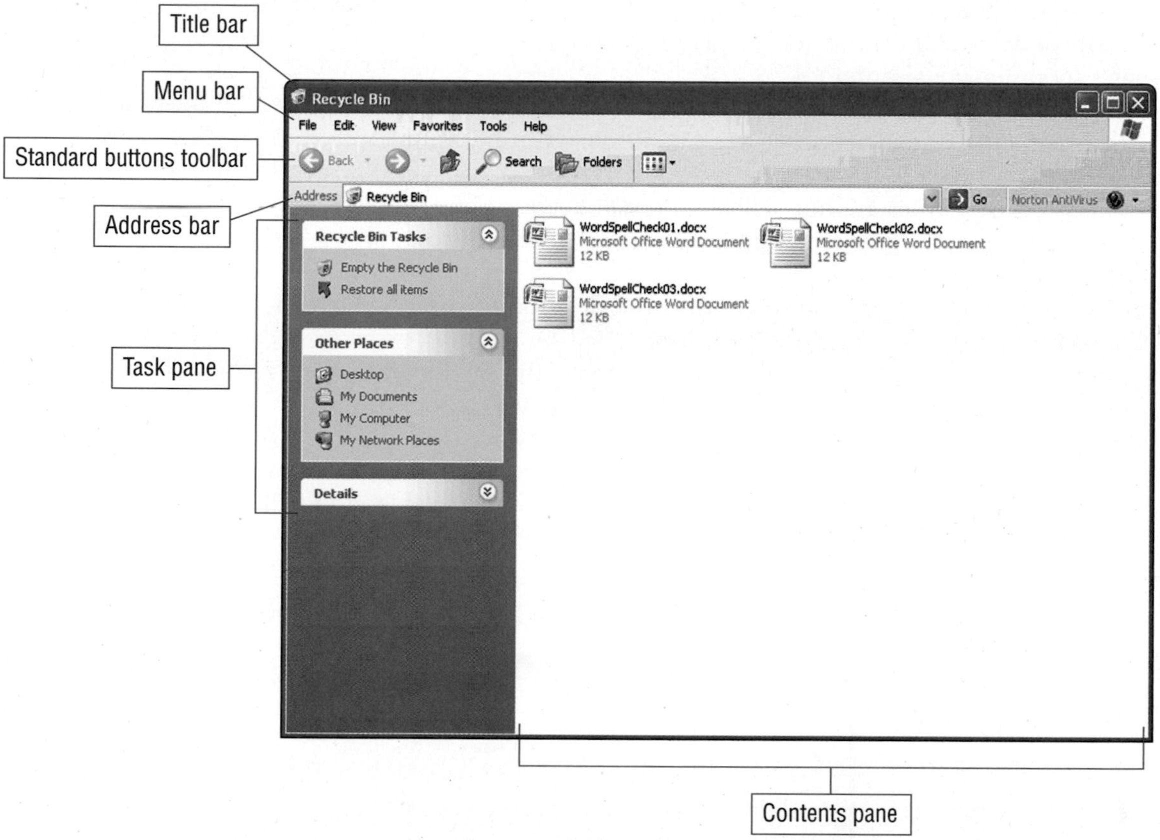

Title bar

Menu bar

Standard buttons toolbar

Address bar

Task pane

Contents pane

Project ⑥ · Deleting Files to and Recovering Files from the Recycle Bin

Before beginning this project, check with your instructor to determine if you can copy files to the hard drive.

1. At the Windows XP desktop, open the My Computer window.
2. Copy files from your storage medium to the My Documents folder on your hard drive by completing the following steps:
   a. Double-click in the contents pane the drive containing your storage medium.
   b. Double-click the *WindowsXP* folder in the contents pane.
   c. Click the Views button on the Standard Buttons toolbar and then click *List* at the drop-down list.
   d. Position the arrow pointer on **WordSpellCheck01.docx** and then click the left mouse button.
   e. Hold down the Shift key, click **WordSpellCheck03.docx**, and then release the Shift key.

f. Click the Copy the selected items hyperlink in the *File and Folder Tasks* section of the task pane.

g. At the Copy Items dialog box, click *My Documents* in the list box.

h. Click the Copy button.

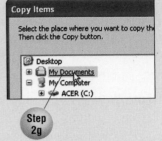

Step 2g

3. Click the <u>My Documents</u> hyperlink in the *Other Places* section of the task pane. (The files you copied, **WordSpellCheck01.docx** through **WordSpellCheck03.docx**, will display in the contents pane in alphabetical order.)

4. Delete **WordSpellCheck01.docx** through **WordSpellCheck03.docx** from the My Documents folder and send them to the Recycle Bin by completing the following steps:

   a. Select **WordSpellCheck01.docx** through **WordSpellCheck03.docx** in the contents pane. (If these files are not visible, you will need to scroll down the list of files.)

   b. Click the <u>Delete the selected items</u> hyperlink in the *File and Folder Tasks* section of the task pane.

   c. At the message asking you to confirm the deletion to the Recycle Bin, click Yes.

5. Click the Close button to close the window.

6. At the desktop, display the contents of the Recycle Bin by double-clicking the *Recycle Bin* icon.

7. At the Recycle Bin window, restore **WordSpellCheck01.docx** through **WordSpellCheck03.docx** to the My Documents folder by completing the following steps:

   a. Select **WordSpellCheck01.docx** through **WordSpellCheck03.docx** in the contents pane of the Recycle Bin window. (If these files are not visible, you will need to scroll down the list of files.)

   b. With the files selected, click the <u>Restore the selected items</u> hyperlink in the *Recycle Bin Tasks* section of the task pane.

8. Close the Recycle Bin window by clicking the Close button located in the upper right corner of the window.

9. Display the My Computer window.

10. Click the <u>My Documents</u> hyperlink in the *Other Places* section of the task pane.

11. Delete the files you restored by completing the following steps:

    a. Select **WordSpellCheck01.docx** through **WordSpellCheck03.docx** in the contents pane. (If these files are not visible, you will need to scroll down the list of files. These are the files you recovered from the Recycle Bin.)

    b. Click the <u>Delete the selected items</u> hyperlink in the *File and Folder Tasks* section of the task pane.

    c. At the message asking you to confirm the deletion, click Yes.

12. Close the window.

Emptying the Recycle Bin

Just like a wastepaper basket, the Recycle Bin can get full. To empty the Recycle Bin, position the arrow pointer on the *Recycle Bin* icon on the desktop and then click the right mouse button. At the shortcut menu that displays, click *Empty Recycle Bin*. At the message asking you to confirm the deletion, click Yes. You can also empty the Recycle Bin by double-clicking the *Recycle Bin* icon. At the Recycle Bin window, click the <u>Empty the Recycle Bin</u> hyperlink in the *Recycle Bin Tasks* section of the task pane. At the message asking you to confirm the deletion, click Yes. (You can also empty the Recycle Bin by clicking File on the Menu bar and then clicking *Empty Recycle Bin* at the drop-down menu.)

Emptying the Recycle Bin deletes all files/folders. You can delete a specific file/folder from the Recycle Bin (rather than all files/folders). To do this, double-click the *Recycle Bin* icon on the desktop. At the Recycle Bin window, select the file/folder or files/folders you want to delete. Click File on the Menu bar and then click *Delete* at the drop-down menu. (You can also right-click a selected file/folder and then click *Delete* at the shortcut menu.) At the message asking you to confirm the deletion, click Yes.

Project 7 — Emptying the Recycle Bin

Before beginning this project, check with your instructor to determine if you can delete files/folders from the Recycle Bin.

1. At the Windows XP desktop, double-click the *Recycle Bin* icon.
2. At the Recycle Bin window, empty the contents of the Recycle Bin by completing the following steps:
   a. Click the <u>Empty the Recycle Bin</u> hyperlink in the *Recycle Bin Tasks* section of the task pane.

   b. At the message asking you to confirm the deletion, click Yes.
3. Close the Recycle Bin window by clicking the Close button located in the upper right corner of the window.

When you empty the Recycle Bin, the files cannot be recovered by the Recycle Bin or by Windows XP. If you have to recover a file, you will need to use a file recovery program such as Norton Utilities. These utilities are separate programs, but might be worth their cost if you ever need them.

Creating a Shortcut

If you use a file or program on a consistent basis, consider creating a shortcut to the file or program. A shortcut is a specialized icon that represents very small files that point the operating system to the actual item, whether it is a file, a folder, or an application. If you create a shortcut to a Word document, the shortcut icon is not the actual document but a path to the document. Double-click the shortcut icon and Windows XP opens the document in Word.

One method for creating a shortcut is to display the My Computer window and then display the drive or folder where the file is located. Right-click the desired file, point to *Send To*, and then click *Desktop (create shortcut)*. You can easily delete a shortcut icon from the desktop by dragging the shortcut icon to the Recycle Bin icon. This deletes the shortcut icon but does not delete the file to which the shortcut pointed.

Project 8 Creating a Shortcut

1. At the Windows XP desktop, display the My Computer window.
2. Double-click the drive containing your storage medium.
3. Double-click the *WindowsXP* folder in the contents pane.
4. Change the display of files to a list by clicking the Views button on the Standard Buttons toolbar and then clicking *List* at the drop-down list.
5. Create a shortcut to the file named **WordLetter01.docx** by right-clicking on **WordLetter01.docx**, pointing to *Send To*, and then clicking *Desktop (create shortcut)*.

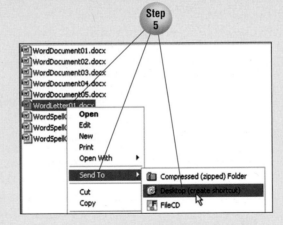

Step 5

Step 7

6. Close the My Computer window by clicking the Close button located in the upper right corner of the window.
7. Open Word and the file named **WordLetter01.docx** by double-clicking the *WordLetter01.docx* shortcut icon on the desktop.
8. After viewing the file in Word, exit Word by clicking the Close button that displays in the upper right corner of the window.
9. Delete the *WordLetter01.docx* shortcut icon by completing the following steps:
   a. At the desktop, position the mouse pointer on the *WordLetter01.docx* shortcut icon.
   b. Hold down the left mouse button, drag the icon on top of the *Recycle Bin* icon, and then release the mouse button.

Customizing the Desktop

You can customize the Windows XP desktop to fit your particular needs and preferences. For example, you can choose a different theme, change the desktop background, add a screen saver, and apply a different appearance to windows, dialog boxes, and menus. To customize the desktop, position the arrow pointer on any empty location on the desktop and then click the right mouse button. At the shortcut menu that displays, click *Properties*. This displays the Display Properties dialog box with the Themes tab selected as shown in Figure W.10.

Figure W.10 Display Properties Dialog Box

Changing the Theme

A Windows XP theme specifies a variety of formatting such as fonts, sounds, icons, colors, mouse pointers, background, and screen saver. Windows XP contains two themes—Windows XP (the default) and Windows Classic (which appears like earlier versions of Windows). Other themes are available as downloads from the Microsoft Web site. Change the theme with the *Theme* option at the Display Properties dialog box with the Themes tab selected.

Changing the Desktop

With options at the Display Properties dialog box with the Desktop tab selected, as shown in Figure W.11, you can choose a different desktop background and customize the desktop. Click any option in the *Background* list box and preview the results in the preview screen. With the *Position* option, you can specify that the background image is centered, tiled, or stretched on the desktop. Use the *Color* option to change the background color and click the Browse button to choose a background image from another location or Web site.

Figure W.11 Display Properties Dialog Box with Desktop Tab Selected

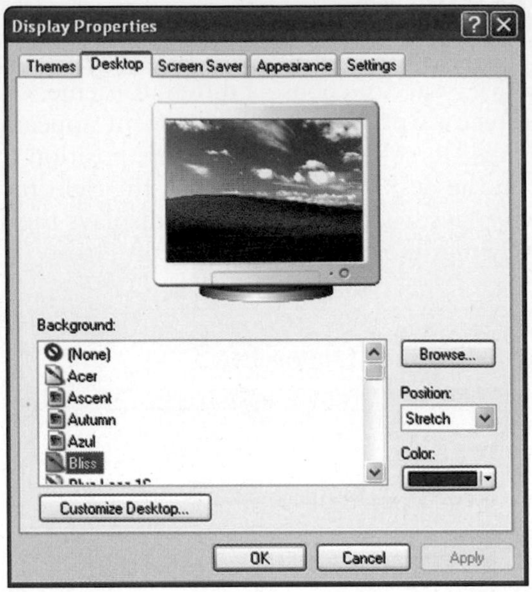

Adding a Screen Saver

If your computer sits idle for periods of time, consider adding a screen saver. A screen saver is a pattern that changes constantly, thus eliminating the problem of an image staying on the screen too long. To add a screen saver, display the Display Properties dialog box and then click the Screen Saver tab. This displays the dialog box as shown in Figure W.12.

Figure W.12 Display Properties Dialog Box with Screen Saver Tab Selected

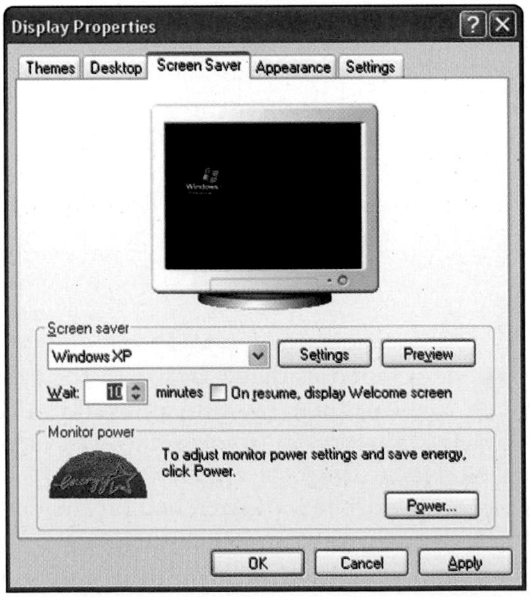

Click the down-pointing arrow at the right side of the *Screen saver* option box to display a list of installed screen savers. Click a screen saver and a preview displays in the monitor located toward the top of the dialog box. Click the Preview button and the dialog box is hidden and the screen saver displays on your monitor. Move the mouse or click a button on the mouse and the dialog box will reappear. Click the Power button in the *Monitor power* section and a dialog box displays with options for choosing a power scheme appropriate to the way you use your computer. The dialog box also includes options for specifying how long the computer can be left unused before the monitor and hard disk are turned off and the system goes to standby or hibernate mode.

Changing Colors

Click the Appearance tab at the Display Properties dialog box and the dialog box displays as shown in Figure W.13. At this dialog box, you can change the desktop scheme. Schemes are predefined collections of colors used in windows, menus, title bars, and system fonts. Windows XP loads with the Windows XP style color scheme. Choose a different scheme with the Windows and buttons option and choose a specific color with the Color scheme option.

Figure W.13 Display Properties Dialog Box with Appearance Tab Selected

Changing Settings

Click the Settings tab at the Display Properties dialog box and the dialog box displays as shown in Figure W.14. At this dialog box, you can set color and screen resolution. The *Color quality* option determines how many colors your monitor displays. The more colors that are shown, the more realistic the images will appear. However, a lot of computer memory is required to show thousands of colors. Your exact choice is determined by the specific hardware you are using. The *Screen resolution* slide bar sets the screen's resolution. The higher the number, the more you can fit onto your screen. Again, your actual values depend on your particular hardware.

Figure W.14 Display Properties Dialog Box with Settings Tab Selected

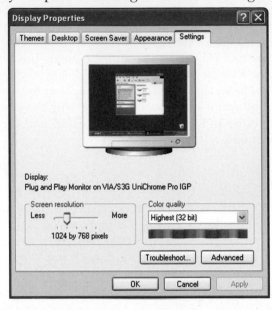

Project 9 Customizing the Desktop

Before beginning this project, check with your instructor to determine if you can customize the desktop.

1. At the Windows XP desktop, display the Display Properties dialog box by positioning the arrow pointer on an empty location on the desktop, clicking the right mouse button, and then clicking *Properties* at the shortcut menu.
2. At the Display Properties dialog box, change the desktop background by completing the following steps:
   a. Click the Desktop tab.
   b. If a background is selected in the *Background* list box (other than the *(None)* option), make a note of this background name.
   c. Click *Blue Lace 16* in the *Background* list box. (If this option is not available, choose another background.)
   d. Make sure *Tile* is selected in the *Position* list box.
   e. Click OK to close the dialog box.

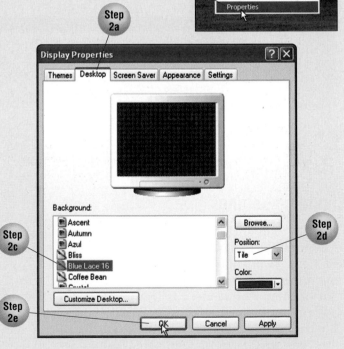

3. After viewing the desktop with the Blue Lace 16 background, remove the background image and change the background color by completing the following steps:
   a. Display the Display Properties dialog box.
   b. At the Display Properties dialog box, click the Desktop tab.
   c. Click *(None)* in the *Background* list box.
   d. Click the down-pointing arrow at the right side of the *Color* option and then click the dark red option at the color palette.
   e. Click OK to close the Display Properties dialog box.

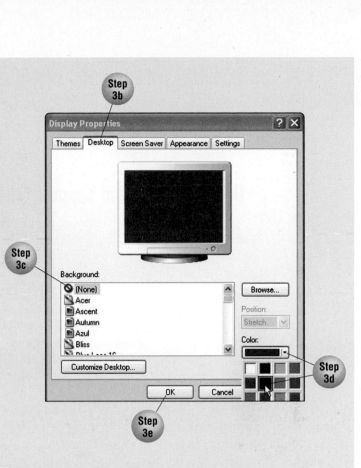

4. After viewing the desktop with the dark red background color, add a screen saver and change the wait time by completing the following steps:
   a. Display the Display Properties dialog box.
   b. At the Display Properties dialog box, click the Screen Saver tab. (If a screen saver is already selected in the *Screen saver* option box, make a note of this screen saver name.)
   c. Click the down-pointing arrow at the right side of the *Screen saver* option box.
   d. At the drop-down list that displays, click a screen saver that interests you. (A preview of the screen saver displays in the screen located toward the top of the dialog box.)
   e. Click a few other screen savers to see how they will display on the monitor.
   f. Click OK to close the Display Properties dialog box.
5. Return all settings back to the default by completing the following steps:
   a. Display the Display Properties dialog box.
   b. Click the Desktop tab.
   c. If a background and color were selected when you began this project, click that background name in the *Background* list box and change the color back to the original color.
   d. Click the Screen Saver tab.
   e. At the Display Properties dialog box with the Screen Saver tab selected, click the down-pointing arrow at the right side of the *Screen saver* option box, and then click *(None)*. (If a screen saver was selected before completing this project, return to that screen saver.)
   f. Click OK to close the Display Properties dialog box.

Exploring Windows XP Help and Support

Windows XP includes an on-screen reference guide providing information, explanations, and interactive help on learning Windows features. The on-screen reference guide contains complex files with hypertext used to access additional information by clicking a word or phrase.

Using the Help and Support Center Window

Display the Help and Support Center window shown in Figure W.15 by clicking the Start button on the Taskbar and then clicking *Help and Support* at the Start menu. The appearance of your Help and Support Center window may vary slightly from what you see in Figure W.15.

If you want to learn about a topic listed in the *Pick a Help topic* section of the window, click the desired topic and information about the topic displays in the window. Use the other options in the Help and Support Center window to get assistance or support from a remote computer or Windows XP newsgroups, pick a specific task, or learn about the additional help features. If you want help on a specific topic and do not see that topic listed in the *Pick a Help topic* section of the window, click inside the *Search* text box (generally located toward the top of the window), type the desired topic, and then press Enter or click the Start searching button (white arrow on a green background).

Figure W.15 Help and Support Center Window

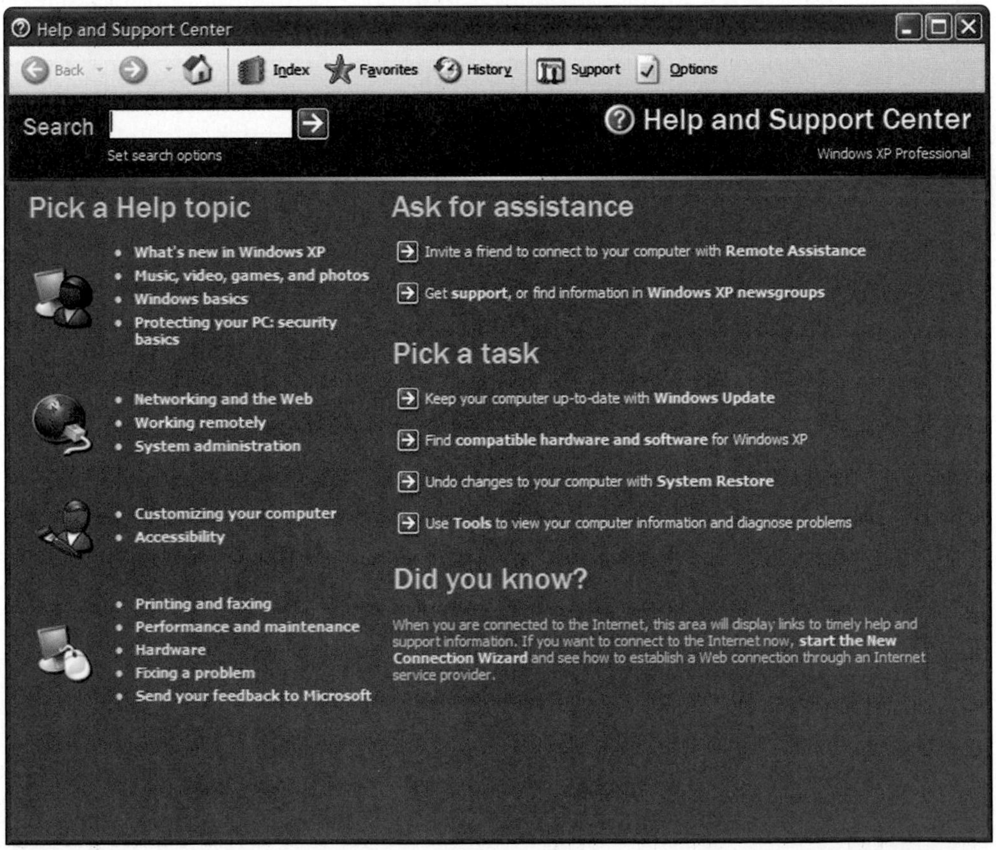

1. At the Windows XP desktop, use the Help and Support feature to learn about new Windows XP features by completing the following steps:
   a. Click the Start button on the Taskbar and then click *Help and Support* at the Start menu.
   b. At the Help and Support Center window, click the <u>What's new in Windows XP</u> hyperlink located in the *Pick a Help topic* section of the window.

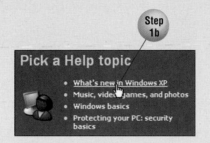

Step 1b

c. Click the <u>What's new</u> hyperlink located in the *What's new in Windows XP* section of the window. (This displays a list of Help options at the right side of the window.)
   d. Click the <u>What's new in Windows XP</u> hyperlink located at the right side of the window below the subheading *Overviews, Articles, and Tutorials*.
   e. Read the information about Windows XP that displays at the right side of the window.
   f. Print the information by completing the following steps:
      1) Click the Print button located on the toolbar that displays above the information titled *What's new in Windows XP Professional*.

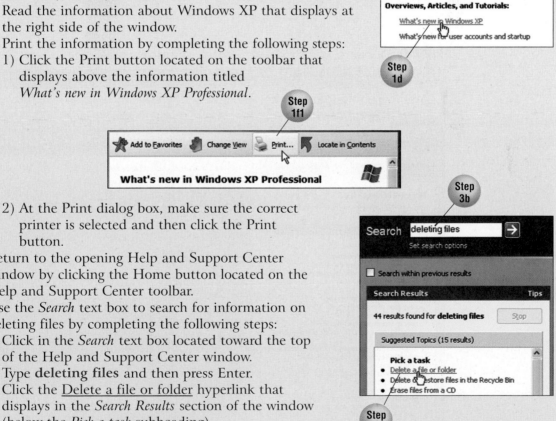

Step 1d

Step 1f1

2) At the Print dialog box, make sure the correct printer is selected and then click the Print button.
2. Return to the opening Help and Support Center window by clicking the Home button located on the Help and Support Center toolbar.
3. Use the *Search* text box to search for information on deleting files by completing the following steps:
   a. Click in the *Search* text box located toward the top of the Help and Support Center window.
   b. Type **deleting files** and then press Enter.
   c. Click the <u>Delete a file or folder</u> hyperlink that displays in the *Search Results* section of the window (below the *Pick a task* subheading).

Step 3b

Step 3c

d. Read the information about deleting a file or folder that displays at the right side of the window and then print the information by clicking the Print button on the toolbar and then clicking the Print button at the Print dialog box.

e. Click the <u>Delete or restore files in the Recycle Bin</u> hyperlink that displays in the *Search Results* section of the window.

f. Read the information that displays at the right side of the window about deleting and restoring files in the Recycle Bin and then print the information.

4. Close the Help and Support Center window by clicking the Close button located in the upper right corner of the window.

Displaying an Index of Help and Support Topics

Display a list of help topics available by clicking the Index button on the Help and Support Center window toolbar. This displays an index of help topics at the left side of the window as shown in Figure W.16. Scroll through this list until the desired topic displays and then double-click the topic. Information about the selected topic displays at the right side of the window. If you are looking for a specific topic or keyword, click in the *Type in the keyword to find* text box, type the desired topic or keyword, and then press Enter.

Figure W.16 Help and Support Center Window with Index Displayed

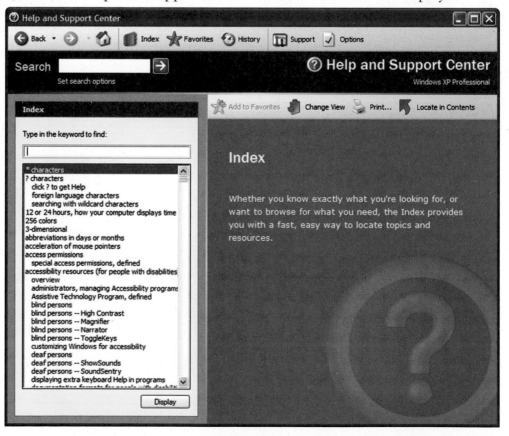

1. At the Windows XP desktop, use the Index to display information on accessing programs by completing the following steps:
   a. Click the Start button on the Taskbar and then click *Help and Support* at the Start menu.
   b. Click the Index button on the Help and Support Center window toolbar.
   c. Scroll down the list of Index topics until *accessing programs* is visible and then double-click the subheading *overview* that displays below *accessing programs*.

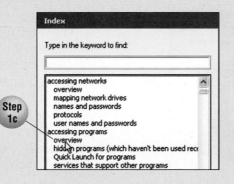

d. Read the information that displays at the right side of the window and then print the information.
2. Find information on adding a shortcut to the desktop by completing the following steps:
   a. Select and delete the text *overview* that displays in the *Type in the keyword to find* text box and then type **shortcuts**.
   b. Double-click the subheading *for specific programs* that displays below the *shortcuts* heading.

c. Read the information that displays at the right side of the window and then print the information.
3. Close the Help and Support Center window by clicking the Close button located in the upper right corner of the window.

Customizing Settings

Before beginning computer projects in this textbook, you may need to customize the monitor settings and turn on the display of file extensions. Projects in the chapters in this textbook assume that the monitor display is set to 1024 by 768 pixels and that the display of file extensions is turned on. To change the monitor display to 1024 by 768, complete the following steps:

1. At the Windows XP desktop, right-click on any empty location on the desktop and then click *Properties* at the shortcut menu.
2. At the Display Properties dialog box, click the Settings tab.
3. Using the mouse, drag the slide bar button in the *Screen resolution* section to the left or right until *1024 by 768* displays below the slider bar.
4. Click the Apply button.
5. Click the OK button.

To turn on the display of file extensions, complete the following steps:

1. At the Windows XP desktop, click the Start button and then click *My Computer*.
2. At the My Computer window, click Tools on the Menu bar and then click *Folder Options* at the drop-down list.

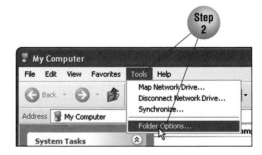

3. At the Folder Options dialog box, click the View tab.
4. Click the *Hide extentions for known file types* check box to remove the check mark.
5. Click the Apply button.
6. Click the OK button.

Browsing the Internet Using Internet Explorer 7.0

Microsoft Internet Explorer 7.0 is a Web browser program with options and features for displaying sites as well as navigating and searching for information on the Internet. The *Internet* is a network of computers connected around the world. Users access the Internet for several purposes: to communicate using instant messaging and/or e-mail, to subscribe to newsgroups, to transfer files, to socialize with other users around the globe in "chat" rooms, and also to access virtually any kind of information imaginable.

Tutorial IE1
Browsing the Internet with Internet Explorer 7.0
Tutorial IE2
Gathering and Downloading Information and Files

Using the Internet, people can find a phenomenal amount of information for private or public use. To use the Internet, three things are generally required: an Internet Service Provider (ISP), a program to browse the Web (called a *Web browser*), and a *search engine*. In this section, you will learn how to:

- Navigate the Internet using URLs and hyperlinks
- Use search engines to locate information
- Download Web pages and images

Browsing the Internet

You will use the Microsoft Internet Explorer Web browser to locate information on the Internet. Uniform Resource Locators, referred to as URLs, are the method used to identify locations on the Internet. The steps for browsing the Internet vary but generally include: opening Internet Explorer, typing the URL for the desired site, navigating the various pages of the site, navigating to other sites using links, and then closing Internet Explorer.

To launch Internet Explorer 7.0, double-click the *Internet Explorer* icon on the Windows desktop. Figure IE.1 identifies the elements of the Internet Explorer, version 7.0, window. The Web page that displays in your Internet Explorer window may vary from what you see in Figure IE.1.

Figure IE.1 Internet Explorer Window

Title bar

Navigation bar

Address bar

Tabbed browsing—display multiple Web pages by inserting new tabs

Instant search box

Toolbar

Status bar

Change zoom level

If you know the URL for the desired Web site, click in the Address bar, type the URL, and then press Enter. The Web site's home page displays in a tab within the Internet Explorer window. URLs (Uniform Resource Locators) are the method used to identify locations on the Internet. The format of a URL is *http://server-name.path*. The first part of the URL, *http*, stands for HyperText Transfer Protocol, which is the protocol or language used to transfer data within the World Wide Web. The colon and slashes separate the protocol from the server name. The server name is the second component of the URL. For example, in the URL http://www.microsoft.com, the server name is *microsoft*. The last part of the URL specifies the domain to which the server belongs. For example, *.com* refers to "commercial" and establishes that the URL is a commercial company. Other examples of domains include *.edu* for "educational," *.gov* for "government," and *.mil* for "military."

Project ① Browsing the Internet Using URLs

1. Make sure you are connected to the Internet through an Internet Service Provider and that the Windows desktop displays. (Check with your instructor to determine if you need to complete steps for accessing the Internet such as typing a user name and password to log on.)
2. Launch Microsoft Internet Explorer by double-clicking the *Internet Explorer* icon located on the Windows desktop.
3. At the Internet Explorer window, explore the Web site for Yosemite National Park by completing the following steps:
   a. Click in the Address bar, type **www.nps.gov/yose**, and then press Enter.

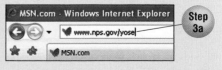

Step 3a

b. Scroll down the home page for Yosemite National Park by clicking the down-pointing arrow on the vertical scroll bar located at the right side of the Internet Explorer window.

c. Print the home page by clicking the Print button located on the Internet Explorer toolbar.

4. Explore the Web site for Glacier National Park by completing the following steps:

a. Click in the Address bar, type **www.nps.gov/glac**, and then press Enter.

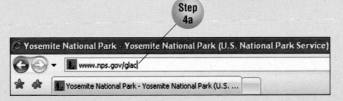

b. Print the home page by clicking the Print button located on the Internet Explorer toolbar.

5. Close Internet Explorer by clicking the Close button (contains an X) located in the upper right corner of the Internet Explorer window.

Navigating Using Hyperlinks

Most Web pages contain "hyperlinks" that you click to connect to another page within the Web site or to another site on the Internet. Hyperlinks may display in a Web page as underlined text in a specific color or as images or icons. To use a hyperlink, position the mouse pointer on the desired hyperlink until the mouse pointer turns into a hand, and then click the left mouse button. Use hyperlinks to navigate within and between sites on the Internet. The navigation bar in the Internet Explorer window contains a Back button that, when clicked, takes you to the previous Web page viewed. If you click the Back button and then want to return to the previous page, click the Forward button. You can continue clicking the Back button to back your way out of several linked pages in reverse order since Internet Explorer maintains a history of the Web sites you visit.

Project ② Navigating Using Hyperlinks

1. Make sure you are connected to the Internet and then double-click the *Internet Explorer* icon on the Windows desktop.

2. At the Internet Explorer window, display the White House Web page and navigate in the page by completing the following steps:

a. Click in the Address bar, type **whitehouse.gov**, and then press Enter.

b. At the White House home page, position the mouse pointer on a hyperlink that interests you until the pointer turns into a hand, and then click the left mouse button.

c. At the linked Web page, click the Back button. (This returns you to the White House home page.)

d. At the White House home page, click the Forward button to return to the previous Web page viewed.

e. Print the Web page by clicking the Print button on the Internet Explorer toolbar.

3. Display the Web site for Amazon.com and navigate in the site by completing the following steps:

a. Click in the Address bar, type www.amazon.com, and then press Enter.

b. At the Amazon.com home page, click a hyperlink related to books.

c. When a book Web page displays, click the Print button on the Internet Explorer toolbar.

4. Close Internet Explorer by clicking the Close button (contains an X) located in the upper right corner of the Internet Explorer window.

Searching for Specific Sites

If you do not know the URL for a specific site or you want to find information on the Internet but do not know what site to visit, complete a search with a search engine. A search engine is a software program created to search quickly and easily for desired information. A variety of search engines are available on the Internet, each offering the opportunity to search for specific information. One method for searching for information is to click in the *Instant Search* box (displays the text *Live Search*) located at the right end of the navigation bar, type a keyword or phrase related to your search, and then click the Search button or press Enter. Another method for completing a search is to visit the Web site for a search engine and use options at the site.

Project ③ Searching for Information by Topic

1. Start Internet Explorer.

2. At the Internet Explorer window, search for sites on bluegrass music by completing the following steps:

a. Click in the *Instant Search* box (may display with *Live Search*) located at the right end of the of the navigation bar.

b. Type **bluegrass music** and then press Enter.

c. When a list of sites displays in the Live Search tab, click a site that interests you.

d. When the page displays, click the Print button.

3. Use the Yahoo! search engine to find sites on bluegrass music by completing the following steps:
   a. Click in the Address bar, type www.yahoo.com, and then press Enter.
   b. At the Yahoo! Web site, with the insertion point positioned in the *Search* text box, type **bluegrass music** and then press Enter. (Notice that the sites displayed vary from sites displayed in the earlier search.)

   c. Click hyperlinks until a Web site displays that interests you.
   d. Print the page.
4. Use the Google search engine to find sites on jazz music by completing the following steps:
   a. Click in the Address bar, type www.google.com, and then press Enter.
   b. At the Google Web site, with the insertion point positioned in the search text box, type **jazz music** and then press Enter.

   c. Click a site that interests you.
   d. Print the page.
5. Close Internet Explorer.

Completing Advanced Searches for Specific Sites

The Internet contains an enormous amount of information. Depending on what you are searching for on the Internet and the search engine you use, some searches can result in several thousand "hits" (sites). Wading through a large number of sites can be very time-consuming and counterproductive. Narrowing a search to very specific criteria can greatly reduce the number of hits for a search. To narrow a search, use the advanced search options offered by the search engine.

Web Search

1. Start Internet Explorer.
2. Search for sites on skydiving in Oregon by completing the following steps:
   a. Click in the Address bar and then type www.yahoo.com.
   b. At the Yahoo! Web site, click the Web Search button next to the Search text box and then click the Advanced Search hyperlink.

   c. At the Advanced Web Search page, click in the search text box next to *all of these words*.
   d. Type skydiving Oregon tandem static line. (This limits the search to Web pages containing all of the words typed in the search text box.)

   e. Choose any other options at the Advanced Web Search page that will narrow your search.
   f. Click the Yahoo! Search button.
   g. When the list of Web sites displays, click a hyperlink that interests you.
   h. Print the page.
3. Close Internet Explorer.

Downloading Images, Text, and Web Pages from the Internet

The image(s) and/or text that display when you open a Web page as well as the Web page itself can be saved as a separate file. This separate file can be viewed, printed, or inserted in another file. The information you want to save in a separate file is downloaded from the Internet by Internet Explorer and saved in a folder of your choosing with the name you specify. Copyright laws protect much of the information on the Internet. Before using information downloaded from the Internet, check the site for restrictions. If you do use information, make sure you properly cite the source.

Project 5 **Downloading Images and Web Pages**

1. Start Internet Explorer.
2. Download a Web page and image from Banff
   National Park by completing the following steps:
   a. Search for sites on the Internet for Banff
      National Park.
   b. From the list of sites that displays, choose a site
      that contains information about Banff National
      Park and at least one image of the park.
   c. Save the Web page as a separate file by clicking
      the Page button on the Internet Explorer toolbar,
      and then clicking *Save As* at the drop-down list.
   d. At the Save Webpage dialog box, click the
      down-pointing arrow at the right side of the *Save in*
      option and then click the drive you are using as
      your storage medium at the drop-down list.
   e. Select the text in the *File name* text box, type
      BanffWebPage, and then press Enter.

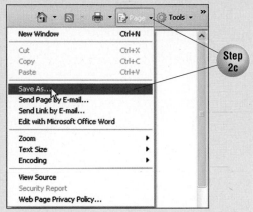

3. Save an image file by completing the following steps:
   a. Right-click an image that displays on the Web site. (The image that displays may vary
      from what you see below.)
   b. At the shortcut menu that displays, click *Save Picture As*.

c. At the Save Picture dialog box, change the *Save in* option to your storage medium.
d. Select the text in the *File name* text box, type **BanffImage**, and then press Enter.
4. Close Internet Explorer.

Step 3c

Step 3d

OPTIONAL

Project **Opening the Saved Web Page and Image in a Word Document**

1. Open Microsoft Word by clicking the Start button on the Taskbar, pointing to *All Programs*, pointing to *Microsoft Office*, and then clicking *Microsoft Office Word 2007*.
2. With Microsoft Word open, insert the image in a document by completing the following steps:
   a. Click the Insert tab and then click the Picture button in the Illustrations group.
   b. At the Insert Picture dialog box, change the *Look in* option to the location where you saved the Banff image and then double-click *BanffImage.jpg*.
   c. When the image displays in the Word document, print the document by clicking the Print button on the Quick Access toolbar.
   d. Close the document by clicking the Office button and then clicking *Close* at the drop-down menu. At the message asking if you want to save the changes, click No.
3. Open the **BanffWebPage.mht** file by completing the following steps:
   a. Click the Office button and then click *Open* at the drop-down menu.
   b. At the Open dialog box, change the *Look in* option to the location where you saved the Banff Web page and then double-click *BanffWebPage.mht*.
   c. Print the Web page by clicking the Print button on the Quick Access toolbar.
   d. Close the **BanffWebPage.mht** file by clicking the Office button and then *Close*.
4. Close Word by clicking the Close button (contains an X) that displays in the upper right corner of the screen.

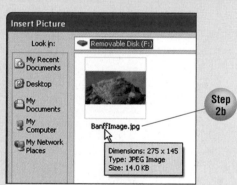

Step 2b

Step 3b

Microsoft® excel

Making Excel Work for You!

DEERING INDUSTRIES

SEMIANNUAL CUSTOMER SALES ANALYSIS

Customer	January	February	March	April	May	June	Average
Lakeside Trucking	$89,450	$75,340	$98,224	$84,231	$73,455	$97,549	$86,375
Gresham Machines	$45,210	$28,340	$53,400	$33,199	$40,390	$50,112	$41,775
Real Photography	$30,219	$28,590	$34,264	$30,891	$35,489	$36,400	$32,642
Genesis Productions	$65,290	$51,390	$79,334	$72,190	$75,390	$83,219	$71,136
Landower Company	$12,168	$19,355	$45,209	$22,188	$14,228	$38,766	$25,319
Jewell Enterprises	$44,329	$21,809	$33,490	$19,764	$50,801	$32,188	$33,730
Total	$286,666	$224,824	$343,921	$262,463	$289,753	$338,234	$290,977

Tracking and analyzing numerical data is a large component of the daily activity in today's workplace. Microsoft Excel 2007 is a popular choice among individuals and companies for organizing, analyzing, and presenting numerical information.

Organizing Information

Numbers are the foundation of every business transaction. Think about all of the numbers that the owner of a retail operation needs to organize to record customer purchases: account numbers, stock numbers, quantities, sale price, cost price, taxes, total due, amount received—just to name a few. Now consider a different scenario in which the manager of an apple orchard wants to track the volume of apples produced by each of 10 hybrids, along with the associated costs, in order to identify which hybrid apple trees are the most cost-effective. Factors to consider might include the number of apples produced weekly plus the costs of seed, fertilizer, general maintenance, and so on. These are just two examples of the type of information management for which you could use Excel.

Formula bar

Column header

Active cell

Row header

| A1 | ▼ | fx |

Active cell

Sheet1 / Sheet2 / Sheet3

Spreadsheet software organizes data in columns and rows—an electronic version of an accountant's ledger—only with a lot more power and versatility. In Microsoft Excel, information is organized by creating column and row *headers*, also called headings or labels. Numbers, called *values*, are entered below and beside the headers and then formulas are created to perform calculations. The completed document is referred to as a *worksheet*. The potential uses for an application like Excel are only limited by your imagination—any type of document that can be set up in the column/row format is a candidate for an Excel worksheet.

Not sure how to set up the information you want to track? Go to Office Online and browse the templates at the Microsoft Web site. Several templates are available that already contain labels and formulas, so all you have to do is fill in the data. You can preview a template before downloading it to make sure it will meet your needs. The templates site is updated continually, so keep checking for new additions.

Cedarview Construction

Corporate Sales Quotas

Salesperson	Current Quota	Projected Quota
Allejandro	$ 95,500	$114,600
Crispin	$ 137,000	$164,400
Frankel	$ 124,000	$148,800
Hiesmann	$ 85,500	$102,600
Jarvis	$ 159,000	$190,800
Littleman	$ 110,500	$132,600
Massey	$ 90,000	$108,000
Silverstein	$ 140,500	$168,600
Ting	$ 100,000	$120,000
Zimmerman	$ 115,500	$138,600
20% Increase	1.2	

What would be the projected sales quotas with a 20% increase?

Answer appears as soon as you change the percentage.

Analyzing Information

The true power of Excel lies in its ability to analyze information at the click of a mouse. Once you have created a worksheet, you can play the *what-if* game. For example, suppose you work in the sales department of a construction company and have used Excel to set up a worksheet that tracks sales quotas. You can use Excel's calculating and protecting features to answer questions: What kind of sales increase could we achieve if we added four more salespeople who each sold an average of the total current sales? What if we increase the existing sales quotas by 20 percent? Whenever you change a value in a worksheet, Excel automatically recalculates other values that are dependent on the number you changed. In an instant, you have your answer.

Excel includes several predefined formulas, called *functions*, that make the task of constructing complex worksheets easier to manage. So math is not your favorite subject? Not a problem with Excel's Insert Function dialog box, which helps you build a formula by prompting you with explanations for each parameter.

Use the sorting and filtering in Excel to help you analyze the data in various arrangements. With the click of a button, you can rearrange the order of the worksheet to sort in ascending or descending order by a single column or by multiple columns. By filtering records, you can reduce the data you are viewing by temporarily hiding rows that do not meet your criteria. For example, in a workplace scenario, you might want to view only those clients that owe the company less than $500.

Original worksheet

Real Photography

Invoices

Invoice #	Client #	Service	Date	Amount	Tax	Amount Due
1199	03-288	Development	9/11/2010	$ 95.00	0.0%	$ 95.00
1326	04-325	Sports Portraits	9/3/2010	$ 750.00	8.5%	$ 813.75
1320	04-325	Sports Portraits	9/7/2010	$ 750.00	8.5%	$ 813.75
1270	04-789	Family Portraits	9/8/2010	$ 560.00	8.8%	$ 609.28
1345	05-335	Development	9/8/2010	$ 400.00	0.0%	$ 400.00
1144	05-335	Development	9/15/2010	$ 140.00	0.0%	$ 140.00
1302	10-226	Wedding Portraits	9/14/2010	$ 2,250.00	8.5%	$ 2,441.25
1233	10-455	Sports Portraits	9/10/2010	$ 600.00	8.5%	$ 651.00
1230	10-788	Family Portraits	9/1/2010	$ 450.00	8.5%	$ 488.25
1277	11-005	Business Portrait	9/14/2010	$ 225.00	8.8%	$ 244.80
1438	11-279	Wedding Portraits	9/1/2010	$ 1,075.00	8.8%	$ 1,169.60
1129	11-279	Development	9/2/2010	$ 225.00	0.0%	$ 225.00
1355	11-279	Development	9/4/2010	$ 350.00	0.0%	$ 350.00
1198	11-325	Wedding Portraits	9/4/2010	$ 875.00	8.5%	$ 949.38

Records sorted by Invoice #

Real Photography

Invoices

Invoice #	Client #	Service	Date	Amount	Tax	Amount Due
1129	11-279	Development	9/2/2010	$ 225.00	0.0%	$ 225.00
1144	05-335	Development	9/15/2010	$ 140.00	0.0%	$ 140.00
1198	11-325	Wedding Portraits	9/4/2010	$ 875.00	8.5%	$ 949.38
1199	03-288	Development	9/11/2010	$ 95.00	0.0%	$ 95.00
1230	10-788	Family Portraits	9/1/2010	$ 450.00	8.5%	$ 488.25
1233	10-455	Sports Portraits	9/10/2010	$ 600.00	8.5%	$ 651.00
1270	04-789	Family Portraits	9/8/2010	$ 560.00	8.8%	$ 609.28
1277	11-005	Business Portrait	9/14/2010	$ 225.00	8.8%	$ 244.80
1302	10-226	Wedding Portraits	9/14/2010	$ 2,250.00	8.5%	$ 2,441.25
1320	04-325	Sports Portraits	9/7/2010	$ 750.00	8.5%	$ 813.75
1326	04-325	Sports Portraits	9/3/2010	$ 750.00	8.5%	$ 813.75
1345	05-335	Development	9/8/2010	$ 400.00	0.0%	$ 400.00
1355	11-279	Development	9/4/2010	$ 350.00	0.0%	$ 350.00
1438	11-279	Wedding Portraits	9/1/2010	$ 1,075.00	8.8%	$ 1,169.60

Real Photog

Records filtered to display amounts less than $500.00

Invoices

Invoice	Client #	Service	Date	Amount	Tax	Amount Due
1199	03-288	Development	9/11/2010	$ 95.00	0.0%	$ 95.00
1345	05-335	Development	9/8/2010	$ 400.00	0.0%	$ 400.00
1144	05-335	Development	9/15/2010	$ 140.00	0.0%	$ 140.00
1230	10-788	Family Portraits	9/1/2010	$ 450.00	8.5%	$ 488.25
1277	11-005	Business Portrait	9/14/2010	$ 225.00	8.8%	$ 244.80
1129	11-279	Development	9/2/2010	$ 225.00	0.0%	$ 225.00
1355	11-279	Development	9/4/2010	$ 350.00	0.0%	$ 350.00

Presenting Information

With information already structured in columns and rows, the task of interpreting the results is already simplified. Add some color and other rich text enhancements to draw the reader's attention to important titles, totals, or other results and you have just made the process even easier! Add clip art, photographs, or other media to a worksheet using the Clip Art task pane.

Since a picture is worth a thousand words, why not use Excel's charting capabilities to turn those numbers into a chart—a pictorial representation that enables a reader to more easily distinguish the impact of the differences between columns of numbers. Excel can render both two-dimensional and three-dimensional charts in several chart types, a sampling of which are: column, bar, line, pie, area, radar, doughnut, and scatter.

Knowing how to use Excel is a prerequisite for many jobs in our information-driven economy. Creating worksheets in Microsoft Excel 2007 is as simple as one, two, three—set up the column and row headings, enter the data, and create the formulas. Within a short period of time, you will *excel* at creating, editing, and formatting worksheets!

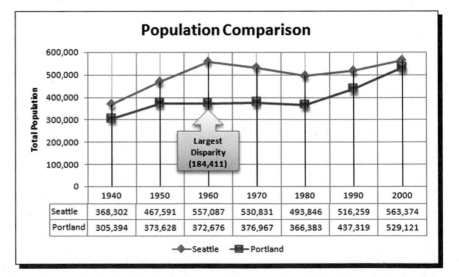

Microsoft®

Unit 1: Preparing and Formatting a Worksheet

- ➤ Preparing an Excel Workbook
- ➤ Inserting Formulas in a Worksheet
- ➤ Formatting an Excel Worksheet
- ➤ Enhancing a Worksheet

excel **Level 1**

Benchmark Microsoft® Excel 2007 Level 1

Microsoft Certified Application Specialist Skills—Unit 1

Reference No.	Skill	Pages
1	**Creating and Manipulating Data**	
1.1	Insert data using AutoFill	
1.1.1	Fill a series	16-19
1.1.2	Copy a series	21
1.4	Change worksheet views	
1.4.1	Change views within a single window	79-80, 115-116
2	**Formatting Data and Content**	
2.1	Format worksheets	
2.1.1	Use themes to format worksheets	81-82
2.1.4	Format worksheet backgrounds	118
2.2	Insert and modify rows and columns	
2.2.1	Insert and delete cells, rows, and columns	71-74
2.2.2	Format rows and columns	75-78
2.2.3	Hide and unhide rows and columns	96-98
2.2.4	Modify row height and column width	68-71
2.3	Format cells and cell content	
2.3.1	Apply number formats	51-52, 82-84
2.3.3	Apply and modify cell styles	25-26
2.3.4	Format text in cells	75-78, 85-87
2.3.6	Merge and split cells	76-78
2.3.7	Add and remove cell borders	91-93
3	**Creating and Modifying Formulas**	
3.1	Reference data in formulas	
3.1.1	Create formulas that use absolute and relative cell references	56-59
3.2	Summarize data using a formula	
3.2.1	Use SUM, COUNT, COUNTA, AVERAGE, MIN, and MAX	43-49
3.8	Display and print formulas	49
5	**Collaborating and Securing Data**	
5.5	Set print options for printing data, worksheets, and workbooks	
5.5.1	Define the area of a worksheet to be printed	120-121
5.5.2	Insert and move a page break	114-116
5.5.3	Set margins	110-112
5.5.4	Add and modify headers and footers	121-123
5.5.5	Change the orientation of a worksheet	112-113
5.5.6	Scale worksheet content to fit a printed page	117-118

Note: The Level 1 and Level 2 texts each address approximately half of the Microsoft Certified Application Specialist skills. Complete coverage of the skills is offered in the combined Level 1 and Level 2 text titled *Benchmark Series Microsoft® Excel 2007: Levels 1 and 2*, which has been approved as certified courseware and which displays the Microsoft Certified Application Specialist logo on the cover.

Preparing an Excel Workbook

PERFORMANCE OBJECTIVES

Upon successful completion of Chapter 1, you will be able to:

- Identify the various elements of an Excel workbook
- Create, save, and print a workbook
- Enter data in a workbook
- Edit data in a workbook
- Insert a formula using the Sum button
- Apply predesigned formatting to cells in a workbook
- Use the Help feature

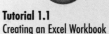

Tutorial 1.1
Creating an Excel Workbook

Many companies use a spreadsheet for numerical and financial data and to analyze and evaluate information. An Excel spreadsheet can be used for such activities as creating financial statements, preparing budgets, managing inventory, and analyzing cash flow. In addition, numbers and values can be easily manipulated to create "what if" situations. For example, using a spreadsheet, a person in a company can ask questions such as "What if the value in this category is decreased? How would that change affect the department budget?" Questions like these can be easily answered in an Excel spreadsheet. Change the value in a category and Excel will recalculate formulas for the other values. In this way, a spreadsheet can be used not only for creating financial statements or budgets, but also as a planning tool.

Note: Before beginning computer projects, copy to your storage medium the Excel2007L1C1 subfolder from the Excel2007L1 folder on the CD that accompanies this textbook. Steps on how to copy a folder are presented on the inside of the back cover of this textbook. Do this every time you start a chapter's projects.

Project 1 Prepare a Worksheet with Employee Information

You will create a worksheet containing employee information, edit the contents, and then save and close the workbook.

Creating a Worksheet

start

Open Excel by clicking the Start button at the left side of the Taskbar, pointing to *All Programs*, pointing to *Microsoft Office*, and then clicking *Microsoft Office Excel 2007*. (Depending on your operating system, these steps may vary.) When Excel is open, you are presented with a blank worksheet like the one shown in Figure 1.1. The elements of a blank Excel worksheet are described in Table 1.1.

Figure 1.1 Blank Excel Worksheet

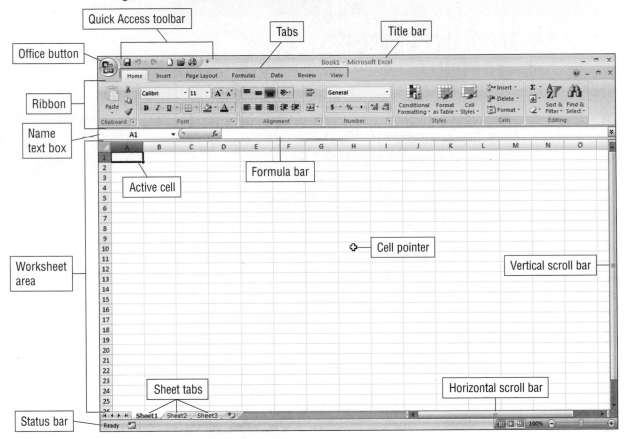

A file created in Excel is referred to as a ***workbook***. An Excel workbook consists of individual worksheets (or *sheets*) like the sheets of paper in a notebook. Notice the tabs located toward the bottom of the Excel window that are named *Sheet1*, *Sheet2*, and so on. The area containing the gridlines in the Excel window is called the ***worksheet area***. Figure 1.2 identifies the elements of the worksheet area. Create a worksheet in the worksheet area that will be saved as part of a workbook. Columns in a worksheet are labeled with letters of the alphabet and rows are numbered.

Table 1.1 Elements of an Excel Worksheet

Feature	Description
Office button	Displays as a Microsoft Office logo and, when clicked, displays a list of options along with the most recently opened workbooks
Quick Access toolbar	Contains buttons for commonly-used commands
Title bar	Displays workbook name followed by program name
Tab	Contains commands and features organized into groups
Ribbon	Area containing the tabs and commands divided into groups
Name box	Displays cell address (also called the cell reference) and includes the column letter and row number
Formula bar	Provides information about active cell; enter and edit formulas in this bar
Scroll bars	Use vertical and horizontal scroll bars to navigate within a worksheet
Sheet tab	Displays towards bottom of screen and identifies current worksheet
Status bar	Displays information about worksheet and active cell, view buttons, and Zoom slider bar

Figure 1.2 Elements of a Worksheet Area

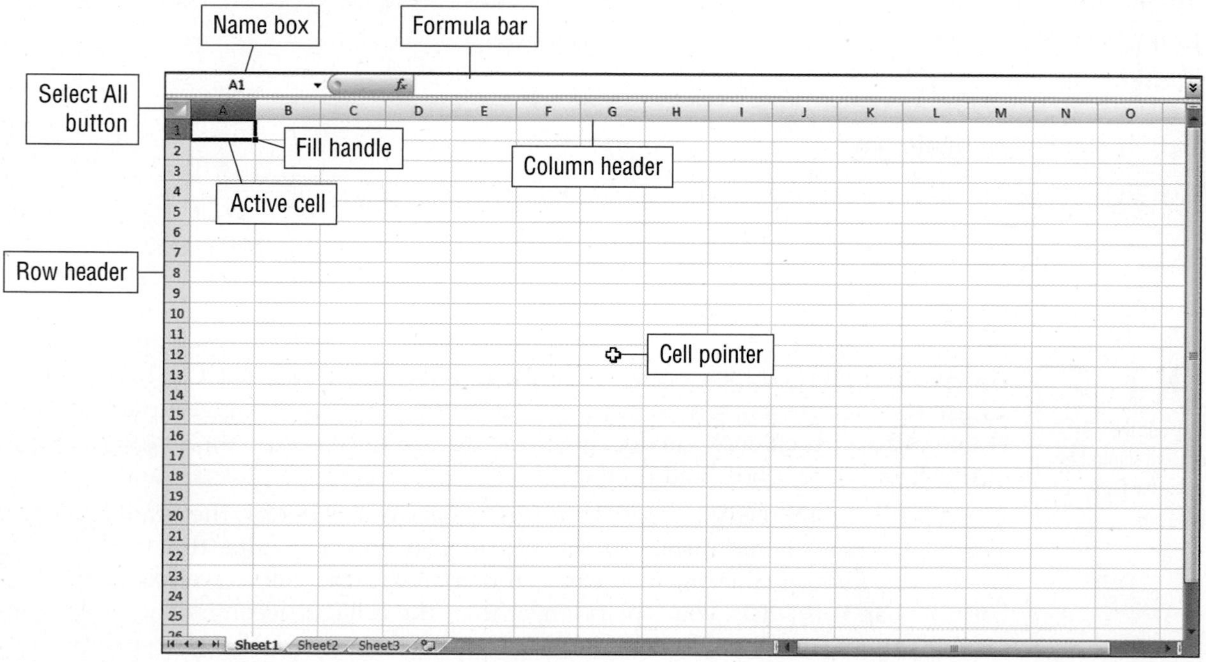

HINT

To make a cell active, position the cell pointer in the cell and then click the left mouse button.

The horizontal and vertical lines that define the cells in the worksheet area are called *gridlines*. When a cell is active (displays with a black border), the *cell address*, also called the *cell reference*, displays in the *Name box*. The cell reference includes the column letter and row number. For example, if the first cell of the worksheet is active, the cell reference *A1* displays in the Name box. A thick black border surrounds the active cell.

Entering Data in a Cell

Enter data such as a heading, number, or value in a cell. To enter data in a cell, make the desired cell active and then type the data. To make the next cell active, press the Tab key. Table 1.2 displays additional commands for making a specific cell active.

Table 1.2 Commands for Making a Specific Cell Active

To make this cell active	Press
Cell below current cell	Enter
Cell above current cell	Shift + Enter
Next cell	Tab
Previous cell	Shift + Tab
Cell at beginning of row	Home
Next cell in the direction of the arrow	Up, Down, Left, or Right Arrow keys
Last cell in worksheet	Ctrl + End
First cell in worksheet	Ctrl + Home
Cell in next window	Page Down
Cell in previous window	Page Up
Cell in window to right	Alt + Page Down
Cell in window to left	Alt + Page Up

HINT

Ctrl + G is the keyboard shortcut to display the Go To dialog box.

Find & Select ▾

Another method for making a specific cell active is to use the Go To feature. To use this feature, click the Find & Select button in the Editing group in the Home tab and then click Go To. At the Go To dialog box, type the cell reference in the *Reference* text box, and then click OK.

When you are ready to type data into the active cell, check the Status bar. The word *Ready* should display at the left side. As you type data, the word *Ready* changes to *Enter*. Data you type in a cell displays in the cell as well as in the Formula bar. If the data you type is longer than the cell can accommodate, the data overlaps the next cell to the right (it does not become a part of the next cell—it simply overlaps it). You will learn how to change column widths to accommodate data later in this chapter.

If the data you enter in a cell consists of text and the text does not fit into the cell, it overlaps the next cell. If, however, you enter a number in a cell, specify it as a number (rather than text) and the number is too long to fit in the cell, Excel changes the display of the number to number symbols *(###)*. This is because Excel does not want you to be misled by a number when you see only a portion of it in the cell.

Along with the keyboard, you can use the mouse to make a specific cell active. To make a specific cell active with the mouse, position the mouse pointer, which displays as a white plus sign (called the **cell pointer**), on the desired cell, and then click the left mouse button. The cell pointer displays as a white plus sign when positioned in a cell in the worksheet and displays as an arrow pointer when positioned on other elements of the Excel window such as options in tabs or scroll bars.

Scroll through a worksheet using the horizontal and/or vertical scroll bars. Scrolling shifts the display of cells in the worksheet area, but does not change the active cell. Scroll through a worksheet until the desired cell is visible and then click the desired cell.

Saving a Workbook

Save an Excel workbook, which may consist of a worksheet or several worksheets, by clicking the Save button on the Quick Access toolbar or by clicking the Office button and then clicking *Save* at the drop-down list. At the Save As dialog box, type a name for the workbook in the *File name* text box and then press Enter or click the Save button. A workbook file name can contain up to 255 characters, including drive letter and any folder names, and can include spaces. Note that you cannot give a workbook the same name in first uppercase and then lowercase letters. Also, some symbols cannot be used in a file name such as:

Save a Workbook
1. Click Save button.
2. Type workbook name.
3. Press Enter.

forward slash (/)	question mark (?)
backslash (\)	quotation mark (")
greater than sign (>)	colon (:)
less than sign (<)	semicolon (;)
asterisk (*)	pipe symbol (|)

To save an Excel workbook in the Excel2007L1C1 folder on your storage medium, display the Save As dialog box and then click the down-pointing arrow at the right side of the *Save in* option box. At the drop-down list that displays, click the drive representing your storage medium and then double-click Excel2007L1C1 in the list box.

HINT
Ctrl + S is the keyboard command to save a document.

Save

Office button

1. Open Excel by clicking the Start button on the Taskbar, pointing to *All Programs*, pointing to *Microsoft Office*, and then clicking *Microsoft Office Excel 2007*. (Depending on your operating system, these steps may vary.)
2. At the Excel worksheet that displays, create the worksheet shown in Figure 1.3 by completing the following steps:

   a. Press the Enter key once to make cell A2 the active cell.
   b. With cell A2 active (displays with a thick black border), type **Employee**.
   c. Press the Tab key. (This makes cell B2 active.)
   d. Type **Location** and then press the Tab key. (This makes cell C2 active.)
   e. Type **Benefits** and then press the Enter key to move the insertion point to cell A3.
   f. With cell A3 active, type the name **Avery**.
   g. Continue typing the data shown in Figure 1.3. (For commands for making specific cells active, refer to Table 1.2.)
3. After typing the data shown in the cells in Figure 1.3, save the workbook by completing the following steps:
   a. Click the Save button on the Quick Access toolbar.
   b. At the Save As dialog box, click the down-pointing arrow to the right of the *Save in* option.
   c. From the drop-down list that displays, click the letter representing your storage medium.
   d. Double-click the Excel2007L1C1 folder that displays in the list box.
   e. Select the text in the *File name* text box and then type **ExcelL1_C1_P1** (for Excel Level 1, Chapter 1, Project 1).
   f. Press the Enter key or click the Save button.

   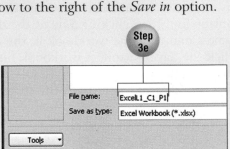

Figure 1.3 Project 1a

	A	B	C	D
1				
2	Employee	Location	Benefits	
3	Avery			
4	Connors			
5	Estrada			
6	Juergens			
7	Mikulich			
8	Talbot			
9				

Editing Data in a Cell

Edit data being typed in a cell by pressing the Backspace key to delete the character to the left of the insertion point or pressing the Delete key to delete the character to the right of the insertion point. To change the data in a cell, click the cell once to make it active and then type the new data. When a cell containing data is active, anything typed will take the place of the existing data.

If you want to edit only a portion of the data in a cell, double-click the cell. This makes the cell active, moves the insertion point inside the cell, and displays the word *Edit* at the left side of the Status bar. Move the insertion point using the arrow keys or the mouse and then make the needed corrections. If you are using the keyboard, you can press the Home key to move the insertion point to the first character in the cell or Formula bar, or press the End key to move the insertion point to the last character.

When you are finished editing the data in the cell, be sure to change out of the Edit mode. To do this, make another cell active. You can do this by pressing Enter, Tab, or Shift + Tab. You can also change out of the Edit mode and return to the Ready mode by clicking another cell or clicking the Enter button on the Formula bar.

If the active cell does not contain data, the Formula bar displays only the cell reference (by column letter and row number). As you type data, the two buttons shown in Figure 1.4 display on the Formula bar to the right of the Name box. Click the Cancel button to delete the current cell entry. You can also delete the cell entry by pressing the Delete key. Click the Enter button to indicate that you are finished typing or editing the cell entry. When you click the Enter button on the Formula bar, the word *Enter* (or *Edit*) located at the left side of the Status bar changes to *Ready*.

Cancel

Enter

Figure 1.4 Buttons on the Formula Bar

Project **1b** **Editing Data in a Cell**

1. With **ExcelL1_C1_P1.xlsx** open, double-click cell A7 (contains *Mikulich*).
2. Move the insertion point immediately left of the *k* and then type a c. (This changes the spelling to *Mickulich*.)
3. Click once in cell A4 (contains *Connors*), type **Bryant**, and then press the Tab key. (Clicking only once allows you to type over the existing data.)
4. Edit cell C2 by completing the following steps:
   a. Click the Find & Select button in the Editing group in the Home tab and then click *Go To* at the drop-down list.
   b. At the Go To dialog box, type C2 in the *Reference* text box, and then click OK.
   c. Type **Classification** (over *Benefits*).
5. Click once in any other cell.
6. Click the Save button on the Quick Access toolbar to save the workbook again.

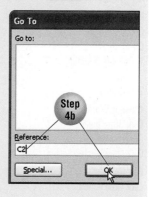

Step 4b

Quick Print

Printing a Workbook

Click the Quick Print button on the Quick Access toolbar to print the active worksheet. If the Quick Print button does not display on the Quick Access toolbar, click the Customize Quick Access Toolbar button that displays at the right side of the toolbar and then click *Quick Print* at the drop-down list. You can also print a worksheet by clicking the Office button, pointing to the *Print* option, and then clicking *Quick Print* at the side menu.

Closing a Workbook

Close Window

To close an Excel workbook, click the Office button and then click *Close* at the drop-down list. You can also close a workbook by clicking the Close Window button located toward the upper right corner of the screen. Position the mouse pointer on the button and a ScreenTip displays with the name *Close Window*.

Exiting Excel

X Exit Excel

Close

To exit Excel, click the Close button that displays in the upper right corner of the screen. The Close button contains an X and if you position the mouse pointer on the button a ScreenTip displays with the name *Close*. You can also exit Excel by clicking the Office button and then clicking the Exit Excel button located at the bottom of the drop-down list.

Using Automatic Entering Features

Excel contains several features that help you enter data into cells quickly and efficiently. These features include ***AutoComplete***, which automatically inserts data in a cell that begins the same as a previous entry; ***AutoCorrect***, which automatically corrects many common typographical errors; and ***AutoFill***, which will automatically insert words, numbers, or formulas in a series.

Using AutoComplete and AutoCorrect

The AutoComplete feature will automatically insert data in a cell that begins the same as a previous entry. If the data inserted by AutoComplete is the data you want in the cell, press Enter. If it is not the desired data, simply continue typing the correct data. This feature can be very useful in a worksheet that contains repetitive data entries. For example, consider a worksheet that repeats the word *Payroll*. The second and subsequent times this word is to be inserted in a cell, simply typing the letter *P* will cause AutoComplete to insert the entire word.

The AutoCorrect feature automatically corrects many common typing errors. To see what symbols and words are in the AutoCorrect feature, click the Office button and then click Excel Options located in the lower right corner of the drop-down list. At the Excel Options dialog box, click *Proofing* in the left panel and then click the AutoCorrect Options button located in the right panel. This displays the AutoCorrect dialog box with the AutoCorrect tab selected as shown in Figure 1.5 with a list box containing the replacement data.

Figure 1.5 AutoCorrect Dialog Box with AutoCorrect Tab Selected

When you type the text displayed in the first column in a worksheet and then press the spacebar, the text is replaced by the text in the second column.

At the AutoCorrect dialog box, type the text shown in the first column in the list box and the text in the second column is inserted in the cell. Along with symbols, the AutoCorrect dialog box contains commonly misspelled words and common typographical errors.

Project 1c — Inserting Data in Cells with AutoComplete

1. With **ExcelL1_C1_P1.xlsx** open make cell A1 active.
2. Type the text in cell A1 as shown in Figure 1.6. Insert the ® symbol by typing (r). (AutoCorrect will change (r) to ®.)
3. Type the remaining text in the cells. When you type the W in *West* in cell B5, the AutoComplete feature will insert *West*. Accept this by pressing the Enter key. (Pressing the Enter key accepts *West* and also makes the cell below active.) Use the AutoComplete feature to enter *West* in B6 and B8 and *North* in cell B7. Use AutoComplete to enter the second and subsequent occurrences of *Salaried* and *Hourly*.
4. Click the Save button on the Quick Access toolbar.
5. Print **ExcelL1_C1_P1.xlsx** by clicking the Quick Print button on the Quick Access toolbar. (The gridlines will not print.) If the Quick Print button does not display on the Quick Access toolbar, click the Customize Quick Access Toolbar button that displays at the right side of the toolbar and then click *Quick Print* at the drop-down list.
6. Close the workbook by clicking the Close Window button (contains an X) that displays in the upper right corner of screen. (Make sure you click the Close Window button and not the Close button.)

Step 5

Step 6

Figure 1.6 Project 1c

	A	B	C	D
1	Team Net®			
2	Employee	Location	Classification	
3	Avery	West	Hourly	
4	Bryant	North	Salaried	
5	Estrada	West	Salaried	
6	Juergens	West	Salaried	
7	Mickulich	North	Hourly	
8	Talbot	West	Hourly	
9				

Project 2 Open and Format a Workbook and Insert Formulas

You will open an existing workbook, insert formulas to find the sum and averages of numbers and apply predesigned formatting with table and cell styles.

Using AutoFill

When a cell is active, a thick black border surrounds it and a small black square displays in the bottom right corner of the border. This black square is called the AutoFill *fill handle* (see Figure 1.2). With the fill handle, you can quickly fill a range of cells with the same data or with consecutive data. For example, suppose you need to insert the year 2010 in a row or column of cells. To do this quickly, type **2010** in the first cell, position the mouse pointer on the fill handle, hold down the left mouse button, drag across the cells in which you want the year inserted, and then release the mouse button.

You can also use the fill handle to insert a series in a row or column of cells. For example, suppose you are creating a worksheet with data for all of the months in the year. Type **January** in the first cell, position the mouse pointer on the fill handle, hold down the left mouse button, drag down or across to 11 more cells, and then release the mouse button. Excel automatically inserts the other 11 months in the year in the proper order. When using the fill handle, the cells must be adjacent. Table 1.3 identifies the sequence inserted in cells by Excel when specific data is entered.

Table 1.3 AutoFill Fill Handle Series

Enter this data (Commas represent data in separate cells.)	And the fill handle will insert this sequence in adjacent cells
January	February, March, April, and so on . . .
Jan	Feb, Mar, Apr, and so on . . .
Jan 08, Jan 09	Jan-10, Jan-11, Jan-12, and so on . . .
Monday	Tuesday, Wednesday, Thursday, and so on . . .
Product 1	Product 2, Product 3, Product 4, and so on . . .
Qtr 1	Qtr 2, Qtr 3, Qtr 4
2, 4	6, 8, 10, and so on . . .

Certain sequences, such as *2, 4* and *Jan 08, Jan 09,* require that both cells be selected before using the fill handle. If only the cell containing *2* is active, the fill handle will insert *2s* in the selected cells. The list in Table 1.3 is only a sampling of what the fill handle can do. You may find a variety of other sequences that can be inserted in a worksheet using the fill handle.

An Auto Fill Options button displays when you fill cells with the fill handle. Click this button and a list of options displays for filling the cells. By default, data and formatting are filled in each cell. You can choose to fill only the formatting in the cells or fill only the data without the formatting.

HINT

If you do not want a series to increment, hold down the Ctrl key while dragging the fill handle.

Auto Fill Options

Opening a Workbook

Open a Workbook
1. Click Open button.
2. Display desired folder.
3. Double-click workbook name.

Open

Open an Excel workbook by displaying the Open dialog box and then double-clicking the desired workbook name. Display the Open dialog box by clicking the Open button on the Quick Access toolbar or clicking the Office button and then clicking *Open* at the drop-down list. If the Open button does not display on the Quick Access toolbar, click the Customize Quick Access Toolbar button that displays at the right side of the toolbar and then click *Open* at the drop-down list. You can also use the keyboard shortcut Ctrl + O to display the Open dialog box.

Project 2a Inserting Data in Cells with the Fill Handle

1. Open **ExcelC01Project02.xlsx**. (This workbook is located in the Excel2007L1C1 folder on your storage medium.)
2. Save the workbook with Save As and name it **ExcelL1_C1_P2**.
3. Add data to cells as shown in Figure 1.7. Begin by making cell B1 active and then typing January.
4. Position the mouse pointer on the fill handle for cell B1, hold down the left mouse button, drag across to cell G1, and then release the mouse button.

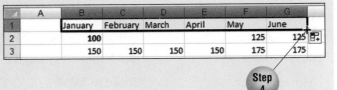

Step 4

5. Type a sequence and then use the fill handle to fill the remaining cells by completing the following steps:
   a. Make cell A2 active and then type **Year 1**.
   b. Make cell A3 active and then type **Year 3**.
   c. Select cells A2 and A3 by positioning the mouse pointer in cell A2, holding down the left mouse button, dragging down to cell A3, and then releasing the mouse button.
   d. Drag the fill handle for cell A3 to cell A5. (This inserts *Year 5* in cell A4 and *Year 7* in cell A5.)
6. Use the fill handle to fill adjacent cells with a number but not the formatting by completing the following steps:
   a. Make cell B2 active. (This cell contains *100* with bold formatting.)
   b. Drag the fill handle for cell B2 to cell E2. (This inserts *100* in cells C2, D2, and E2.)
   c. Click the Auto Fill Options button that displays at the bottom right of the selected cells.
   d. Click the *Fill Without Formatting* option at the drop-down list.

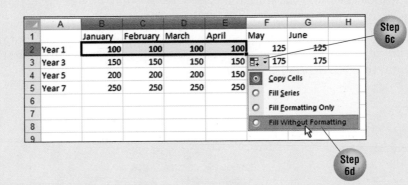

Step 6c

Step 6d

7. Use the fill handle to apply formatting only by completing the following steps:
   a. Make cell B2 active.
   b. Drag the fill handle to cell B5.
   c. Click the Auto Fill Options button and then click *Fill Formatting Only* at the drop-down list.
8. Make cell A10 active and then type **Qtr 1**.
9. Drag the fill handle for cell A10 to cell A13.
10. Save **ExcelL1_C1_P2.xlsx**.

Step 7c

Figure 1.7 Project 2a

	A	B	C	D	E	F	G	H
1		January	February	March	April	May	June	
2	Year 1	100	100	100	100	125	125	
3	Year 3	150	150	150	150	175	175	
4	Year 5	200	200	200	150	150	150	
5	Year 7	250	250	250	250	250	250	
6								
7								
8								
9								
10	Qtr 1	$5,500	$6,250	$7,000	$8,500	$5,500	$4,500	
11	Qtr 2	$6,000	$7,250	$6,500	$9,000	$4,000	$5,000	
12	Qtr 3	$4,500	$8,000	$6,000	$7,500	$6,000	$5,000	
13	Qtr 4	$6,500	$8,500	$7,000	$8,000	$5,500	$6,000	
14								

Inserting Formulas

Excel is a powerful decision-making tool containing data that can be manipulated to answer "what if" situations. Insert a formula in a worksheet and then manipulate the data to make projections, answer specific questions, and use as a planning tool. For example, the manager of a department might use an Excel worksheet to prepare a department budget and then determine the impact on the budget of hiring a new employee or increasing the volume of production.

Insert a formula in a worksheet to perform calculations on values. A formula contains a mathematical operator, value, cell reference, cell range, and a function. Formulas can be written that add, subtract, multiply, and/or divide values. Formulas can also be written that calculate averages, percentages, minimum and maximum values, and much more. Excel includes a Sum button in the Editing group in the Home tab that inserts a formula to calculate the total of a range of cells.

Using the Sum Button to Add Numbers

You can use the Sum button in the Editing group in the Home tab to insert a formula. The Sum button adds numbers automatically with the SUM function. Make active the cell in which you want to insert the formula (this cell should be empty) and then click the Sum button. Excel looks for a range of cells containing numbers above the active cell. If no cell above contains numbers, then Excel looks to the left of the active cell. Excel suggests the range of cells to be added. If the

QUICK STEPS

Insert Formula Using Sum Button
1. Click in desired cell.
2. Click Sum button.
3. Check range identified and make changes if necessary.
4. Press Enter.

HINT
You can use the keyboard shortcut, Alt + = to insert the SUM function in the cell.

Σ ▾

Sum

suggested range is not correct, drag through the desired range with the mouse, and then press Enter. You can also just double-click the Sum button and this will insert the SUM function with the range Excel chooses.

Project 2b   Adding Values with the Sum Button

1. With **ExcelL1_C1_P2.xlsx** open, make cell A6 active and then type **Total**.
2. Make cell B6 active and then calculate the sum of cells by clicking the Sum button in the Editing group in the Home tab.
3. Excel inserts the formula *=SUM(B2:B5)* in cell B6. This is the correct range of cells, so press Enter.

Step 2

	A	B	C	D	E	F	G	H	I	J	K	L	M	N
1		January	February	March	April	May	June							
2	Year 1	100	100	100	100	125	125							
3	Year 3	150	150	150	150	175	175							
4	Year 5	200	200	200	150	150	150							
5	Year 7	250	250	250	250	250	250							
6	Total	=SUM(B2:B5)												
7		SUM(number1, [number2], ...)												

DATE ▼ X ✓ *fx* =SUM(B2:B5)

Step 3

4. Make cell C6 active and then click the Sum button in the Editing group.
5. Excel inserts the formula *=SUM(C2:C5)* in cell C6. This is the correct range of cells, so press Enter.
6. Make cell D6 active.
7. Double-click the Sum button. (This inserts the formula *=SUM(D2:D5)* in cell D6 and inserts the sum *700*.)
8. Insert the sum in cells E6, F6, and G6.
9. Save **ExcelL1_C1_P2.xlsx**.

QUICK STEPS

Using the Sum Button to Average Numbers

Insert Average Formula Using Sum Button
1. Click in desired cell.
2. Click Sum button arrow.
3. Click *Average*.
4. Check range identified and make changes if necessary.
5. Press Enter.

A common function in a formula is the AVERAGE function. With this function, a range of cells is added together and then divided by the number of cell entries. The AVERAGE function is available on the Sum button. Click the Sum button arrow and a drop-down list displays with a number of common functions.

Using the Fill Handle to Copy a Formula

In a worksheet, you may want to insert the same basic formula in other cells. In a situation where a formula is copied to other locations in a worksheet, use a *relative cell reference*. Copy a formula containing relative cell references and the cell references change. For example, if you enter the formula =*SUM(A2:C2)* in cell D2 and then copy it relatively to cell D3, the formula in cell D3 displays as =*SUM(A3:C3)*. You can use the fill handle to copy a formula relatively in a worksheet. To do this, position the mouse pointer on the fill handle until the mouse pointer turns into a thin black cross. Hold down the left mouse button, drag and select the desired cells, and then release the mouse button.

QUICK STEPS

Copy Formula Using Fill Handle
1. Insert formula in cell.
2. Make active the cell containing formula.
3. Using fill handle, drag through cells you want to contain formula.

Project **2c**   **Inserting the AVERAGE Function and Copying a Formula Relatively**

1. With **ExcelL1_C1_P2.xlsx** open, make cell A14 active, and then type **Average**.
2. Insert the average of cells B10 through B13 by completing the following steps:
   a. Make cell B14 active.
   b. Click the Sum button arrow and then click *Average* at the drop-down list.
   c. Excel inserts the formula =*AVERAGE(B10:B13)* in cell B14. This is the correct range of cells, so press Enter.
3. Copy the formula relatively to cells C14 through G14 by completing the following steps:
   a. Make cell B14 active.
   b. Position the mouse pointer on the fill handle, hold down the left mouse button, drag across to cell G14, and then release the mouse button.

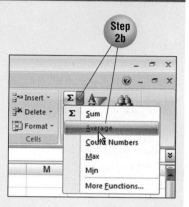

Step 2b

Step 3b

9							
10	Qtr 1	$5,500	$6,250	$7,000	$8,500	$5,500	$4,500
11	Qtr 2	$6,000	$7,250	$6,500	$9,000	$4,000	$5,000
12	Qtr 3	$4,500	$8,000	$6,000	$7,500	$6,000	$5,000
13	Qtr 4	$6,500	$8,500	$7,000	$8,000	$5,500	$6,000
14	Average	$5,625	$7,500	$6,625	$8,250	$5,250	$5,125
15							

4. Save **ExcelL1_C1_P2.xlsx**.

Selecting Cells

You can use a variety of methods for formatting cells in a worksheet. For example, you can change the alignment of data in cells or rows or add character formatting. To identify the cells that are to be affected by the formatting, select the specific cells.

Selecting Cells Using the Mouse

Select specific cells in a worksheet using the mouse or select columns or rows. Methods for selecting cells using the mouse display in Table 1.4.

Selected cells, except the active cell, display with a light blue background (this may vary) rather than a white background. The active cell is the first cell in the selection block and displays in the normal manner (white background with black data). Selected cells remain selected until you click a cell with the mouse or press an arrow key on the keyboard.

Table 1.4 Selecting with the Mouse

To select this	Do this
Column	Position the cell pointer on the column header (a letter) and then click the left mouse button.
Row	Position the cell pointer on the row header (a number) and then click the left mouse button.
Adjacent cells	Drag with mouse to select specific cells.
Nonadjacent cells	Hold down the Ctrl key while clicking column header, row header, or specific cells.
All cells in worksheet	Click Select All button (refer to Figure 1.2).

Selecting Cells Using the Keyboard

You can use the keyboard to select specific cells within a worksheet. Table 1.5 displays the commands for selecting specific cells.

Table 1.5 Selecting Cells Using the Keyboard

To select	Press
Cells in direction of arrow key	Shift + arrow key
To beginning of row	Shift + Home
To beginning of worksheet	Shift + Ctrl + Home
To last cell in worksheet containing data	Shift + Ctrl + End
An entire column	Ctrl + spacebar
An entire row	Shift + spacebar
An entire worksheet	Ctrl + A or Ctrl + Shift + spacebar

Selecting Data within Cells

The selection commands presented select the entire cell. You can also select specific characters within a cell. To do this with the mouse, position the cell pointer in the desired cell, and then double-click the left mouse button. Drag with the I-beam pointer through the data you want selected. Data selected within a cell displays in white with a black background. If you are using the keyboard to select data in a cell, hold down the Shift key, and then press the arrow key that moves the insertion point in the desired direction. Data the insertion point passes through will be selected. You can also press F8 to turn on the Extend Selection mode, move the insertion point in the desired direction to select the data, and then press F8 to turn off the Extend Selection mode. When the Extend Selection mode is on, the words *Extend Selection* display toward the left side of the Status bar.

Formatting with Predesigned Styles

An Excel worksheet contains default formatting. For example, letters and words are aligned at the left of a cell, numbers are aligned at the right, and data is set in 11-point Calibri. Excel provides predesigned styles you can use to apply formatting to cells in a worksheet. Apply table formatting styles with the Format as Table button or the Cell Styles button, both located in the Styles group in the Home tab.

Formatting with Table Styles

Apply table formatting styles to selected cells in a worksheet using the Format as Table button in the Styles group in the Home tab. When you select cells and then click the Format as Table button, a drop-down list displays as shown in Figure 1.8. Click the desired table style and the Format As Table dialog box displays. Click OK at this dialog box and the formatting is applied to the selected cells. Excel also inserts filtering arrows in each cell in the first row of selected cells. The filtering arrows do not print. You can turn off the display of the filtering arrows by clicking the Data tab and then clicking the Filter button in the Sort & Filter group. You will learn more about these filtering arrows in a later chapter.

Figure 1.8 Format as Table Drop-down List

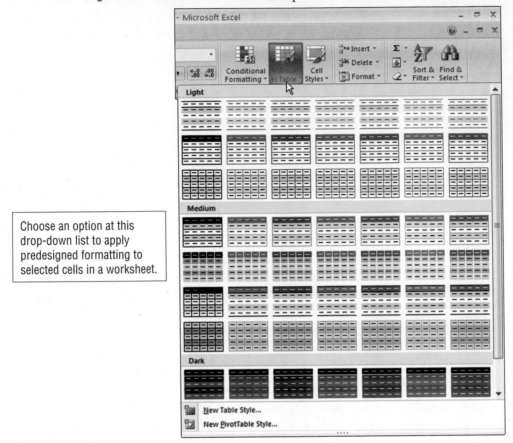

Choose an option at this drop-down list to apply predesigned formatting to selected cells in a worksheet.

Project 2d   Formatting Cells with Table Styles

1. With **ExcelL1_C1_P2.xlsx** open, apply a table style to specific cells by completing the following steps:
   a. Select cells A1 through G6.
   b. Click the Format as Table button in the Styles group in the Home tab.
   c. At the drop-down list, click the *Table Style Light 9* option (second style option from the left in the second row in the *Light* section).

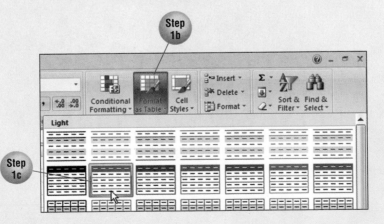

Step 1b

Step 1c

d. At the Format As Table dialog box, click OK. (Excel inserts filtering arrows in the cells in the first row.)

2. Select cells A10 through G14 and then apply the Table Style Light 11 style (fourth style option from the left in the second row in the *Light* section). At the Format As Table dialog box, click OK.

3. Save **ExcelL1_C1_P2.xlsx**. (Excel inserts a row with filtering arrows.)

Format As Table dialog box:

Where is the data for your table?
=$A$1:$G$6
☑ My table has headers

Step 1d → OK   Cancel

Formatting with Cell Styles

QUICK STEPS

Apply Cell Style
1. Select desired cell(s).
2. Click Cell Styles button.
3. Click desired style option.

Cell Styles

In some worksheets, you may want to highlight or accentuate certain cells. You can apply formatting to a cell or selected cells with cell styles. Click the Cell Styles button in the Styles group in the Home tab and a drop-down gallery of style options displays as shown in Figure 1.9. Hover your mouse pointer over a style option and the cell or selected cells display with the style formatting applied. You can hover your mouse over different style options to see how the style formatting affects the cell or selected cells. The Cell Styles button drop-down gallery is an example of the *live preview* feature, which allows you to see how the style formatting affects cells in your worksheet without having to return to the worksheet.

Figure 1.9 Cell Styles Drop-down Gallery

Choose an option at this drop-down gallery to apply a predesigned style to a cell or selected cells in a worksheet.

1. With **ExcelL1_C1_P2.xlsx** open, select cells B2 through G6.
2. Click the Cell Styles button in the Styles group in the Home tab.
3. At the drop-down gallery, hover your mouse over style options to see how the style formatting affects the selected cells.
4. Click the *Currency [0]* option (fourth option from the left in the *Number Format* section).

5. Select cells B6 through G6.
6. Click the Cell Styles button and then click the *Total* option (the last option in the *Titles and Headings* section).

7. Select cells B15 through G15 and then apply the Total cell style.
8. Save, print, and then close **ExcelL1_C1_P2.xlsx**.

Project 3 Use the Help Feature

You will use the Help feature to learn more about entering data in cells and selecting text and saving a workbook. You will also customize Help to search for information offline and for Excel training.

Using Help

Excel's Help feature is an on-screen reference manual containing information about Excel features. Excel's Help feature is similar to the Windows Help and the Help features in Word, PowerPoint, and Access. Get help by clicking the Microsoft Office Excel Help button located in the upper right corner of the screen (a question mark in a circle) or by pressing the keyboard shortcut, F1. This displays the Excel Help window. In this window, type a topic, feature, or question in the *Search* text box and then press Enter. Topics related to the search text display in the Help window. Click a topic that interests you. If the topic window contains a <u>Show All</u> hyperlink in the upper right corner, click this hyperlink and the information expands to show all help information related to the topic. When you click the <u>Show All</u> hyperlink, it becomes the <u>Hide All</u> hyperlink.

QUICK STEPS

Use Help Feature
1. Click Microsoft Office Excel Help button.
2. Type help question.
3. Press Enter.

Help

Project 3a Using the Help Feature

1. At a blank worksheet, click the Microsoft Office Excel Help button located in the upper right corner of the screen.
2. At the Excel Help window, type **enter data in cells** in the *Search* text box.
3. Press the Enter key.
4. When the list of topics displays, click the *Enter data manually in worksheet cells* hyperlink.
5. Click the <u>Show All</u> hyperlink that displays in the upper right corner of the window.

Step 1

Step 2

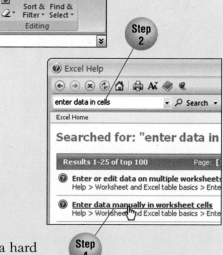

Step 5

Step 4

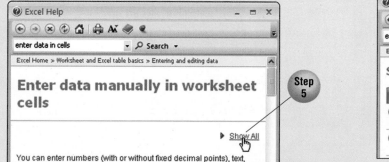

6. Read the information about entering data. (If you want a hard copy of the Help text, click the Print button located toward the top of the Excel Help window, and then click the Print button at the Print dialog box.)
7. Click the Close button to close the Excel Help window.

excel Level 1

Preparing an Excel Workbook   **27**

Getting Help in a Dialog Box

Dialog boxes contain a Help button you can click to display help in the Excel Help window that is specific to the dialog box. This button is located in the upper right corner of the dialog box and displays as a question mark inside a circle. Click this button and the Excel Help window displays with topics related to the dialog box.

Getting Help on a Button

When you position the mouse pointer on a button, a ScreenTip displays with information about the button. Some button ScreenTips display with the message "Press F1 for more help." that is preceded by an image of the Help button. With the ScreenTip visible, press the F1 function key and the Excel Help window opens and displays information about the specific button.

Project 3b — Getting Help in a Dialog Box and Button ScreenTip

1. At a blank worksheet, click the Office button and then click *Save As* at the drop-down list.
2. At the Save As dialog box, click the Help button located in the upper right corner of the dialog box.
3. At the Excel Help window, click the *Save As* hyperlink.
4. In the Save As list box, click *Microsoft Office Excel*.
5. Read the information that displays about saving in Excel and then click the Close button to close the Excel Help window.
6. Close the Save As dialog box.
7. Position the mouse pointer on the Office button until the ScreenTip displays and then press F1.

Step 2

Excel Help

Excel
Help and How-to

Suggestions

- **Export XML data**
  Working with XML
- **Introduction to new file nam Formats**
  Workbook management > File ma
- **Organize quick file access b**
  Workbook management > File ma
- **Publish a workbook to Excel**
  Publishing to SharePoint Server E
- **Publish as PDF or XPS**
- **Save a file**
  Workbook management > Saving
- **Save As**

Step 3

Step 7

Office Button

Click here to open, save, or print, and to see everything else you can do with your document.

Press F1 for more help.

8. At the Excel Help window that displays, click a hyperlink that interests you. Read the information and then close the Excel Help window.

Customizing Help

By default, the Excel Help feature will search for an Internet connection and, if one is found, display help resources from Office Online. If you are connected online to help resources, the message "Connected to Office Online" displays in the lower right corner of the Excel Help window. If you are not connected to the Internet, the message displays as "Offline."

Office Online provides additional help resources such as training and templates. To view the resources, display the Excel Help window and then click the down-pointing arrow at the right side of the Search button. This displays a drop-down list similar to the one shown in Figure 1.10. Generally, the *All Excel* option in the *Content from Office Online* is selected. If you want to search only the Help resources available with your computer (offline), click the *Excel Help* option in the *Content from this computer* section. To access Office Online training, click the *Excel Training* option in the *Content from Office Online* section, type a training topic in the *Search* text box, and then click OK.

Figure 1.10 Excel Help Search Drop-down List

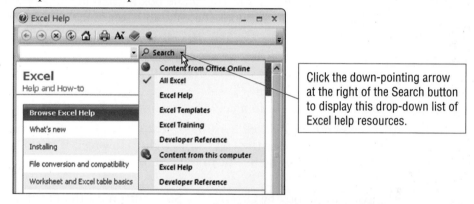

Click the down-pointing arrow at the right of the Search button to display this drop-down list of Excel help resources.

Project 3c Customizing Help

1. At a blank worksheet, click the Microsoft Office Excel Help button located toward the upper right corner of the screen.
2. Click the down-pointing arrow at the right side of the Search button in the Excel Help window.
3. At the drop-down list that displays, click *Excel Help* in the *Content from this computer* section.
4. Click in the *Search* text box, type formulas in the *Search* text box, and then press Enter.
5. Click a hyperlink that interests you and then read the information that displays.
6. Click the down-pointing arrow at the right side of the Search button and then click *Excel Training* in the *Content from Office Online* section.
7. Click in the *Search* text box (this will select *formulas*) and then press Enter.
8. Click the hyperlink of a training about formulas that interests you.
9. After completing the training, close Internet Explorer and then close the Excel Help window.

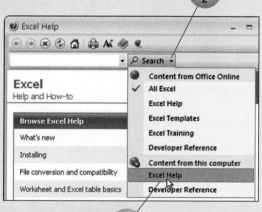

Step 2

Step 3

CHAPTER summary

- Use an Excel spreadsheet to create financial statements, prepare budgets, manage inventory, and analyze cash flow. Numbers and values can be easily manipulated in an Excel spreadsheet to answer "what if" questions.

- A file created in Excel is called a workbook. A workbook consists of individual worksheets. The intersection of columns and rows in a worksheet is referred to as a cell.

- An Excel window contains the following elements: Office button, Quick Access toolbar, Title bar, tabs, ribbon, Name box, Formula bar, scroll bars, sheet tabs, and Status bar.

- The horizontal and vertical lines that define cells in the worksheet area are called gridlines.

- When the insertion point is positioned in a cell, the cell name (also called the cell reference) displays in the Name box located at the left side of the Formula bar. The cell name includes the column letter and row number.

- To enter data in a cell, make the cell active and then type the data. To move the insertion point to the next cell, press the Tab key. To move the insertion point to the previous cell, press Shift + Tab. For other insertion point movement commands, refer to Table 1.2.

- Data being entered in a cell displays in the cell as well as in the Formula bar.

- If data entered in a cell consists of text (letters) and the text does not fit into the cell, it overlaps the cell to the right. However, if the data being entered are numbers and do not fit in the cell, the numbers are changed to number symbols (###).

- Save a workbook by clicking the Save button on the Quick Access toolbar or by clicking the Office button and then clicking *Save* at the drop-down list.

- To replace data in a cell, click the cell once and then type the new data. To edit data within a cell, double-click the cell and then make necessary changes.

- Print a workbook by clicking the Quick Print button on the Quick Access toolbar or by clicking the Office button, pointing to the *Print* option, and then clicking *Quick Print*.

- Close a workbook by clicking the Close Window button located in the upper right corner of the screen or by clicking the Office button and then clicking *Close* at the drop-down list.

- Exit Excel by clicking the Close button located in the upper right corner of the screen or by clicking the Office button and then clicking the Exit Excel button.

- The AutoComplete feature will automatically insert a previous entry if the character or characters being typed in a cell match a previous entry.

- The AutoCorrect feature corrects many common typographical errors.

- Use the AutoFill fill handle to fill a range of cells with the same or consecutive data.

- Open a workbook by clicking the Open button on the Quick Access toolbar or by clicking the Office button and then clicking the *Open* option at the drop-down list. At the Open dialog box, double-click the desired workbook.

- Use the Sum button in the Editing group in the Home tab to find the total or average of data in columns or rows.

- Select all cells in a column by clicking the column header. Select all cells in a row by clicking the row header. Select all cells in a worksheet by clicking the Select All button located immediately to the left of the column headers.
- To select cells with the mouse, refer to Table 1.4; to select cells using the keyboard, refer to Table 1.5.
- Use options from the Format as Table button drop-down gallery to apply predesigned table styles to selected cells.
- Use options from the Cell Styles button drop-down gallery to apply predesigned styles to a cell or selected cells.
- Excel's Help feature is an on-screen reference manual containing information about Excel features.
- Click the Microsoft Office Excel Help button or press F1 to display the Excel Help window. At this window, type a topic and then press Enter.
- Dialog boxes contain a Help button you can click to display the Excel Help window with information specific to the dialog box. The ScreenTip for some buttons displays with a message telling you to press F1. Press F1 and the Excel Help window opens with information about the button.
- Customize Help with options from the Search button drop-down list in the Excel Help window.

COMMANDS review

FEATURE	RIBBON TAB, GROUP	BUTTON	QUICK ACCESS TOOLBAR	OFFICE BUTTON DROP-DOWN LIST	KEYBOARD SHORTCUT
Close workbook		X		Close	Ctrl + F4
Exit Excel		X		Exit Excel	
Go To dialog box	Home, Editing	, Go To			Ctrl + G
Excel Help window					F1
Open workbook				Open	Ctrl + O
Print workbook				Print, Quick Print	
Save workbook				Save	Ctrl + S
Format as Table drop-down list	Home, Styles				
Cell Styles drop-down gallery	Home, Styles				
Sum button drop-down list	Home, Editing	Σ			

CONCEPTS check

Test Your Knowledge

Completion: In the space provided at the right, indicate the correct term, symbol, or command.

1. Columns in a worksheet are labeled with this. — *LETTERS*

2. Rows in a worksheet are labeled with this. — *NUMBERS*

3. The horizontal and vertical lines that define the cells in a worksheet area are referred to as this. — *GRIDLINES*

4. Press this key on the keyboard to move the insertion point to the next cell. — *TAB*

5. Press these keys on the keyboard to move the insertion point to the previous cell. — *SHIFT TAB*

6. If a number entered in a cell is too long to fit inside the cell, the number is changed to this. — *#*

7. Data being typed in a cell displays in the cell as well as here. — *Formula Bar*

8. This is the name of the small black square that displays in the bottom right corner of the active cell. — *Auto Fill fill handle*

9. To select nonadjacent columns using the mouse, hold down this key on the keyboard while clicking the column headers. — *CTRL*

10. Use this button in the Editing group in the Home tab to insert a formula in a cell. — *AUTO SUM*

11. With this function, a range of cells is added together and then divided by the number of cell entries. — *AVERAGE*

12. Click this button in the worksheet area to select all of the cells in the table. — *[△] Select All*

13. This feature allows you to see how style formatting affects cells in your worksheet without having to return to the worksheet. — *Cell Styles*

14. Press this function key to display the Excel Help window. — *F1*

SKILLS check

Demonstrate Your Proficiency

Assessment

1 CREATE AND FORMAT A WORKSHEET WITH A TABLE STYLE

1. Create the worksheet shown in Figure 1.11.
2. Select cells A1 through C5 and then apply the Table Style Medium 3 table style.
3. Save the workbook and name it **ExcelL1_C1_A1**.
4. Print and then close **ExcelL1_C1_A1.xlsx**.

Figure 1.11 Assessment 1

	A	B	C	D
1	Expense	Original	Current	
2	Labor	97000	98500	
3	Material	129000	153000	
4	Permits	1200	1350	
5	Tax	1950	2145	
6				

Assessment

2 CREATE A WORKSHEET USING AUTOCOMPLETE

1. Create the worksheet shown in Figure 1.12. To create the © symbol in cell A1, type (c). Type the misspelled words as shown and let the AutoCorrect feature correct the spelling. Use the AutoComplete feature to insert the second occurrence of *Category*, *Available*, and *Balance*.
2. Apply a table style of your choosing to cells A1 through B7. (Excel inserts a row with filtering arrows.)
3. Save the workbook and name it **ExcelL1_C1_A2**.
4. Print and then close **ExcelL1_C1_A2.xlsx**.

Figure 1.12 Assessment 2

	A	B	C
1	Premiere Plan©		
2	Plan A	Catagory	
3		Availalbe	
4		Balence	
5	Plan B	Category	
6		Available	
7		Balance	
8			

Assessment

3 CREATE A WORKSHEET USING THE FILL HANDLE

1. Create the worksheet shown in Figure 1.13. Type **Monday** in cell B2 and then use the fill handle to fill in the remaining days of the week. Use the fill handle to enter other repetitive data.
2. Apply a table style of your choosing to cells A1 through F4.
3. Save the workbook and name it **ExcelL1_C1_A3**.
4. Print and then close **ExcelL1_C1_A3.xlsx**.

Figure 1.13 Assessment 3

	A	B	C	D	E	F	G
1	CAPITAL INVESTMENTS						
2		Monday	Tuesday	Wednesday	Thursday	Friday	
3	Budget	350	350	350	350	350	
4	Actual	310	425	290	375	400	
5							

Assessment

4 INSERT FORMULAS IN A WORKSHEET

1. Open **ExcelC01Assessment04.xlsx** and then save the workbook and name it **ExcelL1_C1_A4**.
2. Insert a formula in cell B15 that totals the amounts in cells B4 through B14.
3. Use the fill handle to copy relatively the formula in cell B15 to cell C15.
4. Insert a formula in cell D4 that finds the average of cells B4 and C4.
5. Use the fill handle to copy relatively the formula in cell D4 down to cells D5 through D14.
6. Save, print, and then close **ExcelL1_C1_A4.xlsx**.

Assessment

5 USE HELP FEATURE TO LEARN ABOUT SCROLLING

1. Use the Help feature to learn more about how to scroll within an Excel worksheet.
2. Read and then print the information provided by Help.
3. Create a worksheet containing the information. Set this up as a worksheet with two columns (cells will contain only text—not numbers). Create a title for the worksheet.
4. Select the cells in your worksheet containing data and then apply a table style to the cells.
5. Save the completed workbook and name it **ExcelL1_C1_A5**.
6. Print and then close **ExcelL1_C1_A5.xlsx**.

CASE study
Apply Your Skills

Part 1

You are the office manager for Deering Industries. One of your responsibilities is creating a monthly calendar containing information on staff meetings, training, and due dates for time cards. Open **DeeringCalendar.xlsx** and then insert the following information:

- Insert the text **September, 2010** in cell A2.
- Insert the days of the week (*Sunday, Monday, Tuesday, Wednesday, Thursday, Friday*, and *Saturday*) in cells A3 through G3.
- Insert the number *1* in cell D4, number *2* in cell E4, number *3* in cell F4, and number *4* in cell G4.
- Insert in the calendar the remaining numbers of the days (numbers 5-11 in cells A6 through G6, numbers 12 through 18 in cells A8 through G8, numbers 19 through 25 in cells A10 through G10, and numbers 26 through 30 in cells A12 through E12).
- Excel training will be held Thursday, September 2, from 9-11 a.m. Insert this information in cell E5. (Insert the text on two lines by typing **Excel Training**, pressing Alt + Enter to move the insertion point to the next line, and then typing **9-10 a.m.**)
- A staff meeting is held the second and fourth Monday of each month from 9-10 a.m. Insert this information in cell B9 and cell B13.
- Time cards are due the first and third Fridays of the month. Insert in cells F5 and F9 information indicating that time cards are due.
- A production team meeting is scheduled for Tuesday, September 21, from 1-3 p.m. Insert this information in cell C11.

Save the workbook and name it **ExcelL1_C1_CS_P1**. Print and then close the workbook.

Part 2

The manager of the Purchasing Department has asked you to prepare a worksheet containing information on quarterly purchases. Open **DeeringExpenditures.xlsx** and then insert the data as shown in Figure 1.14. After typing the data, insert in the appropriate cells formulas to calculate averages and totals. Save the workbook and name it **ExcelL1_C1_CS_P2**. Print and then close the workbook.

Figure 1.14 Case Study Part 2

	A	B	C	D	E	F	G
1	DEERING INDUSTRIES						
2	PURCHASING DEPARTMENT - EXPENDITURES						
3	Category	1st Qtr.	2nd Qtr.	3rd Qtr.	4th Qtr.	Average	
4	Supplies	$ 645.75	$ 756.25	$ 534.78	$ 78,950.00		
5	Equipment	$ 4,520.55	$ 10,789.35	$ 3,825.00	$ 12,890.72		
6	Furniture	$ 458.94	$ 2,490.72	$ 851.75	$ 743.20		
7	Training	$ 1,000.00	$ 250.00	$ 1,200.00	$ 800.00		
8	Software	$ 249.00	$ 1,574.30	$ 155.45	$ 3,458.70		
9	Total						
10							

Part 3

The manager of the Purchasing Department has asked you to prepare a note to the finances coordinator, Jennifer Strauss. In Word, type a note to Jennifer Strauss explaining that you have prepared an Excel worksheet with the Purchasing Department expenditures. You are including the cells from the worksheet containing the expenditure information. In Excel, open **ExcelL1_C1_CS_P2.xlsx**, copy cells A3 through F9, and then paste them in the Word document. Make any corrections to the table so the information is readable. Save the document and name it **WordExcelL1_C1_CS_P3**. Print and then close the document. Close **ExcelL1_C1_CS_P3.xlsx**.

Part 4

You will be ordering copy machines for several departments in the company and decide to research prices. Using the Internet, find three companies that sell copiers and write down information on different copier models. Open **DeeringCopiers.xlsx** and then type the company, model number, and price in the designated cells. Save the completed workbook and name it **ExcelL1_C1_CS_P4**. Print and then close **ExcelL1_C1_CS_P4.xlsx**.

CHAPTER 2

Inserting Formulas in a Worksheet

PERFORMANCE OBJECTIVES

Upon successful completion of Chapter 2, you will be able to:

- Write formulas with mathematical operators
- Type a formula in the Formula bar
- Copy a formula
- Use the Insert Function feature to insert a formula in a cell
- Write formulas with the AVERAGE, MAX, MIN, COUNT, PMT, FV, DATE, NOW, and IF functions
- Create an absolute and mixed cell reference

Tutorial 2.1
Inserting and Editing Formulas
Tutorial 2.2
Working with Cell References

Excel is a powerful decision-making tool containing data that can be manipulated to answer "what if" situations. Insert a formula in a worksheet and then manipulate the data to make projections, answer specific questions, and use as a planning tool. For example, the owner of a company might prepare a worksheet on production costs and then determine the impact on company revenues if production is increased or decreased.

Insert a formula in a worksheet to perform calculations on values. A formula contains a mathematical operator, value, cell reference, cell range, and a function. Formulas can be written that add, subtract, multiply, and/or divide values. Formulas can also be written that calculate averages, percentages, minimum and maximum values, and much more. As you learned in Chapter 1, Excel includes a Sum button in the Editing group in the Home tab that inserts a formula to calculate the total of a range of cells and also includes some commonly used formulas. Along with the Sum button, Excel includes a Formulas tab that offers a variety of functions to create formulas.

Note: Before beginning computer projects, copy to your storage medium the Excel2007L1C2 subfolder from the Excel2007L1 folder on the CD that accompanies this textbook and make Excel2007L1C2 the active folder.

Project 1   Insert Formulas in a Worksheet

You will open a worksheet containing data and then insert formulas to calculate differences, salaries, and percentages of budgets.

Writing Formulas with Mathematical Operators

HINT

After typing a formula in a cell, press the Enter key, the Tab key, Shift + Tab, or click the Enter button on the Formula bar.

As you learned in Chapter 1, the Sum button in the Editing group in the Home tab creates the formula for you. You can also write your own formulas using mathematical operators. Commonly used mathematical operators and their functions are displayed in Table 2.1. When writing your own formula, begin the formula with the equals (=) sign. For example, to create a formula that divides the contents of cell B2 by the contents of cell C2 and inserts the result in cell D2, you would make D2 the active cell and then type =B2/C2.

Table 2.1 Mathematical Operators

Operator	Function
+	Addition
-	Subtraction
*	Multiplication
/	Division
%	Percent
^	Exponentiation

If a formula contains two or more operators, Excel uses the same order of operations used in algebra. From left to right in a formula, this order, called the *order of operations*, is: negations (negative number—a number preceded by -) first, then percents (%), then exponentiations (^), followed by multiplications (*), divisions (/), additions (+), and finally subtractions (-). If you want to change the order of operations, use parentheses around the part of the formula you want calculated first.

Copying a Formula with Relative Cell References

In many worksheets, the same basic formula is used repetitively. In a situation where a formula is copied to other locations in a worksheet, use a *relative cell reference*. Copy a formula containing relative cell references and the cell references change. For example, if you enter the formula =SUM(A2:C2) in cell D2 and then copy it relatively to cell D3, the formula in cell D3 displays as =SUM(A3:C3). (Additional information on cell references is discussed later in this chapter in the "Using an Absolute Cell Reference in a Formula" section.)

To copy a formula relatively in a worksheet, use the Fill button or the fill handle (you used the fill handle to copy a formula in Chapter 1). To use the Fill button, select the cell containing the formula as well as the cells to which you want the formula copied and then click the Fill button in the Editing group in the Home tab. At the Fill drop-down list, click the desired direction. For example, if you are copying the formula down cells, click the *Down* option.

QUICK STEPS

Copy Relative Formula
1. Insert formula in cell.
2. Select cell containing formula and all cells you want to contain formula.
3. Click Fill button.
4. Click desired direction.

Project 1a — Finding Differences by Inserting and Copying a Formula

1. Open **ExcelC02Project01.xlsx**.
2. Save the workbook with Save As and name it **ExcelL1_C2_P1**.
3. Insert a formula by completing the following steps:
   a. Make cell D3 active.
   b. Type the formula =C3-B3.
   c. Press Enter.
4. Copy the formula to cells D4 through D10 by completing the following steps:
   a. Select cells D3 through D10.
   b. Click the Fill button in the Editing group in the Home tab and then click *Down* at the drop-down list.
5. Save **ExcelL1_C2_P1.xlsx**.
6. With the worksheet open, make the following changes to cell contents:
   B4: Change *$48,290* to *46425*
   C6: Change *$61,220* to *60000*
   B8: Change *$55,309* to *57415*
   B9: Change *$12,398* to *14115*
7. Save **ExcelL1_C2_P1.xlsx**.

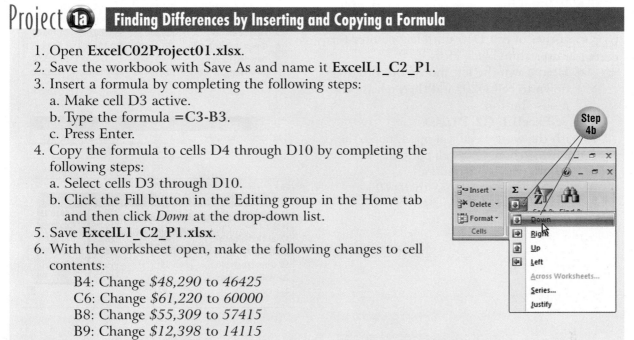

Copying Formulas with the Fill Handle

Use the fill handle to copy a formula up, down, left, or right within a worksheet. To use the fill handle, insert the desired data in the cell (text, value, formula, etc.). With the cell active, position the mouse pointer on the fill handle until the mouse pointer turns into a thin, black cross. Hold down the left mouse button, drag and select the desired cells, and then release the mouse button. If you are dragging a cell containing a formula, a relative version of the formula is copied to the selected cells.

HINT
Use the fill handle to copy a relative version of a formula.

1. With **ExcelL1_C2_P1.xlsx** open, insert a formula by completing the following steps:
   a. Make cell D15 active.
   b. Click in the Formula bar text box and then type =C15*B15.
   c. Click the Enter button on the Formula bar.
2. Copy the formula to cells D16 through D20 by completing the following steps:
   a. Make sure cell D15 is the active cell.
   b. Position the mouse pointer on the fill handle that displays at the lower right corner of cell D15 until the pointer turns into a thin, black cross.
   c. Hold down the left mouse button, drag down to cell D20, and then release the mouse button.
3. Save **ExcelL1_C2_P1.xlsx**.
4. With the worksheet still open, make the following changes to cell contents:
   B16: Change *20* to *28*
   C17: Change *$18.75* to *19.10*
   B19: Change *15* to *24*
5. Save **ExcelL1_C2_P1.xlsx**.

Step 1c

Step 1b

| DATE | ▼ | ⊘ | ✕ | ✓ | *fx* | =C15*B15 |

	A	B	C	D
1	**Highland Construction**			
2	Customer	Actual	Planned	Difference
3	Sellar Corporation	$30,349.00	$34,109.00	$3,760.00
4	Main Street Photos	$46,425.00	$48,100.00	$1,675.00
5	Sunset Automotive	$34,192.00	$32,885.00	-$1,307.00
6	Linstrom Enterprises	$63,293.00	$60,000.00	-$3,293.00
7	Morcos Media	$29,400.00	$30,500.00	$1,100.00
8	Green Valley Optics	$57,415.00	$58,394.00	$979.00
9	Detailed Designs	$14,115.00	$13,100.00	-$1,015.00
10	Arrowstar Company	$87,534.00	$86,905.00	-$629.00
11				
12				
13				
14	Name	Hours	Rate	Salary
15	Carolyn Bentley	35	$23.15	=C15*B15
16	Lindon Cassini	20	$19.00	

13				
14	Name	Hours	Rate	Salary
15	Carolyn Bentley	35	$23.15	$810.25
16	Lindon Cassini	20	$19.00	$380.00
17	Michelle DeFord	40	$18.75	$750.00
18	Javier Farias	24	$16.45	$394.80
19	Deborah Gould	15	$11.50	$172.50
20	William Jarman	15	$11.50	$172.50
21				
22				

Step 2c

Writing a Formula by Pointing

In Project 1a and Project 1b, you wrote formulas using cell references such as *=C3-B3*. Another method for writing a formula is to "point" to the specific cells that are to be part of the formula. Creating a formula by pointing is more accurate than typing the cell reference since a mistake can happen when typing the cell reference.

To write a formula by pointing, click the cell that will contain the formula, type the equals sign to begin the formula, and then click the cell you want to reference in the formula. This inserts a moving border around the cell and also changes the mode from Enter to Point. (The word *Point* displays at the left side of the Status bar.) Type the desired mathematical operator and then click the next cell reference. Continue in this manner until all cell references are specified and then press the Enter key. This ends the formula and inserts the result of the calculation of the formula in the active cell. When writing a formula by pointing, you can also select a range of cells you want included in a formula.

1. With **ExcelL1_C2_P1.xlsx** open, enter a formula by pointing that calculates the percentage of actual budget by completing the following steps:
   a. Make cell D25 active.
   b. Type the equals sign.
   c. Click cell C25. (This inserts a moving border around the cell and the mode changes from Enter to Point.)
   d. Type the forward slash symbol (/).
   e. Click cell B25.

	A	B	C	D	E
22					
23					
24	Expense	Actual	Budget	% of Actual	
25	Salaries	$126,000.00	$124,000.00	=C25/B25	
26	Commissions	$58,000.00	$54,500.00		
27	Media space	$8,250.00	$10,100.00		
28	Travel expenses	$6,350.00	$6,000.00		
29	Dealer display	$4,140.00	$4,500.00		
30	Payroll taxes	$2,430.00	$2,200.00		
31	Telephone	$1,450.00	$1,500.00		
32					

Steps 1a–1e

   f. Make sure the formula looks like this =C25/B25 and then press Enter.
2. Make cell D25 active, position the mouse pointer on the fill handle, drag down to cell D31, and then release the mouse button.
3. Save **ExcelL1_C2_P1.xlsx**.

C	D	E
Budget	% of Actual	
$124,000.00	98%	
$54,500.00	94%	
$10,100.00	122%	
$6,000.00	94%	
$4,500.00	109%	
$2,200.00	91%	
$1,500.00	103%	

Step 2

Using the Trace Error Button

As you are working in a worksheet, you may occasionally notice a button pop up near the active cell. The general term for this button is *smart tag*. The display of the smart tag button varies depending on the action performed. In Project 1d, you will insert a formula that will cause a smart tag button, named the Trace Error button, to appear. When the Trace Error button appears, a small dark green triangle also displays in the upper left corner of the cell. Click the Trace Error button and a drop-down list displays with options for updating the formula to include specific cells, getting help on the error, ignoring the error, editing the error in the Formula bar, and completing an error check. In Project 1d, two of the formulas you insert return the desired results. You will click the Trace Error button, read information on what Excel perceives as the error, and then tell Excel to ignore the error.

Trace Error

1. With **ExcelL1_C2_P1.xlsx** open, enter a
   formula by pointing that computes the
   percentage of equipment down time by
   completing the following steps:
   a. Make cell B45 active.
   b. Type the equals sign followed by the
      left parenthesis (=().
   c. Click cell B37. (This inserts a moving
      border around the cell and the mode
      changes from Enter to Point.)
   d. Type the minus symbol (-).
   e. Click cell B43.
   f. Type the right parenthesis followed by
      the forward slash ()/).
   g. Click cell B37.
   h. Make sure the formula looks like
      this =*(B37-B43)/B37* and then
      press Enter.
2. Make cell B45 active, position the
   mouse pointer on the fill handle,
   drag across to cell G45, and then
   release the mouse button.
3. Enter a formula by dragging
   through a range of cells by
   completing the following steps:
   a. Click in cell B46 and then click
      the Sum button in the Editing
      group in the Home tab.
   b. Select cells B37 through D37.
   c. Click the Enter button on the
      Formula bar. (This inserts *7,260*
      in cell B46.)
4. Click in cell B47 and then complete
   steps similar to those in Step 3 to create a
   formula that totals hours available from April
   through June (cells E37 through G37). (This
   inserts *7,080* in cell B47.)
5. Click in cell B46 and notice the Trace Error
   button that displays. Complete the following
   steps to read about the error and then tell Excel
   to ignore the error:
   a. Click the Trace Error button.
   b. At the drop-down list that displays, click the
      Help on this error option.
   c. Read the information that displays in the
      Excel Help window and then close the
      window.

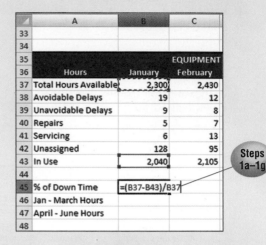

Steps 1a–1g

Step 3c

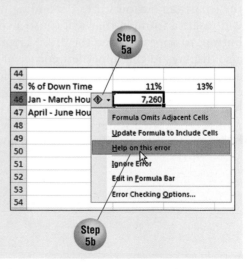

Step 5a

Step 5b

d. Click the Trace Error button again and then click *Ignore Error* at the drop-down list.

6. Remove the dark green triangle from cell B47 by completing the following steps:
   a. Click in cell B47.
   b. Click the Trace Error button and then click *Ignore Error* at the drop-down list.

7. Save, print, and then close **ExcelL1_C2_P1.xlsx**.

44				
45	% of Down Time		11%	13%
46	Jan - March Hou	◈ ▾	7,260	
47	April - June Hou			

Formula Omits Adjacent Cells
Update Formula to Include Cells
Help on this error
Ignore Error
Edit in Formula Bar
Error Checking Options...

Step 5d

Project 2 Insert Formulas with Statistical Functions

You will use the AVERAGE function to determine average test scores, use the MINIMUM and MAXIMUM functions to determine lowest and highest averages, use the COUNT function to count number of students taking a test, and display formulas in a cell rather than the result of the formula.

Inserting Formulas with Functions

In Project 2a in Chapter 1, you used the Sum button to insert the formula =SUM(B2:B5) in a cell. The beginning section of the formula, =SUM, is called a *function*, which is a built-in formula. Using a function takes fewer keystrokes when creating a formula. For example, the =SUM function saved you from having to type each cell to be included in the formula with the plus (+) symbol between cell entries.

Excel provides other functions for writing formulas. A function operates on what is referred to as an *argument*. An argument may consist of a constant, a cell reference, or another function (referred to as a nested function). In the formula =SUM(B2:B5), the cell range *(B2:B5)* is an example of a cell reference argument. An argument may also contain a *constant*. A constant is a value entered directly into the formula. For example, if you enter the formula =SUM(B3:B9,100), the cell range *B3:B9* is a cell reference argument and *100* is a constant. In this formula, 100 is always added to the sum of the cells. If a function is included in an argument within a function, it is called a *nested function*. (You will learn about nested functions later in this chapter.)

When a value calculated by the formula is inserted in a cell, this process is referred to as *returning the result*. The term *returning* refers to the process of calculating the formula and the term *result* refers to inserting the value in the cell.

You can type a function in a cell in a worksheet or you can use the Insert Function button on the Formula bar or in the Formulas tab to help you write the formula. Figure 2.1 displays the Formulas tab. The Formulas tab provides the Insert Function button as well as other buttons for inserting functions in a worksheet. The Function Library group in the Formulas tab contains a number of buttons for inserting functions from a variety of categories such as Financial, Logical, Text, and Date & Time.

Insert Function

Figure 2.1 Formulas Tab

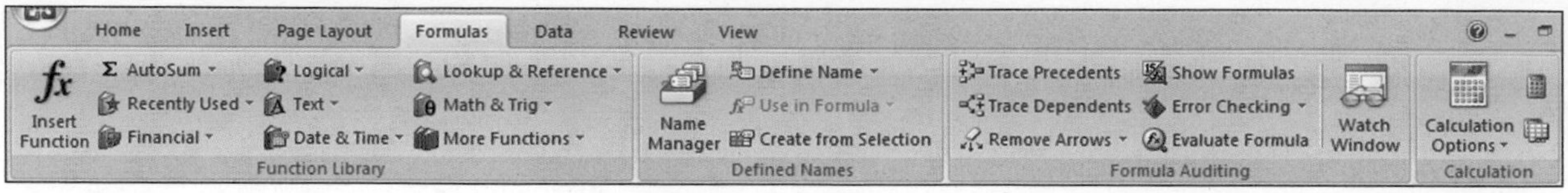

HINT

You can also display the Insert Function dialog box by clicking the down-pointing arrow at the right side of the Sum button and then clicking *More Functions*.

Click the Insert Function button on the Formula bar or in the Formulas tab and the Insert Function dialog box displays as shown in Figure 2.2. At the Insert Function dialog box, the most recently used functions display in the *Select a function* list box. You can choose a function category by clicking the down-pointing arrow at the right side of the *Or select a category* list box and then clicking the desired category at the drop-down list. Use the *Search for a function* option to locate a specific function.

Figure 2.2 Insert Function Dialog Box

The most recently used functions display in this list box.

Click this down-pointing arrow to display a list of categories.

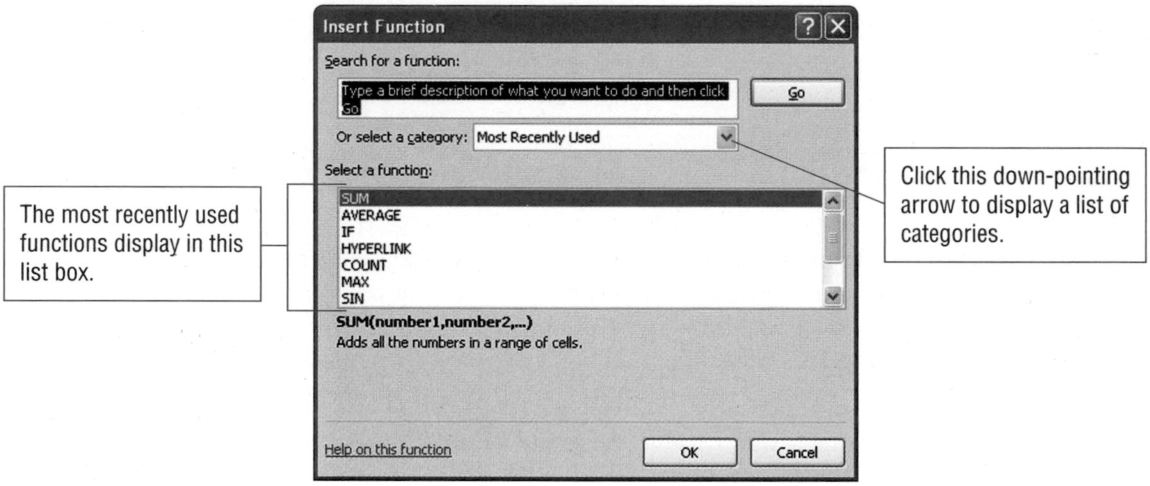

HINT

Click the down-pointing arrow at the right side of the Sum button in the Formulas tab and common functions display in a drop-down list.

With the desired function category selected, choose a function in the *Select a function* list box and then click OK. This displays a Function Arguments palette like the one shown in Figure 2.3. At this palette, enter in the *Number1* text box the range of cells you want included in the formula, enter any constants that are to be included as part of the formula, or enter another function. After entering a range of cells, a constant, or another function, click the OK button. You can include more than one argument in a function. If the function you are creating contains more than one argument, press the Tab key to move the insertion point to the *Number2* text box, and then enter the second argument. If you need to display a specific cell or cells behind the function palette, move the palette by clicking and dragging it.

Figure 2.3 Example Function Arguments Palette

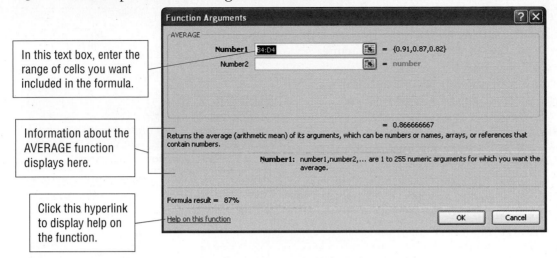

In this text box, enter the range of cells you want included in the formula.

Information about the AVERAGE function displays here.

Click this hyperlink to display help on the function.

Excel includes over 200 functions that are divided into 11 different categories including *Financial, Date & Time, Math & Trig, Statistical, Lookup & Reference, Database, Text, Logical, Information, Engineering,* and *Cube.* Clicking the Sum button in the Function Library group in the Formulas tab or the Editing group in the Home tab automatically adds numbers with the SUM function. The SUM function is included in the *Math & Trig* category. In some projects in this chapter, you will write formulas with functions in other categories including *Statistical, Financial, Date & Time,* and *Logical.*

Excel includes the Formula AutoComplete feature that displays a drop-down list of functions. To use this feature, click in the desired cell or click in the Formula bar text box, type the equals sign (=), and then type the first letter of the desired function. This displays a drop-down list with functions that begin with the letter. Double-click the desired function, enter the cell references, and then press Enter.

Writing Formulas with Statistical Functions

In this section, you will learn to write formulas with the statistical functions AVERAGE, MAX, MIN, and COUNT. The AVERAGE function returns the average (arithmetic mean) of the arguments. The MAX function returns the largest value in a set of values and the MIN function returns the smallest value in a set of values. Use the COUNT function to count the number of cells that contain numbers within the list of arguments.

Finding Averages

A common function in a formula is the AVERAGE function. With this function, a range of cells is added together and then divided by the number of cell entries. In Project 2a you will use the AVERAGE function, which will add all of the test scores for a student and then divide that number by the total number of tests. You will use the Insert Function button to simplify the creation of the formula containing an AVERAGE function.

One of the advantages to using formulas in a worksheet is the ability to easily manipulate data to answer certain questions. In Project 2a you will learn the impact of retaking certain tests on the final average score.

1. Open **ExcelC02Project02.xlsx**.
2. Save the workbook with Save As and name it **ExcelL1_C2_P2**.
3. Use the Insert Function button to find the average of test scores by completing the following steps:
   a. Make cell E4 active.
   b. Click the Insert Function button on the Formula bar.
   c. At the Insert Function dialog box, click the down-pointing arrow at the right side of the *Or select a category* list box and then click *Statistical* at the drop-down list.
   d. Click *AVERAGE* in the *Select a function* list box.
   e. Click OK.
   f. At the Function Arguments palette, make sure *B4:D4* displays in the *Number1* text box. (If not, type **B4:D4** in the *Number1* text box.)
   g. Click OK.
4. Copy the formula by completing the following steps:
   a. Make sure cell E4 is active.
   b. Position the mouse pointer on the fill handle until the pointer turns into a thin black cross.
   c. Hold down the left mouse button, drag down to cell E16, and then release the mouse button.
5. Save and then print **ExcelL1_C2_P2.xlsx**.
6. After viewing the averages of test scores, you notice that a couple of people have a low average. You decide to see what happens to the average score if students make up tests where they scored the lowest. You decide that a student can score a maximum of 70% on a retake of the test. Make the following changes to test scores to see how the changes will affect the test average.

   > B9: Change *50* to *70*
   > C9: Change *52* to *70*
   > D9: Change *60* to *70*
   > B10: Change *62* to *70*
   > B14: Change *0* to *70*
   > D14: Change *0* to *70*
   > D16: Change *0* to *70*

7. Save and then print **ExcelL1_C2_P2.xlsx**. (Compare the test averages for Teri Fisher-Edwards, Stephanie Flanery, Claude Markovits, and Douglas Pherson to see what the effect of retaking the tests has on their final test averages.)

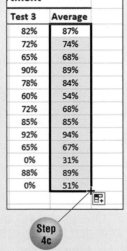

When a formula such as the AVERAGE formula you inserted in a cell in Project 2a calculates cell entries, it ignores certain cell entries. The AVERAGE function will ignore text in cells and blank cells (not zeros). For example, in the worksheet containing test scores, a couple of cells contained a *0%* entry. This entry was included in the averaging of the test scores. If you did not want that particular test to be included in the average, enter text in the cell such as *N/A* (for *not applicable*) or leave the cell blank.

Finding Maximum and Minimum Values

The MAX function in a formula returns the maximum value in a cell range and the MIN function returns the minimum value in a cell range. As an example, you could use the MAX and MIN functions in a worksheet containing employee hours to determine which employee worked the most number of hours and which worked the least. In a worksheet containing sales commissions, you could use the MAX and MIN functions to determine the salesperson who earned the most commission dollars and the one who earned the least.

Insert a MAX and MIN function into a formula in the same manner as an AVERAGE function. In Project 2b, you will use the Formula AutoComplete feature to insert the MAX function in cells to determine the highest test score average and the Insert Function button to insert the MIN function to determine the lowest test score average.

Project **2b** **Finding Maximum and Minimum Values in a Worksheet**

1. With **ExcelL1_C2_P2.xlsx** open, type the following in the specified cells:
   A19: **Highest Test Average**
   A20: **Lowest Test Average**
   A21: **Average of All Tests**
2. Insert a formula to identify the highest test score average by completing the following steps:
   a. Make cell B19 active.
   b. Type **=M.** (This displays the Formula AutoComplete list.)
   c. Double-click *MAX* in the Formula AutoComplete list.
   d. Type **E4:E16)** and then press Enter.
3. Insert a formula to identify the lowest test score average by completing the following steps:
   a. Make cell B20 active.
   b. Click the Insert Function button on the Formula bar.
   c. At the Insert Function dialog box, make sure *Statistical* is selected in the *Or select a category* list box, and then click *MIN* in the *Select a function* list box. (You will need to scroll down the list to display *MIN*.)
   d. Click OK.
   e. At the Function Arguments palette, type **E4:E16** in the *Number1* text box.
   f. Click OK.

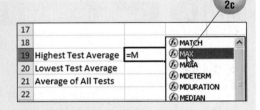

Step 2c

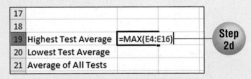

Step 2d

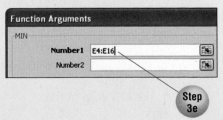

Step 3e

4. Insert a formula to determine the average of all test scores by completing the following steps:
   a. Make cell B21 active.
   b. Click the Formulas tab.
   c. Click the Insert Function button in the Function Library group.
   d. At the Insert Function dialog box, make sure *Statistical* is selected in the *Or select a category* list box and then click *AVERAGE* in the *Select a function* list box.
   e. Click OK.
   f. At the Function Arguments palette, type **E4:E16** in the *Number1* text box, and then click OK.
5. Save and then print **ExcelL1_C2_P2.xlsx**.
6. Change the *70%* values (which were previously *0%*) in cells B14, D14, and D16 to *N/A*. (This will cause the average of test scores for Claude Markovits and Douglas Pherson to increase and will change the minimum number and average of all test scores.)
7. Save and then print **ExcelL1_C2_P2.xlsx**.

Counting Numbers in a Range

Use the COUNT function to count the numeric values in a range. For example, in a range of cells containing cells with text and cells with numbers, you can count how many cells in the range contain numbers. In Project 2c, you will use the COUNT function to specify the number of students taking Test 2 and Test 3. In the worksheet, the cells containing the text N/A are not counted by the COUNT function.

Project 2c Counting the Number of Students Taking Tests

1. With **ExcelL1_C2_P2.xlsx** open, make cell A22 active.
2. Type **Test 2 Completed**.
3. Make cell B22 active.
4. Insert a formula counting the number of students who have taken Test 2 by completing the following steps:
   a. With cell B22 active, click in the Formula bar text box.
   b. Type **=C**.
   c. At the Formula AutoComplete list that displays, scroll down the list until *COUNT* displays and then double-click *COUNT*.
   d. Type **C4:C16)** and then press Enter.
5. Count the number of students who have taken Test 3 by completing the following steps:
   a. Make cell A23 active.
   b. Type **Test 3 Completed**.

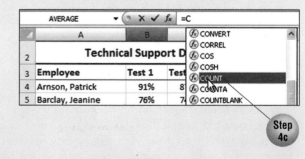

c. Make cell B23 active.
d. Click the Insert Function button on the Formula bar.
e. At the Insert Function dialog box, make sure *Statistical* is selected in the *Or select a category* list box.
f. Scroll down the list of functions in the *Select a function* list box until *COUNT* is visible and then double-click *COUNT*.
g. At the formula palette, type D4:D16 in the *Value1* text box, and then click OK.
6. Save and then print **ExcelL1_C2_P2.xlsx**.
7. Add test scores by completing the following steps:
a. Make cell B14 active and then type 68.
b. Make cell D14 active and then type 70.
c. Make cell D16 active and then type 55.
d. Press Enter.
8. Save and then print **ExcelL1_C2_P2.xlsx**.

Displaying Formulas

In some situations, you may need to display the formulas in a worksheet rather than the results of the formula. You may want to turn on formulas for auditing purposes or check formulas for accuracy. Display all formulas in a worksheet rather than the results by pressing Ctrl + ` (this is the grave accent). Press Ctrl + ` to turn off the display of formulas.

Project 2d Displaying Formulas

1. With **ExcelL1_C2_P2.xlsx** open, make cell A3 active.
2. Press Ctrl + ` to turn on the display of formulas.
3. Print the worksheet with the formulas.
4. Press Ctrl + ` to turn off the display of formulas.
5. Save and then close **ExcelL1_C2_P2.xlsx**.

Project 3 Insert Formulas with Financial and Date and Time Functions

You will use the PMT financial function to calculate payments and the FV function to find the future value of an investment. You will also use the DATE function to return the serial number for a date and the NOW function to insert the current date and time as a serial number.

Writing Formulas with Financial Functions

In this section, you will learn to write formulas with the financial functions PMT and FV. The PMT function calculates the payment for a loan based on constant payments and a constant interest rate. Use the FV function to return the future value of an investment based on periodic, constant payments and a constant interest rate.

Finding the Periodic Payments for a Loan

The PMT function finds the periodic payment for a loan based on constant payments and a constant interest rate. The PMT function contains the arguments Nper, Pv, Fv, and Type. The Nper argument is the number of payments that will be made to an investment or loan, Pv is the current value of amounts to be received or paid in the future, Fv is the value of a loan or investment at the end of all periods, and Type determines whether calculations will be based on payments made in arrears (at the end of each period) or in advance (at the beginning of each period).

Project 3a Calculating Payments

1. Open **ExcelC02Project03.xlsx**.
2. Save the workbook with Save As and name it **ExcelL1_C2_P3**.
3. The owner of Real Photography is interested in purchasing a new developer and needs to determine monthly payments on three different models. Insert a formula that calculates monthly payments and then copy that formula by completing the following steps:
   a. Make cell E5 active.
   b. Click the Formulas tab.
   c. Click the Financial button in the Function Library group, scroll down the drop-down list until *PMT* displays, and then click *PMT*.
   d. At the Function Arguments palette, type **C5/12** in the *Rate* text box. (This tells Excel to divide the interest rate by 12 months.)
   e. Press the Tab key. (This moves the insertion point to the *Nper* text box).
   f. Type **D5**. (This is the total number of months in the payment period.)
   g. Press the Tab key. (This moves the insertion point to the *Pv* text box.)
   h. Type **-B5**. (Excel displays the result of the PMT function as a negative number since the loan represents a negative cash flow to the borrower. Insert a minus sign before *B5* to show the monthly payment as a positive number rather than a negative number.)
   i. Click OK. (This closes the palette and inserts the monthly payment of *$316.98* in cell E5.)
   j. Copy the formula in cell E5 down to cells E6 and E7.
4. Insert a formula in cell F5 that calculates the <u>total amount of the payments</u> by completing the following steps:
   a. Make cell F5 active. MONTHLY PMTS X TERM IN MONTHS
   b. Type **=E5*D5** and then press Enter.
   c. Make cell F5 active and then copy the formula down to cells F6 and F7.
5. Insert a formula in cell G5 that calculates the <u>total amount of interest paid</u> by completing the following steps:
   a. Make cell G5 active. TOTAL PMTS - PURCHASE PRICE
   b. Type **=F5-B5** and then press Enter.
   c. Make cell G5 active and then copy the formula down to cells G6 and G7.
6. Save **ExcelL1_C2_P3.xlsx**.

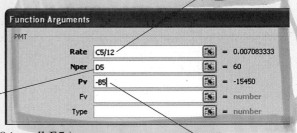

Monthly Payments	Total Payments	Total Interest
$316.98	$ 19,018.82	$ 3,568.82
$615.39	$ 36,923.60	$ 6,928.60
$711.92	$ 42,715.42	$ 8,015.42

Finding the Future Value of a Series of Payments

The FV function calculates the future value of a series of equal payments or an annuity. Use this function to determine information such as how much money can be earned in an investment account with a specific interest rate and over a specific period of time.

Project 3b · Finding the Future Value of an Investment

1. Make sure **ExcelL1_C2_P3.xlsx** is open.
2. The owner of Real Photography has decided to save money to purchase a new developer and wants to compute how much money can be earned by investing the money in an investment account that returns 9% annual interest. The owner determines that $1,200 per month can be invested in the account for three years. Complete the following steps to determine the future value of the investment account by completing the following steps:
   a. Make cell B15 active.
   b. Click the Financial button in the Function Library group in the Formulas tab.
   c. At the drop-down list that displays, scroll down the list until *FV* is visible and then click *FV*.
   d. At the Function Arguments palette, type B12/12 in the *Rate* text box.
   e. Press the Tab key.
   f. Type B13 in the *Nper* text box.
   g. Press the Tab key.
   h. Type B14 in the *Pmt* text box.
   i. Click OK. (This closes the palette and also inserts the future value of *$49,383.26* in cell B15.)
3. Save and then print **ExcelL1_C2_P3.xlsx**.
4. The owner decides to determine the future return after two years. To do this, change the amount in cell B13 from *36* to *24* and then press Enter. (This recalculates the future investment amount in cell B15.)
5. Save and then print **ExcelL1_C2_P3.xlsx**.

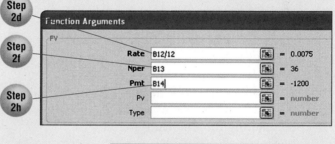

10		
11	**Future Value of Investment**	
12	Rate	9%
13	Number of Months	24
14	Monthly Payment	$ (1,200.00)
15	Future Value	$31,426.16
16		

Step 4

Writing Formulas with Date and Time Functions

In this section, you will learn to write formulas with the date and time functions NOW and DATE. The NOW function returns the serial number of the current date and time. The DATE function returns the serial number that represents a particular date. Excel can make calculations using dates because the dates are represented as serial numbers. To calculate a date's serial number, Excel counts the days since the beginning of the twentieth century. The date serial number for January 1, 1900, is 1. The date serial number for January 1, 2000, is 36,526. To access the DATE and NOW functions, click the Date & Time button in the Function Library group in the Formulas tab.

HINT
Ctrl + ; is the keyboard shortcut to insert the current date in the active cell.

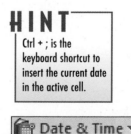

1. Make sure **ExcelL1_C2_P3.xlsx** is open.
2. Certain cells in this worksheet establish overdue dates for Real Photography accounts. Enter a formula in cell D20 that returns the serial number for the date March 17, 2010, by completing the following steps:
   a. Make cell D20 active.
   b. Click the Formulas tab.
   c. Click the Date & Time button in the Function Library group.
   d. At the drop-down list that displays, click *DATE*.
   e. At the Function Arguments palette, type **2010** in the *Year* text box.
   f. Press the Tab key and then type **03** in the *Month* text box.
   g. Press the Tab key and then type **17** in the *Day* text box.
   h. Click OK.

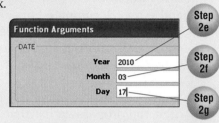

3. Complete steps similar to those in Step 2 to enter the following dates as serial numbers in the specified cells:
   D21 = March 24, 2010
   D22 = March 31, 2010
   D23 = April 7, 2010
4. Enter a formula in cell F20 that inserts the due date (the purchase date plus the number of days in the *Terms* column) by completing the following steps:
   a. Make cell F20 active.
   b. Type **=D20+E20** and then press Enter.
   c. Make cell F20 active and then copy the formula down to cells F21, F22, and F23.
5. Make cell A26 active and then type your name.
6. Insert the current date and time as a serial number by completing the following steps:
   a. Make cell A27 active.
   b. Click the Date & Time button in the Function Library group in the Formulas tab and then click *NOW* at the drop-down list.
   c. At the Function Arguments palette telling you that the function takes no argument, click OK.
7. Save, print, and then close **ExcelL1_C2_P3.xlsx**.

Project **4** Insert Formulas with the IF Logical Function

You will use the IF logical function to calculate sales bonuses, determine letter grades based on test averages, and identify discounts and discount amounts.

Writing a Formula with the IF Logical Function

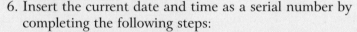

The IF function is considered a ***conditional function***. With the IF function you can perform conditional tests on values and formulas. A question that can be answered with true or false is considered a ***logical test***. The IF function makes a logical test and then performs a particular action if the answer is true and another action if the answer is false.

For example, an IF function can be used to write a formula that calculates a salesperson's bonus as 10% if the quota of $100,000 is met or exceeded, and zero if the quota is less than $100,000. That formula would look like this: =IF(quota=>100000,quota*0.1,0). The formula contains three parts—the condition or logical test IF(quota=>100000), action taken if the condition or logical test is true (quota*0.1), and the action taken if the condition or logical test is false (0). Commas separate the condition and the actions. In the bonus formula, if the quota is equal to or greater than $100,000, then the quota is multiplied by 10%. If the quota is less than $100,000, then the bonus is zero.

In Project 4a, you will write a formula with cell references rather than cell data. The formula in Project 4a is =IF(C5>B5,C5*0.15,0). In this formula the condition or logical test is whether or not the number in cell C5 is greater than the number in cell B5. If the condition is true and the number is greater, then the number in cell C5 is multiplied by 0.15 (providing a 15% bonus). If the condition is false and the number in cell C5 is less than the number in cell B5, then nothing happens (no bonus). Notice how commas are used to separate the logical test from the actions.

Editing a Formula

Edit a formula by making active the cell containing the formula and then editing the formula in the cell or in the Formula bar text box. After editing the formula, press Enter or click the Enter button on the Formula bar and Excel will recalculate the result of the formula.

Enter

Project 4a — Writing a Formula with an IF Function and Editing the Formula

1. Open **ExcelC02Project04.xlsx**.
2. Save the workbook with Save As and name it **ExcelL1_C2_P4**.
3. Write a formula with the IF function by completing the following steps. (The formula will determine if the quota has been met and, if it has, will insert the bonus [15% of the actual sales]. If the quota has not been met, the formula will insert a zero.)
   a. Make cell D5 active.
   b. Type =IF(C5>B5,C5*0.15,0) and then press Enter.
   c. Make cell D5 active and then use the fill handle to copy the formula to cells D6 through D10.
4. Print the worksheet.
5. Revise the formula so it will insert a 25% bonus if the quota has been met by completing the following steps:
   a. Make cell D5 active.
   b. Click in the Formula bar, edit the formula so it displays as =IF(C5>B5,C5*0.25,0), and then click the Enter button on the Formula bar.
   c. Copy the formula down to cells D6 through D10.
6. Save and then print **ExcelL1_C2_P4.xlsx**.

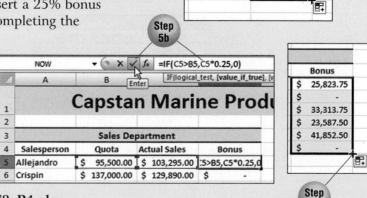

Writing a Nested IF Condition

In Project 4a, the IF function had only two possible actions—the actual sales times 15% or a zero. In a formula where more than two actions are required, use nested IF functions. For example, in Project 4b, you will write a formula with IF conditions that has four possible actions—a letter grade of A, B, C, or D. When writing nested IF conditions, insert symbols such as commas, quotation marks, and parentheses in the proper locations. If you want an IF condition to insert text, insert quotation marks before and after the text. The formula you will be writing in Project 4b is shown below.

$$=IF(E16>89,"A",IF(E16>79,"B",IF(E16>69,"C",IF(E16>59, "D"))))$$

This formula begins with the condition *=IF(E16>89, "A",*. If the number in cell E16 is greater than 89, then the condition is met and the grade of A is returned. The formula continues with a nested condition, *IF(E16>79, "B",*. If the number in cell E16 does not meet the first condition (greater than 89), then Excel looks to the next condition—is the number in cell E16 greater than 79? If it is, then the grade of B is inserted in cell E16. The formula continues with another nested condition, *IF(E16>69, "C",*. If the number in cell E16 does not match the first condition, Excel looks to the second condition, and if that condition is not met, then Excel looks to the third condition. If the number in cell E16 is greater than 69, then the grade of C is inserted in cell E16. The final nested condition is *IF(E16>59, "D"*. If the first three conditions are not met but this one is, then the grade of D is inserted in cell E16. The four parentheses at the end of the formula end each condition in the formula.

Project 4b Writing a Formula with Nested IF Conditions

1. With **ExcelL1_C2_P4.xlsx** open, insert a formula to average the scores by completing the following steps:
   a. Make cell E16 active.
   b. Type =AVERAGE(B16:D16) and then press Enter.
   c. Make cell E16 active and then copy the formula down to cells E17 through E20.
2. Insert a formula with nested IF conditions by completing the following steps:
   a. Make cell F16 active.
   b. Type =IF(E16>89,"A",IF(E16>79,"B",IF(E16>69,"C",IF(E16>59,"D")))) and then press Enter.

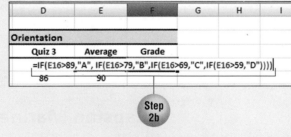

Step 2b

   c. Make cell F16 active and then use the fill handle to copy the formula down to cells F17 through F20.
3. Save **ExcelL1_C2_P4.xlsx**.

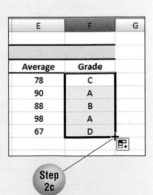

Step 2c

As you typed the formula with nested IF conditions in Step 2b of Project 4b, did you notice that the parentheses were different colors? Each color represents a condition. The four right parentheses at the end of the formula ended each of the conditions and each matched in color a left parenthesis. If an average in column E in **ExcelL1_C2_P4.xlsx** is less than 59, the nested formula inserts *FALSE* in the cell. If you want the formula to insert a letter grade, such as *F*, instead of *FALSE*, include another nested IF condition in the formula. Up to 64 levels of functions can be nested.

You can use the IF function from the Logical button drop-down list in the Function Library in the Formulas tab to write an IF statement. The IF statement you write using the IF function from the Logical button checks whether a condition is met and returns one value if the condition is met and another if the condition is not met. For example, in Project 4c you will insert an IF statement that identifies whether or not a part receives a discount. Parts that sell for more than $499 receive a discount and parts that sell for less do not. If the condition is met (the amount is greater than $499), then the statement will return a *YES* and if the condition is not met, the statement will return a *NO*.

In Project 4c, you will type the second IF statement in the cell rather than using the IF function from the Logical button drop-down list. The IF statement you write will reduce the price by five percent for parts that sell from $500 up to $749, seven percent for parts that sell from $750 up to $999, and ten percent for parts that sell for at least $1,000.

Project 4c Writing IF Statements Identifying Discounts and Discount Amounts

1. With **ExcelL1_C2_P4.xlsx** open, insert an IF statement by completing the following steps:
   a. Make cell C26 active.
   b. Click the Logical button in the Function Library group in the Formulas tab and then click IF at the drop-down list.
   c. At the Function Arguments palette, type B26>499 in the *Logic_test* text box.
   d. Press the Tab key to move the insertion point to the *Value_if_true* text box and then type YES.
   e. Press the Tab key to move the insertion point to the *Value_if_false* text box and then type NO.
   f. Click OK to close the Function Arguments palette.
2. Copy the formula in cell C26 down to cells C27 through C38.
3. Make cell D26 active.
4. Insert the following IF statement in the cell:
   =IF(B26>999,B26*0.1,IF(B26>749,B26*0.07,IF(B26>499,B26*0.05,IF(B26>0,"N/A"))))
5. Copy the formula in cell D26 down to cells D27 through D38.
6. Save, print, and then close **ExcelL1_C2_P4.xlsx**.

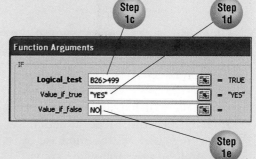

You will insert a formula containing an absolute cell reference that determines the effect on earnings with specific increases, insert a formula with multiple absolute cell references that determine the weighted average of scores, and use mixed cell references to determine simple interest.

Using Absolute and Mixed Cell References in Formulas

A reference identifies a cell or a range of cells in a worksheet and can be relative, absolute, or mixed. Relative cell references refer to cells relative to a position in a formula. Absolute references refer to cells in a specific location. When a formula is copied, a relative cell reference adjusts while an absolute cell reference remains constant. A mixed cell reference does both—either the column remains absolute and the row is relative or the column is relative and the row is absolute. Distinguish between relative, absolute, and mixed cell references using the dollar sign ($). Type a dollar sign before the column and/or row cell reference in a formula to specify that the column or row is an absolute cell reference.

Using an Absolute Cell Reference in a Formula

In this chapter you have learned to copy a relative formula. For example, if the formula =SUM(A2:C2) in cell D2 is copied relatively to cell D3, the formula changes to =SUM(A3:C3). In some situations, you may want a formula to contain an absolute cell reference, which always refers to a cell in a specific location. In Project 5a, you will add a column for projected job earnings and then perform "what if" situations using a formula with an absolute cell reference. To identify an absolute cell reference, insert a $ symbol before the row and the column. For example, the absolute cell reference C12 would be typed as $C$12 in a formula.

Project ⑤ⓐ Inserting and Copying a Formula with an Absolute Cell Reference

1. Open **ExcelC02Project05.xlsx**.
2. Save the workbook with Save As and name it **ExcelL1_C2_P5**.
3. Determine the effect on actual job earnings with a 20% increase by completing the following steps:
   a. Make cell C3 active, type the formula =B3*$B$12, and then press Enter.
   b. Make cell C3 active and then use the fill handle to copy the formula to cells C4 through C10.
4. Save and then print **ExcelL1_C2_P5.xlsx**.

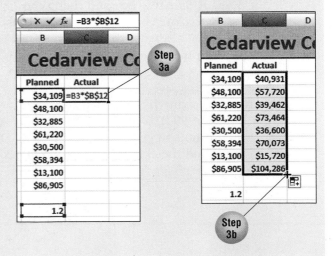

5. With the worksheet still open, determine the effect on actual job earnings with a 10% decrease by completing the following steps:
   a. Make cell B12 active.
   b. Type 0.9 and then press Enter.
6. Save and then print the **ExcelL1_C2_P5.xlsx**.
7. Determine the effects on actual job earnings with a 10% increase. (To do this, type 1.1 in cell B12.)
8. Save and then print **ExcelL1_C2_P5.xlsx**.

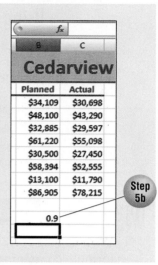

	fx	
	B	C
	Cedarview	
	Planned	Actual
	$34,109	$30,698
	$48,100	$43,290
	$32,885	$29,597
	$61,220	$55,098
	$30,500	$27,450
	$58,394	$52,555
	$13,100	$11,790
	$86,905	$78,215
	0.9	

Step 5b

In Project 5a, you created a formula with one absolute cell reference. You can also create a formula with multiple absolute cell references. For example, in Project 5b you will create a formula that contains both relative and absolute cell references to determine the average of training scores based on specific weight percentages.

Project 5b   Inserting and Copying a Formula with Multiple Absolute Cell References

1. With **ExcelL1_C2_P5.xlsx** open, insert the following formulas:
   a. Insert a formula in cell B23 that averages the percentages in cells B17 through B22.
   b. Copy the formula in cell B23 to the right to cells C23 and D23.
2. Insert a formula that determines the weighted average of training scores by completing the following steps:
   a. Make cell E17 active.
   b. Type the following formula:
      =$B$24*B17+$C$24*C17+$D$24*D17
   c. Press the Enter key.
   d. Copy the formula in cell E17 down to cells E18 through E22.
3. Save and then print the **ExcelL1_C2_P5.xlsx**.
4. With the worksheet still open, determine the effect on weighted training scores if the weighted values change by completing the following steps:
   a. Make cell B24 active, type 30, and then press Enter.
   b. Make cell D24 active, type 40, and then press Enter.
5. Save and then print **ExcelL1_C2_P5.xlsx**.

15	Employee Training				
16	Name	Plumbing	Electrical	Carpentry	Weighted Average
17	Allesandro	76%	80%	84%	89%
18	Ellington	66%	72%	64%	73%
19	Goodman	90%	88%	94%	100%
20	Huntington	76%	82%	88%	91%
21	Kaplan-Downing	90%	84%	92%	98%
22	Larimore	58%	62%	60%	66%
23	Training Averages	76%	78%	80%	
24	Training Weights	30%	30%	50%	
25					

Step 4a

Using a Mixed Cell Reference in a Formula

The formula you created in Step 3a in Project 5a contained a relative cell reference (B3) and an absolute cell reference ($B$12). A formula can also contain a mixed cell reference. In a mixed cell reference either the column remains absolute and the row is relative or the column is relative and the row is absolute. In Project 5c you will insert a number of formulas, two of which will contain mixed cell references. You will insert the formula =E29*E$26 to calculate withholding tax and =E29*H$36 to calculate Social Security tax. The dollar sign before the rows indicates that the row is an absolute cell reference.

 **Project 5c** **Determining Payroll Using Formulas with Absolute and Mixed Cell References**

1. With **ExcelL1_C2_P5.xlsx** open, make cell E29 active and then insert the following formula containing mixed cell references:
    =(B29*C29+(B29*$B$36*D29))
2. Copy the formula in cell E29 down to cells E30 through E34.
3. Make cell F29 active and then insert the following formula that calculates the amount of withholding tax:
    =E29*E$36
4. Copy the formula in cell F29 down to cells F30 through F34.
5. Make cell G29 active and then insert the following formula that calculates the amount of Social Security tax:
    =E29*H$36
6. Copy the formula in cell G29 down to cells G30 through G34.
7. Make cell H29 active and then insert the following formula that calculates net pay:
    =E29-(F29+G29)
8. Copy the formula in cell H29 down to cells H30 through H34.
9. Save **ExcelL1_C2_P5.xlsx**.

As you learned in Project 5c, a formula can contain a mixed cell reference. In a mixed cell reference either the column remains absolute and the row is relative or the column is relative and the row is absolute. In Project 5d, you will create the formula =$A41*B$40. In the first cell reference in the formula, $A41, the column is absolute and the row is relative. In the second cell reference, B$40, the column is relative and the row is absolute. The formula containing the mixed cell references allows you to fill in the column and row data using only one formula.

Identify an absolute or mixed cell reference by typing a dollar sign before the column and/or row reference or press the F4 function key to cycle through the various cell references. For example, type =A41 in a cell, press F4, and the cell reference changes to =$A$41. Press F4 again and the cell reference changes to =A$41. The next time you press F4, the cell reference changes to =$A41 and press it again to change the cell reference back to =A41.

Project **5d** **Determining Simple Interest Using a Formula with Mixed Cell References**

1. With **ExcelL1_C2_P5.xlsx** open, make cell B41 the active cell and then insert a formula containing mixed cell references by completing the following steps:
   a. Type =A41 and then press the F4 function key three times. (This changes the cell reference to *$A41*.)
   b. Type *B40 and then press the F4 function key twice. (This changes the cell reference to *B$40*.)
   c. Make sure the formula displays as *=$A41*B$40* and then press Enter.

39		SIMPLE INTEREST LOAN TABLE					
40		$ 1,000	$ 2,000	$ 3,000	$ 4,000	$ 5,000	
41	5%	=$A41*B$40					
42	6%						
43	7%						

Step 1c

2. Copy the formula to the right by completing the following steps:
   a. Make cell B41 active and then use the fill handle to copy the formula right to cell F41.

39		SIMPLE INTEREST LOAN TABLE					
40		$ 1,000	$ 2,000	$ 3,000	$ 4,000	$ 5,000	
41	5%	$ 50	$ 100	$ 150	$ 200	$ 250	
42	6%						
43	7%						

Step 2a

   b. With cells B41 through F41 selected, use the fill handle to copy the formula down to cell F51.

39		SIMPLE INTEREST LOAN TABLE					
40		$ 1,000	$ 2,000	$ 3,000	$ 4,000	$ 5,000	
41	5%	$ 50	$ 100	$ 150	$ 200	$ 250	
42	6%	$ 60	$ 120	$ 180	$ 240	$ 300	
43	7%	$ 70	$ 140	$ 210	$ 280	$ 350	
44	8%	$ 80	$ 160	$ 240	$ 320	$ 400	
45	9%	$ 90	$ 180	$ 270	$ 360	$ 450	
46	10%	$ 100	$ 200	$ 300	$ 400	$ 500	
47	11%	$ 110	$ 220	$ 330	$ 440	$ 550	
48	12%	$ 120	$ 240	$ 360	$ 480	$ 600	
49	13%	$ 130	$ 260	$ 390	$ 520	$ 650	
50	14%	$ 140	$ 280	$ 420	$ 560	$ 700	
51	15%	$ 150	$ 300	$ 450	$ 600	$ 750	
52							

Step 2b

3. Save, print, and then close **ExcelL1_C2_P5.xlsx**. (This worksheet will print on two pages.)

CHAPTER summary

- Type a formula in a cell and the formula displays in the cell as well as in the Formula bar. If cell entries are changed, a formula will automatically recalculate the values and insert the result in the cell.

- Create your own formula with commonly used operators such as addition (+), subtraction (-), multiplication (*), division (/), percent (%), and exponentiation (^). When writing a formula, begin with the equals (=) sign.

- Copy a formula to other cells in a row or column with the Fill button in the Editing group in the Home tab or with the fill handle that displays in the bottom right corner of the active cell.

- Another method for writing a formula is to point to specific cells that are part of the formula.

- If Excel detects an error in a formula, a Trace Error button appears and a dark green triangle displays in the upper left corner of the cell containing the formula.

- Excel includes over 200 functions that are divided into eleven categories. Use the Insert Function feature to create formulas using built-in functions.

- A function operates on an argument, which may consist of a cell reference, a constant, or another function. When a value calculated by a formula is inserted in a cell, this is referred to as returning the result.

- The AVERAGE function returns the average (arithmetic mean) of the arguments. The MAX function returns the largest value in a set of values, and the MIN function returns the smallest value in a set of values. The COUNT function counts the number of cells containing numbers within the list of arguments.

- Use the keyboard shortcut, Ctrl + ` (grave accent) to turn on the display of formulas in a worksheet.

- The PMT function calculates the payment for a loan based on constant payments and a constant interest rate. The FV function returns the future value of an investment based on periodic, constant payments and a constant interest rate.

- The NOW function returns the serial number of the current date and time and the DATE function returns the serial number that represents a particular date.

- Use the IF function, considered a conditional function, to perform conditional tests on values and formulas.

- Use nested IF functions in a formula where more than two actions are required.

- A reference identifies a cell or a range of cells in a worksheet and can be relative, absolute, or mixed. Identify an absolute cell reference by inserting a $ symbol before the column and row. Cycle through the various cell reference options by typing the cell reference and then pressing F4.

COMMANDS review

FEATURE	RIBBON TAB, GROUP	BUTTON	KEYBOARD SHORTCUT
SUM function	Home, Editing OR Formulas, Function Library	Σ AutoSum ▾	Alt + =
Insert Function dialog box	Formulas, Function Library	*fx*	Shift + F3
Display formulas			Ctrl + `

CONCEPTS check
Test Your Knowledge

Completion: In the space provided at the right, indicate the correct term, symbol, or command.

1. When typing a formula, begin the formula with this sign. =

2. This is the operator for division that is used when writing a formula. /

3. This is the operator for multiplication that is used when writing a formula. *

4. This is the name of the small black box located at the bottom right corner of a cell that can be used to copy a formula to adjacent cells. *fill handle*

5. A function operates on this, which may consist of a constant, a cell reference, or other function. *an argument*

6. This function returns the largest value in a set of values. *MAX*

7. This is the keyboard shortcut to display formulas in a worksheet. *Ctrl + `*

8. This function finds the periodic payment for a loan based on constant payments and a constant interest rate. *FV*

9. This function returns the serial number of the current date and time. *Now*

10. This function is considered a conditional function. *IF*

11. To identify an absolute cell reference, type this symbol before the column and row.

(handwritten: $)

12. Suppose that cell B2 contains the budgeted amount and cell C2 contains the actual amount. Write the formula (including the IF conditions) that would insert the word *under* if the actual amount was less than the budgeted amount and insert the word *over* if the actual amount was greater than the budgeted amount.

(handwritten: =if(C2<b2,"under","over")

SKILLS check
Demonstrate Your Proficiency

Assessment

(handwritten: Hand In →)

1 INSERT AVERAGE, MAX, AND MIN FUNCTIONS

1. Open **ExcelC02Assessment01.xlsx**.
2. Save the workbook with Save As and name it **ExcelL1_C2_A1**.
3. Use the AVERAGE function to determine the monthly sales (cells H4 through H9).
4. Total each monthly column including the Average column (cells B10 through H10).
5. Use the MAX function to determine the highest monthly total (for cells B4 through G9) and insert the amount in cell B11.
6. Use the MIN function to determine the lowest monthly total (for cells B4 through G9) and insert the amount in cell B12.
7. Save, print, and then close **ExcelL1_C2_A1.xlsx**.

Assessment

2 INSERT PMT FUNCTION

1. Open **ExcelC02Assessment02.xlsx**.
2. Save the workbook with Save As and name it **ExcelL1_C2_A2**.
3. The manager of Clearline Manufacturing is interested in refinancing a loan for either $125,000 or $300,000 and wants to determine the monthly payments, total payments, and total interest paid. Insert a formula with the following specifications:
   a. Make cell E5 active.
   b. Use the Insert Function button on the Formula bar to insert a formula using the PMT function. At the formula palette, enter the following:
      Rate = C5/12
      Nper = D5
      Pv = -B5
   c. Copy the formula in cell E5 down to cells E6 through E8.
4. Insert a formula in cell F5 that multiplies the amount in E5 by the amount in D5.

5. Copy the formula in cell F5 down to cells F6 through F8.
6. Insert a formula in cell G5 that subtracts the amount in B5 from the amount in F5. (The formula is =F5-B5.)
7. Copy the formula in cell G5 down to cells G6 through G8.
8. Save, print, and then close **ExcelL1_C2_A2.xlsx**.

Assessment

 3   INSERT FV FUNCTION

1. Open **ExcelC02Assessment03.xlsx**.
2. Save the workbook with Save As and name it **ExcelL1_C2_A3**.
3. Make the following changes to the worksheet:
   a. Change the percentage in cell B3 from *9%* to *10%*.
   b. Change the number in cell B4 from *36* to *60*.
   c. Change the amount in cell B5 from *($1,200) to -500*.
   d. Use the FV function to insert a formula that calculates the future value of the investment. ***Hint: For help with the formula, refer to Project 3b.***
4. Save, print, and then close **ExcelL1_C2_A3.xlsx**.

Assessment

4   WRITE IF STATEMENT FORMULAS

1. Open **ExcelC02Assessment04.xlsx**.
2. Save the workbook with Save As and name it **ExcelL1_C2_A4**.
3. Insert a formula in cell C4 that contains an IF statement with the following details:
   > If the contents of cell B4 are greater than 150000, then insert the word Platinum.
   > If the contents of cell B4 are greater than 100000, then insert the word Gold.
   > If the contents of cell B4 are greater than 75000, then insert the word Silver.
   > If the contents of cell B4 are greater than 0 (zero), then insert the word Bronze.

   When writing the IF statement, make sure you insert quotes around the words *Platinum*, *Gold*, *Silver*, and *Bronze*. Copy the formula in cell C4 down to cell C14.
4. Insert a formula in cell D4 that contains in IF statement with the following details:
   > If the content of cell C4 is Bronze, then insert the word None.
   > If the content of cell C4 is Silver, then insert $3,000.
   > If the content of cell C4 is Gold, then insert $5,000.
   > If the content of cell C4 is Platinum, then insert $10,000.

   When writing the IF statement, you will need to insert quotes around the words *Platinum*, *Gold*, *Silver*, *Bronze*, and *None* as well as the amounts *$3,000*, *$5,000*, and *$10,000*. Copy the formula in cell D4 down to cell D14.
5. Save and then print **ExcelL1_C2_A4.xlsx**.

6. Display the formulas in the worksheet.
7. Print **ExcelL1_C2_A4.xlsx**.
8. Turn off the display of the formulas.
9. Save and then close **ExcelL1_C2_A4.xlsx**.

Assessment

5 WRITE FORMULAS WITH ABSOLUTE CELL REFERENCES

1. Open **ExcelC02Assessment05.xlsx**.
2. Save the workbook with Save As and name it **ExcelL1_C2_A5**.
3. Make the following changes to the worksheet:
   a. Insert a formula using an absolute reference to determine the projected quotas at 10% of the current quotas.
   b. Save and then print **ExcelL1_C2_A5.xlsx**.
   c. Determine the projected quotas at 15% of the current quota by changing cell A15 to *15% Increase* and cell B15 to *1.15*.
   d. Save and then print **ExcelL1_C2_A5.xlsx**.
   e. Determine the projected quotas at 20% of the current quota.
4. Save, print, and then close **ExcelL1_C2_A5.xlsx**.

Assessment

6 USE HELP TO LEARN ABOUT EXCEL OPTIONS

1. Learn about specific options in the Excel Options dialog box by completing the following steps:
   a. Display the Excel Options dialog box by clicking the Office button and then clicking the Excel Options button that displays in the lower right corner of the drop-down list.
   b. At the Excel Options dialog box, click the *Advanced* option located in the left panel.
   c. Click the Help button that displays in the upper right corner of the dialog box, read the information that displays about advanced features, and then close the Excel Help window.
   d. Write down the check box options available in the *Display options for this workbook* section and the *Display options for this worksheet* section of the dialog box and identify whether or not the check box contains a check mark. (Record only check box options and ignore buttons and options preceded by circles.)
2. With the information you wrote down about the options, create an Excel spreadsheet with the following information:
   a. In column C, type each option you wrote down. (Include an appropriate heading.)
   b. In column B, insert an X in the cell that precedes any option that contains a check mark in the check box. (Include an appropriate heading.)
   c. In column A, write a formula with the IF function that inserts the word ON in the cell if the cell in column B contains an X and inserts the word OFF if it does not (the cell is blank). (Include an appropriate heading.)
   d. Apply formatting to improve the visual appeal of the worksheet.

3. Save the workbook and name it **ExcelL1_C2_A6**.
4. Turn on the display of formulas.
5. Print the worksheet.
6. Turn off the display of formulas.
7. Save, print, and then close **ExcelL1_C2_A6.xlsx**.

CASE study
Apply Your Skills

Part 1

You are a loan officer for Dollar Wise Financial Services and work in the department that specializes in home loans. You have decided to prepare a sample home mortgage worksheet to show prospective clients. This sample home mortgage worksheet will show the monthly payments on variously priced homes with varying interest rates. Open the **DollarWise.xlsx** worksheet and then complete the home mortgage worksheet by inserting the following formulas:

- Since many homes in your area sell for at least $400,000, you decide to add that amount to the worksheet with a 5%, 10%, 15%, and 20% down payment.
- In column C, insert a formula that determines the down payment amount.
- In column D, insert a formula that determines the loan amount.
- In column G, insert a formula using the PMT function (the monthly payment will display as a negative number).

Save the worksheet and name it **ExcelL1_C2_CS_P1**.

Part 2

If home buyers put down less than twenty percent of the home's purchase price, mortgage insurance is required. With **ExcelL1_C2_C1.xlsx** open, insert an IF statement in the cells in column H that inserts the word "No" if the percentage in column B is equal to or greater than 20% or inserts the word "Yes" if the percentage in column B is less than 20%. Save and then print **ExcelL1_C2_CS_P1.xlsx**.

Part 3

Interest rates fluctuate on a regular basis. Using the resources available to you, determine a current interest rate in your area. Delete the interest rate of 7% in the Dollar Wise worksheet and insert the interest rate for your area. Save and then print **ExcelL1_C2_CS_P1.xlsx**.

Part 4

When a client is required to purchase mortgage insurance, you would like to provide information to the client concerning this insurance. Use the Help feature to learn about creating hyperlinks in Excel. Locate a helpful Web site that specializes in private mortgage insurance. Create a hyperlink in the worksheet that will display the Web site. Save, print, and then close **ExcelL1_C2_CS_P1.xlsx**.

Part 5

Once a loan has been approved and finalized, a letter is sent to the client explaining the details of the loan. Use a letter template in Word to create a letter that is sent to the client. Copy and link the information in the **ExcelL1_C2_CS_P1.xlsx** worksheet to the client letter. Save the letter document and name it **WordDollarWiseLetter**. Print and then close **WordDollarWiseLetter.docx**.

Formatting an Excel Worksheet

PERFORMANCE OBJECTIVES

Upon successful completion of Chapter 3, you will be able to:

- Change column widths
- Change row heights
- Insert rows and columns in a worksheet
- Delete cells, rows, and columns in a worksheet
- Clear data in cells
- Apply formatting to data in cells
- Apply formatting to selected data using the Mini toolbar
- Preview a worksheet
- Apply a theme and customize the theme font and color
- Format numbers
- Repeat the last action
- Automate formatting with Format Painter
- Hide and unhide rows and columns

Tutorial 3.1
Working with Excel
Tutorial 3.2
Enhancing the Appearance of a
Worksheet

The appearance of a worksheet on the screen and how it looks when printed is called the *format*. In Chapter 1, you learned how to apply formatting to a table with the Format as Table button in the Styles group in the Home tab and apply formatting to a cell or selected cells with the Cell Styles button. Other types of formatting you may want to apply to a worksheet include changing column width and row height; applying character formatting such as bold, italics, and underlining; specifying number formatting; inserting and deleting rows and columns; and applying borders, shading, and patterns to cells. You can also apply formatting to a worksheet with a theme. A theme is a set of formatting choices that include colors and fonts.

Note: Before beginning computer projects, copy to your storage medium the Excel2007L1C3 subfolder from the Excel2007L1 folder on the CD that accompanies this textbook and then make Excel2007L1C3 the active folder.

Project ① Format a Product Pricing Worksheet

You will open a workbook containing a worksheet with product pricing data, and then format the worksheet by changing column widths and row heights, inserting and deleting rows and columns, deleting rows and columns, and clearing data in cells. You will also apply font and alignment formatting to data in cells and then preview the worksheet.

Changing Column Width

Columns in a worksheet are the same width by default. In some worksheets you may want to change column widths to accommodate more or less data. You can change column width using the mouse on column boundaries or at a dialog box.

Changing Column Width Using Column Boundaries

You can use the mouse to change the width of a column or selected columns. For example, to change the width of column B, you would position the mouse pointer on the blue boundary line between columns B and C in the column header until the mouse pointer turns into a double-headed arrow pointing left and right and then drag the boundary to the right to increase the size or to the left to decrease the size.

HINT

To change the width of all columns in a worksheet, click the Select All button and then drag a column boundary to the desired position.

You can change the width of selected adjacent columns at the same time. To do this, select the columns and then drag one of the column boundaries within the selected columns. As you drag the boundary the column width changes for all selected columns. To select adjacent columns, position the cell pointer on the first desired column header (the mouse pointer turns into a black, down-pointing arrow), hold down the left mouse button, drag the cell pointer to the last desired column header, and then release the mouse button.

As a column boundary is being dragged, the column width displays in a box above the mouse pointer. The column width number that displays represents the average number of characters in the standard font that can fit in a cell.

A column width in an existing worksheet can be adjusted to fit the longest entry in the column. To automatically adjust a column width to the longest entry, position the cell pointer on the column boundary at the right side of the column and then double-click the left mouse button.

Project ⓛⓐ Changing Column Width Using a Column Boundary

1. Open **ExcelC03Project01.xlsx**.
2. Save the workbook with Save As and name it **ExcelL1_C3_P1**.
3. Insert a formula in cell D2 that multiplies the price in cell B2 with the number in cell C2. Copy the formula in cell D2 down to cells D3 through D14.

4. Change the width of column D by completing the following steps:
   a. Position the mouse pointer on the column boundary in the column header between columns D and E until it turns into a double-headed arrow pointing left and right.
   b. Hold down the left mouse button, drag the column boundary to the right until *Width: 11.00 (82 pixels)* displays in the box, and then release the mouse button.

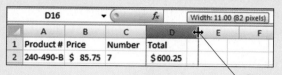

5. Make cell D15 active and then insert the sum of cells D2 through D14.

Step 4b

6. Change the width of columns A and B by completing the following steps:
   a. Select columns A and B. To do this, position the cell pointer on the column A header, hold down the left mouse button, drag the cell pointer to the column B header, and then release the mouse button.
   b. Position the cell pointer on the column boundary between columns A and B until it turns into a double-headed arrow pointing left and right.
   c. Hold down the left mouse button, drag the column boundary to the right until *Width: 10.14 (76 pixels)* displays in the box, and then release the mouse button.

Step 6c

7. Adjust the width of column C to accommodate the longest entry in the column by completing the following steps:
   a. Position the cell pointer on the column boundary between columns C and D until it turns into a double-headed arrow pointing left and right.
   b. Double-click the left mouse button.
8. Save **ExcelL1_C3_P1.xlsx**.

Changing Column Width at the Column Width Dialog Box

At the Column Width dialog box shown in Figure 3.1, you can specify a column width number. Increase the column width number to make the column wider or decrease the column width number to make the column narrower.

To display the Column Width dialog box, click the Format button in the Cells group in the Home tab and then click *Column Width* at the drop-down list. At the Column Width dialog box, type the number representing the average number of characters in the standard font that you want to fit in the column, and then press Enter or click OK.

Figure 3.1 Column Width Dialog Box

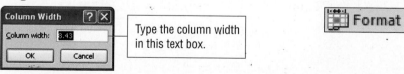

QUICK STEPS

Change Column Width
Drag column boundary line.
OR
Double-click column boundary.
OR
1. Click Format button.
2. Click *Column Width* at drop-down list.
3. Type desired width.
4. Click OK.

Format ▾

Project 1b — Changing Column Width at the Column Width Dialog Box

1. With **ExcelL1_C3_P1.xlsx** open, change the width of column A by completing the following steps:
   a. Make any cell in column A active.
   b. Click the Format button in the Cells group in the Home tab and then click *Column Width* at the drop-down list.
   c. At the Column Width dialog box, type 12.75 in the *Column width* text box.
   d. Click OK to close the dialog box.
2. Make any cell in column B active and then change the width of column B to *12.75* by completing steps similar to those in Step 1.
3. Make any cell in column C active and then change the width of column C to *8* by completing steps similar to those in Step 1.
4. Save **ExcelL1_C3_P1.xlsx**.

Step 1c

Step 1d

Column Width
Column width: 12.75
OK   Cancel

QUICK STEPS

Change Row Height
Drag row boundary line.
OR
1. Click Format button.
2. Click *Row Height* at drop-down list.
3. Type desired height.
4. Click OK.

Changing Row Height

Row height can be changed in much the same manner as column width. For example, you can change the row height using the mouse on a row boundary, or at the Row Height dialog box. Change row height using a row boundary in the same manner as you learned to change column width. To do this, position the cell pointer on the boundary between rows in the row header until it turns into a double-headed arrow pointing up and down, hold down the left mouse button, drag up or down until the row is the desired height, and then release the mouse button.

The height of selected rows that are adjacent can be changed at the same time. (The height of nonadjacent rows will not all change at the same time.) To do this, select the rows and then drag one of the row boundaries within the selected rows. As the boundary is being dragged the row height changes for all selected rows.

As a row boundary is being dragged, the row height displays in a box above the mouse pointer. The row height number that displays represents a point measurement. A vertical inch contains approximately 72 points. Increase the point size to increase the row height; decrease the point size to decrease the row height.

At the Row Height dialog box shown in Figure 3.2, you can specify a row height number. To display the Row Height dialog box, click the Format button in the Cells group in the Home tab and then click *Row Height* at the drop-down list.

HINT
To change the height of all rows in a worksheet, click the Select All button and then drag a row boundary to the desired position.

Figure 3.2 Row Height Dialog Box

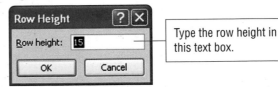

Row Height
Row height: 15
OK   Cancel

Type the row height in this text box.

Project 1c Changing Row Height

1. With **ExcelL1_C3_P1.xlsx** open, change the height of row 1 by completing the following steps:
   a. Position the cell pointer in the row header on the row boundary between rows 1 and 2 until it turns into a double-headed arrow pointing up and down.
   b. Hold down the left mouse button, drag the row boundary down until *Height: 19.50 (26 pixels)* displays in the box, and then release the mouse button.
2. Change the height of rows 2 through 14 by completing the following steps:
   a. Select rows 2 through 14. To do this, position the cell pointer on the number 2 in the row header, hold down the left mouse button, drag the cell pointer to the number 14 in the row header, and then release the mouse button.
   b. Position the cell pointer on the row boundary between rows 2 and 3 until it turns into a double-headed arrow pointing up and down.
   c. Hold down the left mouse button, drag the row boundary down until *Height: 16.50 (22 pixels)* displays in the box, and then release the mouse button.
3. Change the height of row 15 by completing the following steps:
   a. Make cell A15 active.
   b. Click the Format button in the Cells group in the Home tab and then click *Row Height* at the drop-down list.
   c. At the Row Height dialog box, type 20 in the *Row height* text box, and then click OK.
4. Save **ExcelL1_C3_P1.xlsx**.

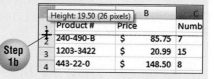

Step 1b

Step 2c

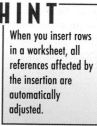

Step 3c

Inserting/Deleting Cells, Rows, and Columns

New data may need to be included in an existing worksheet. For example, a row or several rows of new data may need to be inserted into a worksheet, or data may need to be removed from a worksheet.

Inserting Rows

After you create a worksheet, you can add (insert) rows to the worksheet. Insert a row with the Insert button in the Cells group in the Home tab or with options at the Insert dialog box. By default, a row is inserted above the row containing the active cell. To insert a row in a worksheet, select the row below where the row is to be inserted, and then click the Insert button. If you want to insert more than one row, select the number of rows in the worksheet that you want inserted and then click the Insert button.

HINT
When you insert rows in a worksheet, all references affected by the insertion are automatically adjusted.

⊟ Insert ▾

Insert Row
Click Insert button.
OR
1. Click Insert button
   arrow.
2. Click *Insert Sheet Rows*
   at drop-down list.
OR
1. Click Insert button
   arrow.
2. Click *Insert Cells.*
3. Click *Entire row* in
   dialog box.
4. Click OK.

You can also insert a row by making a cell active in the row below where the row is to be inserted, clicking the Insert button arrow, and then clicking *Insert Sheet Rows*. Another method for inserting a row is to click the Insert button arrow and then click *Insert Cells*. This displays the Insert dialog box as shown in Figure 3.3. At the Insert dialog box, click *Entire row*. This inserts a row above the active cell.

Figure 3.3 Insert Dialog Box

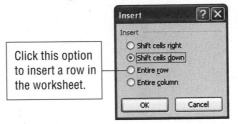

Click this option to insert a row in the worksheet.

Project 1d Inserting Rows

1. With **ExcelL1_C3_P1.xlsx** open, insert two rows at the beginning of the worksheet by completing the following steps:
   a. Make cell A1 active.
   b. Click the Insert button arrow in the Cells group in the Home tab.
   c. At the drop-down list that displays, click *Insert Sheet Rows*.
   d. With cell A1 active, click the Insert button arrow and then click *Insert Sheet Rows* at the drop-down list.

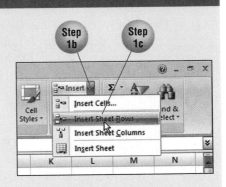

2. Type the text **Capstan Marine Products** in cell A1.
3. Make cell A2 active and then type **Purchasing Department**.
4. Change the height of row 1 to *42.00 (56 pixels)*.
5. Change the height of row 2 to *21.00 (28 pixels)*.
6. Insert two rows by completing the following steps:
   a. Select rows 7 and 8 in the worksheet.
   b. Click the Insert button in the Cells group in the Home tab.

7. Type the following data in the specified cells (you do not need to type the dollar sign in cells containing money amounts):

   A7 = 855-495
   B7 = 42.75
   C7 = 5
   A8 = ST039
   B8 = 12.99
   C8 = 25

8. Make D6 the active cell and then use the fill handle to copy the formula down to cells D7 and D8.
9. Save **ExcelL1_C3_P1.xlsx**.

Inserting Columns

Insert columns in a worksheet in much the same way as rows. Insert a column with options from the Insert button drop-down list or with options at the Insert dialog box. By default, a column is inserted immediately to the left of the column containing the active cell. To insert a column in a worksheet, make a cell active in the column immediately to the right of where the new column is to be inserted, click the Insert button arrow and then click *Insert Sheet Columns* at the drop-down list. If you want to insert more than one column, select the number of columns in the worksheet that you want inserted, click the Insert button arrow and then click *Insert Sheet Columns*.

You can also insert a column by making a cell active in the column immediately to the right of where the new column is to be inserted, clicking the Insert button arrow, and then clicking *Insert Cells* at the drop-down list. This causes the Insert dialog box to display. At the Insert dialog box, click *Entire column*. This inserts an entire column immediately to the left of the active cell.

Excel includes an especially helpful and time-saving feature related to inserting columns. When you insert columns in a worksheet, all references affected by the insertion are automatically adjusted.

QUICK STEPS

Insert Column
Click Insert button.
OR
1. Click Insert button arrow.
2. Click *Insert Sheet Columns* at drop-down list.
OR
1. Click Insert button arrow.
2. Click *Insert Cells*.
3. Click *Entire column*.
4. Click OK.

Project 1e Inserting a Column

1. With **ExcelL1_C3_P1.xlsx** open, insert a column by completing the following steps:
   a. Click in any cell in column A.
   b. Click the Insert button arrow in the Cells group in the Home tab and then click *Insert Sheet Columns* at the drop-down list.
2. Type the following data in the specified cell:

A3	=	Company
A4	=	RD Manufacturing
A8	=	Smithco, Inc.
A11	=	Sunrise Corporation
A15	=	Geneva Systems

3. Make cell A1 active and then adjust the width of column A to accommodate the longest entry.
4. Insert another column by completing the following steps:
   a. Make cell B1 active.
   b. Click the Insert button arrow and then click *Insert Cells* at the drop-down list.
   c. At the Insert dialog box, click *Entire column*.
   d. Click OK.
5. Type Date in cell B3 and then press Enter.
6. Save **ExcelL1_C3_P1.xlsx**.

Step 2

Step 4c

Step 4d

	A	B
1		Capstan Marine
2		Purchasing Dep
3	Company	Product #
4	RD Manufacturing	240-490-B
5		1203-3422
6		443-22-0
7		855-495
8	Smithco, Inc.	ST039
9		A-4302-5
10		43-GB-39
11	Sunrise Corporation	341-453
12		CT-342
13		83-492
14		L-756-M
15	Geneva Systems	340-19
16		T-3491-S
17		900-599
18		43-49CE
19		Total
20		

Insert

Insert
○ Shift cells right
○ Shift cells down
○ Entire row
● Entire column

OK   Cancel

Deleting Cells, Rows, or Columns

You can delete specific cells in a worksheet or rows or columns in a worksheet. To delete a row, select the row and then click the Delete button in the Cells group in the Home tab. To delete a column, select the column and then click the Delete button. Delete a specific cell by making the cell active, clicking the Delete button arrow, and then clicking *Delete Cells* at the drop-down list. This displays the Delete dialog box shown in Figure 3.4. At the Delete dialog box, specify what you want deleted, and then click OK. You can also delete adjacent cells by selecting the cells and then displaying the Delete Cells dialog box.

⊟ Delete ▾

Figure 3.4 Delete Dialog Box

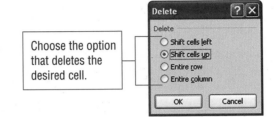

Choose the option that deletes the desired cell.

Clearing Data in Cells

If you want to delete cell contents but not the cell, make the cell active or select desired cells and then press the Delete key. A quick method for clearing the contents of a cell is to right-click the cell and then click *Clear Contents* at the shortcut menu. Another method for deleting cell contents is to make the cell active or select desired cells, click the Clear button in the Editing group in the Home tab, and then click *Clear Contents* at the drop-down list.

With the options at the Clear button drop-down list you can clear the contents of the cell or selected cells as well as formatting and comments. Click the *Clear Formats* option to remove formatting from cells or selected cells while leaving the data. You can also click the *Clear All* option to clear the contents of the cell or selected cells as well as the formatting.

Project ⑪ **Deleting and Clearing Rows in a Worksheet**

1. With **ExcelL1_C3_P1.xlsx** open, delete column B in the worksheet by completing the following steps:
   a. Click in any cell in column B.
   b. Click the Delete button arrow in the Cells group in the Home tab and then click *Delete Sheet Columns* at the drop-down list.
2. Delete row 5 by completing the following steps:
   a. Select row 5.
   b. Click the Delete button in the Cells group.

Step 1b

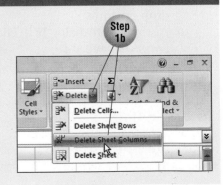

3. Clear row contents by completing the following steps:
   a. Select rows 7 and 8.
   b. Click the Clear button in the Editing group in the Home tab and then click *Clear Contents* at the drop-down list.
4. Type the following data in the specified cell:

A7	=	Ray Enterprises
B7	=	S894-T
C7	=	4.99
D7	=	30
B8	=	B-3448
C8	=	25.50
D8	=	12

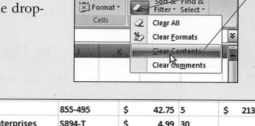

Step 3b

Step 4

6		855-495	$	42.75	5	$	213.75
7	Ray Enterprises	S894-T	$	4.99	30		
8		B-3448	$	25.50	12		
9		43-GB-39	$	45.00	20	$	900.00

5. Make cell E6 active and then copy the formula down to cells E7 and E8.
6. Save **ExcelL1_C3_P1.xlsx**.

Applying Formatting

With many of the groups in the Home tab you can apply formatting to text in the active cells or selected cells. Use buttons in the Font group to apply font formatting to text and use buttons in the Alignment group to apply alignment formatting to text.

Applying Font Formatting

You can apply a variety of formatting to cells in a worksheet with buttons in the Font group in the Home tab. With buttons in the Font group shown in Figure 3.5, you can change the font, font size, and font color; bold, italicize, and underline data in cells; change the text color; and apply a border or add fill to cells.

Figure 3.5 Font Group

Use buttons in the font group to apply formatting to cells or data in cells.

Calibri (Body) — *Font*

11 — *Font Size*

B *Bold*   *I* *Italic*

U *Underline*

A *Increase Font Size*   A *Decrease Font Size*

Use the Font button in the Font group to change the font of text in a cell and use the Font Size button to specify size for the text. Apply bold formatting to text in a cell with the Bold button, italic formatting with the Italic button, and underlining with the Underline button.

Click the Increase Font Size button and the text in the active cell or selected cells increases from 11 points to 12 points. Click the Increase Font Size button again and the font size increases to 14. Each additional time you click the button, the font size increases by two points. Click the Decrease Font Size button and text in the active cell or selected cells decreases in point size.

Border

Fill Color

Font Color

With the Borders button in the Font group, you can insert a border on any or all sides of the active cell or any or all sides of selected cells. The name of the button changes depending on the most recent border applied to a cell or selected cells. Use the Fill Color button to insert color in the active cell or in selected cells. With the Font Color button, you can change the color of text within a cell.

Formatting with the Mini Toolbar

Double-click in a cell and then select data within the cell and the Mini toolbar displays in a dimmed fashion above the selected data. Hover the mouse pointer over the Mini toolbar and it becomes active. The Mini toolbar contains buttons for applying font formatting such as font, font size, and font color as well as bold and italic formatting. Click a button on the Mini toolbar to apply formatting to selected text.

Applying Alignment Formatting

The alignment of data in cells depends on the type of data entered. Enter words or text combined with numbers in a cell and the text is aligned at the left edge of the cell. Enter numbers in a cell and the numbers are aligned at the right side of the cell. Use options in the Alignment group to align text at the left, center, or right side of the cell; align text at the top, center, or bottom of the cell; increase and/or decrease the indent of text; and change the orientation of text in a cell. Click the Merge & Center button to merge selected cells and center data within the merged cells. If you have merged cells and want to split them again, select the cells and then click the Merge & Center button.

Merge & Center

Orientation

Wrap Text

Click the Orientation button to rotate data in a cell. Click the Orientation button and a drop-down list displays with options for rotating text in a cell. If data typed in a cell is longer than the cell, it overlaps the next cell to the right. If you want data to remain in a cell and wrap to the next line within the same cell, click the Wrap Text button in the Alignment group.

Project 1g | **Applying Font and Alignment Formatting**

1. With **ExcelL1_C3_P1.xlsx** open, make cell B1 active and then click the Wrap Text button in the Alignment group in the Home tab. (This wraps the company name within the cell.)
2. Make cell B2 active and then click the Wrap Text button.
3. Instead of wrapping text within cells, you decide to spread out the text over several cells and vertically align text in cells by completing the following steps:
   a. Select cells A1 through E1.
   b. Click the Merge & Center button in the Alignment group in the Home tab.
   c. Click the Middle Align button in the Alignment group.
   d. Select cells A2 through E2, click the Merge & Center button, and then click the Middle Align button.

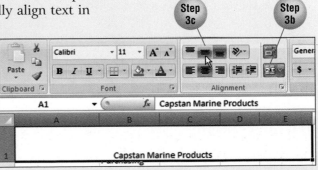

4. Rotate text in the third row by completing the following steps:

a. Select cells A3 through E3.

b. Click the Orientation button in the Alignment group and then click *Angle Counterclockwise* at the drop-down list.

c. After looking at the rotated text, you decide to return the orientation back to the horizontal by clicking the Undo button on the Quick Access toolbar.

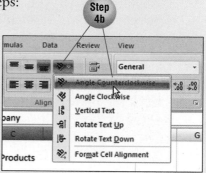

5. Change the font, font size, and font color for text in specific cells by completing the following steps:

a. Make cell A1 active.

b. Click the Font button arrow in the Font group in the Home tab, scroll down the drop-down gallery, and then click *Bookman Old Style*.

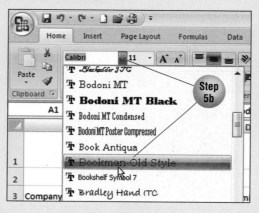

c. Click the Font Size button arrow in the Font group and then click *22* at the drop-down gallery.

d. Click the Font Color button arrow and then click *Dark Blue* in the *Standard* section of the drop-down color palette.

6. Make cell A2 active and then complete steps similar to those in Step 5 to change the font to Bookman Old Style, the font size to 16, and the font color to Dark Blue.

7. Select cells A3 through E3 and then click the Center button in the Alignment group.

8. With cells A3 through E3 still selected, click the Bold button in the Font group and then click the Italic button.

9. Select cells A3 through E18 and then change the font to Bookman Old Style.

10. Apply formatting to selected data using the Mini toolbar by completing the following steps:

a. Double-click cell A4.

b. Select the letters *RD*. (This displays the dimmed Mini toolbar above the selected word.)

c. Click the Increase Font Size button on the Mini toolbar.

d. Double-click cell A14.

e. Select the word *Geneva* and then click the Italic button on the Mini toolbar.

11. Adjust columns A through E to accommodate the longest entry in each column.

12. Select cells D4 through D17 and then click the Center button in the Alignment group.

13. Add a double-line bottom border to cell A2 by completing the following steps:

a. Make cell A2 active.

b. Click the Borders button arrow in the Font group in the Home tab.

c. Click the *Bottom Double Border* option at the drop-down list.

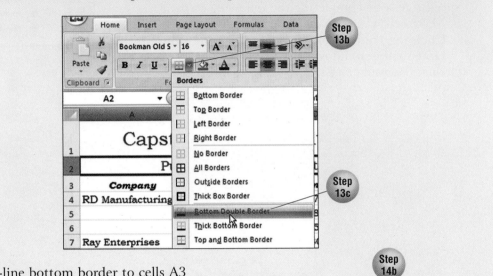

14. Add a single-line bottom border to cells A3 through E3 by completing the following steps:

a. Select cells A3 through E3.

b. Click the Borders button arrow and then click the *Bottom Border* option.

15. Apply fill color to specific cells by completing the following steps:

a. Select cells A1 through E3.

b. Click the Fill Color button arrow in the Font group.

c. Click the *Aqua, Accent 5, Lighter 80%* color option.

16. Save **ExcelL1_C3_P1.xlsx**.

Previewing a Worksheet

Before printing a worksheet, consider previewing it to see how it will appear when printed. To preview a worksheet, click the Office button, point to the *Print* option, and then click the *Print Preview* option. You can also display a worksheet in Print Preview by clicking the Preview button that displays in the lower left corner of the Print dialog box. A document displays in Print Preview as it will appear when printed. Figure 3.6 displays the **ExcelL1_C3_P1.xlsx** worksheet in Print Preview. Notice that the gridlines in the worksheet do not print.

Figure 3.6 Worksheet in Print Preview

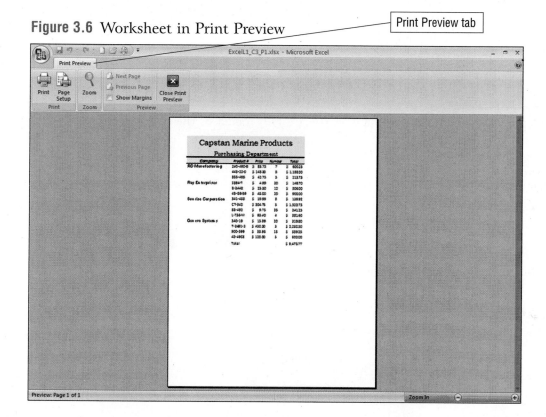

To zoom in on the worksheet, position the mouse pointer (displays as a magnifying glass) in the worksheet text and then click the left mouse button. You can also click the Zoom In option located at the left slide of the Zoom slider bar located at the right side of the Status bar (lower right corner of the Excel window). Click the Print button in the Print Preview tab to send the worksheet to the printer. Click the Page Setup button in the Print Preview tab and the Page Setup dialog box displays with options for changing the paper size and orientation of the page. Insert a check mark in the *Show Margins* check box and margin boundary lines display around the worksheet. Insert a check mark in the *Show Margins* check box and you can change worksheet margins by dragging margin borders. Close Print Preview by clicking the Close Print Preview button.

Preview a Worksheet
1. Click Office button.
2. Point to *Print*.
3. Click *Print Preview*.

Changing the Zoom Setting

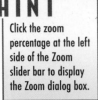

In Print Preview, you can zoom in on the worksheet and make the display bigger. You can also change the size of worksheet display in Normal view using the Zoom slider bar that displays at the right side of the Status bar. To change the percentage of display, drag the button on the Zoom slider bar to increase or decrease the percentage of display. You can also click the Zoom Out button located at the left side of the slider bar to decrease the percentage of display or click the Zoom In button located at the right side of the slider bar to increase the percentage of display.

Project 1h — Previewing a Worksheet

1. With **ExcelL1_C3_P1.xlsx** open, click the Office button, point to the *Print* option, and then click the *Print Preview* option.
2. At the print preview screen, click in the worksheet. (This increases the display of the worksheet cells.)
3. After viewing the worksheet, click the Close Print Preview button.
4. At the worksheet, drag the button on the Zoom slider bar to the right until the zoom displays as 190%. (The percentage amount displays at the left side of the slider.)

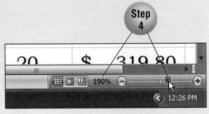

Step 4

5. After viewing the worksheet at 190% display, click the Zoom Out button located at the left side of the slider until the display percentage is 100%.

Step 5

6. Save, print, and then close **ExcelL1_C3_P1.xlsx**.

Project 2 — Apply a Theme to a Payroll Worksheet

You will open a workbook containing a worksheet with payroll information and then insert text, apply formatting to cells and cell contents, apply a theme, and then change the theme font and colors.

Applying a Theme

Excel provides a number of themes you can use to format text and cells in a worksheet. A theme is a set of formatting choices that include a color theme (a set of colors), a font theme (a set of heading and body text fonts), and an effects theme (a set of lines and fill effects). To apply a theme, click the Page Layout tab and then click the Themes button in the Themes group. At the drop-down gallery that displays, click the desired theme. Position the mouse pointer over a theme and the *live preview* feature will display the worksheet with the theme formatting applied. With the live preview feature you can see how the theme formatting affects your worksheet before you make your final choice.

HINT

Apply a theme to give your worksheet a professional look.

Project ② Applying a Theme

1. Open **ExcelC03Project02.xlsx** and then save it and name it **ExcelL1_C3_P2**.
2. Make G4 the active cell and then insert a formula that calculates the amount of Social Security tax (multiply the gross pay amount in E4 with the Social Security rate in cell H11 [you will need to use the mixed cell reference H$11 when writing the formula]).
3. Copy the formula in cell G4 down to cells G5 through G9.
4. Make H4 the active cell and then insert a formula that calculates the net pay (gross pay minus withholding and Social Security tax).
5. Automatically adjust the width of column H.
6. Copy the formula in H4 down to cells H5 through H9.
7. Increase the height of row 1 to 36.00.
8. Make A1 the active cell, click the Middle Align button in the Alignment group, click the Font Size button arrow and click *18* at the drop-down list, and then click the Bold button.
9. Type Stanton & Barnett Associates in cell A1.
10. Select cells A2 through H3 and then click the Bold button in the Font group.
11. Apply a theme and customize the font and colors by completing the following steps:
    a. Click the Page Layout tab.
    b. Click the Themes button in the Themes group and then click *Aspect* at the drop-down gallery. (You might want to point the mouse to various themes to see how the theme formatting affects the worksheet).

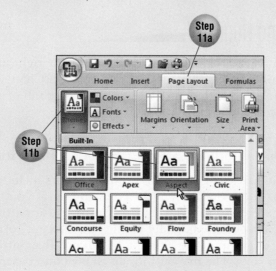

c. Click the Colors button in the Themes group and then click *Flow* at the drop-down gallery.
d. Click the Fonts button in the Themes group, scroll down the drop-down gallery, and then click *Opulent*.

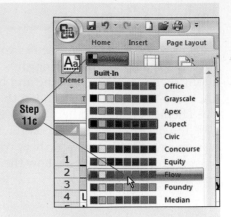

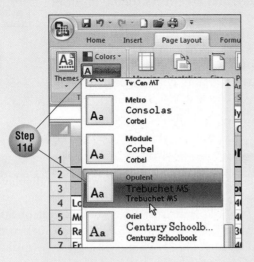

12. Select columns A through H and then adjust the width of the columns to accommodate the longest entries.
13. Save, print, and then close **ExcelL1_C3_P2.xlsx**.

Project ③ Format an Invoices Worksheet

You will open a workbook containing an invoice worksheet and apply number formatting to numbers in cells.

Formatting Numbers

Numbers in a cell, by default, are aligned at the right and decimals and commas do not display unless they are typed in the cell. Change the format of numbers with buttons in the Number group in the Home tab or with options at the Format Cells dialog box with the Number tab selected.

Formatting Numbers Using Number Group Buttons

Format symbols you can use to format numbers include a percent sign (%), a comma (,), and a dollar sign ($). For example, if you type the number *$45.50* in a cell, Excel automatically applies Currency formatting to the number. If you type *45%*, Excel automatically applies the Percent formatting to the number. The Number group in the Home tab contains five buttons you can use to format numbers in cells. The five buttons are shown and described in Table 3.1.

Table 3.1 Number Formatting Buttons on Formatting Toolbar

	Click this button	To do this
$ ▾	Accounting Number Format	Add a dollar sign, any necessary commas, and a decimal point followed by two decimal digits, if none are typed; right-align number in cell
%	Percent Style	Multiply cell value by 100 and display result with a percent symbol; right-align number in cell
,	Comma Style	Add any necessary commas and a decimal point followed by two decimal digits, if none are typed; right-align number in cell
←.0 .00	Increase Decimal	Increase number of decimal places displayed after decimal point in selected cells
.00 →.0	Decrease Decimal	Decrease number of decimal places displayed after decimal point in selected cells

Specify the formatting for numbers in cells in a worksheet before typing the numbers, or format existing numbers in a worksheet. The Increase Decimal and Decrease Decimal buttons in the Number group in the Home tab will change decimal places for existing numbers only.

Increase Decimal   Decrease Decimal

The Number group in the Home tab also contains the Number Format button. Click the Number Format button arrow and a drop-down list displays of common number formats. Click the desired format at the drop-down list to apply the number formatting to the cell or selected cells.

General ▾

Number Format

Project 3a   Formatting Numbers with Buttons in the Number Group

1. Open **ExcelC03Project03.xlsx**.
2. Save the workbook with Save As and name it **ExcelL1_C3_P3**.
3. Make the following changes to column widths:
   a. Change the width of column C to 17.00.
   b. Change the width of column D to 10.00.
   c. Change the width of column E to 7.00.
   d. Change the width of column F to 12.00.
4. Select row 1 and then click the Insert button in the Cells group.
5. Change the height of row 1 to 42.00.
6. Select cells A1 through F1 and then make the following changes:
   a. Click the Merge & Center button in the Alignment group.
   b. With cell A1 active, change the font size to 24 points.
   c. Click the Fill Color button arrow in the Font group and then click *Olive Green, Accent 3, Lighter 80%*.

Step 6c

d. Click the Borders button arrow in the Font group and then click the *Top and Thick Bottom Border* option.

e. With cell A1 active, type **REAL PHOTOGRAPHY** and then press Enter.

7. Change the height of row 2 to 24.00.

8. Select cells A2 through F2 and then make the following changes:

a. Click the Merge & Center button in the Alignment group.

b. With cell A2 active, change the font size to 18.

c. Click the Fill Color button in the Font group. (This will fill the cell with light green color.)

d. Click the Borders button arrow in the Font group and then click the *Bottom Border* option.

9. Make the following changes to row 3:

a. Change the height of row 3 to 18.00.

b. Select cells A3 through F3, click the Bold button in the Font group, and then click the Center button in the Alignment group.

c. With the cells still selected, click the Borders button arrow and then click the *Bottom Border* option.

10. Make the following number formatting changes:

a. Select cells E4 through E16 and then click the *Percent Style* button in the Number group.

b. With the cells still selected, click once on the Increase Decimal button in the Number group. (The percent numbers should contain one decimal place.)

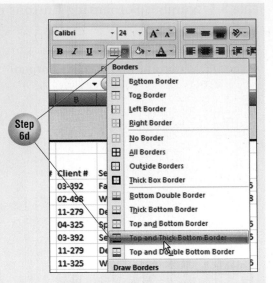

Step 6d

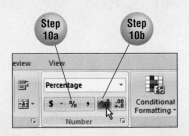

Step 10a

Step 10b

c. Select cells A4 through B16.

d. Click the Number Format button arrow, scroll down the drop-down list, and then click *Text*.

e. With A4 through B16 still selected, click the Center button in the Alignment group.

11. Save **ExcelL1_C3_P3.xlsx**.

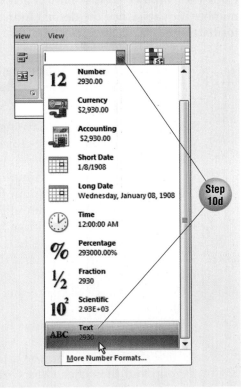

Step 10d

Formatting Numbers Using the Format Cells Dialog Box

Along with buttons in the Number group, you can format numbers with options at the Format Cells dialog box with the Number tab selected as shown in Figure 3.7. Display this dialog box by clicking the Number group dialog box launcher or by clicking the Number Format button arrow and then clicking *More Number Formats* at the drop-down list. The left side of the dialog box displays number categories with a default category of *General.* At this setting no specific formatting is applied to numbers except right-aligning numbers in cells. The other number categories are described in Table 3.2.

Figure 3.7 Format Cells Dialog Box with Number Tab Selected

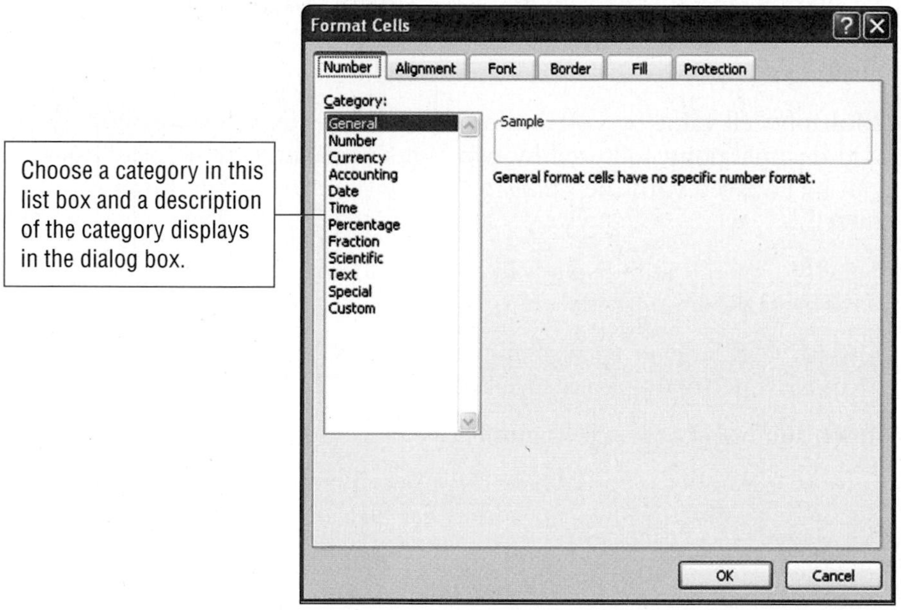

Choose a category in this list box and a description of the category displays in the dialog box.

Table 3.2 Number Categories at the Format Cells Dialog Box

Click this category	To apply this number formatting
Number	Specify number of decimal places and whether or not a thousand separator should be used; choose the display of negative numbers; right-align numbers in cell.
Currency	Apply general monetary values; dollar sign is added as well as commas and decimal points, if needed; right-align numbers in cell.
Accounting	Line up the currency symbol and decimal points in a column; add dollar sign and two digits after a decimal point; right-align numbers in cell.
Date	Display date as date value; specify the type of formatting desired by clicking an option in the *Type* list box; right-align date in cell.
Time	Display time as time value; specify the type of formatting desired by clicking an option in the *Type* list box; right-align time in cell.
Percentage	Multiply cell value by 100 and display result with a percent symbol; add decimal point followed by two digits by default; number of digits can be changed with the *Decimal places* option; right-align number in cell.
Fraction	Specify how fraction displays in cell by clicking an option in the *Type* list box; right-align fraction in cell.
Scientific	Use for very large or very small numbers. Use the letter *E* to tell Excel to move a decimal point a specified number of positions.
Text	Treat number in cell as text; number is displayed in cell exactly as typed.
Special	Choose a number type, such as Zip Code, Phone Number, or Social Security Number in the *Type* option list box; useful for tracking list and database values.
Custom	Specify a numbering type by choosing an option in the *Type* list box.

Project 3b Formatting Numbers at the Format Cells Dialog Box

1. With **ExcelL1_C3_P3.xlsx** open, make cell F4 active and then insert the following formula: =(D4*E4)+D4.
2. Make cell F4 active and then copy the formula down to cells F5 through F16.
3. Change number formatting by completing the following steps:
   a. Select cells D4 through D16.
   b. Click the Number group dialog box launcher.

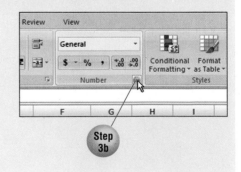

Step 3b

c. At the Format Cells dialog box with the Number tab selected, click *Accounting* in the *Category* section.

d. Make sure a *2* displays in the *Decimal places* option box and a dollar sign *$* displays in the *Symbol* option box.

e. Click OK.

4. Apply Accounting formatting to cells F4 through F16 by completing steps similar to those in Step 3.

5. Save, print, and then close **ExcelL1_C3_P3.xlsx**.

Project 4 Format a Company Budget Worksheet

You will open a workbook containing a company budget worksheet and then apply formatting to cells with options at the Format Cells dialog box, use the Format Painter to apply formatting, and hide and unhide rows and columns in the worksheet.

Formatting Cells Using the Format Cells Dialog Box

In the previous section, you learned how to format numbers with options at the Format Cells dialog box with the Number tab selected. This dialog box contains a number of other tabs you can select to format cells.

Aligning and Indenting Data

You can align and indent data in cells using buttons in the Alignment group in the Home tab or with options at the Format Cells dialog box with the Alignment tab selected as shown in Figure 3.8. Display this dialog box by clicking the Alignment group dialog box launcher.

Figure 3.8 Format Cells Dialog Box with Alignment Tab Selected

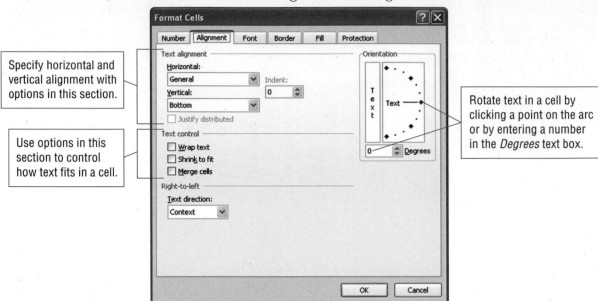

Specify horizontal and vertical alignment with options in this section.

Use options in this section to control how text fits in a cell.

Rotate text in a cell by clicking a point on the arc or by entering a number in the *Degrees* text box.

In the *Orientation* section, you can choose to rotate data. A portion of the *Orientation* section shows points on an arc. Click a point on the arc to rotate the text along that point. You can also type a rotation degree in the *Degrees* text box. Type a positive number to rotate selected text from the lower left to the upper right of the cell. Type a negative number to rotate selected text from the upper left to the lower right of the cell.

If data typed in a cell is longer than the cell, it overlaps the next cell to the right. If you want data to remain in a cell and wrap to the next line within the same cell, click the *Wrap text* option in the *Text control* section of the dialog box. Click the *Shrink to fit* option to reduce the size of the text font so all selected data fits within the column. Use the *Merge cells* option to combine two or more selected cells into a single cell.

If you want to enter data on more than one line within a cell, enter the data on the first line and then press Alt + Enter. Pressing Alt + Enter moves the insertion point to the next line within the same cell.

Project 4a Aligning and Rotating Data in Cells

1. Open **ExcelC03Project04.xlsx**.
2. Save the workbook with Save As and name it **ExcelL1_C3_P4**.
3. Make the following changes to the worksheet:
   a. Insert a new row at the beginning of the worksheet.
   b. Change the height of row 1 to 66.00.
   c. Merge and center cells A1 through E1.
   d. Type **Harris & Briggs** in cell A1 and then press Alt + Enter. (This moves the insertion point down to the next line in the same cell.)
   e. Type **Construction** and then press Enter.
   f. With cell A2 active, type **Preferred**, press Alt + Enter, type **Customer**, and then press Enter.

g. Change the width of column A to 20.00.

h. Change the width of column B to 7.00.

i. Change the width of columns C, D, and E to 10.00.

4. Change number formatting for specific cells by completing the following steps:

a. Select cells C3 through E11.

b. Click the Number group dialog box launcher.

c. At the Format Cells dialog box with the Number tab selected, click *Accounting* in the *Category* section.

d. Click the down-pointing arrow at the right side of the *Decimal places* option until *0* displays.

e. Make sure a dollar sign *$* displays in the *Symbol* option box.

f. Click OK.

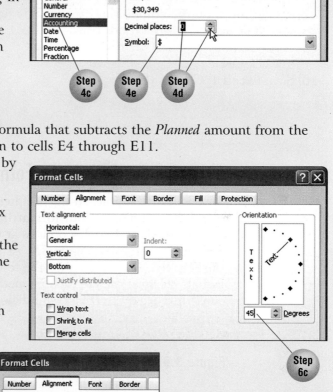

5. Make cell E3 active and then insert a formula that subtracts the *Planned* amount from the *Actual* amount. Copy this formula down to cells E4 through E11.

6. Change the orientation of data in cells by completing the following steps:

a. Select cells B2 through E2.

b. Click the Alignment group dialog box launcher.

c. At the Format Cells dialog box with the Alignment tab selected, select *0* in the *Degrees* text box and then type 45.

d. Click OK.

7. Change the vertical alignment of text in cells by completing the following steps:

a. Select cells A1 through E2.

b. Click the Alignment group dialog box launcher.

c. At the Format Cells dialog box with the Alignment tab selected, click the down-pointing arrow at the right side of the *Vertical* alignment option.

d. Click *Center* at the drop-down list.

e. Click OK.

8. Change the horizontal alignment of text in cells by completing the following steps:

a. Select cells A2 through E2.

b. Click the Alignment group dialog box launcher.

c. At the Format Cells dialog box with the Alignment tab selected, click the down-pointing arrow at the right side of the *Horizontal* alignment option.

d. Click *Center* at the drop-down list.

e. Click OK.

9. Change the horizontal alignment and indent of text in cells by completing the following steps:
   a. Select cells B3 through B11.
   b. Click the Alignment group dialog box launcher.
   c. At the Format Cells dialog box with the Alignment tab selected, click the down-pointing arrow at the right side of the *Horizontal* alignment option and then click *Right (Indent)* at the drop-down list.
   d. Click once on the up-pointing arrow at the right side of the *Indent* option box (this displays *1* in the box).
   e. Click OK.
10. Save **ExcelL1_C3_P4.xlsx**.

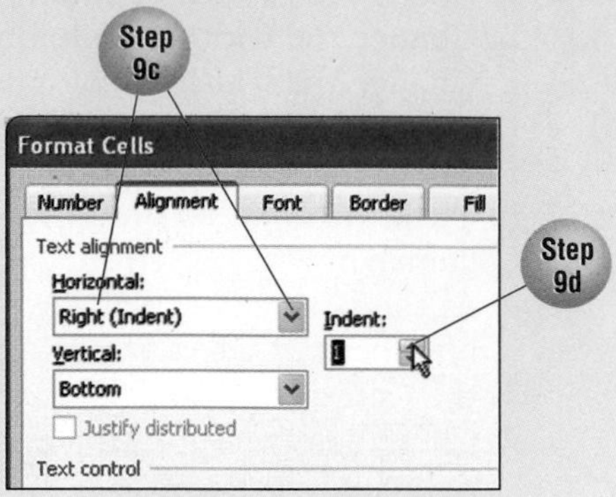

Changing the Font at the Format Cells Dialog Box

As you learned earlier in this chapter, the Font group in the Home tab contains buttons for applying font formatting to data in cells. You can also change the font for data in cells with options at the Format Cells dialog box with the Font tab selected as shown in Figure 3.9. At the Format Cells dialog box with the Font tab selected, you can change the font, font style, font size, and font color. You can also change the underlining method and add effects such as superscript and subscript. Click the Font group dialog box launcher to display this dialog box.

Figure 3.9 Format Cells Dialog Box with Font Tab Selected

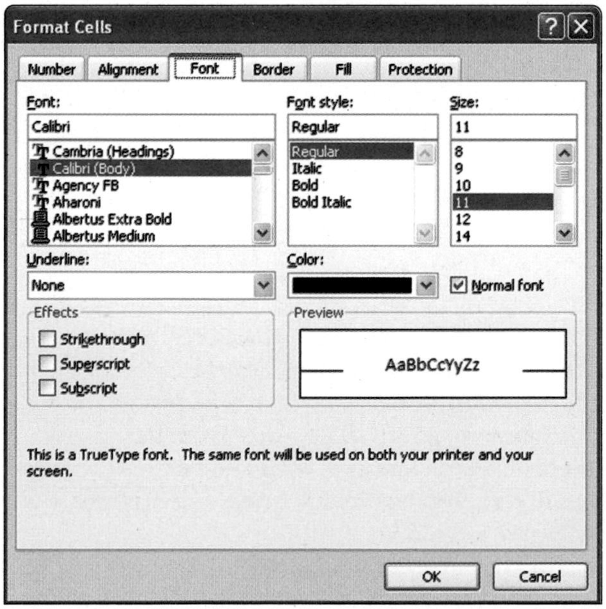

Project 4b Applying Font Formatting at the Format Cells Dialog Box

1. With **ExcelL1_C3_P4.xlsx** open, change the font and font color by completing the following steps:
   a. Select cells A1 through E11.
   b. Click the Font group dialog box launcher.
   c. At the Format Cells dialog box with the Font tab selected, click *Garamond* in the *Font* list box (you will need to scroll down the list to make this font visible).
   d. Click *12* in the *Size* list box.
   e. Click the down-pointing arrow at the right of the *Color* option box.
   f. At the palette of color choices that displays, click the *Dark Red* color (first color option from the left in the *Standard Colors* section).
   g. Click OK to close the dialog box.
2. Make cell A1 active and then change the font to 24-point Garamond bold.
3. Select cells A2 through E2 and then apply bold formatting.
4. Save and then print **ExcelL1_C3_P4.xlsx**.

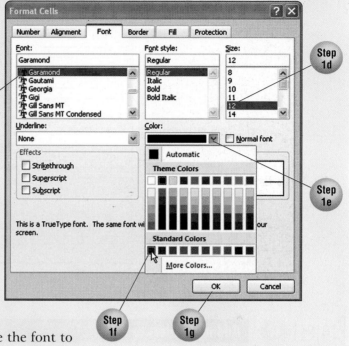

Adding Borders to Cells

The gridlines that display in a worksheet do not print. As you learned earlier in this chapter, you can use the Borders button in the Font group to add borders to cells that will print. You can also add borders to cells with options at the Format Cells dialog box with the Border tab selected as shown in Figure 3.10. Display this dialog box by clicking the Borders button arrow in the Font group and then clicking *More Borders* at the drop-down list.

With options in the *Presets* section, you can remove borders with the *None* option, add only outside borders with the *Outline* option, or click the *Inside* option to add borders to the inside of selected cells. In the *Border* section of the dialog box, specify the side of the cell or selected cells to which you want to apply a border. Choose the style of line desired for the border with the options that display in the *Style* list box. Add color to border lines with choices from the color palette that displays when you click the down-pointing arrow located at the right side of the *Color* option box.

QUICK STEPS

Add Borders to Cells
1. Select cells.
2. Click Borders button arrow.
3. Click desired border.
OR
1. Select cells.
2. Click Borders button arrow.
3. Click *More Borders*.
4. Use options in dialog box to apply desired border.
5. Click OK.

Figure 3.10 Format Cells Dialog Box with Border Tab Selected

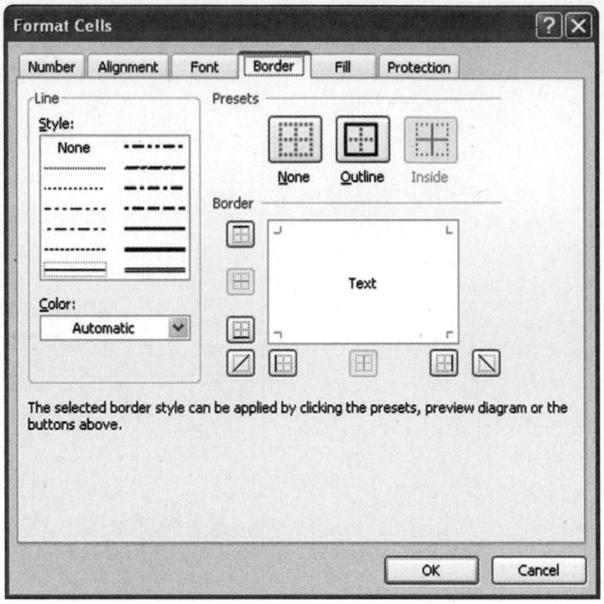

Project 4C · Adding Borders to Cells

1. With **ExcelL1_C3_P4.xlsx** open, remove the 45 degrees orientation you applied in Project 4a by completing the following steps:
   a. Select cells B2 through E2.
   b. Click the Alignment group dialog box launcher.
   c. At the Format Cells dialog box with the Alignment tab selected, select *45* in the *Degrees* text box and then type 0.
   d. Click OK.

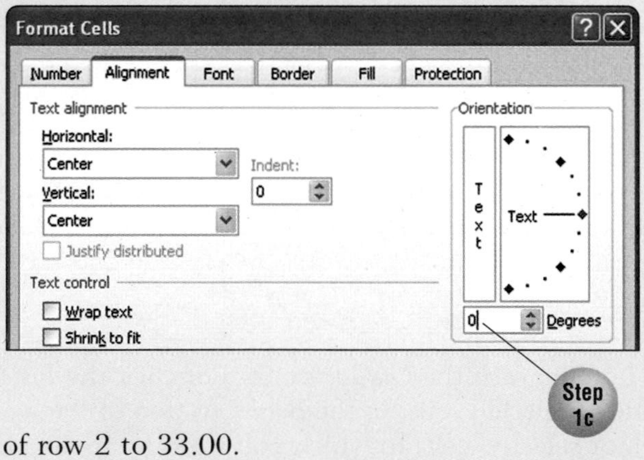

Step 1c

2. Change the height of row 2 to 33.00.
3. Add a thick, dark red border line to cells by completing the following steps:
   a. Select cells A1 through E11 (cells containing data).
   b. Click the Border button arrow in the Font group and then click the *More Borders* option at the drop-down list.

c. At the Format Cells dialog box with the Border tab selected, click the down-pointing arrow at the right side of the *Color* option and then click *Dark Red* at the color palette (first color option from the left in the *Standard Colors* section).

d. Click the thick single line option located in the second column (sixth option from the top) in the *Style* option box in the *Line* section.

e. Click the *Outline* option in the *Presets* section.

f. Click OK.

4. Add a border above and below cells by completing the following steps:

a. Select cells A2 through E2.

b. Click the Border button arrow in the Font group and then click *More Borders* at the drop-down list.

c. At the Format Cells dialog box with the Border tab selected, make sure the color is Dark Red.

d. Make sure the thick single line option (sixth option from the top in the second column) is selected in the *Style* option box in the *Line* section.

e. Click the top border of the sample cell in the *Border* section of the dialog box.

f. Click the double-line option (bottom option in the second column) in the *Style* option box.

g. Click the bottom border of the sample cell in the *Border* section of the dialog box.

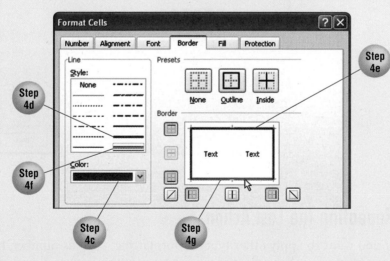

h. Click OK.

5. Save **ExcelL1_C3_P4.xlsx**.

QUICK STEPS

Add Shading to Cells

1. Select cells.
2. Click Fill Color button arrow.
3. Click desired color.

OR

1. Select cells.
2. Click Format button.
3. Click *Format Cells* at drop-down list.
4. Click Fill tab.
5. Use options in dialog box to apply desired shading.
6. Click OK.

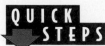

Adding Fill and Shading to Cells

To enhance the visual display of cells and data within cells, consider adding fill and/or shading to cells. As you learned earlier in this chapter, you can add fill color to cells with the Fill Color button in the Font group. You can also add fill color and/or shading to cells in a worksheet with options at the Format Cells dialog box with the Fill tab selected as shown in Figure 3.11. Display the Format Cells dialog box by clicking the Format button in the Cells group and then clicking *Format Cells* at the drop-down list. You can also display the dialog box by clicking the Font group, Alignment group, or Number group dialog box launcher. At the Format Cells dialog box, click the Fill tab.

Choose a fill color for a cell or selected cells by clicking a color choice in the *Color* palette. To add shading to a cell or selected cells, click the Fill Effects button, and then click the desired shading style at the Fill Effects dialog box.

Figure 3.11 Format Cells Dialog Box with Fill Tab Selected

QUICK STEPS

Repeat Last Action

1. Apply formatting.
2. Move to desired location.
3. Press F4 or Ctrl + Y.

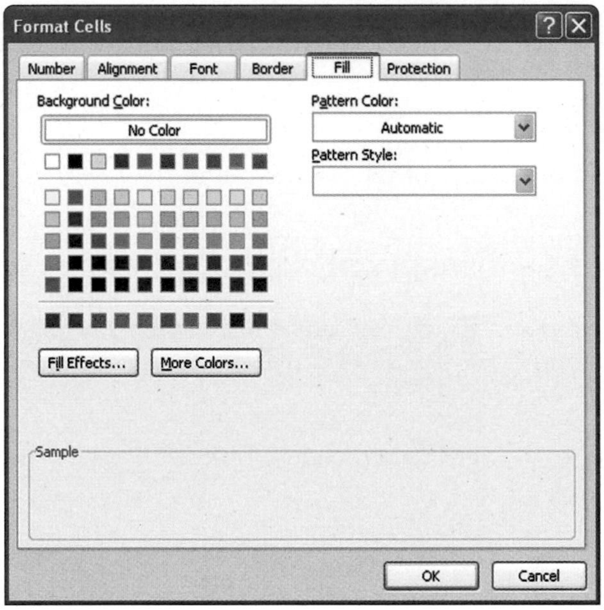

Repeating the Last Action

If you want to apply other types of formatting, such as number, border, or shading formatting to other cells in a worksheet, use the Repeat command by pressing F4 or Ctrl + Y. The Repeat command repeats the last action performed.

Project 4d Adding Fill Color and Shading to Cells

1. With **ExcelL1_C3_P4.xlsx** open, add fill color to cell A1 and repeat the formatting by completing the following steps:
   a. Make cell A1 active.
   b. Click the Format button in the Cells group and then click *Format Cells* at the drop-down list.
   c. At the Format Cells dialog box, click the Fill tab.
   d. Click a light purple color in the *Color* section (click the eighth color from the left in the second row).

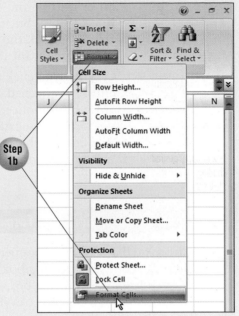

Step 1b

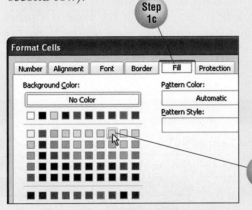

Step 1c

Step 1d

   e. Click OK.
   f. Select cells A2 through E2 and then press the F4 function key. (This repeats the light purple fill.)
2. Select row 2, insert a new row, and then change the width of the new row to 12.00.
3. Add shading to cells by completing the following steps:
   a. Select cells A2 through E2.
   b. Click the Format button in the Cells group and then click *Format Cells* at the drop-down list.
   c. At the Format Cells dialog box, if necessary, click the Fill tab.
   d. Click the Fill Effects button.
   e. At the Fill Effects dialog box, click the down-pointing arrow at the right side of the *Color 2* option box and then click *Purple, Accent 4* (eighth color from the left in the top row).
   f. Click *Horizontal* in the *Shading styles* section of the dialog box.
   g. Click OK to close the Fill Effects dialog box.
   h. Click OK to close the Format Cells dialog box.
4. Save **ExcelL1_C3_P4.xlsx**.

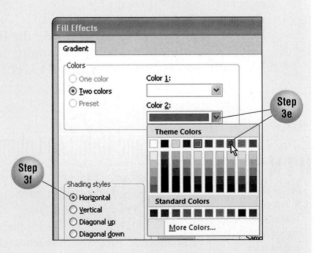

Step 3e

Step 3f

Formatting with Format Painter

The Clipboard group in the Home tab contains a button you can use to copy formatting to different locations in the worksheet. This button is the Format Painter button and displays in the Clipboard group as a paintbrush. To use the Format Painter button, make a cell or selected cells active that contain the desired formatting, click the Format Painter button, and then click the cell or selected cells to which you want the formatting applied.

When you click the Format Painter button, the mouse pointer displays with a paintbrush attached. If you want to apply formatting a single time, click the Format Painter button once. If, however, you want to apply the character formatting in more than one location in the worksheet, double-click the Format Painter button. If you have double-clicked the Format Painter button, turn off the feature by clicking the Format Painter button once.

Project 4e   Formatting with Format Painter

1. With **ExcelL1_C3_P4.xlsx** open, select cells A5 through E5.
2. Click the Font group dialog box launcher.
3. At the Format Cells dialog box, click the Fill tab.
4. Click the light green color (seventh color from the left in the second row).
5. Click OK to close the dialog box.
6. Use Format Painter to "paint" formatting to rows by completing the following steps:
   a. With A5 through E5 selected, double-click the Format Painter button in the Clipboard group.
   b. Select cells A7 through E7.
   c. Select cells A9 through E9.
   d. Select cells A11 through E11.
   e. Turn off Format Painter by clicking the Format Painter button in the Clipboard group.
7. Save and then print **ExcelL1_C3_P4.xlsx**.

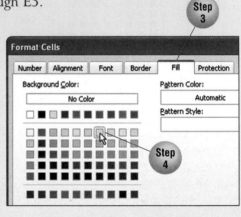

Hiding and Unhiding Columns/Rows

HINT
Set the column width to zero and the column is hidden. Set the row height to zero and the row is hidden.

If a worksheet contains columns and/or rows of sensitive data or data that you are not using or do not want to view, consider hiding the columns and/or rows. To hide columns in a worksheet, select the columns to be hidden, click the Format button in the Cells group in the Home tab, point to *Hide & Unhide*, and then click *Hide Columns*. To hide selected rows, click the Format button in the Cells group, point to *Hide & Unhide*, and then click *Hide Rows*. To make a hidden column visible, select the column to the left and the column to the right of the hidden column, click the Format button in the Cells group, point to *Hide & Unhide*, and then click *Unhide Columns*. To make a hidden row visible, select the row above and the row below the hidden row, click the Format button in the Cells group, point to *Hide & Unhide*, and then click *Unhide Rows*.

If the first row or column is hidden, use the Go To feature to make the row or column visible. To do this, click the Find & Select button in the Editing group in the Home tab and then click *Go To* at the drop-down list. At the Go To dialog box, type A1 in the *Reference* text box, and then click OK. At the worksheet, click the Format button in the Cells group, point to *Hide & Unhide*, and then click *Unhide Columns* or click *Unhide Rows*.

You can also unhide columns or rows using the mouse. If a column or row is hidden, the light blue boundary line in the column or row header displays as a slightly thicker blue line. To unhide a column, position the mouse pointer on the slightly thicker blue line that displays in the column header until the mouse pointer changes to left- and right-pointing arrows with a double line between. (Make sure the mouse pointer displays with two lines between the arrows. If a single line displays, you will simply change the size of the visible column.) Hold down the left mouse button, drag to the right until the column displays at the desired width, and then release the mouse button. Unhide a row in a similar manner. Position the mouse pointer on the slightly thicker blue line in the row header until the mouse pointer changes to up- and down-pointing arrows with a double line between. Drag down to display the row and then release the mouse button. If two or more adjacent columns or rows are hidden, you will need to unhide each column or row separately.

Project ④ Hiding/Unhiding Columns and Rows

1. With **ExcelL1_C3_P4.xlsx** open, hide the row for Linstrom Enterprises and the row for Summit Services by completing the following steps:
   a. Click the row 7 header to select the entire row.
   b. Hold down the Ctrl key and then click the row 11 header to select the entire row.
   c. Click the Format button in the Cells group in the Home tab, point to *Hide & Unhide*, and then click *Hide Rows*.
2. Hide the column containing the planned amounts by completing the following steps:
   a. Click cell D3 to make it the active cell.
   b. Click the Format button in the Cells group, point to *Hide & Unhide*, and then click *Hide Columns*.
3. Save and then print **ExcelL1_C3_P4.xlsx**.

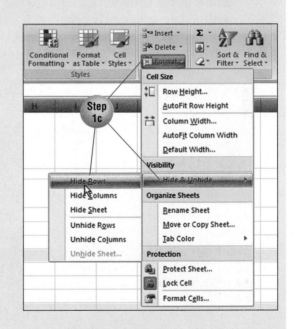

4. Unhide the rows by completing the following steps:
   a. Select rows 6 through 12.
   b. Click the Format button in the Cells group, point to *Hide & Unhide*, and then click *Unhide Rows*.
   c. Click in cell A4.

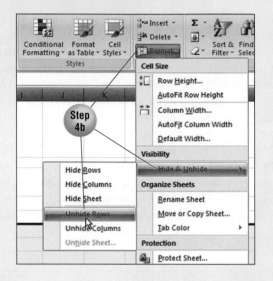

5. Unhide column D by completing the following steps:
   a. Position the mouse pointer on the thicker blue line that displays between columns C and E in the column header until the pointer turns into arrows pointing left and right with a double line between.
   b. Hold down the left mouse button, drag to the right until *Width: 12.57 (93 pixels)* displays in a box above the mouse pointer, and then release the mouse button.

6. Save, print, and then close **ExcelL1_C3_P4.xlsx**.

CHAPTER summary

- Change column width using the mouse on column boundaries or with options at the Column Width dialog box.
- To automatically adjust a column to accommodate the longest entry in the column, double-click the column header boundary on the right.
- Change row height using the mouse on row boundaries or with options at the Row Height dialog box.
- Insert a row in a worksheet with the Insert button in the Cells group in the Home tab or with options at the Insert dialog box.
- Insert a column in a worksheet with the Insert button in the Cells group or with options at the Insert dialog box.
- Delete a specific cell by clicking the Delete button arrow and then clicking *Delete Cells* at the drop-down list. At the Delete dialog box, specify if you want to delete just the cell or an entire row or column.
- Delete a selected row(s) or column(s) by clicking the Delete button in the Cells group.
- Delete cell contents by pressing the Delete key or clicking the Clear button in the Editing group and then clicking *Clear Contents* at the drop-down list.
- Apply font formatting with buttons in the Font group in the Home tab.
- Use the Mini toolbar to apply font formatting to selected data in a cell.
- Apply alignment formatting with buttons in the Alignment group in the Home tab.
- Preview a worksheet by clicking the Office button, pointing to *Print*, and then clicking *Print Preview*.
- Change the size of the worksheet display with the Zoom button in the Print Preview tab or with the Zoom slider bar that displays at the right side of the Status bar.
- Use the Themes button in the Themes group in the Page Layout tab to apply a theme to cells in a worksheet that applies formatting such as color, font, and effects. Use the other buttons in the Themes group to customize the theme.
- Format numbers in cells with the Accounting Number Format, Percent Style, Comma Style, Increase Decimal, and Decrease Decimal buttons in the Number group in the home tab. You can also apply number formatting with options at the Format Cells dialog box with the Number tab selected.
- Apply formatting to cells in a worksheet with options at the Format Cells dialog box. This dialog box includes the following tabs for formatting cells: Number, Alignment, Font, Border, and Fill.
- Press F4 or Ctrl + Y to repeat the last action performed.
- Use the Format Painter button in the Clipboard group in the Home tab to apply formatting to different locations in a worksheet.
- Hide selected columns or rows in a worksheet by clicking the Format button in the Cells group in the Home tab, pointing to *Hide & Unhide*, and then clicking *Hide Columns* or *Hide Rows*.

- To make a hidden column visible, select the column to the left and right, click the Format button in the Cells group, point to *Hide & Unhide*, and then click *Unhide Columns*.
- To make a hidden row visible, select the row above and below, click the Format button in the Cells group, point to *Hide & Unhide*, and then click *Unhide Rows*.

COMMANDS review

FEATURE	RIBBON TAB, GROUP	BUTTON	KEYBOARD SHORTCUT
Format	Home, Cells	Format	
Insert cells, rows, columns	Home, Cells	Insert	
Delete cells, rows, columns	Home, Cells	Delete	
Clear cell or cell contents	Home, Editing		
Font	Home, Font	Calibri	
Font size	Home, Font	11	
Increase Font Size	Home, Font	A	
Decrease Font Size	Home, Font	A	
Bold	Home, Font	B	Ctrl + B
Italic	Home, Font	I	Ctrl + I
Underline	Home, Font	U	Ctrl + U
Borders	Home, Font		
Fill Color	Home, Font		
Font Color	Home, Font	A	
Top Align	Home, Alignment		
Middle Align	Home, Alignment		
Bottom Align	Home, Alignment		
Orientation	Home, Alignment		
Align Text Left	Home, Alignment		

continued

FEATURE	RIBBON TAB, GROUP	BUTTON	KEYBOARD SHORTCUT
Center	Home, Alignment		
Align Text Right	Home, Alignment		
Decrease Indent	Home, Alignment		Ctrl + Alt + Shift + Tab
Increase Indent	Home, Alignment		Ctrl + Alt + Tab
Wrap Text	Home, Alignment		
Merge & Center	Home, Alignment		
Print Preview		, Print, Print Preview	Ctrl + F2
Themes	Page Layout, Themes		
Number Format	Home, Number	General	
Accounting Number Format	Home, Number	$	
Percent Style	Home, Number	%	Ctrl + Shift + %
Increase Decimal	Home, Number		
Decrease Decimal	Home, Number		
Format Painter	Home, Clipboard		
Repeat			F4 or Ctrl + Y

CONCEPTS check

Test Your Knowledge

Completion: In the space provided at the right, indicate the correct term, symbol, or command.

1. To automatically adjust a column width to accommodate the longest entry in the cell, do this with the mouse on the column boundary.

   double click

2. By default, a column is inserted in this direction from the column containing the active cell.

   left

3. To delete a row, select the row and then click the Delete button in this group in the Home tab.

   cells

4. With the options at this button drop-down list, you can clear the contents of the cell or selected cells.

clear button

5. Use this button to insert color in the active cell or selected cells.

fill colour

6. By default, numbers are aligned at this side of a cell.

right

7. Click this button to merge selected cells and center data within the merged cells.

merge + center

8. Select data in a cell and this displays in a dimmed fashion above the selected text.

mini tool bar

9. Click this button in the Alignment group in the Home tab to rotate data in a cell.

orientation

10. Use this bar, located at the right side of the Status bar, to zoom the display of the worksheet.

zoom slide bar

11. The Themes button is located in this tab.

page layout

12. If you type a number with a dollar sign, such as $50.25, Excel automatically applies this formatting to the number.

currency

13. If you type a number with a percent sign, such as 25%, Excel automatically applies this formatting to the number.

percent

14. Align and indent data in cells using buttons in the Alignment group in the Home tab or with options at this dialog box with the Alignment tab selected.

format cells dialog box

15. You can repeat the last action performed with the command Ctrl + Y or pressing this function key.

F4

16. The Format Painter button is located in this group in the Home tab.

clipboard

17. To hide a column, select the column, click this button in the Cells group in the Home tab, point to *Hide & Unhide*, and then click *Hide Columns*.

format

SKILLS check

Demonstrate Your Proficiency

Assessment

1 FORMAT A SALES AND BONUSES WORKSHEET

1. Open **ExcelC03Assessment01.xlsx**.
2. Save the workbook with Save As and name it **ExcelL1_C3_A1**.
3. Change the width of columns as follows:

   Column A   =   14.00

   Columns B - E   =   10.00

   Column F   =   6.00
4. Select row 2 and then insert a new row.
5. Merge and center cells A2 through F2.
6. Type **Sales Department** in cell A2 and then press Enter.
7. Increase the height of row 1 to 33.00.
8. Increase the height of row 2 to 21.00.
9. Increase the height of row 3 to 18.00.
10. Make the following formatting changes to the worksheet:
    a. Make cell A1 active, change the font size to 18 points, and turn on bold.
    b. Make cell A2 active, change the font size to 14 points, and turn on bold.
    c. Select cells A3 through F3, click the Bold button in the Font group, and then click the Center button in the Alignment group.
    d. Select cells A1 through F3, change the vertical alignment to Middle Align.
    e. Select cells B4 through E11 and then change the number formatting to Accounting with 0 decimal places and a dollar sign.
11. Insert the following formulas in the worksheet:
    a. Insert a formula in D4 that adds the amounts in B4 and C4. Copy the formula down to cells D5 through D11.
    b. Insert a formula in E4 that averages the amounts in B4 and C4. Copy the formula down to cells E5 through E11.
    c. Insert an IF statement in cell F4 that says that if the amount in cell E4 is greater than 74999, then insert the word "Yes" and if the amount is less than 75000, then insert the word "No." Copy this formula down to cells F5 through F11.
12. Make the following changes to the worksheet:
    a. Select cells F4 through F11 and then click the Center button in the Alignment group.
    b. Add a double-line border around cells A1 through F11.
    c. Select cells A1 and A2 and then apply a light orange fill color.
    d. Select cells A3 through F3 and then apply an orange fill color.
13. Save and then print the worksheet.
14. Apply the Verve theme to the worksheet.
15. Save, print, and then close **ExcelL1_C3_A1.xlsx**.

Assessment

2 FORMAT AN OVERDUE ACCOUNTS WORKSHEET

1. Open **ExcelC03Assessment02.xlsx**.
2. Save the workbook with Save As and name it **ExcelL1_C3_A2**.
3. Change the width of columns as follows:

Column A	=	21.00
Column B	=	10.00
Column C	=	10.00
Column D	=	12.00
Column E	=	7.00
Column F	=	12.00

4. Make cell A1 active and then insert a new row.
5. Merge and center cells A1 through F1.
6. Type **Compass Corporation** in cell A1 and then press Enter.
7. Increase the height of row 1 to 42.00.
8. Increase the height of row 2 to 24.00.
9. Make the following formatting changes to the worksheet:
   a. Select cells A1 through F11 and then change the font to 10-point Bookman Old Style.
   b. Make cell A1 active, change the font size to 24 points, and turn on bold.
   c. Make cell A2 active, change the font size to 18 points, and turn on bold.
   d. Select cells A3 through F3, click the Bold button in the Font group and then click the Center button in the Alignment group.
   e. Select cells A1 through F3, click the Middle Align button in the Alignment group.
   f. Select cells B4 through C11 and then click the Center button in the Alignment group.
   g. Select cells E4 through E11 and then click the Center button in the Alignment group.
10. Use the DATE function in the following cells to enter a formula that returns the serial number for the following dates:

D4	=	September 1, 2010
D5	=	September 3, 2010
D6	=	September 8, 2010
D7	=	September 22, 2010
D8	=	September 15, 2010
D9	=	September 30, 2010
D10	=	October 6, 2010
D11	=	October 13, 2010

11. Enter a formula in cell F4 that inserts the due date (the purchase date plus the number of days in the Terms column). Copy the formula down to cells F5 through F11.
12. Apply the following borders and fill color:
    a. Add a thick line border around cells A1 through F11.
    b. Make cell A2 active and then add a double-line border at the top and bottom of the cell.
    c. Select cells A3 through F3 and then add a single line border to the bottom of the cells.
    d. Select cells A1 and A2 and then apply a light blue fill color.
13. Save, print, and then close **ExcelL1_C3_A2.xlsx**.

Assessment

3 FORMAT A SUPPLIES AND EQUIPMENT WORKSHEET

1. Open **ExcelC03Assessment03.xlsx**.
2. Save the workbook with Save As and name it **ExcelL1_C3_A3**.
3. Select cells A1 through D19 and then change the font to Garamond and the font color to dark blue.
4. Select and then merge and center cells A1 through D1.
5. Select and then merge and center cells A2 through D2.
6. Make cell A1 active and then change the font size to 22 points and turn on bold.
7. Make cell A2 active and then change the font size to 12 points and turn on bold.
8. Change the height of row 1 to 36.00.
9. Change the height of row 2 to 21.00.
10. Change the width of column A to 15.00.
11. Select cells A3 through A17, turn on bold, and then click the Wrap Text button in the Alignment group.
12. Select cells A1 and A2 and then click the Middle Align button in the Alignment group.
13. Make cell B3 active and then change the number formatting to Currency with no decimal places.
14. Select cells C6 through C19 and then change the number formatting to Percentage with one decimal place.
15. Automatically adjust the width of column B.
16. Make cell D6 active and then type a formula that multiplies the absolute cell reference $B$3 with the percentage in cell C6. Copy the formula down to cells D7 through D19.
17. With cells D6 through D19 selected, change the number formatting to Currency with no decimal places.
18. Make cell D8 active and then clear the cell contents. Use the Repeat command, F4, to clear the contents from cells D11, D14, and D17.
19. Add light green fill color to the following cells: A1, A2, A5–D5, A8–D8, A11–D11, A14–D14, and A17–D17.
20. Add borders and/or shading of your choosing to enhance the visual appeal of the worksheet.
21. Save, print, and then close **ExcelL1_C3_A3.xlsx**.

Assessment

4 FORMAT A FINANCIAL ANALYSIS WORKSHEET

1. Use the Help feature to learn how to use the shrink to fit option to show all data in a cell (with an option at the Format Cells dialog box with the Alignment tab selected).
2. Open **ExcelC03Assessment04.xlsx**.
3. Save the workbook with Save As and name it **ExcelL1_C3_A4**.
4. Make cell B9 active and then insert a formula that averages the percentages in cells B3 through B8. Copy the formula to the right to cells C9 and D9.

5. Select cells B3 through D9, display the Format Cells dialog box with the Alignment tab selected, change the horizontal alignment to Right (Indent) and the indent to *2*, and then close the dialog box.
6. Select cells A1 through D9 and then change the font size to 14.
7. Select cells B2 through D2 and then change the orientation to 45 degrees.
8. With cells B2 through D2 still selected, shrink the font size to show all data in the cells.
9. Save, print, and then close **ExcelL1_C3_A4.xlsx**.

CASE study
Apply Your Skills

Part 1

You are the office manager for HealthWise Fitness Center and you decide to prepare an Excel worksheet that displays the various plans offered by the health club. In this worksheet, you want to include yearly dues for each plan as well as quarterly and monthly payments. Open the **HealthWise.xlsx** workbook and then save it and name it **ExcelL1_C3_CS_P1A**. Make the following changes to the worksheet:

- Select cells B3 through D8 and then change the number formatting to Accounting with two decimal places and a dollar sign.
- Make cell B3 active and then insert *500.00*.
- Make cell B4 active and then insert a formula that adds the amount in B3 with the product (multiplication) of B3 multiplied by 10%. (The formula should look like this: **=B3+(B3*10%)**. The Economy plan is the base plan and each additional plan costs 10% more than the previous plan.)
- Copy the formula in cell B4 down to cells B5 through B8.
- Insert a formula in cell C3 that divides the amount in cell B3 by 4 and then copy the formula down to cells C4 through C8.
- Insert a formula in cell D3 that divides the amount in cell B3 by 12 and then copy the formula down to cells D4 through D8.
- Apply formatting to enhance the visual display of the worksheet.

Save and print the completed worksheet.

With **ExcelL1_C3_CS_P1A.xlsx** open, save the workbook with Save As and name it **ExcelL1_C3_CS_P1B**, and then make the following changes:

- You have been informed that the base rate for yearly dues has increased from $500.00 to $600.00. Change this amount in cell B3 of the worksheet.
- If clients are late with their quarterly or monthly dues payments, a late fee is charged. You decide to add the late fee information to the worksheet. Insert a new column to the right of Column C. Type **Late Fees** in cell D2 and also in cell F2.
- Insert a formula in cell D3 that multiplies the amount in C3 by 5%. Copy this formula down to cells D4 through D8.
- Insert a formula in cell F3 that multiplies the amount in E3 by 7%. Copy this formula down to cells F4 through F8. If necessary, change the number formatting for cells F3 through F8 to Accounting with two decimal places and a dollar sign.
- Apply any additional formatting to enhance the visual display of the worksheet.

Save, print, and then close **ExcelL1_C3_CS_P1B.xlsx**.

Part 2

Prepare a payroll sheet for the employees of the fitness center and include the following information:

HealthWise Fitness Center
Weekly Payroll

Employee	Hourly Wage	Hours	Weekly Salary	Benefits
Heaton, Kelly	$26.50	40		
Severson, Joel	$25.00	40		
Turney, Amanda	$20.00	15		
Walters, Leslie	$19.65	30		
Overmeyer, Jean	$18.00	20		
Haddon, Bonnie	$16.00	20		
Baker, Grant	$15.00	40		
Calveri, Shannon	$12.00	15		
Dugan, Emily	$10.50	10		
Joyner, Daniel	$10.50	10		
Lee, Alexander	$10.50	10		

Insert a formula in the *Weekly Salary* column that multiplies the hourly wage by the number of hours. Insert an IF statement in the *Benefits* column that states that if the number in the *Hours* column is greater than 19, then insert "Yes" and if the number is less than 20, then insert "No." Apply formatting to enhance the visual display of the worksheet. Save the workbook and name it **ExcelL1_C3_CS_P2**. Print **ExcelL1_C3_CS_P2.xlsx**. Press Ctrl + ` to turn on the display of formulas, print the worksheet, and then press Ctrl + ` to turn off the display of formulas.

Make the following changes to the worksheet:

- Change the hourly wage for Amanda Turney to $22.00.
- Increase the hours for Emily Dugan to 20.
- Remove the row for Grant Baker.
- Insert a row between Jean Overmeyer and Bonnie Haddon and then type the following information in the cells in the new row: Employee: Tonya McGuire; Hourly Wage: $17.50; Hours: 15.

Save and then print **ExcelL1_C3_CS_P2.xlsx**. Press Ctrl + ` to turn on the display of formulas and then print the worksheet. Press Ctrl + ` to turn off the display of formulas and then save and close **ExcelL1_C3_CS_P2.xlsx**.

Part 3

Your boss is interested in ordering new equipment for the health club. She is interested in ordering three elliptical machines, three recumbent bikes, and three upright bikes. She has asked you to use the Internet to research models and prices for this new equipment. She then wants you to prepare a worksheet with the information. Using the Internet, search for the following equipment:

- Search for elliptical machines for sale. Locate two different models and, if possible, find at least two companies that sell each model. Make a note of the company names, model numbers, and prices.

- Search for recumbent bikes for sale. Locate two different models and, if possible, find at least two companies that sell each model. Make a note of the company names, model numbers, and prices.
- Search for upright bikes for sale. Locate two different models and, if possible, find at least two companies that sell each model. Make a note of the company names, model numbers, and prices.

Using the information you found on the Internet, prepare an Excel worksheet with the following information:

- Equipment name
- Equipment model
- Price
- A column that multiplies the price by the number required (which is 3).

Include the fitness center name, HealthWise Fitness Center, and any other information you determine is necessary to the worksheet. Apply formatting to enhance the visual display of the worksheet. Save the workbook and name it **ExcelL1_C3_CS_P3**. Print and then close **ExcelL1_C3_CS_P3.xlsx**.

Part 4

When a prospective client contacts HealthWise about joining, you send a letter containing information about the fitness center, the plans offered, and the dues amounts. Use a letter template in Word to create a letter to send to a prospective client (you determine the client's name and address). Copy the cells in **ExcelL1_C3_CS_P1B.xlsx** containing data and paste them into the body of the letter. Make any formatting changes to make the data readable. Save, print, and then close the letter.

Enhancing a Worksheet

PERFORMANCE OBJECTIVES

Upon successful completion of Chapter 4, you will be able to:

- Change worksheet margins
- Center a worksheet horizontally and vertically on the page
- Insert a page break in a worksheet
- Print gridlines and row and column headings
- Set and clear a print area
- Insert headers and footers
- Customize print jobs
- Complete a spelling check on a worksheet
- Find and replace data and cell formatting in a worksheet
- Sort data in cells in ascending and descending order
- Filter a list using AutoFilter
- Plan and create a worksheet

Tutorial 4.1
Printing Worksheets
Tutorial 4.2
Finding, Sorting, and Filtering
Data

Excel contains features you can use to enhance and control the formatting of a worksheet. In this chapter, you will learn how to change worksheet margins, orientation, size, and scale; print column and row titles; print gridlines; and center a worksheet horizontally and vertically on the page. You will also learn how to complete a spell check on text in a worksheet, find and replace specific data and formatting in a worksheet, sort and filter data, and plan and create a worksheet.

Note: Before beginning computer projects, copy to your storage medium the Excel2007L1C4 subfolder from the Excel2007L1 folder on the CD that accompanies this textbook and make Excel2007L1C4 the active folder.

Project ① Format a Yearly Budget Worksheet

You will format a yearly budget worksheet by inserting formulas; changing margins, page orientation, and page size; inserting a page break; printing column headings on multiple pages; scaling data to print on one page; inserting a background picture; inserting headers and footers; and identifying a print area and customizing print jobs.

Change Worksheet Margins
1. Click Page Layout tab.
2. Click Margins button.
3. Click desired predesigned margin.
OR
1. Click Page Layout tab.
2. Click Margins button.
3. Click *Custom Margins* at drop-down list.
4. Change the top, left, right, and/or bottom measurements.
5. Click OK.

Margins

Formatting a Worksheet Page

An Excel worksheet contains default page formatting. For example, a worksheet contains left and right margins of 0.7 inch and top and bottom margins of 0.75 inch, a worksheet prints in portrait orientation, and the worksheet page size is 8.5 inches by 11 inches. These default settings as well as additional options can be changed and/or controlled with options in the Page Layout tab.

Changing Margins

The Page Setup group in the Page Layout tab contains buttons for changing margins, the page orientation and size, as well as buttons for establishing a print area, inserting a page break, applying a picture background, and printing titles.

Change the worksheet margins by clicking the Margins button in the Page Setup group in the Page Layout tab. This displays a drop-down list of predesigned margin choices. If one of the predesigned choices is what you want to apply to the worksheet, click the option. If you want to customize margins, click the *Custom Margins* option at the bottom of the Margins drop-down list. This displays the Page Setup dialog box with the Margins tab selected as shown in Figure 4.1.

Figure 4.1 Page Setup Dialog Box with Margins Tab Selected

Changes made to margin measurements are reflected in the sample worksheet page.

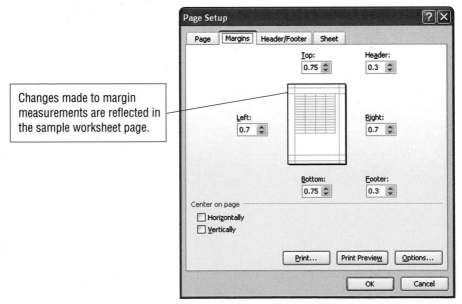

A worksheet page showing the cells and margins displays in the dialog box. As you increase or decrease the top, bottom, left, or right margin measurements, the sample worksheet page reflects the change. You can also increase or decrease the measurement from the top of the page to the header with the *Header* option or the measurement from the footer to the bottom of the page with the *Footer* option. (You will learn about headers and footers later in this chapter.)

Centering a Worksheet Horizontally and/or Vertically

By default, worksheets print in the upper left corner of the page. You can center a worksheet on the page by changing the margins; however, an easier method for centering a worksheet is to use the *Horizontally* and/or *Vertically* options that display at the bottom of the Page Setup dialog box with the Margins tab selected. If you choose one or both of these options, the worksheet page in the preview section displays how the worksheet will print on the page.

QUICK STEPS

Center Worksheet Horizontally/ Vertically
1. Click Page Layout tab.
2. Click *Custom Margins* at drop-down list.
3. Click *Horizontally* option and/or click *Vertically* option.
4. Click OK.

Project 1a **Changing Margins and Horizontally and Vertically Centering a Worksheet**

1. Open **ExcelC04Project01.xlsx**.
2. Save the workbook with Save As and name it **ExcelL1_C4_P1**.
3. Insert the following formulas in the worksheet:
   a. Insert formulas in column N, rows 5 through 10 that sum the totals for each income item.
   b. Insert formulas in row 11, columns B through N that sum the income as well as the total for all income items.
   c. Insert formulas in column N, rows 14 through 19 that sum the totals for each expense item.
   d. Insert formulas in row 20, columns B through N that sum the expenses as well as the total of expenses.
   e. Insert formulas in row 21, columns B through N that subtract the total expenses from the income. (To begin the formula, make cell B21 active and then type the formula =B11-B20. Copy this formula to columns C through N.)
4. Click the Page Layout tab.
5. Click the Margins button in the Page Setup group and then click *Custom Margins* at the drop-down list.

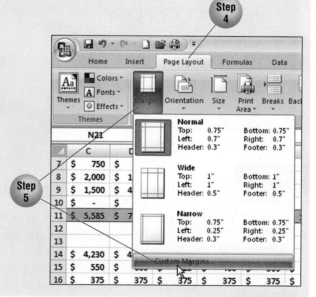

6. At the Page Setup dialog box with the Margins tab selected, click the up-pointing arrow at the right side of the *Top* text box until *3.5* displays.
7. Click the up-pointing arrow at the right side of the *Bottom* text box until *1.5* displays.
8. Preview the worksheet by clicking the Print Preview button located toward the bottom of the Page Setup dialog box. The worksheet appears to be a little low on the page so you decide to horizontally and vertically center it by completing the following steps:
   a. Click the Close Print Preview button.
   b. Click the Margins button in the Page Setup group and then click *Custom Margins* at the drop-down list.
   c. At the Page Setup dialog box with the Margins tab selected, change the *Top* and *Bottom* measurements to *1*.
   d. Click the *Horizontally* option. (This inserts a check mark.)
   e. Click the *Vertically* option. (This inserts a check mark.)
   f. Click OK to close the dialog box.
9. Save **ExcelL1_C4_P1.xlsx**.

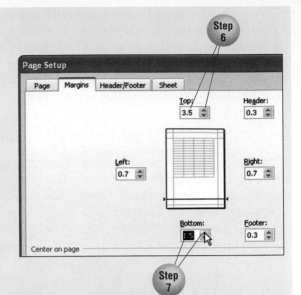

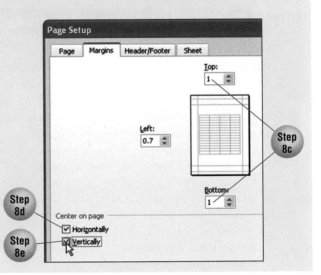

QUICK STEPS Changing Page Orientation

Change Page Orientation
1. Click Page Layout tab.
2. Click Orientation button.
3. Click desired orientation at drop-down list.

Click the Orientation button in the Page Setup group and a drop-down list displays with two choices, *Portrait* and *Landscape*. The two choices are represented by sample pages. A sample page that is taller than it is wide shows how the default orientation (*Portrait*) prints data on the page. The other choice, *Landscape*, will rotate the data and print it on a page that is wider than it is tall.

Changing the Page Size

An Excel worksheet page size, by default, is set at 8.5 × 11 inches. You can change this default page size by clicking the Size button in the Page Setup group. At the drop-down list that displays, notice that the default setting is *Letter* and the measurement *8.5" × 11"* displays below *Letter*. This drop-down list also contains a number of page sizes such as *Executive*, *Legal*, and a number of envelope sizes.

QUICK STEPS

Change Page Size
1. Click Page Layout tab.
2. Click Size button.
3. Click desired size at drop-down list.

 1b | **Changing Page Orientation and Size**

1. With **ExcelL1_C4_P1.xlsx** open, click the Orientation button in the Page Setup group in the Page Layout tab and then click *Landscape* at the drop-down list.

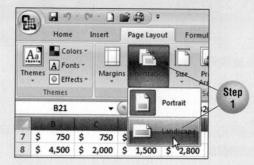

2. Click the Size button in the Page Setup group and then click *Legal* at the drop-down list.

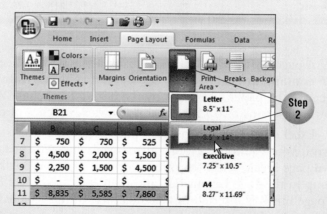

3. Preview the worksheet by clicking the Office button, pointing to *Print*, and then clicking *Print Preview*. After viewing the worksheet in Print Preview, click the Close Print Preview button.
4. Save **ExcelL1_C4_P1.xlsx**.

Inserting and Removing Page Breaks

The default left and right margins of 0.7 inch allow approximately 7 inches of cells across the page (8.5 inches minus 1.4 inches equals 7.1 inches). If a worksheet contains more than 7 inches of cells across the page, a page break is inserted in the worksheet and the remaining columns are moved to the next page. A page break displays as a broken line along cell borders. Figure 4.2 shows the page break in **ExcelL1_C4_P1.xlsx**.

Figure 4.2 Page Break

A page break also displays horizontally in a worksheet. By default, a worksheet can contain approximately 9.5 inches of cells vertically down the page. This is because the paper size is set by default at 11 inches. With the default top and bottom margins of 0.75 inch, this allows 9.5 inches of cells to print on one page.

Excel automatically inserts a page break in a worksheet. You can insert your own if you would like more control over what cells print on a page. To insert your own page break, select the column or row, click the Breaks button in the Page Setup group in the Page Layout tab, and then click *Insert Page Break* at the drop-down list. A page break is inserted immediately left of the selected column or immediately above the selected row.

If you want to insert both a horizontal and vertical page break at the same time, make a cell active, click the Breaks button in the Page Setup group and then click *Insert Page Break*. This causes a horizontal page break to be inserted immediately above the active cell, and a vertical page break to be inserted at the left side of the active cell. To remove a page break, select the column or row or make the desired cell active, click the Breaks button in the Page Setup group, and then click *Remove Page Break* at the drop-down list.

The page break automatically inserted by Excel may not be visible initially in a worksheet. One way to display the page break is to preview the worksheet. When you close Print Preview, the page break will display in the worksheet.

QUICK STEPS

Insert Page Break
1. Select column or row.
2. Click Page Layout tab.
3. Click Breaks button.
4. Click *Insert Page Break* at drop-down list.

Breaks

Displaying a Worksheet in Page Break Preview

Excel provides a page break view that displays worksheet pages and page breaks. To display this view, click the Page Break Preview button located in the view area at the right side of the Status bar or click the View tab and then click the Page Break Preview button in the Workbook Views group. This causes the worksheet to display similar to the worksheet shown in Figure 4.3. The word *Page* along with the page number is displayed in gray behind the cells in the worksheet. A solid blue line indicates a page break inserted by Excel and a dashed blue line indicates a page break inserted manually.

You can move the page break by positioning the arrow pointer on the blue line, holding down the left mouse button, dragging the line to the desired location, and then releasing the mouse button. To return to the Normal view, click the Normal button in the view area on the Status bar or click the View tab and then click the Normal button in the Workbook Views group.

HINT
You can edit a worksheet in Page Break Preview.

Page Break Preview

Normal

Figure 4.3 Worksheet in Page Break Preview

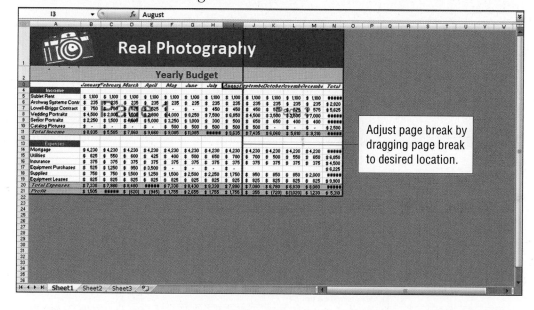

Adjust page break by dragging page break to desired location.

 Project ❿ **Inserting a Page Break in a Worksheet**

1. With **ExcelL1_C4_P1.xlsx** open, click the Size button in the Page Setup group in the Page Layout tab and then click *Letter* at the drop-down list.
2. Click the Margins button and then click *Custom Margins* at the drop-down list.
3. At the Page Setup dialog box with the Margins tab selected, click *Horizontally* to remove the check mark, click *Vertically* to remove the check mark, and then click OK to close the dialog box.
4. Insert a page break between columns I and J by completing the following steps:
   a. Select column J.
   b. Click the Breaks button in the Page Setup group and then click *Insert Page Break* at the drop-down list. Click in any cell in column I.

Step 4b

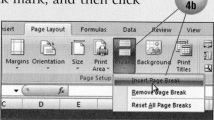

5. View the worksheet in Page Break Preview by completing the following steps:

a. Click the Page Break Preview button located in the view area on the Status bar. (If a welcome message displays, click OK.)

b. View the pages and page breaks in the worksheet.

c. You decide to include the first six months of the year on one page. To do this, position the arrow pointer on the vertical blue line, hold down the left mouse button, drag the line to the left so it is positioned between columns G and H, and then release the mouse button.

d. Click the Normal button located in the view area on the Status bar.

6. Save **ExcelL1_C4_P1.xlsx**.

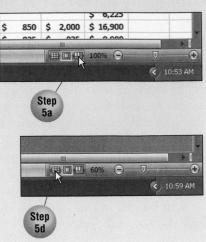

Step 5a

Step 5d

Printing Column and Row Titles on Multiple Pages

Columns and rows in a worksheet are usually titled. For example, in **ExcelL1_C4_P1.xlsx**, column titles include *Income*, *Expenses*, *January*, *February*, *March*, and so on. Row titles include the income and expenses categories. If a worksheet prints on more than one page, having column and/or row titles printing on each page can be useful. To do this, click the Print Titles button in the Page Setup group in the Page Layout tab. This displays the Page Setup dialog box with the Sheet tab selected as shown in Figure 4.4.

Figure 4.4 Page Setup Dialog Box with Sheet Tab Selected

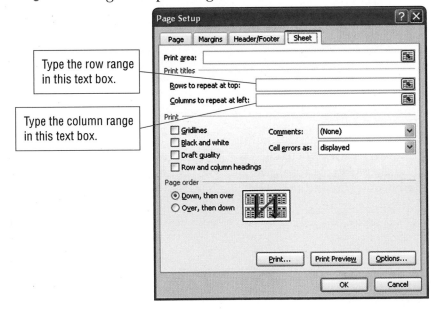

Type the row range in this text box.

Type the column range in this text box.

At the Page Setup dialog box with the Sheet tab selected, specify the range of row cells you want to print on every page in the *Rows to repeat at top* text box. Type a cell range using a colon. For example, if you want cells A1 through J1 to print on every page, you would type A1:J1 in the *Rows to repeat at top* text box. Type the range of column cells you want to print on every page in the *Columns to repeat at left* text box. To make rows and columns easier to identify on the printed page, specify that row and/or column headings print on each page.

QUICK STEPS

Print Column and Row Titles
1. Click Page Layout tab.
2. Click Print Titles button.
3. Type row range in *Rows to repeat at top* option.
4. Type column range in *Columns to repeat at left* option.
5. Click OK.

Project 1d Printing Column Titles on Each Page of a Worksheet

1. With **ExcelL1_C4_P1.xlsx** open, click the Page Layout tab and then click the Print Titles button in the Page Setup group.
2. At the Page Setup dialog box with the Sheet tab selected, click in the *Columns to repeat at left* text box.
3. Type A1:A21.

Page Setup		? X
Page	Margins	Header/Footer	**Sheet**

Print area: [   ]
Print titles
Rows to repeat at top: [   ]
Columns to repeat at left: [A1:A21]

Step 3

4. Click OK to close the dialog box.
5. Save, preview, and then print **ExcelL1_C4_P1.xlsx**.

Scaling Data

With buttons in the Scale to Fit group in the Page Layout tab, you can adjust the printed output by a percentage to fit the number of pages specified. For example, if a worksheet contains too many columns to print on one page, click the down-pointing arrow at the right side of the *Width* box in the Scale to Fit group in the Page Layout tab and then click *1 page*. This causes the data to shrink so all columns display and print on one page.

Project 1e Scaling Data to Fit on One Page

1. With **ExcelL1_C4_P1.xlsx** open, click the down-pointing arrow at the right side of the *Width* box in the Scale to Fit group in the Page Layout tab.
2. At the drop-down list that displays, click the *1 page* option.

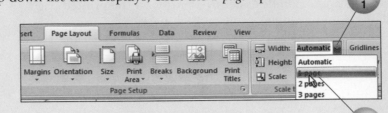

Step 1

Step 2

3. Preview the worksheet to make sure it displays on one page.
4. Save and then print **ExcelL1_C4_P1.xlsx**.

Insert Background Picture
1. Click Page Layout tab.
2. Click Background button.
3. Navigate to desired picture and double-click picture.

Inserting a Background Picture

With the Background button in the Page Setup group in the Page Layout tab you can insert a picture as a background to the worksheet. The picture displays only on the screen and does not print. To insert a picture, click the Background button in the Page Setup group. At the Sheet Background dialog box navigate to the folder containing the desired picture and then double-click the picture. To remove the picture from the worksheet, click the Delete Background button.

Project 1f Inserting a Background Picture

1. With **ExcelL1_C4_P1.xlsx** open, change the scaling back to the default by completing the following steps:
   a. Click the down-pointing arrow at the right side of the *Width* box in the Scale to Fit group and then click *Automatic* at the drop-down list.
   b. Click the up-pointing arrow at the right side of the *Scale* measurement box until *100%* displays in the box.
2. Remove titles from printing on second and subsequent pages by completing the following steps:
   a. Click the Print Titles button in the Page Setup group.
   b. At the Page Setup dialog box with the Sheet tab selected, select the text that displays in the *Columns to repeat at left* text box and then press the Delete key.
   c. Click OK to close the dialog box.
3. Insert a background picture by completing the following steps:
   a. Click the Background button in the Page Setup group.
   b. At the Sheet Background dialog box, navigate to the Excel2007L1C4 folder, and then double-click **Mountain.jpg**.
4. Preview the worksheet. (Notice that the picture does not display in Print Preview.)
5. Remove the picture by clicking the Delete Background button in the Page Setup group.
6. Save **ExcelL1_C4_P1.xlsx**.

Sheet Background

Look in: Excel2007L1C4

My Recent Documents

Desktop

Mountain.jpg

Step 3b

Printing Gridlines and Row and Column Headings

By default, the gridlines that create the cells in a worksheet and the row numbers and column letters do not print. The Sheet Options group in the Page Layout tab contain check boxes for gridlines and headings. The *View* check boxes for Gridlines and Headings contain check marks. At these settings, gridlines and row and column headings display on the screen but do not print. If you want them to print, insert check marks in the *Print* check boxes. Complex worksheets may be easier to read with the gridlines printed.

You can also control the display and printing of gridlines and headings with options at the Page Setup dialog box with the Sheet tab selected. Display this dialog box by clicking the Sheet Options dialog box launcher. To print gridlines and headings, insert check marks in the check boxes located in the *Print* section of the dialog box. The *Print* section contains two additional options—*Black and white* and *Draft quality*. If you are printing with a color printer, you can print the worksheet in black and white by inserting a check mark in the *Black and white* check box. Insert a check mark in the *Draft* option if you want to print a draft of the worksheet. With this option checked, some formatting such as shading and fill are not printed.

QUICK STEPS

Print Gridlines
1. Click Page Layout tab.
2. Click *Print* check box in Gridlines section in Sheet Options group.
OR
1. Click Page Layout tab.
2. Click Sheet Options dialog box launcher.
3. Click *Gridlines* option.
4. Click OK.

Print Row and Column Headings
1. Click Page Layout tab.
2. Click *Print* check box in Headings section in Sheet Options group.
OR
1. Click Page Layout tab.
2. Click Sheet Options dialog box launcher.
3. Click *Row and column headings* option.
4. Click OK.

Project 1g — Printing Gridlines and Row and Column Headings

1. With **ExcelL1_C4_P1.xlsx** open, click in the *Print* check box below Gridlines in the Sheet Options group to insert a check mark.
2. Click in the *Print* check box below Headings in the Sheet Options group to insert a check mark.

Width:	Automatic	Gridlines	Headings	Bring to Front
Height:	Automatic	✓ View	✓ View	Send to Back
Scale:	100%	✓ Print	✓ Print	Selection Pane
Scale to Fit		Sheet Options		Arrange

Step 1   Step 2

3. Click the Margins button in the Page Setup group and then click *Custom Margins* at the drop-down list.
4. At the Page Setup dialog box with the Margins tab selected, click in the *Horizontally* check box to insert a check mark.
5. Click in the *Vertically* check box to insert a check mark.
6. Click OK to close the dialog box.
7. Save, preview, and then print **ExcelL1_C4_P1.xlsx**.
8. Click in the *Print* check box below Headings in the Sheet Options group to remove the check mark.
9. Click in the *Print* check box below Gridlines in the Sheet Options group to remove the check mark.
10. Save **ExcelL1_C4_P1.xlsx**.

Printing a Specific Area of a Worksheet

With the Print Area button in the Page Setup group in the Page Layout tab you can select and print specific areas in a worksheet. To do this, select the cells you want to print, click the Print Area button in the Page Setup group in the Page Layout tab, and then click *Set Print Area* at the drop-down list. This inserts a border around the selected cells. Click the Quick Print button on the Quick Access toolbar and the cells within the border are printed.

You can specify more than one print area in a worksheet. To do this, select the first group of cells, click the Print Area button in the Page Setup group, and then click *Set Print Area*. Select the next group of cells, click the Print Area button, and then click *Add to Print Area*. Clear a print area by clicking the Print Area button in the Page Setup group and then clicking *Clear Print Area* at the drop-down list.

Each area specified as a print area will print on a separate page. If you want nonadjacent print areas to print on the same page, consider hiding columns and/or rows in the worksheet to bring the areas together.

Project 1h   Printing Specific Areas

1. With **ExcelL1_C4_P1.xlsx** open, print the first half expenses by completing the following steps:
   a. Select cells A3 through G21.
   b. Click the Print Area button in the Page Setup group in the Page Layout tab and then click *Set Print Area* at the drop-down list.

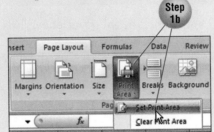

Step 1b

   c. With the border surrounding the cells A3 through G21, click the Quick Print button on the Quick Access toolbar.
   d. Clear the print area by clicking the Print Area button in the Page Setup group and then clicking *Clear Print Area* at the drop-down list.
2. Suppose you want to print the income and expenses information as well as the totals for the month of April. To do this, hide columns and select a print area by completing the following steps:
   a. Select columns B through D.
   b. Click the Home tab.
   c. Click the Format button in the Cells group, point to *Hide & Unhide*, and then click *Hide Columns*.
   d. Click the Page Layout tab.
   e. Select cells A3 through E21. (Columns A and E are now adjacent.)
   f. Click the Print Area button in the Page Setup group and then click *Set Print Area* at the drop-down list.

3. Click the Quick Print button on the Quick Access toolbar.
4. Clear the print area by making sure cells A3 through E21 are selected, clicking the Print Area button in the Page Setup group, and then clicking *Clear Print Area* at the drop-down list.
5. Unhide the columns by completing the following steps:
   a. Click the Home tab.
   b. Select columns A and E (these columns are adjacent).
   c. Click the Format button in the Cells group, point to *Hide & Unhide*, and then click *Unhide Columns*.
   d. Deselect the text by clicking in any cell containing data in the worksheet.
6. Save **ExcelL1_C4_P1.xlsx**.

Inserting Headers/Footers

Text that prints at the top of each worksheet page is called a ***header*** and text that prints at the bottom of each worksheet page is called a ***footer***. You can create a header and/or footer with the Header & Footer button in the Text group in the Insert tab, in Page Layout View, or with options at the Page Setup dialog box with the Header/Footer tab selected.

To create a header with the Header & Footer button, click the Insert tab and then click the Header & Footer button in the Text group. This displays the worksheet in Page Layout view and displays the Header & Footer Tools Design tab. Use buttons in this tab, shown in Figure 4.5, to insert predesigned headers and/or footers or insert header and footer elements such as the page number, date, time, path name, and file name. You can also create a different header or footer on the first page of the worksheet or create a header or footer for even pages and another for odd pages.

QUICK STEPS

Insert a Header or Footer
1. Click Insert tab.
2. Click Header & Footer button.
3. Click Header button and then click predesigned header or click Footer button and then click predesigned footer.
OR
1. Click Insert tab.
2. Click Header & Footer button.
3. Click desired header or footer elements.

HINT
Close the header or footer pane by clicking in the worksheet or pressing Esc.

Figure 4.5 Header & Footer Tools Design Tab

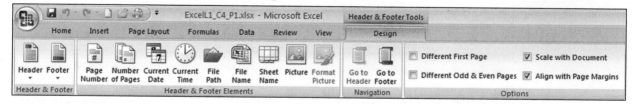

1. With **ExcelL1_C4_P1.xlsx** open, create a header by completing the following steps:
   a. Click the Insert tab.
   b. Click the Header & Footer button in the Text group.

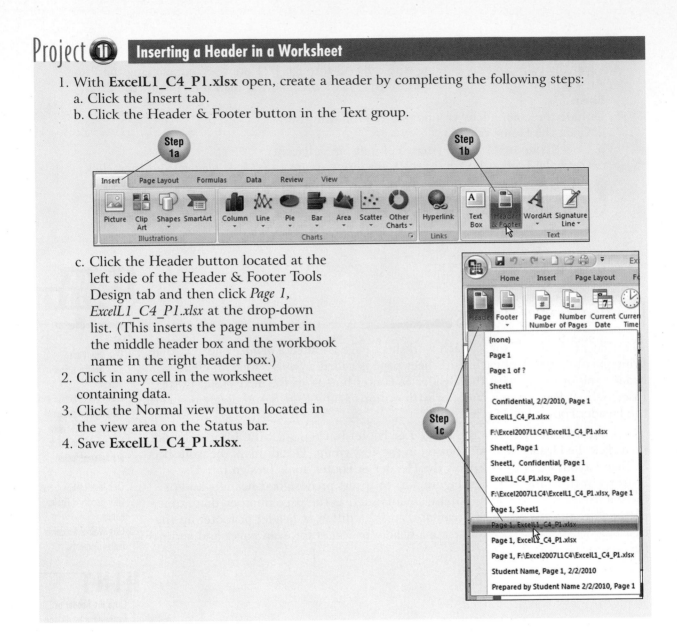

   c. Click the Header button located at the left side of the Header & Footer Tools Design tab and then click *Page 1, ExcelL1_C4_P1.xlsx* at the drop-down list. (This inserts the page number in the middle header box and the workbook name in the right header box.)
2. Click in any cell in the worksheet containing data.
3. Click the Normal view button located in the view area on the Status bar.
4. Save **ExcelL1_C4_P1.xlsx**.

You also can insert a header and/or footer by switching to Page Layout view. In Page Layout view, the top of the worksheet page displays with the text *Click to add header*. Click this text and the insertion point is positioned in the middle header box. Type the desired header in this box or click in the left box or the right box and then type the header. Create a footer in a similar manner. Scroll down the worksheet until the bottom of the page displays and then click the text *Click to add footer*. Type the footer in the center footer box or click the left or right box and then type the footer.

Project ❶   Inserting a Footer and Modifying a Header in a Worksheet

1. With **ExcelL1_C4_P1.xlsx** open, click the Page Layout button located in the view area on the Status bar.
2. Scroll down the worksheet until the text *Click to add footer* displays and then click the text.

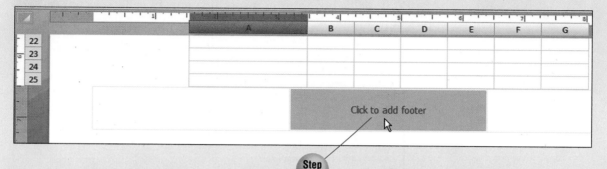

Step 2

3. Type your first and last names.
4. Click in the left footer box and then click the Current Date button in the Header & Footer Elements group in the Header & Footer Tools Design tab.
5. Click in the right footer box and then click the Current Time button in the Header & Footer Elements group.
6. Click in a cell in the worksheet.
7. Save and then print **ExcelL1_C4_Pl.xlsx**.
8. Modify the header by completing the following steps:
    a. Scroll to the beginning of the worksheet and display the header text.
    b. Click the page number in the middle header box. (This displays the Header & Footer Tools Design tab, changes the header to a field, and selects the field.)
    c. Press the Delete key to delete the header.
    d. Click the header text that displays in the right header box and then press the Delete key.
    e. Insert the page number by clicking the Page Number button in the Header & Footer Elements group.
    f. Click in the left header box and then click the File Name button in the Header & Footer Elements group.

    Step 8f

9. Click in any cell in the worksheet containing data.
10. Click the Normal button in the view area on the Status bar.
11. Preview the worksheet to determine how the header and footer print on each page.
12. Save and then print **ExcelL1_C4_P1.xlsx**.

Customizing Print Jobs

The Print dialog box provides options for customizing a print job. Display the Print dialog box shown in Figure 4.6 by clicking the Office button and then clicking *Print* at the drop-down list or by pressing the keyboard shortcut Ctrl + P. Use options at the Print dialog box to print a specific range of cells, selected cells, or multiple copies of a workbook.

Figure 4.6 Print Dialog Box

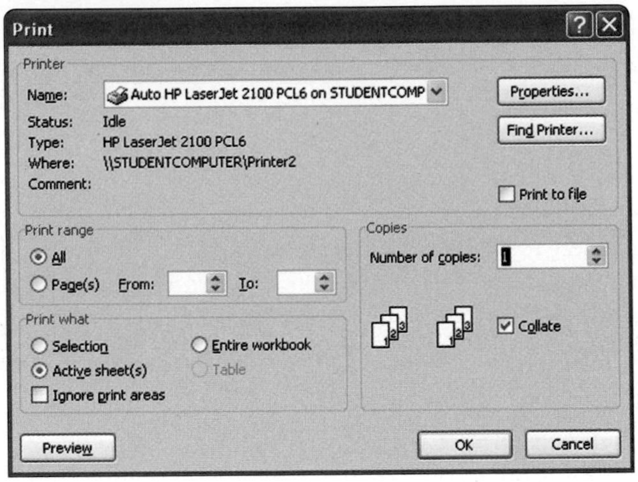

At the Print dialog box, the currently selected printer name displays in the *Name* option box. If other printers are installed, click the down-pointing arrow at the right side of the *Name* option box to display a list of printers.

The *Active sheet(s)* option in the *Print what* section is selected by default. At this setting, the currently active worksheet will print. If you want to print an entire workbook that contains several worksheets, click *Entire workbook* in the *Print what* section. Click the *Selection* option in the *Print what* section to print the currently selected cells.

If you want more than one copy of a worksheet or workbook printed, change the desired number of copies with the *Number of copies* option in the *Copies* section. If you want the copies collated, make sure the *Collate* check box in the *Copies* section contains a check mark.

A worksheet within a workbook can contain more than one page. If you want to print specific pages of a worksheet within a workbook, click *Page(s)* in the *Print range* section, and then specify the desired page numbers in the *From* and *To* text boxes.

If you want to preview the worksheet before printing, click the Preview button that displays at the bottom left corner of the dialog box. This displays the worksheet as it will appear on the printed page. After viewing the worksheet, click the Close Print Preview button that displays at the right side of the Print Preview tab.

Project 1k Printing Specific Cells in a Worksheet

1. With **ExcelL1_C4_P1.xlsx** open, print selected cells by completing the following steps:
   a. Select cells A3 through G11.
   b. Click the Office button and then click *Print* at the drop-down list.
   c. At the Print dialog box, click *Selection* in the *Print what* section.
   d. Click OK.
2. Close **ExcelL1_C4_P1.xlsx**.

Project 2 Format a May Sales and Commissions Worksheet

You will format a sales commission worksheet by inserting a formula, completing a spelling check, and finding and replacing data and cell formatting.

Completing a Spelling Check

Excel includes a spelling checker you can use to check the spelling of text in a worksheet. Before checking the spelling in a worksheet, make the first cell active. The spell checker checks the worksheet from the active cell to the last cell in the worksheet that contains data.

To use the spelling checker, click the Review tab and then click the Spelling button. Figure 4.7 displays the Spelling dialog box. At this dialog box, you can click a button to tell Excel to ignore a word or you can replace a misspelled word with a word from the *Suggestions* list box.

Figure 4.7 Excel Spelling Dialog Box

The word in the worksheet not found in the spell check dictionary displays here.

Suggested spellings display in the *Suggestions* list box.

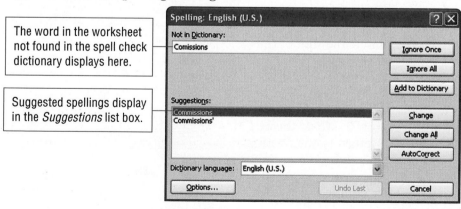

Using Undo and Redo

Undo

Redo

Excel includes an Undo button on the Quick Access toolbar that will reverse certain commands or delete the last data typed in a cell. For example, if you apply an autoformat to selected cells in a worksheet and then decide you want the autoformatting removed, click the Undo button on the Quick Access toolbar. If you decide you want the autoformatting back again, click the Redo button on the Quick Access toolbar.

Excel maintains actions in temporary memory. If you want to undo an action performed earlier, click the down-pointing arrow at the right side of the Undo button and a drop-down list displays containing the actions performed on the worksheet. Click the desired action at the drop-down list. Any actions preceding a chosen action are also undone. You can do the same with the Redo drop-down list. Multiple actions must be undone or redone in sequence.

Project 2a — Spell Checking and Formatting a Worksheet

1. Open **ExcelC04Project02.xlsx**.
2. Save the workbook with Save As and name it **ExcelL1_C4_P2**.
3. Complete a spelling check on the worksheet by completing the following steps:
   a. Make sure cell A1 is the active cell.
   b. Click the Review tab.
   c. Click the Spelling button.
   d. Click the Change button as needed to correct misspelled words in the worksheet. (When the spell checker stops at proper names *Pirozzi*, *Valona*, and *Yonemoto*, click the Ignore All button.)
   e. At the message telling you the spelling check is completed, click OK.

Step 3c · Step 3b

4. Make cell G4 active and then insert a formula that multiplies the sale price by the commission percentage. Copy the formula down to cells G5 through G26.
5. Make cell G27 active and then insert the sum of cells G4 through G26.
6. Apply a theme by clicking the Page Layout button, clicking the Themes button, and then clicking *Civic* at the drop-down gallery.
7. After looking at the worksheet with the Civic theme applied, you decide you want to return to the original formatting. To do this, click the Undo button on the Quick Access toolbar.
8. You realize that copying the formula in cell G4 down to cells G5 through G26 caused the yellow fill to be removed from certain cells and you decide to insert the shading. To do this, complete the following steps:
   a. Make cell G5 active.
   b. Click the Home tab.

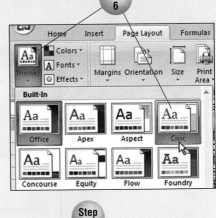

Step 6

Step 7

c. Click the Fill Color button arrow and then click *More Colors* at the drop-down gallery.

d. At the Colors dialog box with the Standard tab selected, click the yellow color as shown at the right.

e. Click OK to close the dialog box.

f. Make cell G7 active and then press F4 (the Repeat command).

g. Use F4 to apply yellow shading to cells G9, G11, G13, G15, G17, G19, G21, G23, and G25.

9. Save **ExcelL1_C4_P2.xlsx**.

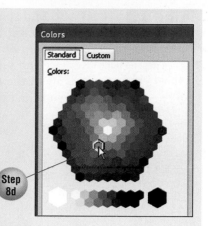

Step 8d

Finding and Replacing Data in a Worksheet

Excel provides a Find feature you can use to look for specific data and either replace it with nothing or replace it with other data. This feature is particularly helpful in a large worksheet with data you want to find quickly. Excel also includes a find and replace feature. Use this to look for specific data in a worksheet and replace it with other data.

To find specific data in a worksheet, click the Find & Select button located in the Editing group in the Home tab and then click *Find* at the drop-down list. This displays the Find and Replace dialog box with the Find tab selected as shown in Figure 4.8. Type the data you want to find in the *Find what* text box and then click the Find Next button. Continue clicking the Find Next button to move to the next occurrence of the data. If the Find and Replace dialog box obstructs your view of the worksheet, use the mouse pointer on the title bar to drag the box to a different location.

QUICK STEPS

Find Data
1. Click Find & Select button.
2. Click *Find* at drop-down list.
3. Type data in *Find what* text box.
4. Click Find Next button.

Find & Select

Figure 4.8 Find and Replace Dialog Box with Find Tab Selected

Type the data you want to find in this text box.

Click this button to expand the dialog box.

QUICK STEPS

Find and Replace Data
1. Click Find & Select button.
2. Click *Replace* at drop-down list.
3. Type data in *Find what* text box.
4. Type data in *Replace with* text box.
5. Click Replace button or Replace All button.

To find specific data in a worksheet and replace it with other data, click the Find & Select button in the Editing group in the Home tab and then click *Replace* at the drop-down list. This displays the Find and Replace dialog box with the Replace tab selected as shown in Figure 4.9. Enter the data for which you are looking in the *Find what* text box. Press the Tab key or click in the *Replace with* text box and then enter the data that is to replace the data in the *Find what* text box.

Figure 4.9 Find and Replace Dialog Box with Replace Tab Selected

Type the data you want to find in this text box.

Type the data that is to replace the data in the *Find what* text box.

Click the Find Next button to tell Excel to find the next occurrence of the data. Click the Replace button to replace the data and find the next occurrence. If you know that you want all occurrences of the data in the *Find what* text box replaced with the data in the *Replace with* text box, click the Replace All button. Click the Close button to close the Replace dialog box.

Display additional find and replace options by clicking the Options button. This expands the dialog box as shown in Figure 4.10. By default, Excel will look for any data that contains the same characters as the data in the *Find what* text box, without concern for the characters before or after the entered data. For example, in Project 2b, you will be looking for sale prices of $450,000 and replacing with $475,000. If you do not specify to Excel that you want to find cells that contain only *450000*, Excel will stop at any cell containing *450000*. In this example, Excel would stop at a cell containing *$1,450,000* or a cell containing *$2,450,000*. To specify that the only data that should be contained in the cell is what is entered in the *Find what* text box, click the Options button to expand the dialog box, and then insert a check mark in the *Match entire cell contents* check box.

Figure 4.10 Expanded Find and Replace Dialog Box

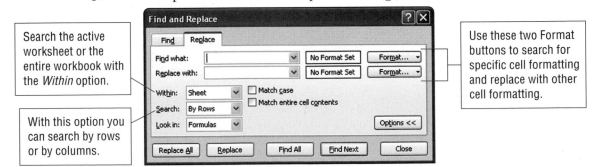

Search the active worksheet or the entire workbook with the *Within* option.

With this option you can search by rows or by columns.

Use these two Format buttons to search for specific cell formatting and replace with other cell formatting.

If the *Match case* option is active (contains a check mark), Excel will look for only that data that exactly matches the case of the data entered in the *Find what* text box. Remove the check mark from this check box if you do not want Excel to find exact case matches. Excel will search in the current worksheet. If you want Excel to search an entire workbook, change the *Within* option to *Workbook*. Excel, by default, searches by rows in a worksheet. You can change this to *By Columns* with the *Search* option.

Project 2b Finding and Replacing Data

1. With **ExcelL1_C4_P2.xlsx** open, find all occurrences of *Land* in the worksheet and replace with *Acreage* by completing the following steps:

   a. Click the Find & Select button in the Editing group in the Home tab and then click *Replace* at the drop-down list.

   b. At the Find and Replace dialog box with the Replace tab selected, type Land in the *Find what* text box.

   c. Press the Tab key (this moves the insertion point to the *Replace with* text box).

   d. Type Acreage.

   e. Click the Replace All button.

   f. At the message telling you that four replacements were made, click OK.

   g. Click the Close button to close the Find and Replace dialog box.

2. Find all occurrences of *$450,000* and replace with *$475,000* by completing the following steps:

   a. Click the Find & Select button in the Editing group and then click *Replace* at the drop-down list.

   b. At the Find and Replace dialog box with the Replace tab selected, type 450000 in the *Find what* text box.

   c. Press the Tab key.

   d. Type 475000.

   e. Click the Options button to display additional options. (If additional options already display, skip this step.)

   f. Click the *Match entire cell contents* option to insert a check mark in the check box.

   g. Click Replace All.

   h. At the message telling you that two replacements were made, click OK.

   i. At the Find and Replace dialog box, click the *Match entire cell contents* option to remove the check mark.

   j. Click the Close button to close the Find and Replace dialog box.

3. Save **ExcelL1_C4_P2.xlsx**.

Finding and Replacing Cell Formatting

Use the Format buttons at the expanded Find and Replace dialog box (see Figure 4.10) to search for specific cell formatting and replace with other formatting. Click the down-pointing arrow at the right side of the Format button and a drop-down list displays. Click the *Format* option and the Find Format dialog box displays with the Number, Alignment, Font, Border, Fill, and Protection tabs. Specify formatting at this dialog box. Click the *Choose Format From Cell* option and the mouse pointer displays with a pointer tool attached. Click in the cell containing the desired formatting and the formatting displays in the *Preview* box to the left of the Format button. Click the *Clear Find Format* option and any formatting in the *Preview* box is removed.

Project 2c   Finding and Replacing Cell Formatting

1. With **ExcelL1_C4_P2.xlsx** open, search for light turquoise fill color and replace with a purple fill color by completing the following steps:
   a. Click the Find & Select button in the Editing group and then click *Replace* at the drop-down list.
   b. At the Find and Replace dialog box with the Replace tab selected, make sure the dialog box is expanded. (If not, click the Options button.)
   c. Select and then delete any text that displays in the *Find what* text box.
   d. Select and then delete any text that displays in the *Replace with* text box.
   e. Make sure the boxes immediately preceding the two Format buttons display with the text *No Format Set*. (If not, click the down-pointing arrow at the right of the Format button, and then click the *Clear Find Format* option at the drop-down list. Do this for each Format button.)
   f. Click the top Format button.
   g. At the Find Format dialog box, click the Fill tab.
   h. Click the More Colors button.
   i. At the Colors dialog box with the Standard tab selected, click the light turquoise color shown at the right.
   j. Click OK to close the Colors dialog box.
   k. Click OK to close the Find Format dialog box.
   l. Click the bottom Format button.
   m. At the Replace Format dialog box with the Fill tab selected, click the purple color shown at the right.
   n. Click OK to close the dialog box.
   o. At the Find and Replace dialog box, click the Replace All button.
   p. At the message telling you that ten replacements were made, click OK.

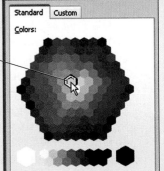

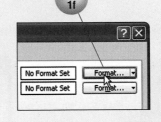

2. Search for yellow fill color and replace with a green fill color by completing the following steps:

   a. At the Find and Replace dialog box, click the top Format button.
   b. At the Find Format dialog box, click the Fill tab.
   c. Click the More Colors button.
   d. At the Colors dialog box with the Standard tab selected, click the yellow color as shown at the right.
   e. Click OK to close the Colors dialog box.
   f. Click OK to close the Find Format dialog box.
   g. Click the bottom Format button.
   h. At the Replace Format dialog box with the Fill tab selected, click the green color shown at the right.
   i. Click OK to close the dialog box.
   j. At the Find and Replace dialog box, click the Replace All button.
   k. At the message telling you that 78 replacements were made, click OK.

3. Search for 11-point Calibri formatting and replace with 10-point Arial formatting by completing the following steps:

   a. With the Find and Replace dialog box open, clear formatting from the top Format button by clicking the down-pointing arrow and then clicking the *Clear Find Format* option at the drop-down list.
   b. Clear formatting from the bottom Format button by clicking the down-pointing arrow and then clicking *Clear Replace Format*.
   c. Click the top Format button.
   d. At the Find Format dialog box, click the Font tab.
   e. Click *Calibri* in the *Font* list box (you may need to scroll down the list to display this typeface).
   f. Click *11* in the *Size* text box.
   g. Click OK to close the dialog box.
   h. Click the bottom Format button.
   i. At the Replace Format dialog box with the Font tab selected, click *Arial* in the *Font* list box (you may need to scroll down the list to display this typeface).
   j. Click *10* in the *Size* list box.
   k. Click OK to close the dialog box.
   l. At the Find and Replace dialog box, click the Replace All button.
   m. At the message telling you that 174 replacements were made, click OK.
   n. At the Find and Replace dialog box, remove formatting from both Format buttons.
   o. Click the Close button to close the Find and Replace dialog box.

4. Save, print, and then close **ExcelL1_C4_P2.xlsx**.

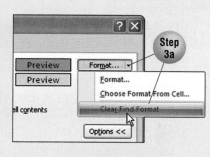

Project ③ Format a Billing Worksheet

You will insert a formula in a weekly billing worksheet and then sort and filter specific data in the worksheet.

QUICK STEPS

Sort Data
1. Select cells.
2. Click Sort & Filter button.
3. Click desired sort option at drop-down list.

HINT

If you are not satisfied with the results of the sort, immediately click the Undo button.

Sorting Data

Excel is primarily a spreadsheet program, but it also includes some basic database functions. With a database program, you can alphabetize information or arrange numbers numerically. Data can be sorted by columns in a worksheet. Sort data in a worksheet with the Sort & Filter button in the Editing group in the Home tab.

To sort data in a worksheet, select the cells containing data you want to sort, click the Sort & Filter button in the Editing group and then click the option representing the desired sort. The sort option names vary depending on the data in selected cells. For example, if the first column of selected cells contains text, the sort options in the drop-down list display as *Sort A to Z* and *Sort Z to A*. If the selected cells contain dates, the sort options in the drop-down list display as *Sort Oldest to Newest* and *Sort Newest to Oldest* and if the cells contain numbers or values, the sort options display as *Sort Smallest to Largest* and *Sort Largest to Smallest*. If you select more than one column in a worksheet, Excel will sort the data in the first selected column.

Project ③a · Sorting Data

1. Open **ExcelC04Project03.xlsx** and save it and name it **ExcelL1_C4_P3**.
2. Insert a formula in cell F4 that multiplies the rate by the hours. Copy the formula down to cells F5 through F29.
3. Sort the data in the first column in descending order by completing the following steps:
   a. Make cell A4 active.
   b. Click the Sort & Filter button in the Editing group.
   c. Click the *Sort Largest to Smallest* option at the drop-down list.
4. Sort in ascending order by clicking the Sort & Filter button and then clicking *Sort Smallest to Largest* at the drop-down list.
5. Save and then print **ExcelL1_C4_P3.xlsx**.

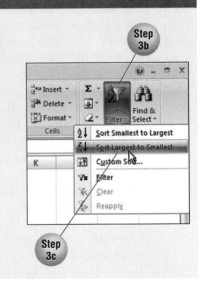

Step 3b

Step 3c

Completing a Custom Sort

If you want to sort data in a column other than the first column, use the Sort dialog box. If you select just one column in a worksheet, click the Sort & Filter button, and then click the desired sort option, only the data in that column is sorted. If this data is related to data to the left or right of the data in the sorted column, that relationship is broken. For example, if you sort cells C4 through C29 in **ExcelL1_C4_P3.xlsx**, the client number, treatment, hours, and total would no longer match the date.

Use the Sort dialog box to sort data and maintain the relationship of all cells. To sort using the Sort dialog box, select the cells you want sorted, click the Sort & Filter button, and then click *Custom Sort*. This displays the Sort dialog box shown in Figure 4.11.

The data displayed in the *Sort by* option box will vary depending on what you have selected. Generally, the data that displays is the title of the first column of selected cells. If the selected cells do not have a title, the data may display as *Column A*. Use this option to specify what column you want sorted. Using the Sort dialog box to sort data in a column maintains the relationship of the data.

Figure 4.11 Sort Dialog Box

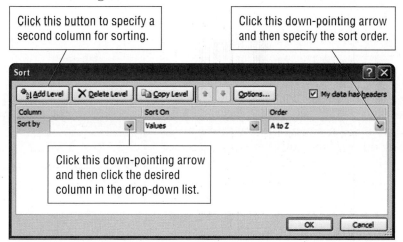

Project **3b**   **Sorting Data Using the Sort Dialog Box**

1. With **ExcelL1_C4_P3.xlsx** open, sort the rates in cells E4 through E29 in ascending order and maintain the relationship to the other data by completing the following steps:
   a. Select cells A3 through F29.
   b. Click the Sort & Filter button and then click *Custom Sort*.
   c. At the Sort dialog box, click the down-pointing arrow at the right of the *Sort by* option box, and then click *Rate* at the drop-down list.
   d. Click the down-pointing arrow at the right of the *Order* option box and then click *Largest to Smallest* at the drop-down list.
   e. Click OK to close the Sort dialog box.
   f. Deselect the cells.
2. Save and then print **ExcelL1_C4_P3.xlsx**.
3. Sort the dates in ascending order (oldest to newest) by completing steps similar to those in Step 1.
4. Save and then print **ExcelL1_C4_P3.xlsx**.

Sorting More Than One Column

When sorting data in cells, you can sort in more than one column. For example, in Project 3c you will be sorting the date from oldest to newest and then sorting client numbers from lowest to highest. In this sort, the dates are sorted first and then client numbers are sorted in ascending order within the same date.

To sort in more than one column, select all columns in the worksheet that need to remain relative and then display the Sort dialog box. At the Sort dialog box, specify the first column you want sorted in the *Sort by* option box, click the *Add Level* button, and then specify the second column in the first *Then by* option box. In Excel, you can sort on multiple columns. Add additional *Then by* option boxes by clicking the *Add Level* button.

Project 3c · Sorting Data in Two Columns

1. With **ExcelL1_C4_P3.xlsx** open, select cells A3 through F29.
2. Click the Sort & Filter button and then click *Custom Sort*.
3. At the Sort dialog box, click the down-pointing arrow at the right side of the *Sort by* option box, and then click *Date* in the drop-down list.
4. Make sure *Oldest to Newest* displays in the *Order* option box.
5. Click the *Add Level* button.
6. Click the down-pointing arrow at the right of the first *Then by* option box and then click *Client #* in the drop-down list.
7. Click OK to close the dialog box.
8. Deselect the cells.
9. Save and then print **ExcelL1_C4_P3.xlsx**.

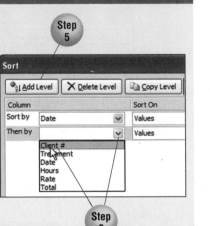

Step 5

Step 6

Filtering Data

You can place a restriction, called a *filter*, on data in a worksheet to isolate temporarily specific data. To turn on filtering, make a cell containing data active, click the Filter & Sort button in the Editing group in the Home tab, and then click *Filter* at the drop-down list. This turns on filtering and causes a filter arrow to appear in each column label in the worksheet as shown in Figure 4.12. You do not need to select before turning on filtering because Excel automatically searches for column labels in a worksheet.

To filter data in a worksheet, click the filter arrow in the heading you want to filter. This causes a drop-down list to display with options to filter all records, create a custom filter, or select an entry that appears in one or more of the cells in the column. When you filter data, the filter arrow changes to a funnel icon. The funnel icon indicates that rows in the worksheet have been filtered. To turn off filtering, click the Sort & Filter button and then click *Filter*.

If a column contains numbers, click the filter arrow, point to *Number Filters*, and a side menu displays with options for filtering numbers. For example, you can filter numbers that are equal to, greater than, or less than a number you specify; filter the top ten numbers; and filter numbers that are above or below a specified number.

Figure 4.12 Filtering Data

Turn on the filter feature and filter arrows display in column headings.

Click the filter in the Client # heading, click the *(Select All)* check box to remove the check mark, and then click the *3102* check box to display only those rows containing Client # 3102.

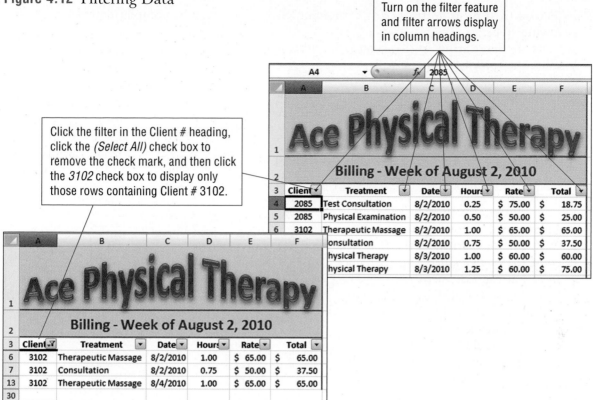

Project **3d**   **Filtering Data**

1. With **ExcelL1_C4_P3.xlsx** open, click in cell A4.
2. Turn on filtering by clicking the Sort & Filter button in the Editing group in the Home tab and then clicking *Filter* at the drop-down list.
3. Filter and then print rows for client number 3102 by completing the following steps:
   a. Click the filter arrow in the *Client #* heading.
   b. Click the *(Select All)* check box to remove the check mark.
   c. Scroll down the list box and then click *3102* to insert a check mark in the check box.
   d. Click OK.
   e. Print the worksheet by clicking the Quick Print button on the Quick Access toolbar.
4. Redisplay all rows containing data by completing the following steps:
   a. Click the funnel icon in the *Client #* heading.
   b. Click the *(Select All)* check box to insert a check mark (this also inserts a check mark for all items in the list).
   c. Click OK.

5. Filter and then print a list of clients receiving physical therapy by completing the following steps:
   a. Click the filter arrow in the *Treatment* heading.
   b. Click the *(Select All)* check box.
   c. Click the *Physical Therapy* check box.
   d. Click OK.
   e. Click the Quick Print button on the Quick Access toolbar.
6. Redisplay all rows containing data by completing the following steps:
   a. Click the funnel icon in the *Treatment* heading.
   b. Click the *(Select All)* check box to insert a check mark (this also inserts a check mark for all items in the list).
   c. Click OK.
7. Display the top two highest rates by completing the following steps:
   a. Click the filter arrow in the *Rate* heading.
   b. Point to *Number Filters* and then click *Top 10* at the side menu.
   c. At the Top 10 AutoFilter dialog box, select the *10* that displays in the middle text box and then type 2.
   d. Click OK to close the dialog box.
   e. Click the Quick Print button on the Quick Access toolbar.
8. Redisplay all rows containing data by completing the following steps:
   a. Click the funnel icon in the *Rate* heading.
   b. Click the *(Select All)* check box to insert a check mark (this also inserts a check mark for all items in the list).
   c. Click OK.

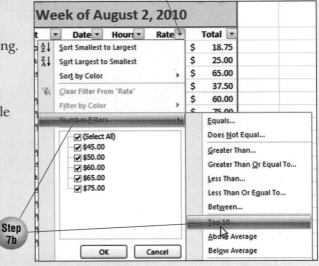

9. Display totals greater than $60 by completing the following steps:
   a. Click the filter arrow in the *Total* heading.
   b. Point to *Number Filters* and then click *Greater Than*.
   c. At the Custom AutoFilter dialog box, type 60 and then click OK.

   d. Click the Quick Print button on the Quick Access toolbar.
10. Turn off the filtering feature by clicking the Sort & Filter button and then clicking *Filter* at the drop-down list.
11. Save and then close **ExcelL1_C4_P3.xlsx**.

Project ④ Plan and Create a Worksheet

You will use steps presented to plan a worksheet and then create, save, print, and then close the worksheet.

Planning a Worksheet

The worksheets you have worked with so far basically have already been planned. If you need to plan a worksheet yourself, some steps you can follow are listed below. These are basic steps—you may think of additional steps or additional information to help you plan a worksheet.

- **Step 1: Identify the purpose of the worksheet.** The more definite you are about your purpose, the easier organizing your data into an effective worksheet will be. Consider things such as the purpose of the worksheet, the intended audience, the desired output or results, and the data required.

- **Step 2: Design the worksheet.** To do this, you need to determine how the data is to be organized, the titles of columns and rows, and how to emphasize important information. Designing the worksheet also includes determining any calculations that need to be performed.

- **Step 3: Create a sketch of the worksheet.** A diagram or sketch can help create a logical and well-ordered worksheet. With a sketch, you can experiment with alternative column and row configurations and titles and headings. When creating a sketch, start with the heading or title of the worksheet, which should provide a quick overview of what the data represents in the worksheet. Determine appropriate column and row titles that clearly identify the data.

- **Step 4: Enter the data in the worksheet.** Type the data in the worksheet, including the worksheet title, column titles, row titles, and data within cells. Enter any required formulas into the worksheet and then format the worksheet to make it appealing and easy to read.

- **Step 5: Test the worksheet data.** After preparing the worksheet and inserting any necessary formulas, check the data to be sure that the calculations are performed correctly. Consider verifying the formula results by completing the formula on a calculator.

Project ④ Planning and Creating a Worksheet

1. Look at the data shown in Figure 4.13. (The first paragraph is simply a description of the data—do not include this in the worksheet.) After reviewing the data, complete the following steps:
   a. Create a sketch of how you think the worksheet should be organized.
   b. Create a worksheet from the sketch. (Be sure to include the necessary formula to calculate the total costs.)
   c. Apply formatting to enhance the appearance of the worksheet.
2. Save the workbook and name it **ExcelL1_C4_P4**.
3. Print and then close **ExcelL1_C4_P4.xlsx**.

Figure 4.13 Project 4

The following data itemizes budgeted direct labor hours and dollars by department for planning purposes. This data is prepared quarterly and sent to the plant manager and production manager.

DIRECT LABOR BUDGET

	Labor Rate	Total Hours	Total Costs
April			
Assembly	12.75	723	
Electronics	16.32	580	
Machining	27.34	442	
May			
Assembly	12.75	702	
Electronics	16.32	615	
Machining	27.34	428	
June			
Assembly	12.75	694	
Electronics	16.32	643	
Machining	27.34	389	

CHAPTER summary

- The Page Setup group in the Page Layout tab contains buttons for changing margins, page orientation and size, and buttons for establishing a print area, inserting page break, applying a picture background, and printing titles.

- The default left and right margins are 0.7 inch and the default top and bottom margins are 0.75 inch. Change these default margins with the Margins button in the Page Setup group in the Page Layout tab.

- Display the Page Setup dialog box with the Margins tab selected by clicking the Margins button and then clicking *Custom Margins* at the drop-down list.

- Center a worksheet on the page with the *Horizontally* and *Vertically* options at the Page Setup dialog box with the Margins tab selected.

- Click the Orientation button in the Page Setup group in the Page Layout tab to display the two orientation choices—*Portrait* and *Landscape*.

- Insert a page break by selecting the column or row, clicking the Breaks button in the Page Setup group in the Page Layout tab, and then clicking *Insert Page Break* at the drop-down list.

- To insert both a horizontal and vertical page break at the same time, make a cell active, click the Breaks button, and then click *Insert Page Break* at the drop-down list.

- Display a worksheet in page break preview by clicking the Page Break Preview button in the view area on the Status bar or clicking the View tab and then clicking the Page Break Preview button.

- Use options at the Page Setup dialog box with the Sheet tab selected to specify that you want column or row titles to print on each page. Display this dialog box by clicking the Print Titles button in the Page Setup group in the Page Layout tab.

- Use options in the Scale to Fit group in the Page Layout tab to scale data to fit on a specific number of pages.

- Use the Background button in the Page Setup group in the Page Layout tab to insert a worksheet background picture. A background picture displays on the screen but does not print.

- Use options in the Sheet Options group in the Page Layout tab to specify if you want gridlines and headings to view and/or print.

- Specify a print area by selecting the desired cells, clicking the Print Area button in the Page Setup group in the Page Layout tab and then clicking *Set Print Area* at the drop-down list. Add another print area by selecting the desired cells, clicking the Print Area button, and then clicking *Add to Print Area* at the drop-down list.

- Create a header and/or footer with the Header & Footer button in the Text group in the Insert tab, in Page Layout view, or with options at the Page Setup dialog box with the Header/Footer tab selected.

- Customize print jobs with options at the Print dialog box.

- To check spelling in a worksheet, click the Review tab and then click the Spelling button.

- Click the Undo button on the Quick Access toolbar to reverse the most recent action and click the Redo button to redo a previously reversed action.
- Use options at the Find and Replace dialog box with the Find tab selected to find specific data and/or formatting in a worksheet.
- Use options at the Find and Replace dialog box with the Replace tab selected to find specific data and/or formatting and replace with other data and/or formatting.
- Sort data in a worksheet with options from the Sort & Filter button in the Editing group in the Home tab.
- Create a custom sort with options at the Sort dialog box. Display this dialog box by clicking the Sort & Filter button and then clicking *Custom Sort* at the drop-down list.
- Use the filter feature to temporarily isolate specific data. Turn on the filter feature by clicking the Sort & Filter button in the Editing group in the Home tab and then clicking *Filter* at the drop-down list. This inserts filter arrows in each column label. Click a filter arrow and then use options at the drop-down list that displays to specify the filter data.
- Plan a worksheet by completing these basic steps: identify the purpose of the worksheet, design the worksheet, create a sketch of the worksheet, enter the data in the worksheet, and test the worksheet data.

COMMANDS review

FEATURE	RIBBON TAB, GROUP	BUTTON, OPTION	KEYBOARD SHORTCUT
Margins	Page Layout, Page Setup		
Page Setup dialog box with Margins tab selected	Page Layout, Page Setup	, Custom Margins	
Orientation	Page Layout, Page Setup		
Size	Page Layout, Page Setup		
Insert page break	Page Layout, Page Setup	, Insert Page Break	
Remove page break	Page Layout, Page Setup	, Remove Page Break	
Page Break Preview	View, Workbook Views		
Page Setup dialog box with Sheet tab selected	Page Layout, Page Setup		
Scale width	Page Layout, Scale to Fit	Width: Automatic	
Scale height	Page Layout, Scale to Fit	Height: Automatic	
Scale	Page Layout, Scale to Fit	Scale: 100%	
Background picture	Page Layout, Page Setup		
Print Area	Page Layout, Page Setup		
Header and footer	Insert, Text		
Page Layout view	View, Workbook Views		
Spelling	Review, Proofing	ABC	F7
Find and Replace dialog box with Find tab selected	Home, Editing	, Find	Ctrl + F
Find and Replace dialog box with Replace tab selected	Home, Editing	, Replace	Ctrl + H
Sort data	Home, Editing		
Filter data	Home, Editing		

CONCEPTS check

Test Your Knowledge

Completion: In the space provided at the right, indicate the correct term, symbol, or command.

1. This is the default left and right margin measurement.   _0.7 inch_

2. This is the default top and bottom margin measurement.   _0.75 inch_

3. The Margins button is located in this tab.   _Page Layout_

4. By default, a worksheet prints in this orientation on a page.   _Portrait_

5. Click the Print Titles button in the Page Setup group in the Page Layout tab and the Page Setup dialog box displays with this tab selected.   _Sheet tab_

6. Use options in this group in the Page Layout tab to adjust the printed output by a percentage to fit the number of pages specified.   _Scale to fit_

7. Use this button in the Page Setup group in the Page Layout tab to select and print specific areas in a worksheet.   _Print Area_

8. Click the Header & Footer button in the Text group in the Insert tab and the worksheet displays in this view.   _Page Layout_

9. This tab contains options for formatting and customizing a header and/or footer.   _Header + Footer tools design_

10. Click this tab to display the Spelling button.   _Review Tab_

11. The Undo and Redo buttons are located on this toolbar.   _Quick Access Toolbar_

12. Click this button in the Find and Replace dialog box to expand the dialog box.   _Options Button_

13. Use these two buttons at the expanded Find and Replace dialog box to search for specific cell formatting and replace with other formatting.   _Format ▽ buttons_

14. Use this button in the Home tab to sort data in a worksheet.   _Sort + Filter_

15. Use this feature to isolate temporarily a specific data in a worksheet.   _Filter Feature_

SKILLS check
Demonstrate Your Proficiency

Assessment

1 FORMAT A DATA ANALYSIS WORKSHEET

1. Open **ExcelC04Assessment01.xlsx**.
2. Save the workbook with Save As and name it **ExcelL1_C4_A1**.
3. Make the following changes to the worksheet:
   a. Insert a formula in cell H4 that averages the amounts in cells B4 through G4.
   b. Copy the formula in cell H4 down to cells H5 through H9.
   c. Insert a formula in cell B10 that adds the amounts in cells B4 through B9.
   d. Copy the formula in cell B10 over to cells C10 through H10. (Click the AutoFill Options button and then click *Fill With Formatting* at the drop-down list.)
   e. Change the orientation of the worksheet to landscape.
   f. Change the top margin to 3 inches and the left margin to 1.5 inches.
4. Save and then print **ExcelL1_C4_A1.xlsx**.
5. Make the following changes to the worksheet:
   a. Change the top margin to 1 inch and the left margin to 0.7 inch.
   b. Change the orientation back to portrait.
   c. Horizontally and vertically center the worksheet on the page.
   d. Scale the worksheet so it fits on one page.
6. Save, print, and then close **ExcelL1_C4_A1.xlsx**.

Assessment

2 FORMAT A TEST RESULTS WORKSHEET

1. Open **ExcelC04Assessment02.xlsx**.
2. Save the workbook with Save As and name it **ExcelL1_C4_A2**.
3. Make the following changes to the worksheet.
   a. Insert a formula in cell N4 that averages the test scores in cells B4 through M4.
   b. Copy the formula in cell N4 down to cells N5 through N21.
   c. Type **Average** in cell A22.
   d. Insert a formula in cell B22 that averages the test scores in cells B4 through B21.
   e. Copy the formula in cell B22 across to cells C22 through N22.
   f. Insert a page break between columns G and H.
4. View the worksheet in Page Break Preview.
5. Change back to the Normal view.
6. Specify that the column row titles (A3 through A22) are to print on each page.
7. Create a header that prints the page number at the right side of the page.
8. Create a footer that prints your name at the left side of the page and the workbook file name at the right side of the page.
9. Save and then print the worksheet.
10. Set a print area for cells N4 through N22 and then print the cells.
11. Clear the print area.
12. Save and then close **ExcelL1_C4_A2.xlsx**.

Assessment

3 FORMAT AN EQUIPMENT RENTAL WORKSHEET

1. Open **ExcelC04Assessment03.xlsx**.
2. Save the workbook with Save As and name it **ExcelL1_C4_A3**.
3. Insert a formula in cell H3 that multiplies the rate in cell G3 by the hours in cell F3. Copy the formula in cell H3 down to cells H4 through H16.
4. Insert a formula in cell H17 that sums the amounts in cells H3 through H16.
5. Complete the following find and replaces:
    a. Find all occurrences of cells containing *75* and replace with *90*.
    b. Find all occurrences of cells containing *55* and replace with *60*.
    c. Find all occurrences of *Barrier Concrete* and replace with *Lee Sand and Gravel*.
    d. Find all occurrences of 11-point Calibri and replace with 10-point Cambria.
6. Insert a header that prints the date at the left side of the page and the time at the right side of the page.
7. Insert a footer that prints your name at the left side of the page and the workbook name at the right side of the page.
8. Print the worksheet horizontally and vertically centered on the page.
9. Save and then close **ExcelL1_C4_A3.xlsx**.

Assessment

4 FORMAT AN INVOICES WORKSHEET

1. Open **ExcelC04Assessment04.xlsx**.
2. Save the workbook with Save As and name it **ExcelL1_C4_A4**.
3. Search for the light green fill (the lightest fill in the worksheet that fills cells in every other row beginning with row 5) and replace it with no fill. (Do this at the Find and Replace dialog box with the Replace tab selected.)
4. Insert a formula in G4 that multiplies the amount in E4 with the percentage in F4 and then adds the product to cell E4. (If you write the formula correctly, the result in G4 will display as *$488.25*.)
5. Copy the formula in cell G4 down to cells G5 through G17.
6. Complete a spelling check on the worksheet.
7. Find all occurrences of *Picture* and replace with *Portrait*. (Do not type a space after *Picture* or *Portrait* because you want to find occurrences that end with an "s.")
8. Sort the records by invoice number in ascending order (smallest to largest).
9. Sort the records by client number in ascending order (A to Z) and then by date in ascending order (oldest to newest).
10. Insert a footer in the worksheet that prints your name at the left side of the page and the current date at the right side of the page.
11. Center the worksheet horizontally and vertically on the page.
12. Save and then print **ExcelL1_C4_A4.xlsx**.
13. Select cells A3 through G3 and then turn on the filter feature and complete the following filters:
    a. Filter and then print a list of rows containing client number 11-279.

b. Filter and then print a list of rows containing the top three highest amounts due.

c. Filter and then print a list of rows containing amounts due that are less than $500.

14. Save and then close **ExcelL1_C4_A4.xlsx**.

Assessment

5 CREATE A WORKSHEET CONTAINING SORT ORDER INFORMATION

1. Use Excel's Help feature and learn about the default sort order. After reading and printing the information presented, create a worksheet containing a summary of the information. Create the worksheet with the following features:

a. Create a title for the worksheet.

b. Set the data in cells in a serif typeface and change the data color.

c. Add borders to the cells (you determine the border style).

d. Add a color shading to cells (you determine the color—make it complementary to the data color).

e. Create a footer that prints your name at the left margin and the file name at the right margin.

2. Save the workbook and name it **ExcelL1_C4_A5**.

3. Print and then close **ExcelL1_C4_A5.xlsx**.

CASE study

Part 1

Apply Your Skills

You are the sales manager for Macadam Realty. You decide that you want to display sample mortgage worksheets in the reception area display rack. Open the **MacadamMortgages.xlsx** workbook, save it with Save As and name it **ExcelL1_C4_CS_P1A**, and then add the following information and make the following changes:

• In column C, insert a formula that determines the down payment amount.

• In column D, insert a formula that determines the loan amount.

• In column G, insert a formula using the PMT function (enter the *Pv* as a negative).

• Insert the date and time as a header and your name and the workbook name (**ExcelL1_C4_CS_P1A.xlsx**) as a footer.

• Find 11-point Calibri formatting and replace with 11-point Candara formatting.

• Scale the worksheet so it prints on one page.

Save and then print **ExcelL1_C4_CS_P1A.xlsx**. After looking at the printed worksheet, you decide that you need to make the following changes:

- Sort the *Price of Home* column from smallest to largest.
- Change the percentage amount in column E from 6% to 7%.
- Shade the cells in row 4 in the light yellow color that matches the fill in cell A2. Copy this shading to every other row of cells in the worksheet (stopping at row 46).

Save the edited worksheet with Save As and name it **ExcelL1_C4_CS_P1B**. Edit the footer to reflect the workbook name change (from *ExcelL1_C4_CS_P1A.xlsx* to *ExcelL1_C4_CS_P1B.xlsx*). Save, print and then close **ExcelL1_C4_CS_P1B.xlsx**. (Make sure the worksheet prints on one page.)

Part 2

You are preparing for a quarterly sales meeting during which you will discuss retirement issues with the sales officers. You want to encourage them to consider opening an Individual Retirement Account (IRA) to supplement the retirement contributions made by Macadam Realty. You have begun an IRA worksheet but need to complete it. Open **MacadamIRA.xlsx** and then save it with Save As and name it **ExcelL1_C4_CS_P2A**. Make the following changes to the worksheet:

- Insert in cell C6 a formula that calculates the future value of an investment. Use the FV function to write the formula. You must use absolute and mixed cell references for the formula. When entering the *Rate* (percentage), the column letter is variable but the row number is fixed; when entering the *Nper* (years), the column letter is fixed but the row number is variable; and when entering the *Pmt* (the contribution amount), both the column letter and row number are absolute.
- Copy the formula in cell C6 down to cells C7 through C19. Copy the formula in cell C6 across to cells D6 through K6. Continue in this manner until the amounts are entered in all the appropriate cells.
- Select and then merge and center cells A6 through A19. Type the text **Number of Years** and then rotate the text up. Make sure the text is centered in the merged cell. Apply 12-point Calibri bold formatting to the text.
- Adjust the column widths so all text is visible in the cells.
- Change the page orientation to landscape.
- Vertically and horizontally center the worksheet.
- Include a header that prints the page number and insert a footer that prints your name.

Save the worksheet and then print it so that the row titles print on both pages. After looking at the worksheet, you decide to make the following changes:

- Remove the header containing the page number.
- Edit the footer so the date prints at the left margin and your name prints at the right margin.
- Scale the worksheet so it prints on one page.

Save the workbook and name it **ExcelL1_C4_CS_P2B** and then print the worksheet. Change the amount in cell D3 to *$2,500* and then print the worksheet again. Change the amount in cell D3 to *$3,000* and then print the worksheet again. Save and then close **ExcelL1_C4_CS_P2B.xlsx**.

Part 3

You have clients living in Canada that are interested in purchasing real estate in the United States. For those clients, you like to keep a conversion worksheet available. Using the Internet, search for the MS MoneyCentral Investor Currency Rates site. Determine the current currency exchange rate for Canada and then create a worksheet with the following specifications:

- Apply formatting that is similar to the formatting in the worksheets you worked with in the first two parts of the case study.
- Create the following columns:
    ◦ Column for home price in American dollars.
    ◦ Column for home price in Canadian dollars.
    ◦ Column for amount of down payment.
    ◦ Column for loan total.
    ◦ Column for monthly payment.
- In the column for home prices, insert home amounts beginning with $100,000, incrementing every $50,000, and ending with $1,000,000.
- Insert a formula in the home price in the Canadian dollars column that displays the home price in Canadian dollars.
- Insert a formula in the down payment column that multiplies the Canadian home price by 20%.
- Insert a formula in the loan total column that subtracts the down payment from the Canadian home price.
- Insert a formula in the monthly payment column that determines the monthly payment using the PMT function. Use 6% as the rate (be sure to divide by 12 months), 360 as the number of payments, and the loan amount as a negative as the present value.
- Apply any other formatting you feel necessary to improve the worksheet.

Save the completed workbook and name it **ExcelL1_C4_CS_P3**. Display formulas and then print the worksheet. Redisplay the formulas and then save and close the workbook.

Part 4

After working with the commissions worksheet, you decide to maintain the information in an Access table. Before importing the information to an Access table, open **MacadamCommissions.xlsx** and then save the workbook with Save As and name it **ExcelL1_C4_CS_P4**. Insert a formula in G4 that multiplies the sale price by the commission percentage. Copy the formula down to cells G5 through G24. Insert a formula in cell G25 that totals the commissions and then adjust the column width so the entire total is visible. Select cells A3 through G25 and then save the selected cells in a separate workbook named **ExcelMacadamComm**. Create a database in Access named **Macadam** and then import the **ExcelMacadamComm.xlsx** Excel workbook as an Access table. Save the database and print the newly imported table.

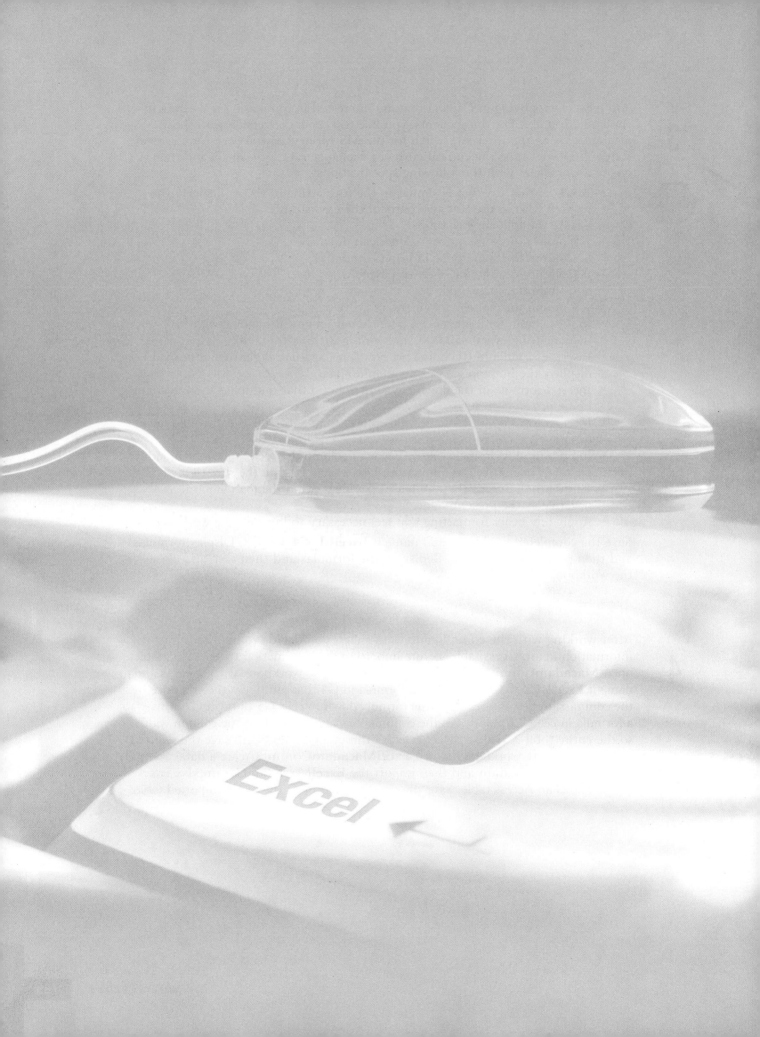

Preparing and Formatting a Worksheet

Unit 1

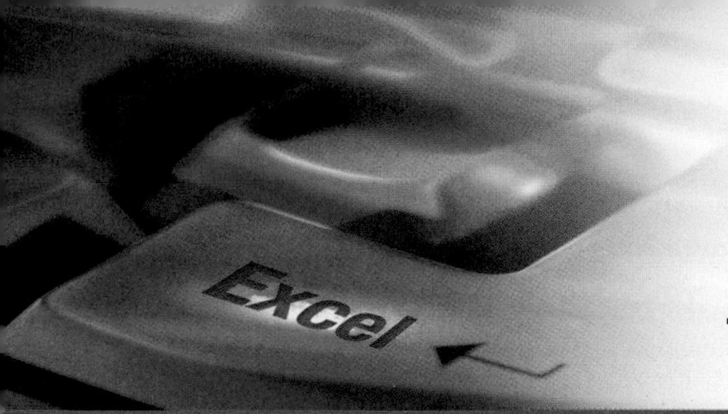

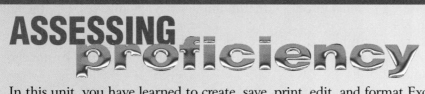

ASSESSING proficiency

In this unit, you have learned to create, save, print, edit, and format Excel worksheets; create and insert formulas; and enhance worksheets with features such as headers and footers, page numbering, sorting, and filtering.

Excel Unit 1

Note: Before beginning computer assessments, copy to your storage medium the Excel2007L1U1 subfolder from the Excel2007L1 folder on the CD that accompanies this textbook and then make Excel2007L1U1 the active folder.

Assessment 1 Create Sales Bonuses Workbook

1. Create the Excel worksheet shown in Figure U1.1. Format the cells as you see them in the figure. Format the money amounts in Accounting format with no decimal places.
2. Insert an IF statement in cell C4 that inserts *7%* if B4 is greater than 99999 and inserts *5%* if B4 is less than 100000.
3. Format the number in cell C4 so it displays as a percentage with no decimal places. Copy the formula in cell C4 down to cells C5 through C11.
4. Insert a formula in cell D4 that multiplies the amount in B4 with the percentage in cell C4. Copy the formula in D4 down to cells D5 through D11.
5. Insert a footer that contains your first and last names and the current date.
6. Print the worksheet horizontally and vertically centered on the page.
7. Save the workbook and name it **ExcelL1_U1_A1**.
8. Close **ExcelL1_U1_A1.xlsx**.

Figure U1.1 Assessment 1

	A	B	C	D	E
1	**Capstan Marine Products**				
2	**Sales Department**				
3	**Salesperson**	**Sales**	**Bonus**	**Bonus Amount**	
4	Allejandro, Eduardo	$ 105,345			
5	Crispin, Juliette	$ 96,345			
6	Frankel, Hayden	$ 89,234			
7	Hiesmann, Denae	$ 120,455			
8	Jarvis, Robert	$ 131,095			
9	Littleman, Marcus	$ 99,850			
10	Weisen, George	$ 103,125			
11	Schoenfeld, Allie	$ 78,495			
12					

Assessment 2 Format Equipment Purchase Plan Workbook

1. Open **ExcelU01Assessment02.xlsx** and then save the workbook and name it **ExcelL1_U1_A2**.
2. The owner of Hilltop Equipment Rental is interested in purchasing a new tractor and needs to determine monthly payments on three different models. Insert a formula in cell E4 that uses the PMT function to calculate monthly payments. Copy the formula down to cells E5 and E6.
3. Insert a formula in cell F4 that multiplies the amount in E4 by the amount in D4.
4. Copy the formula in cell F4 down to cells F5 and F6.
5. Insert a formula in cell G4 that subtracts the amount in B4 from the amount in F4.
6. Copy the formula in cell G4 down to cells G5 and G6.
7. Change the vertical alignment of cell A2 to Middle Align.
8. Change the vertical alignment of cells A3 through G3 to Bottom Align.
9. Save, print, and then close **ExcelL1_U1_A2.xlsx**.

Assessment 3 Format Accounts Due Workbook

1. Open **ExcelU01Assessment03.xlsx** and then save the workbook and name it **ExcelL1_U1_A3**.
2. Using the DATE function, enter a formula in each of the specified cells that returns the serial number for the specified date:

C4	=	October 26, 2010
C5	=	October 27, 2010
C6	=	October 27, 2010
C7	=	October 29, 2010
C8	=	November 3, 2010
C9	=	November 5, 2010
C10	=	November 5, 2010
C11	=	November 12, 2010
C12	=	November 12, 2010

3. Enter a formula in cell E4 that inserts the due date (date of service plus the number of days in the *Terms* column).
4. Copy the formula in cell E4 down to cells E5 through E12.
5. Make cell A14 active and then type your name.
6. Make cell A15 active and then use the NOW function to insert the current date as a serial number.
7. Save, print, and then close **ExcelL1_U1_A3.xlsx**.

Assessment 4 Format First Quarter Sales Workbook

1. Open **ExcelU01Assessment04.xlsx** and then save the workbook and name it **ExcelL1_U1_A4**.
2. Insert a formula in cell E4 that totals the amounts in B4, C4, and D4. Copy the formula in cell E4 down to cells E5 through E18.
3. Insert an IF statement in cell F4 that inserts *10%* if E4 is greater than 99999 and inserts *7%* if E4 is greater than 49999 and inserts *5%* if E4 is greater than 24999 and inserts *0%* if E4 is greater than 0.
4. Make sure the result of the IF formula displays in cell F4 as a percentage with no decimal points and then copy the formula down to cells F5 through F18.

5. Select cells A5 through F5 and then insert the same yellow fill as cell A2. Apply the same yellow fill to cells A7 through F7, A9 through F9, A11 through F11, A13 through F13, A15 through F15, and cells A17 through F17.

6. Insert a footer that prints your name at the left, the current date at the middle, and the current time at the right.

7. Print the worksheet horizontally and vertically centered on the page.

8. Save, print, and then close **ExcelL1_U1_A4.xlsx**.

Assessment 5 Format Weekly Payroll Workbook

1. Open **ExcelU01Assessment05.xlsx** and then save the workbook and name it **ExcelL1_U1_A5**.

2. Insert a formula in cell E4 that multiplies the hourly wage by the hours and then adds that to the multiplication of the hourly wage by the overtime pay rate (1.5) and then overtime hours. (Use parentheses in the formula and use an absolute cell reference for the overtime pay rate (1.5). Refer to Chapter 2, Project 5c.) Copy the formula down to cells E5 through E17.

3. Insert a formula in cell F4 that multiplies the gross pay by the withholding tax rate (W/H Rate). (Use a mixed cell reference for the cell containing the withholding rate. Refer to Chapter 2, Project 5c.) Copy the formula down to cells F5 through F17.

4. Insert a formula in cell G4 that multiplies the gross pay by the Social Security rate (SS Rate). (Use a mixed cell reference for the cell containing the Social Security rate. Refer to Chapter 2, Project 5c.) Copy the formula down to cells G5 through G17.

5. Insert a formula in cell H4 that adds together the Social Security tax and the withholding tax and subtracts that from the gross pay. Copy the formula down to cells H5 through H17.

6. Sort the employee last names alphabetically in ascending order (A to Z).

7. Center the worksheet horizontally and vertically on the page.

8. Insert a footer that prints your name at the left side of the page and the worksheet name at the right side of the page.

9. Save, print, and then close **ExcelL1_U1_A5.xlsx**.

Assessment 6 Format Customer Sales Analysis Workbook

1. Open **ExcelU01Assessment06.xlsx** and then save the workbook and name it **ExcelL1_U1_A6**.

2. Insert formulas and drag down formulas to complete the worksheet.

3. Change the orientation to landscape.

4. Insert a header that prints the page number at the right side of the page.

5. Insert a footer that prints your name at the right side of the page.

6. Horizontally and vertically center the worksheet on the page.

7. Specify that the column headings in cells A3 through A9 print on both pages.

8. Save, print, and then close **ExcelL1_U1_A6.xlsx**.

Assessment 7 Format Invoices Workbook

1. Open **ExcelU01Assessment07.xlsx** and then save the workbook and name it **ExcelL1_U1_A7**.

2. Insert a formula in cell G4 that multiplies the amount in E4 by the percentage in F4 and then adds that total to the amount in E4. (Use parentheses in this formula.)

3. Copy the formula in cell G4 down to cells G5 through G18.

4. Find all occurrences of cells containing *11-279* and replace with *10-005*.
5. Find all occurrences of cells containing *8.5* and replace with *9.0*.
6. Search for the Calibri font and replace with the Candara font (do not specify a type size so that Excel replaces all sizes of Calibri with Candara).
7. Print **ExcelL1_U1_A7.xlsx**.
8. Filter and then print a list of rows containing only the client number *04-325*. (After printing, return the list to *(All)*.)
9. Filter and then print a list of rows containing only the service *Development*. (After printing, return the list to *(All)*.)
10. Filter and then print a list of rows containing the top three highest totals in the *Amount Due* column. (After printing, turn off the filter feature.)
11. Save and then close **ExcelL1_U1_A7.xlsx**.

WRITING activities

The following activities give you the opportunity to practice your writing skills along with demonstrating an understanding of some of the important Excel features you have mastered in this unit. Use correct grammar, appropriate word choices, and clear sentence construction.

Activity 1 Plan and Prepare Orders Summary Workbook

Plan and prepare a worksheet with the information shown in Figure U1.2. Apply formatting of your choosing to the worksheet either with a cell or table style or with formatting at the Format Cells dialog box. Save the completed worksheet and name it **ExcelL1_U1_Act01**. Print and then close **ExcelL1_U1_Act01.xlsx**.

Figure U1.2 Activity 1

Prepare a weekly summary of orders taken that itemizes the products coming into the company and the average order size.

The products and average order size include:

Black and gold wall clock—$2,450 worth of orders, average order size of $125
Traveling alarm clock—$1,358 worth of orders, average order size of $195
Water-proof watch—$890 worth of orders, average order size of $90
Dashboard clock—$2,135 worth of orders, average order size of $230
Pyramid clock—$3,050 worth of orders, average order size of $375
Gold chain watch—$755 worth of orders, average order size of $80

In the worksheet, total the amount ordered and also calculate the average weekly order size. Sort the data in the worksheet by the order amount in descending order.

Activity 2 Prepare Depreciation Workbook

Assets within a company, such as equipment, can be depreciated over time. Several methods are available for determining the amount of depreciation such as the straight-line depreciation method, fixed-declining balance method, and the double-declining method. Use Excel's Help feature to learn about two depreciation methods—straight-line and double-declining depreciation. After reading about the two methods, create an Excel worksheet with the following information:

- An appropriate title
- A heading for straight-line depreciation
- The straight-line depreciation function
- The name and a description for each straight-line depreciation function argument category
- A heading for double-declining depreciation
- The double-declining depreciation function
- The name and a description for each double-declining depreciation function argument category

Apply formatting of your choosing to the worksheet. Save the completed workbook and name it **ExcelL1_U1_Act02**. Print the worksheet horizontally and vertically centered on the page. Close **ExcelL1_U1_Act02.xlsx**.

Activity 3 Insert Straight-Line Depreciation Formula

Open **ExcelU01Activity03.xlsx** and then save the workbook and name it **ExcelL1_U1_Act03**. Insert the function to determine straight-line depreciation in cell E3. Copy the formula down to cells E4 through E10. Apply formatting of your choosing to the worksheet. Print the worksheet horizontally and vertically centered on the page. Save and then close **ExcelL1_U1_Act03.xlsx**.

Optional: Briefly research the topic of straight-line and double-declining depreciation to find out why businesses depreciate their assets. What purpose does it serve? Locate information about the topic on the Internet or in your school library. Then use Word 2007 to write a half-page, single-spaced report explaining the financial reasons for using depreciation methods. Save the document and name it **ExcelL1_U1_Act03Report**. Print and then close the document.

Create a Travel Planning Worksheet

Make sure you are connected to the Internet. Use a search engine of your choosing to look for information on traveling to a specific country that interests you. Find sites that provide cost information for airlines, hotels, meals, entertainment, and car rentals. Create a travel planning worksheet for the country that includes the following:

- appropriate title
- appropriate headings
- airline costs

- hotel costs (off-season and in-season rates if available)
- estimated meal costs
- entertainment costs
- car rental costs

Save the completed workbook and name it **ExcelL1_U1_Act04**. Print and then close the workbook.

Level 1

Microsoft®

Unit 2: Enhancing the Display of Workbooks

- ➤ Moving Data within and between Workbooks

- ➤ Maintaining Workbooks

- ➤ Creating a Chart in Excel

- ➤ Adding Visual Interest to Workbooks

Benchmark Microsoft® Excel 2007 Level 1

Microsoft Certified Application Specialist Skills—Unit 2

Reference No.	Skill	Pages
1	**Creating and Manipulating Data**	
1.3	Modify cell contents and formats	
1.3.1	Cut, copy, and paste data and cell contents	158-164, 181-182
1.4	Change worksheet views	
1.4.1	Change views within a single window	171-174
1.4.2	Split windows	171-174
1.4.3	Open and arrange new windows	177-180
1.5	Manage worksheets	
1.5.1	Copy worksheets	167-168, 207-208
1.5.2	Reposition worksheets within workbooks	167-168
1.5.3	Rename worksheets	167-168
1.5.4	Hide and unhide worksheets	169-170
1.5.5	Insert and delete worksheets	164-166
2	**Formatting Data and Content**	
2.1	Format worksheets	
2.1.3	Add color to worksheet tabs	167-168
2.1.4	Format worksheet backgrounds	291-292
2.3	Format cells and cell content	
2.3.8	Insert, modify, and remove hyperlinks	275-277
4	**Presenting Data Visually**	
4.1	Create and format charts	
4.1.1	Select appropriate data sources for charts	239-243
4.1.2	Select appropriate chart types to represent data sources	243-245
4.1.3	Format charts using Quick Styles	246-248, 257-259
4.2	Modify charts	
4.2.1	Add and remove chart elements	249-253
4.2.2	Move and size charts	241-243, 260-261
4.2.3	Change chart types	243-245
4.4	Insert and modify illustrations	
4.4.1	Insert and modify pictures from files (not clip art files)	255-256, 288-289
4.4.2	Insert and modify SmartArt graphics	292-297
4.4.3	Insert and modify shapes	284-287
5	**Collaborating and Securing Data**	
5.1	Manage changes to workbooks	
5.1.2	Insert, display, modify, and delete comments	222-226
5.4	Save workbooks	
5.4.1	Save workbooks for use in a previous version of Excel	211-212
5.4.2	Using the correct format, save a workbook as a template, a Web page, a macro-enabled document, or another appropriate format	213-214, 272-274

Note: The Level 1 and Level 2 texts each address approximately half of the Microsoft Certified Application Specialist skills. Complete coverage of the skills is offered in the combined Level 1 and Level 2 text titled *Benchmark Series Microsoft® Excel 2007: Levels 1 and 2,* which has been approved as certified courseware and which displays the Microsoft Certified Application Specialist logo on the cover.

CHAPTER 5

Moving Data within and between Workbooks

PERFORMANCE OBJECTIVES

Upon successful completion of Chapter 5, you will be able to:

- Create a workbook with multiple worksheets
- Move, copy, and paste cells within a worksheet
- Split a worksheet into windows and freeze panes
- Name a range of cells and use a range in a formula
- Open multiple workbooks
- Arrange, size, and move workbooks
- Copy and paste data between workbooks
- Link data between worksheets
- Link worksheets with a 3-D reference
- Copy and paste a worksheet between programs

excel Chapter 5

SNAP

Tutorial 5.1
Managing Worksheets and Workbooks
Tutorial 5.2
Working with Multiple Worksheets

Up to this point, the workbooks in which you have been working have consisted of only one worksheet. In this chapter, you will learn to create a workbook with several worksheets and complete tasks such as copying and pasting data within and between worksheets. Moving and pasting or copying and pasting selected cells in and between worksheets is useful for rearranging data or for saving time. You will also work with multiple workbooks and complete tasks such as arranging, sizing, and moving workbooks, and opening and closing multiple workbooks.

Note: Before beginning computer projects, copy to your storage medium the Excel2007L1C5 subfolder from the Excel2007L1 folder on the CD that accompanies this textbook and then make Excel2007L1C5 the active folder.

Project ① Manage Data in a Multiple-Worksheet Account Workbook

You will open an account workbook containing three worksheets and then move, copy, and paste data between the worksheets. You will also hide and unhide worksheets, and format and print multiple worksheets in the workbook.

Creating a Workbook with Multiple Worksheets

An Excel workbook can contain multiple worksheets. You can create a variety of worksheets within a workbook for related data. For example, a workbook may contain a worksheet for the expenses for each salesperson in a company and another worksheet for the monthly payroll for each department within the company. Another example is recording sales statistics for each quarter in individual worksheets within a workbook.

By default, a workbook contains three worksheets named *Sheet1*, *Sheet2*, and *Sheet3*. (Later in this chapter, you will learn how to change these default names.) Display various worksheets in the workbook by clicking the desired tab.

Project 1a — Displaying Worksheets in a Workbook

1. Open **ExcelC05Project01.xlsx** and then save the workbook and name it **ExcelL1_C5_P1**.
2. This workbook contains three worksheets. Display the various worksheets by completing the following steps:

   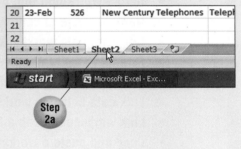

   a. Display the second worksheet by clicking the Sheet2 tab that displays immediately above the Status bar.
   b. Display the third worksheet by clicking the Sheet3 tab that displays immediately above the Status bar.
   c. Return to the first worksheet by clicking the Sheet1 tab.
3. Make the following changes to worksheets in the workbook:
   a. Click the Sheet2 tab and then change the column width for columns E, F, and G to 11.00.
   b. Click the Sheet3 tab and then change the column width for columns E, F, and G to 11.00.
   c. Click the Sheet1 tab to display the first worksheet.
4. Save **ExcelL1_C5_P1.xlsx**.

Cutting, Copying, and Pasting Selected Cells

Situations may arise where you need to move cells to a different location within a worksheet, or you may need to copy repetitive data in a worksheet. You can perform these actions by selecting cells and then using the Cut, Copy, and/or Paste buttons in the Clipboard group in the Home tab. You can also perform these actions with the mouse.

Moving Selected Cells

Cut   Paste

You can move selected cells and cell contents in a worksheet and between worksheets. Move selected cells with the Cut and Paste buttons in the Clipboard group in the Home tab or by dragging with the mouse.

To move selected cells with buttons in the Home tab, select the cells and then click the Cut button in the Clipboard group. This causes a moving dashed line border (called a marquee) to display around the selected cells. Click the cell where you want the first selected cell inserted and then click the Paste button in the Clipboard group. If you change your mind and do not want to move the selected cells, press the Esc key to remove the moving dashed line border or double-click in any cell.

To move selected cells with the mouse, select the cells and then position the mouse pointer on any border of the selected cells until the pointer turns into an arrow pointer with a four-headed arrow attached. Hold down the left mouse button, drag the outline of the selected cells to the desired location, and then release the mouse button.

QUICK STEPS

Move and Paste Cells
1. Select cells.
2. Click Cut button.
3. Click desired cell.
4. Click Paste button.

HINT

Ctrl + X is the keyboard shortcut to cut selected data. Ctrl + V is the keyboard shortcut to paste data.

Project **1b** **Moving Selected Cells**

1. With **ExcelL1_C5_P1.xlsx** open, you realize that the sublet rent deposit was recorded on the wrong day. The correct day is January 11. To move the cells containing information on the deposit, complete the following steps:
   a. Make cell A13 active and then insert a row. (The new row should display above the row containing information on *Rainer Suppliers*.)
   b. Select cells A7 through F7.
   c. Click the Cut button in the Clipboard group in the Home tab.

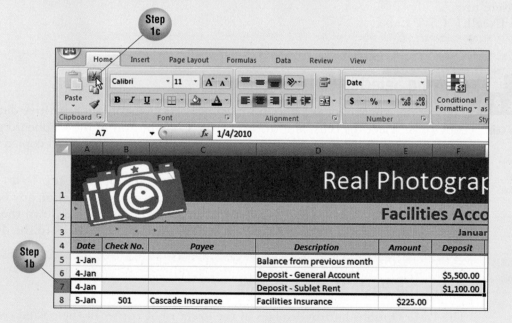

   d. Click cell A13 to make it active.
   e. Click the Paste button in the Clipboard group.

f. Change the date of the deposit from January 4 to January 11.

g. Select row 7 and then delete it.

2. Click the Sheet2 tab and then complete steps similar to those in Step 1 to move the sublet deposit row so it is positioned above the *Rainier Suppliers* row and below the *Clear Source* row. Change the date of the deposit to February 11 and make sure you delete row 7.

3. Move cells using the mouse by completing the following steps:

a. Click the Sheet3 tab.

b. Make cell A13 active and then insert a new row.

c. Using the mouse, select cells A7 through F7.

d. Position the mouse pointer on any boundary of the selected cells until it turns into an arrow pointer with a four-headed arrow attached.

e. Hold down the left mouse button, drag the outline of the selected cells to row 13, and then release the mouse button.

4	Date	Check No.	Payee	Description	Amount	Deposit
5	1-Mar			Balance from previous month		
6	1-Mar			Deposit - General Account		$5,500.00
7	1-Mar			Deposit - Sublet Rent		$1,100.00
8	2-Mar	527				
9	3-Mar	528				
10	3-Mar	529				
11	8-Mar	530	Stationery Plus	Paper Supplies	$113.76	
12	9-Mar	531	Clear Source	Developer Supplies	$251.90	
13						
14	10-Mar	532	Rainier S A13:F13	Camera Supplies	$119.62	
15	11-Mar	533	A1 Wedding Supplies	Photo Albums	$323.58	

Step 3c

Step 3e

f. Change the date of the deposit to March 10.

g. Delete row 7.

4. Save **ExcelL1_C5_P1.xlsx**.

Copy

Paste Options

Copying Selected Cells

Copying selected cells can be useful in worksheets that contain repetitive data. To copy cells, select the cells, and then click the Copy button in the Clipboard group in the Home tab. Click the cell where you want the first selected cell copied and then click the Paste button in the Clipboard group.

You can also copy selected cells using the mouse and the Ctrl key. To do this, select the cells you want to copy and then position the mouse pointer on any border around the selected cells until it turns into an arrow pointer. Hold down the Ctrl key and the left mouse button, drag the outline of the selected cells to the desired location, release the left mouse button, and then release the Ctrl key.

Using the Paste Options Button

The Paste Options button displays in the lower right corner of the pasted cell(s) when you paste a cell or cells. Hover the mouse over this button until it displays with a down-pointing arrow and then click the left mouse button. This causes a drop-down list to display as shown in Figure 5.1. With the options from this list you can specify what you want pasted. You can specify that you want to keep source formatting or use destination themes or destination formatting. You can also keep the column widths of the source worksheet.

Figure 5.1 Paste Options Button Drop-down List

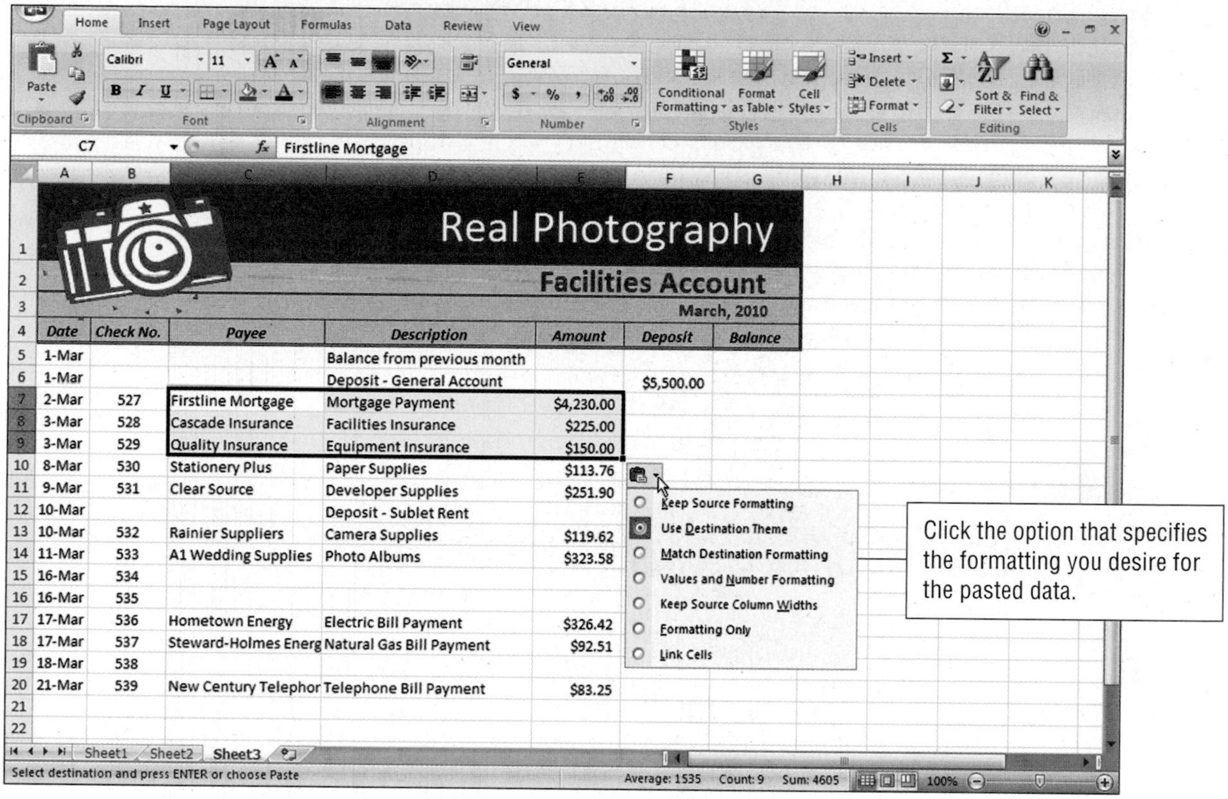

Click the option that specifies the formatting you desire for the pasted data.

Project 1C Copying Selected Cells in a Worksheet

1. With **ExcelL1_C5_P1.xlsx** open, make Sheet2 active.
2. Select cells C7 through E9.
3. Click the Copy button in the Clipboard group in the Home tab.

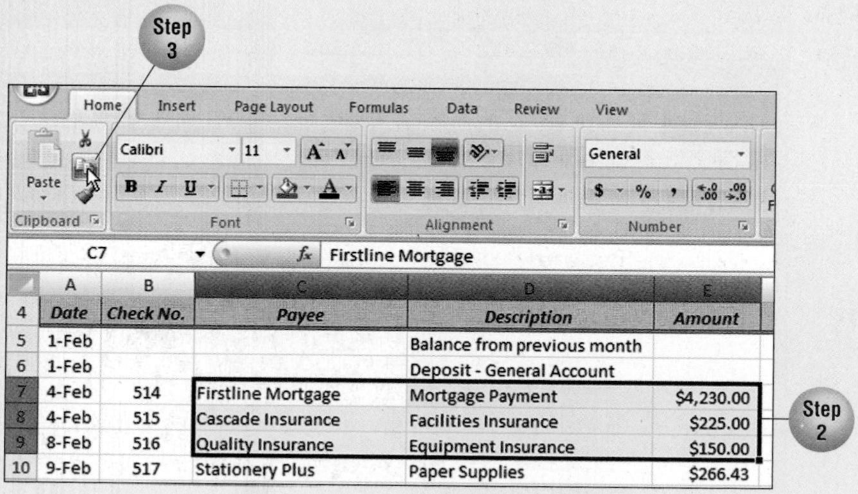

Step 3

Step 2

4. Make Sheet3 active.
5. Make cell C7 active.
6. Click the Paste button in the Clipboard group.
7. Click the Paste Options button that displays in the lower right corner of the pasted cells and then click *Keep Source Column Widths* at the drop-down list.
8. Make Sheet2 active and then press the Esc key to remove the moving marquee.
9. Save **ExcelL1_C5_P1.xlsx**.

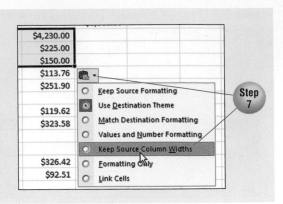

Step 7

Copy and Paste Multiple Items
1. Click Clipboard group dialog box launcher.
2. Select desired cells.
3. Click Copy button.
4. Continue selecting desired cells and then clicking the Copy button.
5. Make active the desired cell.
6. Click item in Clipboard task pane that you want inserted in the worksheet.
7. Continue pasting desired items from the Clipboard task pane.

Using the Office Clipboard

Use the Office Clipboard feature to collect and paste multiple items. To use the Office Clipboard, display the Clipboard task pane by clicking the Clipboard group dialog box launcher. This button is located in the lower right corner of the Clipboard group in the Home tab. The Clipboard task pane displays at the left side of the screen in a manner similar to what you see in Figure 5.2.

Figure 5.2 Clipboard Task Pane

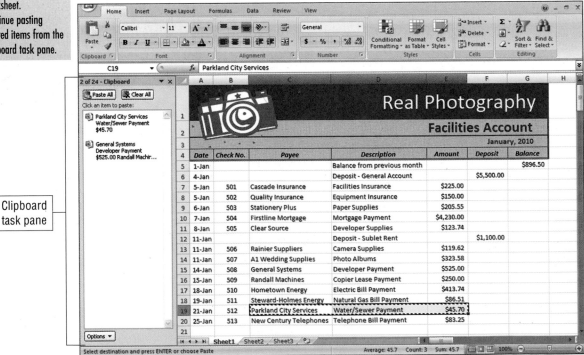

Clipboard task pane

Select data or an object you want to copy and then click the Copy button in the Clipboard group. Continue selecting text or items and clicking the Copy button. To insert an item, position the insertion point in the desired location and then click the item in the Clipboard task pane. If the copied item is text, the first 50 characters display. When all desired items are inserted, click the Clear All button to remove any remaining items. Sometimes, you may have a situation in which you want to copy all of the selected items to a single location. If so, position the insertion point in the desired location and then click the Paste All button in the Clipboard task pane.

Project 1d — Copying and Pasting Cells Using the Office Clipboard

1. With **ExcelL1_C5_P1.xlsx** open, select cells for copying by completing the following steps:
   a. Display the Clipboard task pane by clicking the Clipboard group dialog box launcher. (If the Clipboard contains any copied data, click the Clear All button.)
   b. Click the Sheet1 tab.
   c. Select cells C15 through E16.
   d. Click the Copy button in the Clipboard group.
   e. Select cells C19 through E19.
   f. Click the Copy button in the Clipboard group.
2. Paste the copied cells by completing the following steps:
   a. Click the Sheet2 tab.
   b. Make cell C15 active.
   c. Click the item in the Clipboard task pane representing *General Systems Developer*.
   d. Click the Sheet3 tab.
   e. Make C15 active.
   f. Click the item in the Clipboard task pane representing *General Systems Developer*.
   g. Make cell C19 active.
   h. Click the item in the Clipboard task pane representing *Parkland City Services*.
3. Click the Clear All button located toward the top of the Clipboard task pane.
4. Close the Clipboard task pane by clicking the Close button (contains an X) located in the upper right corner of the task pane.
5. Save **ExcelL1_C5_P1.xlsx**.

Pasting Values Only

When you copy and then paste a cell containing a value as well as a formula, the Paste Options button contains the options shown in Figure 5.1 as well as the additional option *Values Only*. Click this option if you want to copy only the value and not the formula.

Project 1e　Copying and Pasting Values

1. With **ExcelL1_C5_P1.xlsx** open, make Sheet1 active.
2. Make cell G6 active, insert the formula =(F6-E6)+G5, and then press Enter.
3. Copy the formula in cell G6 down to cells G7 through G20.
4. Copy the final balance amount from Sheet1 to Sheet2 by completing the following steps:
   a. Make cell G20 active.
   b. Click the Copy button in the Clipboard group.
   c. Click the Sheet2 tab.
   d. Make cell G5 active and then click the Paste button in the Clipboard group.
   e. Hover the mouse over the Paste Options button until the button displays with a down-pointing arrow and then click the left mouse button.
   f. At the drop-down list, click the *Values Only* option. (This inserts the value and not the formula.)

Step 4e

February, 2010	
Deposit	Balance
◈	#VALUE!
$5,500.00	

○ Keep Source Formatting
◉ Use Destination Theme
○ Match Destination Formatting
◉ Values Only
○ Values and Number Formatting
○ Values and Source Formatting
○ Keep Source Column Widths
○ Formatting Only
○ Link Cells

$1,100.00　**Step 4f**

5. Make cell G6 active, insert a formula that determines the balance, and then copy the formula down to cells G7 through G20.
6. Copy the amount in cell G20 and then paste the value only into cell G5 in Sheet3.
7. With Sheet3 active, make cell G6 active, insert a formula that determines the balance, and then copy the formula down to cells G7 through G20.
8. Save **ExcelL1_C5_P1.xlsx**.

QUICK STEPS

Insert Worksheet
Click Insert Worksheet tab.
OR
Press Shift + F11.

Inserting a Worksheet

A workbook, by default, contains three worksheets. You can insert additional worksheets in a workbook. To do this, click the Insert Worksheet tab located to the right of the Sheet3 tab. This inserts a new worksheet labeled *Sheet4* at the right of the Sheet3 tab. You can also press Shift + F11 to insert a new worksheet. Or, you can insert a worksheet by clicking the Insert button arrow in the Cells group in the Home tab and then clicking *Insert Sheet*.

Project 1f　Inserting a Worksheet

1. With **ExcelL1_C5_P1.xlsx** open, make the following changes:
   a. Make Sheet1 active.
   b. Make cell D21 active, turn on bold, and then type Total.
   c. Make cell E21 active and then click once on the Sum button located in the Editing group in the Home tab. (This inserts the formula =SUM(E13:E20).)
   d. Change the formula to =SUM(E7:E20) and then press Enter.

Water/Sewer Payment	$45.70
Telephone Bill Payment	$83.25
Total	=SUM(E7:E20)
	SUM(number1, [number2], ...)

Step 1d

e. Make cell F21 active and then click once on the Sum button in the Editing group. (This inserts the formula =SUM(F12:F20).)

f. Change the formula to =SUM(F6:F20) and then press Enter.

2. Make Sheet2 active and then complete the steps in Step 1 to insert the totals of the *Amount* and *Deposit* columns.

3. Make Sheet3 active and then complete the steps in Step 1 to insert the totals of the *Amount* and *Deposit* columns.

4. Insert a new worksheet by clicking the Insert Worksheet tab located to the right of the Sheet3 tab.

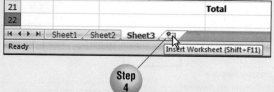

Step 4

5. Make Sheet1 active, copy cells A1 through G3, make Sheet4 active (with cell A1 active), and then paste the cells. (When copying the cells, position the cell pointer to the right of the image, make sure the pointer displays as a white plus symbol, and then drag to select the cells.)

6. Make the following changes to the worksheet:

a. Make cell A3 active and then type **First Quarter Summary, 2010**.

b. Change the width of column A to 20.00.

c. Change the width of columns B, C, and D to 12.00.

d. Select cells B4 through D4, click the Bold button in the Font group in the Home tab, and then click the Center button in the Alignment group.

e. Select cells B5 through D7 and then change the number formatting to Currency with two decimal places and include the dollar sign symbol.

f. Type the following text in the specified cells:

B4 = January
C4 = February
D4 = March
A5 = Checks Amount
A6 = Deposit Amount
A7 = End-of-month Balance

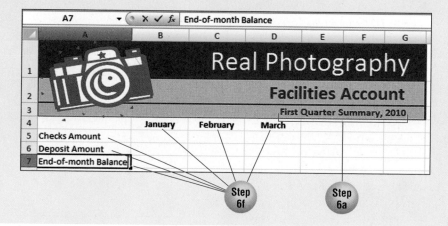

Step 6f

Step 6a

7. Copy a value by completing the following steps:
   a. Make Sheet1 active.
   b. Make cell E21 active and then click the Copy button in the Clipboard group in the Home tab.
   c. Make Sheet4 active.
   d. Make cell B5 active and then click the Paste button in the Clipboard group.
   e. Click the Paste Options button and then click *Values Only* at the drop-down list.

Step 7e

3				First Quarte
4		January	February	March
5	Checks Amount	#REF!		
6	Deposit Amount			
7	End-of-month Balance			

○ Keep Source Formatting
◉ Use Destination Theme
○ Match Destination Formatting
○ Values Only
○ Values and Number Formatting

   f. Make Sheet1 active.
   g. Press the Esc key to remove the moving marquee.
   h. Make cell F21 active and then click the Copy button.
   i. Make Sheet4 active.
   j. Make cell B6 active and then click the Paste button.
   k. Click the Paste Options button and then click *Values Only* at the drop-down list.
   l. Make Sheet1 active.
   m. Press the Esc key to remove the moving marquee.
   n. Make cell G20 active and then click the Copy button.
   o. Make Sheet4 active.
   p. Make cell B7 active and then click the Paste button.
   q. Click the Paste Options button and then click *Values Only* at the drop-down list.
8. Complete steps similar to those in Step 7 to insert amounts and balances for February and March.
9. Save **ExcelL1_C5_P1.xlsx**.

Managing Worksheets

Right-click a sheet tab and a shortcut menu displays as shown in Figure 5.3 with the options for managing worksheets. For example, remove a worksheet by clicking the *Delete* option. Move or copy a worksheet by clicking the *Move or Copy* option. Clicking this option causes a Move or Copy dialog box to display where you specify before what sheet you want to move or copy the selected sheet. By default, Excel names worksheets in a workbook *Sheet1, Sheet2, Sheet3,* and so on. To rename a worksheet, click the *Rename* option (this selects the default sheet name) and then type the desired name.

QUICK STEPS

Move or Copy a Worksheet
1. Right-click sheet tab.
2. Click *Move or Copy*.
3. At Move or Copy dialog box, click desired worksheet name in *Before sheet* list box.
4. Click OK.
OR
Drag worksheet tab to the desired position (to copy, hold down Ctrl key while dragging).

Figure 5.3 Sheet Tab Shortcut Menu

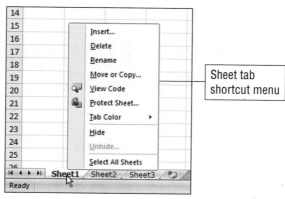

Sheet tab shortcut menu

HINT
Use the tab scroll buttons, located to the left of the sheet tabs, to bring into view any worksheet tabs not currently visible.

In addition to the shortcut menu options, you can use the mouse to move or copy worksheets. To move a worksheet, position the mouse pointer on the worksheet tab, hold down the left mouse button (a page icon displays next to the mouse pointer), drag the page icon to the desired position, and then release the mouse button. For example, to move Sheet2 tab after Sheet3 tab you would position the mouse pointer on the Sheet2 tab, hold down the left mouse button, drag the page icon so it is positioned after the Sheet3 tab, and then release the mouse button. To copy a worksheet, hold down the Ctrl key while dragging the sheet tab.

Use the *Tab Color* option at the shortcut menu to apply a color to a worksheet tab. Right-click a worksheet tab, point to *Tab Color* at the shortcut menu, and then click the desired color at the color palette.

QUICK STEPS

Recolor Sheet Tab
1. Right-click sheet tab.
2. Point to *Tab Color*.
3. Click desired color at color palette.

1. With **ExcelL1_C5_P1.xlsx** open, move Sheet4 by completing the following steps:
   a. Right-click Sheet4 and then click *Move or Copy* at the shortcut menu.

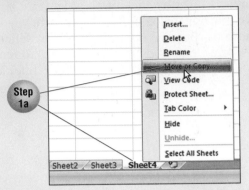

   b. At the Move or Copy dialog box, make sure *Sheet1* is selected in the *Before sheet* section, and then click OK.

2. Rename Sheet4 by completing the following steps:
   a. Right-click the Sheet4 tab and then click *Rename*.
   b. Type **Summary** and then press Enter.

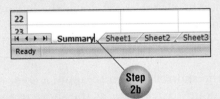

3. Complete steps similar to those in Step 2 to rename Sheet1 to *January*, Sheet2 to *February*, and Sheet3 to *March*.
4. Change the color of the Summary sheet tab by completing the following steps:
   a. Right-click the Summary sheet tab.
   b. Point to *Tab Color* at the shortcut menu.
   c. Click a red color of your choosing at the color palette.
5. Follow steps similar to those in Step 4 to change the January sheet tab to a blue color, the February sheet tab to a purple color, and the March sheet tab to a green color.
6. Save **ExcelL1_C5_P1.xlsx**.

Hiding a Worksheet in a Workbook

In a workbook containing multiple worksheets, you can hide a worksheet that may contain sensitive data or data you do not want to display or print with the workbook. To hide a worksheet in a workbook, click the Format button in the Cells group in the Home tab, point to *Hide & Unhide*, and then click *Hide Sheet*. You can also hide a worksheet by right-clicking a worksheet tab and then clicking the *Hide* option at the shortcut menu. To make a hidden worksheet visible, click the Format button in the Cells group, point to *Hide & Unhide*, and then click *Unhide Sheet*, or right-click a worksheet tab and then click *Unhide* at the shortcut menu. At the Unhide dialog box shown in Figure 5.4, double-click the name of the hidden worksheet you want to display.

Figure 5.4 Unhide Dialog Box

The names of hidden worksheets display in this list box.

Formatting Multiple Worksheets

When you apply formatting to a worksheet, such as changing margins, orientation, or inserting a header or footer, and so on, the formatting is applied only to the active worksheet. If you want formatting to apply to multiple worksheets in a workbook, select the tabs of the desired worksheets and then apply the formatting. For example, if a workbook contains three worksheets and you want to apply formatting to the first and second worksheets only, select the tabs for the first and second worksheets and then apply the formatting.

To select adjacent worksheet tabs, click the first tab, hold down the Shift key, and then click the last tab. To select nonadjacent worksheet tabs, click the first tab, hold down the Ctrl key, and then click any other tabs you want selected.

1. With **ExcelL1_C5_P1.xlsx** open, hide the Summary worksheet by completing the following steps:
   a. Click the Summary tab.
   b. Click the Format button in the Cells group in the Home tab, point to *Hide & Unhide*, and then click *Hide Sheet*.

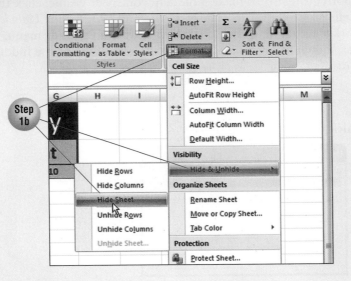

2. Unhide the worksheet by completing the following steps:
   a. Click the Format button in the Cells group, point to *Hide & Unhide*, and then click *Unhide Sheet*.
   b. At the Unhide dialog box, make sure *Summary* is selected and then click OK.

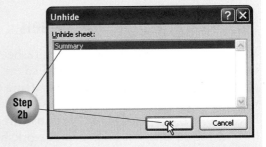

3. Insert a header for each worksheet by completing the following steps:
   a. Click the Summary tab.
   b. Hold down the Shift key and then click the March tab. (This selects all four tabs.)
   c. Click the Insert tab.
   d. Click the Header & Footer button in the Text group.
   e. Click the Header button in the Header & Footer group in the Header & Footer Tools Design tab and then click the option at the drop-down list that prints your name at the left side of the page, the page number in the middle, and the date at the right side of the page.
4. With all the sheet tabs selected, horizontally and vertically center each worksheet on the page. *Hint: Do this at the Page Setup dialog box with the Margins tab selected.*
5. With all of the sheet tabs still selected, change the page orientation to landscape. *Hint: Do this with the Orientation button in the Page Layout tab.*
6. Save **ExcelL1_C5_P1.xlsx**.

Printing a Workbook Containing Multiple Worksheets

By default, Excel prints the currently displayed worksheet. If you want to print all worksheets in a workbook, display the Print dialog box by clicking the Office button and then clicking *Print*. At the Print dialog box, click *Entire workbook* in the *Print what* section, and then click OK. You can also print specific worksheets in a workbook by selecting the tabs of the worksheets you want to print.

QUICK STEPS

Print all Worksheets in a Workbook
1. Click Office button, *Print*.
2. Click *Entire workbook*.
3. Click OK.

Project 1i Printing All Worksheets in a Workbook

1. With **ExcelL1_C5_P1.xlsx** open, click the Office button and then click *Print*.
2. At the Print dialog box, click the *Entire workbook* option in the *Print what* section.
3. Click OK.
4. Close **ExcelL1_C5_P1.xlsx**.

Step 2

Project 2 Write Formulas Using Ranges in an Equipment Usage Workbook

You will open an equipment usage workbook and then split the window and edit cells. You will also name ranges and then use the range names to write formulas in the workbook.

Splitting a Worksheet into Windows and Freezing and Unfreezing Panes

In some worksheets, not all cells display at one time in the worksheet area (such as ExcelC05Project02.xlsx). When working in worksheets with more cells than can display at one time, you may find splitting the worksheet window into panes helpful. Split the worksheet window into panes with the Split button in the Window group in the View tab or with the split bars that display at the top of the vertical scroll bar and at the right side of the horizontal scroll bar. Figure 5.5 identifies these split bars.

QUICK STEPS

Split a Worksheet
1. Click View tab.
2. Click Split button.
OR
Drag horizontal and/or vertical split bars.

Figure 5.5 Split Bars

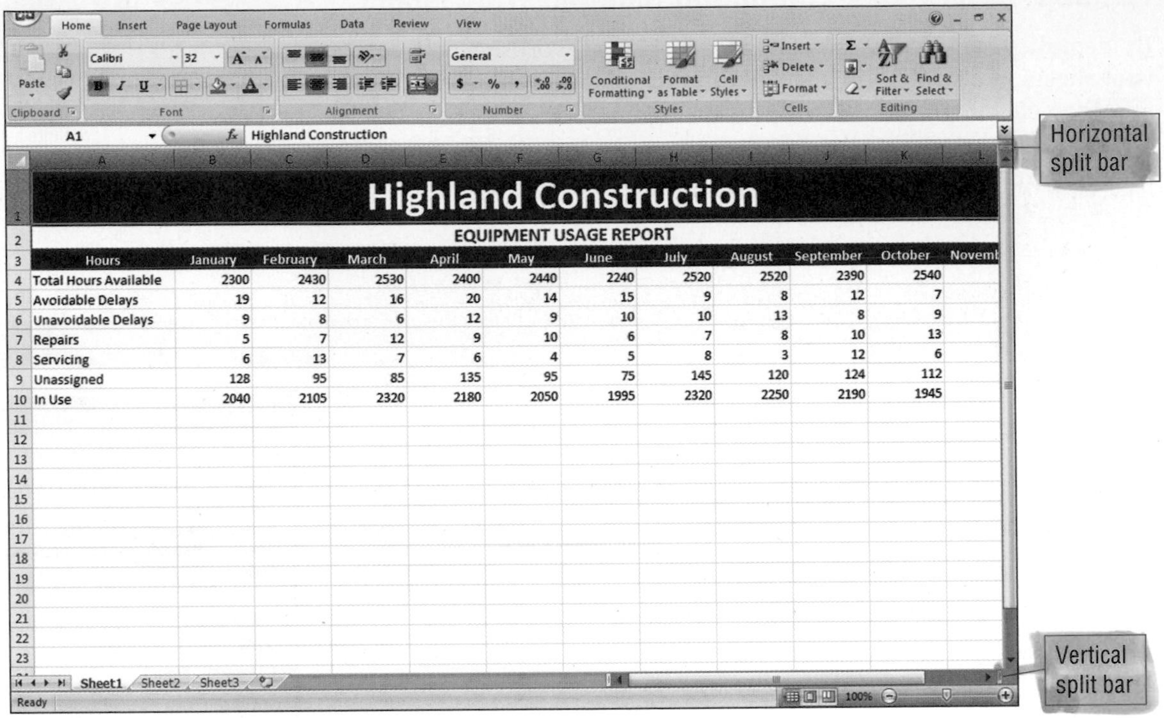

Horizontal split bar

Vertical split bar

HINT

Restore a split window by double-clicking anywhere on the split bar that divides the panes.

To split a window with the split bar located at the top of the vertical scroll bar, position the mouse pointer on the split bar until it turns into a double-headed arrow with a short double line in the middle. Hold down the left mouse button, drag down the thick gray line that displays until the pane is the desired size, and then release the mouse button. Split the window vertically with the split bar at the right side of the horizontal scroll bar.

To split a worksheet window with the Split button, click the View tab, and then click the Split button. This causes the worksheet to split into four window panes as shown in Figure 5.6. The windows are split by thick, light blue lines (with a three-dimensional look). To remove a split from a worksheet click the Split button to deactivate it or drag the split bars to the upper left corner of the worksheet.

Figure 5.6 Split Window

Highland Construction

EQUIPMENT USAGE REPORT

Hours	January	February	March	April	May	June	July	August	September	October	Novem
Total Hours Available	2300	2430	2530	2400	2440	2240	2520	2520	2390	2540	
Avoidable Delays	19	12	16	20	14	15	9	8	12	7	
Unavoidable Delays	9	8	6	12	9	10	10	13	8	9	
Repairs	5	7	12	9	10	6	7	8	10	13	
Servicing	6	13	7	6	4	5	8	3	12	6	
Unassigned	128	95	85	135	95	75	145	120	124	112	
In Use	2040	2105	2320	2180	2050	1995	2320	2250	2190	1945	

A window pane will display the active cell. As the insertion point is moved through the pane, another active cell with a blue background may display. This additional active cell displays when the insertion point passes over one of the light blue lines that creates the pane. As you move through a worksheet, you may see both active cells—one with a normal background and one with a blue background. If you make a change to the active cell, the change is made in both. If you want only one active cell to display, freeze the window panes by clicking the Freeze Panes button in the Window group in the View tab and then clicking *Freeze Panes* at the drop-down list. You can maintain the display of column headings while editing or typing text in cells by clicking the Freeze Panes button and then clicking *Freeze Top Row*. Maintain the display of row headings by clicking the Freeze Panes button and then clicking *Freeze First Column*. Unfreeze window panes by clicking the Freeze Panes button and then clicking *Unfreeze Panes* at the drop-down list.

Using the mouse, you can move the thick, light blue lines that divide the window into panes. To do this, position the mouse pointer on the line until the pointer turns into a double-headed arrow with a double line in the middle. Hold down the left mouse button, drag the outline of the light blue line to the desired location, and then release the mouse button. If you want to move both the horizontal and vertical lines at the same time, position the mouse pointer on the intersection of the thick, light blue lines until it turns into a four-headed arrow. Hold down the left mouse button, drag the thick, light blue lines in the desired direction, and then release the mouse button.

Project 2a **Splitting Windows and Editing Cells**

1. Open **ExcelC05Project02.xlsx** and then save the workbook and name it **ExcelL1_C5_P2**.
2. Make sure cell A1 is active and then split the window by clicking the View tab and then clicking the Split button in the Window group. (This splits the window into four panes.)
3. Drag the vertical light blue line by completing the following steps:
   a. Position the mouse pointer on the vertical split line until the pointer turns into a double-headed arrow pointing left and right with a double-line between.
   b. Hold down the left mouse button, drag to the left until the vertical light blue line is immediately to the right of the first column, and then release the mouse button.

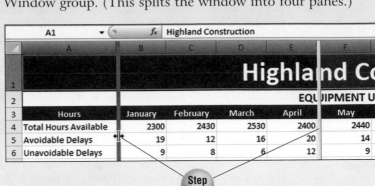

4. Freeze the window panes by clicking the Freeze Panes button in the Window group in the View tab and then clicking *Freeze Panes* at the drop-down list.

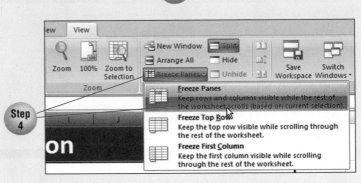

5. Make cell L4 active and then type the following data in the specified cells:

L4	=	2310	M4	=	2210
L5	=	12	M5	=	5
L6	=	5	M6	=	7
L7	=	9	M7	=	8
L8	=	11	M8	=	12
L9	=	95	M9	=	120
L10	=	2005	M10	=	1830

6. Unfreeze the window panes by clicking the Freeze Panes button and then clicking *Unfreeze Panes* at the drop-down list.
7. Remove the panes by clicking the Split button in the Window group to deactivate it.
8. Save **ExcelL1_C5_P2.xlsx**.

QUICK STEPS

Name a Range
1. Select cells.
2. Click in Name box.
3. Type range name.
4. Press Enter.

Working with Ranges

A selected group of cells is referred to as a ***range***. A range of cells can be formatted, moved, copied, or deleted. You can also name a range of cells and then move the insertion point to the range or use a named range as part of a formula.

To name a range, select the cells, and then click in the Name box located at the left of the Formula bar. Type a name for the range (do not use a space) and then press Enter. To move the insertion point to a specific range and select the range, click the down-pointing arrow at the right side of the Name box and then click the range name.

You can also name a range using the Define Name button in the Formulas tab. To do this, click the Formulas tab and then click the Define Name button in the Defined Names group. At the New Name dialog box, type a name for the range and then click OK.

You can use a range name in a formula. For example, if a range is named *Profit* and you want to insert the average of all cells in the *Profit* range, you would make the desired cell active and then type =AVERAGE(Profit). You can use a named range in the current worksheet or in another worksheet within the workbook.

Define Name ▾

Project 2b   Naming a Range and Using a Range in a Formula

1. With **ExcelL1_C5_P2.xlsx** open, click the Sheet2 tab and then type the following text in the specified cells:

   A1 = EQUIPMENT USAGE REPORT
   A2 = Yearly Hours
   A3 = Avoidable Delays
   A4 = Unavoidable Delays
   A5 = Total Delay Hours
   A6 = (leave blank)
   A7 = Repairs
   A8 = Servicing
   A9 = Total Repair/Servicing Hours

2. Make the following formatting changes to the worksheet:
   a. Automatically adjust the width of column A.
   b. Center and bold the text in cells A1 and A2.

3. Select a range of cells in worksheet 1, name the range, and use it in a formula in worksheet 2 by completing the following steps:
   a. Click the Sheet1 tab.
   b. Select cells B5 through M5.
   c. Click in the Name box located to the left of the Formula bar.
   d. Type **adhours** (for Avoidable Delays Hours) and then press Enter.
   e. Click the Sheet2 tab.
   f. Make cell B3 active.
   g. Type the equation =SUM(adhours) and then press Enter.

4. Click the Sheet1 tab and then complete the following steps:
   a. Select cells B6 through M6.
   b. Click the Formulas tab.
   c. Click the Define Name button in the Defined Names group.

Step 1

	A	B	C	D
1	EQUIPMENT USAGE REPORT			
2	Yearly Hours			
3	Avoidable Delays			
4	Unavoidable Delays			
5	Total Delay Hours			
6				
7	Repairs			
8	Servicing			
9	Total Repair/Servicing Hours			
10				

Step 3d

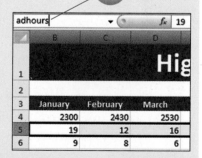

adhours   ▾   *fx*   19

	B	C	D
1			Hig
2			
3	January	February	March
4	2300	2430	2530
5	19	12	16
6	9	8	6

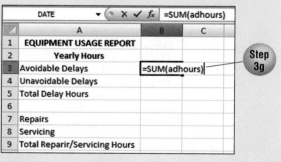

DATE   ▾   X ✓ *fx*   =SUM(adhours)

	A	B	C
1	EQUIPMENT USAGE REPORT		
2	Yearly Hours		
3	Avoidable Delays	=SUM(adhours)	
4	Unavoidable Delays		
5	Total Delay Hours		
6			
7	Repairs		
8	Servicing		
9	Total Reparir/Servicing Hours		

Step 3g

d. At the New Name dialog box, type **udhours** and then click OK.

e. Make worksheet 2 active, make cell B4 active, and then insert the equation *=SUM(udhours)*.

Step 4d

5. Make worksheet 1 active and then complete the following steps:

a. Select cells B7 through M7 and then name the range *rhours*.

b. Make worksheet 2 active, make cell B7 active, and then insert the equation *=SUM(rhours)*.

c. Make worksheet 1 active.

d. Select cells B8 through M8 and then name the range *shours*.

e. Make worksheet 2 active, make cell B8 active, and then insert the equation *=SUM(shours)*.

6. With worksheet 2 still active, make the following changes:

a. Make cell B5 active.

b. Double-click the Sum button in the Editing group in the Home tab.

c. Make cell B9 active.

d. Double-click the Sum button in the Editing group in the Home tab.

7. Make worksheet 1 active and then move to the range *adhours* by clicking the down-pointing arrow at the right side of the Name box and then clicking *adhours* at the drop-down list.

8. Select both sheet tabs, change the orientation to landscape, scale the contents to fit on one page (in Page Layout tab, change width to *1 page*), and insert a custom footer with your name, page number, and date.

Step 7

9. Print both worksheets in the workbook.

10. Save and then close **ExcelL1_C5_P2.xlsx**.

Project 3 Arrange, Size, and Copy Data between Workbooks

You will open, arrange, hide, unhide, size, and move multiple workbooks. You will also copy cells from one workbook and paste in another workbook.

Working with Windows

You can open multiple workbooks in Excel and arrange the open workbooks in the Excel window. With multiple workbooks open, you can cut and paste or copy and paste cell entries from one workbook to another using the same techniques discussed earlier in this chapter with the exception that you activate the destination workbook before executing the Paste command.

Opening Multiple Workbooks

With multiple workbooks open, you can move or copy information between workbooks or compare the contents of several workbooks. When you open a new workbook, it is placed on top of the original workbook. Once multiple workbooks are opened, you can resize the workbooks to see all or a portion of them on the screen.

Open multiple workbooks at one time at the Open dialog box. If workbooks are adjacent, display the Open dialog box, click the first workbook name to be opened, hold down the Shift key, and then click the last workbook name to be opened. If the workbooks are nonadjacent, click the first workbook name to be opened and then hold down the Ctrl key while clicking the remaining desired workbook names. Release the Shift key or the Ctrl key and then click the Open button.

To see what workbooks are currently open, click the View tab and then click the Switch Windows button in the Window group. The names of the open workbooks display in a drop-down list and the workbook name preceded by a check mark is the active workbook. To make one of the other workbooks active, click the desired workbook name at the drop-down list.

Switch Windows

QUICK STEPS

Arrange Workbooks
1. Click View tab.
2. Click Arrange All button.
3. At Arrange Windows dialog box, click desired arrangement.
4. Click OK.

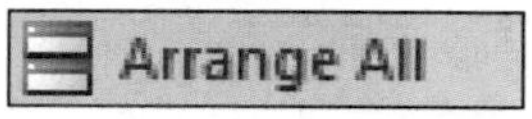

Arranging Workbooks

If you have more than one workbook open, you can arrange the workbooks at the Arrange Windows dialog box shown in Figure 5.7. To display this dialog box, open several workbooks, and then click the Arrange All button in the Window group in the View tab. At the Arrange Windows dialog box, click *Tiled* to display a portion of each open workbook. Figure 5.8 displays four tiled workbooks.

Arrange All

Figure 5.7 Arrange Windows Dialog Box

Use options at this dialog box to choose an arrange method.

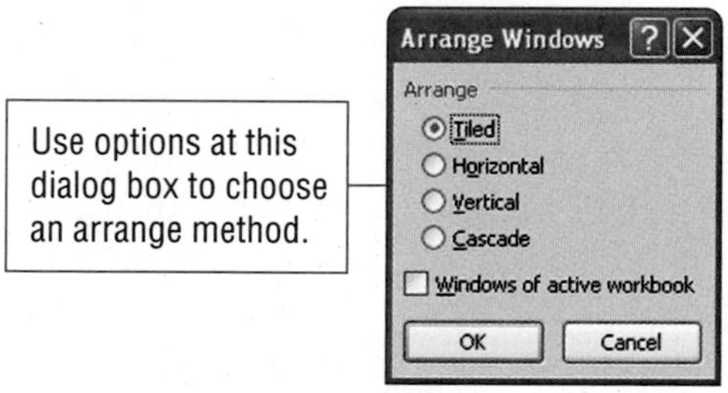

Figure 5.8 Tiled Workbooks

Choose the *Horizontal* option at the Arrange Windows dialog box and the open workbooks display across the screen. The *Vertical* option displays the open workbooks up and down the screen. The last option, *Cascade*, displays the Title bar of each open workbook. Figure 5.9 shows four cascaded workbooks.

The option you select for displaying multiple workbooks depends on which part of the workbooks is most important to view simultaneously. For example, the tiled workbooks in Figure 5.8 allow you to view the company logos and the first few rows and columns of each workbook.

Figure 5.9 Cascaded Workbooks

![Screenshot of Microsoft Excel showing cascaded workbooks ExcelC05Project02.xlsx, ExcelC05Project04.xlsx, ExcelC05Assessment01.xlsx, and ExcelC05Project01.xlsx with a "Real Photography Facilities Account January, 2010" worksheet.]

The active worksheet contains the following table:

Date	Check No.	Payee	Description	Amount	Deposit	Balance
1-Jan			Balance from previous month			$896.50
4-Jan			Deposit - General Account		$5,500.00	
4-Jan			Deposit - Sublet Rent		$1,100.00	
5-Jan	501	Cascade Insurance	Facilities Insurance	$225.00		
5-Jan	502	Quality Insurance	Equipment Insurance	$150.00		
6-Jan	503	Stationery Plus	Paper Supplies	$205.55		
7-Jan	504	Firstline Mortgage	Mortgage Payment	$4,230.00		
8-Jan	505	Clear Source	Developer Supplies	$123.74		
11-Jan	506	Rainier Suppliers	Camera Supplies	$119.62		
11-Jan	507	A1 Wedding Supplies	Photo Albums	$323.58		
14-Jan	508	General Systems	Developer Payment	$525.00		
15-Jan	509	Randall Machines	Copier Lease Payment	$250.00		

Hiding/Unhiding Workbooks

With the Hide button in the Window group in the View tab, you can hide the active workbook. If a workbook has been hidden, redisplay the workbook by clicking the Unhide button in the Window group in the View tab. At the Unhide dialog box, make sure the desired workbook is selected in the list box, and then click OK.

Hide

Unhide

Project 3a   Opening, Arranging, and Hiding/Unhiding Workbooks

1. Open several workbooks at the same time by completing the following steps:
   a. Display the Open dialog box.
   b. Click the workbook named *ExcelC05Project01.xlsx*.
   c. Hold down the Ctrl key, click *ExcelC05Project02.xlsx*, click *ExcelC05Project04.xlsx*, and click *ExcelC05Assessment01.xlsx*.
   d. Release the Ctrl key and then click the Open button in the dialog box.

2. Make **ExcelC05Assessment01.xlsx** the active workbook by clicking the View tab, clicking the Switch Windows button in the Window group, and then clicking 4 at the drop-down list.

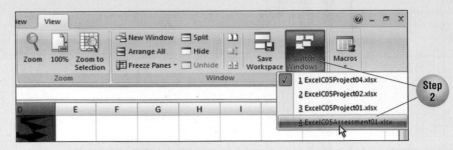

Step 2

3. Make **ExcelC05Project01.xlsx** the active workbook by clicking the Switch Windows button and then clicking *ExcelC05Project01.xlsx* at the drop-down list.
4. Tile the workbooks by completing the following steps:
   a. Click the Arrange All button in the Window group in the View tab.
   b. At the Arrange Windows dialog box, make sure *Tiled* is selected and then click OK.
5. Tile the workbooks horizontally by completing the following steps:
   a. Click the Arrange All button.
   b. At the Arrange Windows dialog box, click *Horizontal*.
   c. Click OK.

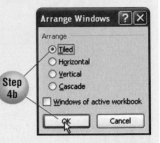

Step 4b

6. Cascade the workbooks by completing the following steps:
   a. Click the Arrange All button.
   b. At the Arrange Windows dialog box, click *Cascade*.
   c. Click OK.
7. Hide and unhide workbooks by completing the following steps:
   a. Make sure **ExcelC05Project01.xlsx** is the active workbook (displays on top of the other workbooks).
   b. Click the Hide button in the Window group in the View tab.
   c. Make sure **ExcelC05Assessment01.xlsx** is the active workbook (displays on top of the other workbooks).
   d. Click the Hide button.
   e. Click the Unhide button.
   f. At the Unhide dialog box, click *ExcelC05Project01.xlsx* in the list box, and then click OK.

Step 7f

   g. Click the Unhide button.
   h. At the Unhide dialog box, make sure **ExcelC05Assessment01.xlsx** is selected in the list box and then click OK.
8. Close all of the open workbooks without saving changes.

Sizing and Moving Workbooks

You can use the Maximize and Minimize buttons located in the upper right corner of the active workbook to change the size of the window. The Maximize button is the button in the upper right corner of the active workbook immediately to the left of the Close button. (The Close button is the button containing the *X*.) The Minimize button is located immediately to the left of the Maximize button.

Maximize Minimize

Close Restore

If you arrange all open workbooks and then click the Maximize button in the active workbook, the active workbook expands to fill the screen. In addition, the Maximize button changes to the Restore button. To return the active workbook back to its size before it was maximized, click the Restore button.

Clicking the Minimize button causes the active workbook to be reduced and positioned as a button on the Taskbar. In addition, the Minimize button changes to the Restore button. To maximize a workbook that has been reduced, click the button on the Taskbar representing the workbook.

Project 3b | Minimizing, Maximizing, and Restoring Workbooks

1. Open **ExcelC05Project01.xlsx**.
2. Maximize **ExcelC05Project01.xlsx** by clicking the Maximize button at the right side of the workbook Title bar. (The Maximize button is the button at the right side of the Title bar, immediately to the left of the Close button.)
3. Open **ExcelC05Project02.xlsx** and **ExcelC05Project03.xlsx**.
4. Make the following changes to the open workbooks:
   a. Tile the workbooks.
   b. Make **ExcelC05Project01.xlsx** the active workbook (Title bar displays with a light blue background [the background color may vary depending on how Windows is customized]).
   c. Minimize **ExcelC05Project01.xlsx** by clicking the Minimize button that displays at the right side of the Title bar.
   d. Make **ExcelC05Project02.xlsx** the active workbook and then minimize it.
   e. Minimize **ExcelC05Project03.xlsx**.
5. Close all workbooks.

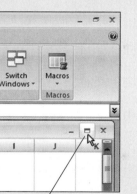

Step 2

Step 4c

Moving, Copying, and Pasting Data

With more than one workbook open, you can move, copy, and/or paste data from one workbook to another. To move, copy, and/or paste data between workbooks, use the cutting and pasting options you learned earlier in this chapter, together with the information about windows in this chapter.

1. Open **ExcelC05Project03.xlsx**.
2. If you just completed Project 3b, click the Maximize button so the worksheet fills the entire worksheet window.
3. Save the workbook and name it **ExcelL1_C5_P3**.
4. With **ExcelL1_C5_P3.xlsx** open, open **ExcelC05Deering.xlsx**.
5. Select and then copy text from **ExcelC05Deering.xlsx** to **ExcelL1_C5_P3.xlsx** by completing the following steps:
   a. With **ExcelC05Deering.xlsx** the active workbook, select cells A3 through D10.
   b. Click the Copy button in the Clipboard group in the Home tab.
   c. Click the button on the Taskbar representing **ExcelL1_C5_P3.xlsx**.

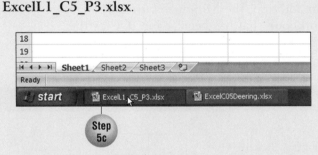

Step 5c

Step 5d

   d. Make cell A8 the active cell and then click the Paste button in the Clipboard group in the Home tab.
   e. Make cell E7 active and then drag the fill handle down to cell E15.
6. Print **ExcelL1_C5_P3.xlsx** horizontally and vertically centered on the page.
7. Save and then close **ExcelL1_C5_P3.xlsx**.
8. Close **ExcelC05Deering.xlsx**.

Project 4 Link Cells between Quarterly Expenses Worksheets

You will open a workbook containing worksheets with quarterly expenses data and then link cells between the worksheets.

Linking Data between Worksheets

You may want to create a link between worksheets or workbooks with data in cells in related workbooks or workbooks containing multiple worksheets. When data is linked, a change made in a linked cell is automatically made to the other cells in the link. You can make links with individual cells or with a range of cells.

Linking cells between worksheets creates what is called a *dynamic link*. Dynamic links are useful in worksheets or workbooks that need to maintain consistency and control over critical data. The worksheet that contains the original data is called the *source* worksheet and the worksheet relying on the source worksheet for the data in the link is called the *dependent* worksheet.

To create a link, make active the cell containing the data to be linked (or select the cells), and then click the Copy button in the Clipboard group in the Home tab. Make active the worksheet where you want to paste the cell or cells, click the Paste button arrow, and then click *Paste Link* at the drop-down list. When a change is made to the cell or cells in the source worksheet, the change is automatically made to the linked cell or cells in the dependent worksheet. You can also create a link by clicking the Paste button, clicking the Paste Options button, and then clicking the *Link Cells* option.

You can also link cells with options at the Paste Special dialog box. Display this dialog box by clicking the Paste button arrow and then clicking *Paste Special* at the drop-down list. At the Paste Special dialog box, specify what in the cell you want to copy and what operators you want to include and then click the Paste Link button.

QUICK STEPS

Link Data between Worksheets
1. Select cells.
2. Click Copy button.
3. Click desired worksheet tab.
4. Click in desired cell.
5. Click Paste button arrow.
6. Click *Paste Link* at drop-down list.

Project ④ Linking Cells between Worksheets

1. Open **ExcelC05Project04.xlsx** and then save the workbook and name it **ExcelL1_C5_P4**.
2. Link cells in the first quarter worksheet to the other three worksheets by completing the following steps:
   a. Select cells C4 through C10.
   b. Click the Copy button in the Clipboard group in the Home tab.
   c. Click the 2nd Qtr. tab.
   d. Make cell C4 active.
   e. Click the Paste button arrow and then click *Paste Link* at the drop-down list.
   f. Click the 3rd Qtr. tab.
   g. Make cell C4 active.
   h. Click the Paste button.
   i. Click the Paste Options button that displays in the lower right corner of the pasted cell and then click *Link Cells* at the drop-down list.
   j. Click the 4th Qtr. tab.
   k. Make cell C4 active.
   l. Click the Paste button arrow and then click *Paste Link*.
   m. Click the 1st Qtr. tab and then press the Esc key to remove the moving marquee.

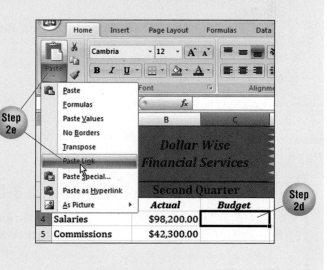

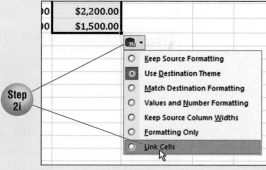

3. Insert a formula in all worksheets that subtracts the Budget amount from the Variance amount by completing the following steps:
   a. Make sure the first quarter worksheet displays.
   b. Hold down the Shift key and then click the 4th Qtr. tab. (This selects all four tabs.)
   c. Make cell D4 active and then insert the formula =C4-B4.
   d. Copy the formula in cell D4 down to cells D5 through D10.
   e. Click the 2nd Qtr. tab and notice that the formula was inserted and copied in this worksheet.
   f. Click the other worksheet tabs and notice the formula.
   g. Click the 1st Qtr. tab.

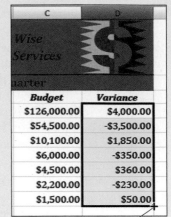

C	D
Wise Services	
uarter	
Budget	**Variance**
$126,000.00	$4,000.00
$54,500.00	-$3,500.00
$10,100.00	$1,850.00
$6,000.00	-$350.00
$4,500.00	$360.00
$2,200.00	-$230.00
$1,500.00	$50.00

Step 3d

4. With the first quarter worksheet active, make the following changes to some of the linked cells:
   C4: Change $126,000 to 128,000
   C5: Change $54,500 to 56,000
   C9: Change $2,200 to 2,400
5. Click the 2nd Qtr. tab and notice that the values in cells C4, C5, and C9 automatically changed (because they are linked to the first quarter worksheet).
6. Click the 3rd Qtr. tab and notice that the values in cells C4, C5, and C9 automatically changed.
7. Click the 4th Qtr. tab and notice that the values in cells C4, C5, and C9 automatically changed.
8. Save **ExcelL1_C5_P4.xlsx** and then print all the worksheets in the workbook.
9. Close **ExcelL1_C5_P4.xlsx**.

Project 5 Link Worksheets with 3-D References

You will open a workbook containing worksheets with quarterly sales data and then link the sales data in the worksheets with a 3-D reference.

Linking Worksheets with a 3-D Reference

In multiple worksheet workbooks, you can use a 3-D reference to analyze data in the same cell or range of cells. A 3-D reference includes the cell or range of cells, preceded by a range of worksheet names. For example, you can add all of the values contained in cells in B2 through B5 in worksheets 1 and 2 in a workbook using a 3-D reference. To do this, you would complete these basic steps:

1. Make active the cell where you want to enter the function.
2. Type =SUM(and then click the Sheet1 tab.
3. Hold down the Shift key and then click the Sheet2 tab.
4. Select cells B2 through B5 in the worksheet.
5. Type) (this is the closing parenthesis that ends the formula) and then press Enter.

Project ⑤ Linking Worksheets with a 3-D Reference

1. Open **ExcelC05Project05.xlsx** and then save the workbook and name it **ExcelL1_C5_P5**.
2. Make sure Sales 2007 is the active worksheet.
3. Make the following changes to the Sales 2007 worksheet:
   a. Make cell B12 active.
   b. Click the Center button in the Alignment group and then click the Bold button in the Font group.
   c. Type **January Sales** and then press Alt + Enter.
   d. Type **2007-2009** and then press Enter.
4. Link the Sales 2007, Sales 2008, and Sales 2009 worksheets with a 3-D reference by completing the following steps:
   a. With cell B13 active, type =SUM(.
   b. Hold down the Shift key, click the Sales 2009 sheet tab, and then release the Shift key. (This selects all three sheet tabs.)
   c. Select cells B5 through B10.
   d. Type) and then press Enter.

3	FIRST-QUARTER SALES - 2007					
4	*Customer*	*January*		*February*		*March*
5	Lakeside Trucking	$	84,231	$	73,455	$ 97,549
6	Gresham Machines	$	33,199	$	40,390	$ 50,112
7	Real Photography	$	30,891	$	35,489	$ 36,400
8	Genesis Productions	$	72,190	$	75,390	$ 83,219
9	Landower Company	$	22,188	$	14,228	$ 38,766
10	Jewell Enterprises	$	19,764	$	50,801	$ 32,188
11						
12		January Sales 2007-2009				
13		=SUM('Sales 2007:Sales 2009'!B5:B10)				
14						

Steps 4a–4d

5. Complete steps similar to those in Step 3 to add *February Sales 2007-2009* (on two lines) in cell C12 and complete steps similar to those in Step 4 to insert the formula with the 3-D reference in cell C13. (Select cells C5 through C10.)
6. Complete steps similar to those in Step 3 to add *March Sales 2007-2009* (on two lines) in cell D12 and complete steps similar to those in Step 4 to insert the formula with the 3-D reference in cell D13. (Select cells D5 through D10.)
7. Save the workbook.
8. Print only the Sales 2007 worksheet.
9. Close **ExcelL1_C5_P5.xlsx**.

Project ⑥ Copy and Paste a Worksheet in a Word Document

You will copy cells in a worksheet and paste the cells in a Word letter document. You will then edit some of the data in cells in the Word document.

Copying and Pasting a Worksheet between Programs

Microsoft Office is a suite that allows integration, which is the combining of data from two or more programs into one file. Integration can occur by copying and pasting data between programs. The program containing the data to be copied is called the *source* program and the program where the data is pasted is called the *destination* program. For example, you can create a worksheet in Excel and then copy it to a Word document. The steps to copy and paste between programs are basically the same as copying and pasting within the same program.

When copying data between worksheets or from one program to another, you can copy and paste, copy and link, or copy and embed the data. Consider the following when choosing a method for copying data:

- Copy data in the source program and paste it in the destination program when the data will not need to be edited.
- Copy data in the source program and then link it in the destination program when the data is updated regularly in the source program and you want the update reflected in the destination program.
- Copy data in the source program and then embed it in the destination program when the data will be edited in the destination program (with the tools of the source program).

Earlier in this chapter, you copied and pasted cells within and between worksheets and you also copied and linked cells between worksheets. You can also copy and link data between programs. Copy and embed data using options at the Paste Special dialog box. In Project 6, you will copy cells in a worksheet and then embed the cells in a Word document. With the worksheet embedded in a Word document, double-click the worksheet and Excel tools display in the document for editing the worksheet.

Project ⑥   Copying and Pasting a Worksheet into a Word Document

1. Open the Word program and then open **WordC05_Letter01.docx**.
2. Save the document and name it **WordExcelL1_C5_P6**.
3. With **WordExcelL1_C5_P6.docx** open, make Excel the active program.
4. Open **ExcelC05Project06.xlsx** and then save the workbook and name it **ExcelL1_C5_P6**.
5. Copy the worksheet to the letter by completing the following steps:
   a. Select cells A1 through D8.
   b. Click the Copy button in the Clipboard group in the Home tab.
   c. Click the button on the Taskbar representing the Word document **WordExcelL1_C5_P6.docx**.
   d. Position the insertion point on the blank line below the first paragraph of text in the body of the letter.
   e. Click the Paste button arrow in the Clipboard group in the Home tab and then click *Paste Special* at the drop-down list.
   f. At the Paste Special dialog box, click *Microsoft Office Excel Worksheet Object* in the *As* list box, and then click OK.

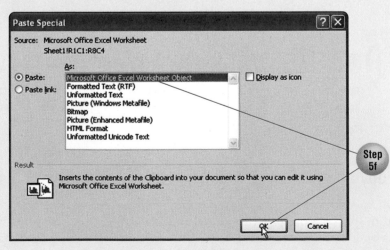

6. Edit a few of the cells in the worksheet by completing the following steps:
   a. Double-click anywhere in the worksheet. (This displays the Excel ribbon for editing.)
   b. Click in each of the following cells and make the change indicated:
      B6: Change *196%* to *110%*.
      C6: Change *190%* to *104%*.
      D6: Change *187%* to *101%*.

and securities. The financial picture looks optimistic and we anticipate a h

	A	B	C	D
1	ANALYSIS OF FINANCIAL CONDITION			
2		Actual	Planned	Prior Year
3	Stockholder's equity ratio	62%	60%	57%
4	Bond holder's equity ratio	45%	39%	41%
5	Liability liquidity ratio	122%	115%	120%
6	Fixed obligation security ratio	110%	104%	101%
7	Fixed interest ratio	23%	20%	28%
8	Earnings ratio	7%	6%	6%

Sheet1 Sheet2 Sheet3

As you can see from the table, the highest increase of percentage was in
security ratio. If you have any questions about this table or about other f

Step
6b

   c. Click outside the worksheet to remove the Excel tools (and deselect the worksheet).
7. Save, print, and then close **WordExcelL1_C5_P6.docx**.
8. Exit Word.
9. With Excel the active program, close **ExcelL1_C5_P6.xlsx**.

CHAPTER summary

- An Excel workbook, by default, contains three worksheets. Click a worksheet tab to display the worksheet.

- Move selected cells and cell contents in and between worksheets using the Cut, Copy, and Paste buttons in the Clipboard group in the Home tab or by dragging with the mouse.

- Move selected cells with the mouse by dragging the outline of the selected cells to the desired position.

- Copy selected cells with the mouse by holding down the Ctrl key and the left mouse button, dragging the outline of the selected cells to the desired location, releasing the left mouse button, and then releasing the Ctrl key.

- When pasting data, use the Paste Options button to specify what you want pasted. Click the Paste Options button and a drop-down list displays with options to specify that you want to keep source formatting, use destination themes, use destination formatting, or keep the column widths of the source worksheet. If you are pasting a cell containing a value as well as a formula, the Paste Options button drop-down list also includes the *Values Only* option.

- Use the Clipboard task pane to collect and paste data within and between worksheets and workbooks. Display the Clipboard task pane by clicking the Clipboard group dialog box launcher.

- Insert a worksheet in a workbook by clicking the Insert Worksheet tab located to the right of the Sheet3 tab or pressing Shift + F11.

- Perform maintenance activities, such as deleting and renaming, on worksheets within a workbook by clicking the *right* mouse button on a sheet tab and then clicking the desired option at the shortcut menu.

- You can use the mouse to move or copy worksheets. To move a worksheet, drag the worksheet tab with the mouse. To copy a worksheet, hold down the Ctrl key and then drag the worksheet tab with the mouse.

- Use the *Tab Color* option at the sheet tab shortcut menu to apply a color to a worksheet tab.

- Hide and unhide a worksheet by clicking the Format button in the Cells group and then clicking the desired option at the drop-down list, or by right-clicking the worksheet tab and then clicking the desired option at the shortcut menu.

- Manage more than one worksheet at a time by first selecting the worksheets. Use the mouse together with the Shift key to select adjacent worksheet tabs and use the mouse together with the Ctrl key to select nonadjacent worksheet tabs.

- If you want formatting to apply to multiple worksheets in a workbook, select the tabs of the desired worksheets and then apply the formatting.

- To print all worksheets in a workbook, click *Entire workbook* in the *Print what* section of the Print dialog box. You can also print specific worksheets by selecting the tabs of the worksheets you want to print.

- Split the worksheet window into panes with the Split button in the Window group in the View tab or with the split bars on the horizontal and vertical scroll bars.

- To remove a split from a worksheet, click the Split button to deactivate it or drag the split bars to the upper left corner of the worksheet.

- Freeze window panes by clicking the Freeze Panes button in the Window group in the View tab and then clicking *Freeze Panes* at the drop-down list. Unfreeze window panes by clicking the Freeze Panes button and then clicking *Unfreeze Panes* at the drop-down list.

- A selected group of cells is referred to as a range. A range can be named and used in a formula. Name a range by typing the name in the Name box located to the left of the Formula bar or at the New Name dialog box.

- To open multiple workbooks that are adjacent, display the Open dialog box, click the first workbook, hold down the Shift key, click the last workbook, and then click the Open button. If workbooks are nonadjacent, click the first workbook, hold down the Ctrl key, click the desired workbooks, and then click the Open button.

- To see a list of open workbooks, click the View tab and then click the Switch Windows button in the Window group.

- Arrange multiple workbooks in a window with options at the Arrange Windows dialog box.

- Hide the active workbook by clicking the Hide button and unhide a workbook by clicking the Unhide button in the Window group in the View tab.

- Click the Maximize button located in the upper right corner of the active workbook to make the workbook fill the entire window area. Click the Minimize button to shrink the active workbook to a button on the Taskbar. Click the Restore button to return the workbook to its previous size.

- You can move, copy, and/or paste data between workbooks.

- Copy and then link data if you make changes in the source worksheet and you want the changes reflected in the destination worksheet. The worksheet containing the original data is called the source worksheet and the worksheet relying on the source worksheet for data in the link is called the dependent worksheet.

- Copy and link data using the Paste Special dialog box or the *Link Cells* option at the Paste Options button drop-down list.

- You can copy data from a file in one program (called the source program) and paste the data into a file in another program (called the destination program).

- Use a 3-D reference to analyze data in the same cell or range of cells.

- You can copy and then paste, link, or embed data between programs in the Office suite. Integrating is the combining of data from two or more programs in the Office suite.

COMMANDS review

FEATURE	RIBBON TAB, GROUP	BUTTON, OPTION	KEYBOARD SHORTCUT
Cut selected cells	Home, Clipboard	✂	Ctrl + X
Copy selected cells	Home, Clipboard	📋	Ctrl + C
Paste selected cells	Home, Clipboard	📋	Ctrl + V
Clipboard task pane	Home, Clipboard	📋	
Insert worksheet		📋	Shift + F11
Hide worksheet	Home, Cells	Format ▾, Hide & Unhide, Hide Sheet	
Unhide worksheet	Home, Cells	Format ▾, Hide & Unhide, Unhide Sheet	
Split window into pane	View, Window	Split	
Freeze window panes	View, Window	Freeze Panes ▾, Freeze Panes	
Unfreeze window panes	View, Window	Freeze Panes ▾, Unfreeze Panes	
New Name dialog box	Formulas, Defined Names	Define Name ▾	
Arrange Windows dialog box	View, Window	Arrange All	
Maximize window		◻	
Restore		◻	
Minimize window		▬	
Paste Special dialog box	Home, Clipboard	📋, Paste Special	

CONCEPTS check

Test Your Knowledge

Completion: In the space provided at the right, indicate the correct term, symbol, or command.

1. By default, a workbook contains this number of worksheets. — *THREE*

2. To copy selected cells with the mouse, hold down this key while dragging the outline of the selected cells to the desired location. — *CTRL KEY*

3. The Cut, Copy, and Paste buttons are located in this group in the Home tab. — *CLIPBOARD*

4. This button displays in the lower right corner of pasted cells. — *PASTE OPTIONS BUTTON*

5. Use this task pane to collect and paste multiple items. — *CLIPBOARD TASK PANE*

6. Click this tab to insert a new worksheet. — *INSERT WORKSHEET TAB*

7. Click this option at the sheet tab shortcut menu to apply a color to a worksheet tab. — *TAB COLOR*

8. To select adjacent worksheet tabs, click the first tab, hold down this key, and then click the last tab. — *SHIFT KEY*

9. To select nonadjacent worksheet tabs, click the first tab, hold down this key, and then click any other tabs you want selected. — *CTRL KEY*

10. Click this option in the *Print what* section of the Print dialog box to print all worksheets in a workbook. — *ENTIRE WORKBOOK*

11. The Split button is located in this tab. — *VIEW TAB*

12. Display the Arrange Windows dialog box by clicking this button in the Window group in the View tab. — *ARRANGE ALL*

13. Click this button to make the active workbook expand to fill the screen. — *MAXIMIZE BUTTON*

14. Click this button to reduce the active workbook to a button on the Taskbar. — *MINIMIZE BUTTON*

15. When copying and pasting data between programs, the program containing the original data is called this. — *SOURCE WORKSHEET*

SKILLS check

Demonstrate Your Proficiency

Assessment

1 COPY AND PASTE DATA BETWEEN WORKSHEETS IN A SALES WORKBOOK

1. Open **ExcelC05Assessment01.xlsx** and then save the workbook and name it **ExcelL1_C5_A1**.
2. Turn on the display of the Clipboard task pane, click the Clear All button to clear any content, and then complete the following steps:
   a. Select and copy cells A7 through C7.
   b. Select and copy cells A10 through C10.
   c. Select and copy cells A13 through C13.
   d. Display the second worksheet, make cell A7 active, and then paste the *Avalon Clinic* cells.
   e. Make cell A10 active and then paste the *Stealth Media* cells.
   f. Make A13 active and then paste the *Danmark Contracting* cells.
   g. Make the third worksheet active and then complete similar steps to paste the cells in the same location as the second worksheet.
   h. Clear the contents of the Clipboard task pane and then close the task pane.
3. Change the name of the Sheet1 tab to *2007 Sales*, the name of the Sheet2 tab to *2008 Sales*, and the name of the Sheet3 tab to *2009 Sales*.
4. Change the color of the 2007 Sales tab to blue, the color of the 2008 Sales tab to green, and the color of the 2009 Sales tab to yellow.
5. Display the 2007 Sales worksheet, select all three tabs, and then insert a formula in cell D4 that sums the amounts in cells B4 and C4. Copy the formula in cell D4 down to cells D5 through D14.
6. Make cell D15 active and then insert a formula that sums the amounts in cells D4 through D14.
7. Insert a footer on all three worksheets that prints your name at the left side and the current date at the right.
8. Save, print, and then close **ExcelL1_C5_A1.xlsx**.

Assessment

2 COPY, PASTE, AND FORMAT WORKSHEETS IN AN INCOME STATEMENT WORKBOOK

1. Open **ExcelC05Assessment02.xlsx** and then save the workbook and name it **ExcelL1_C5_A2**.
2. Copy cells A1 through B17 in Sheet1 and paste them into Sheet2. (Click the Paste Options button and then click *Keep Source Column Widths* at the drop-down list.)
3. Make the following changes to the Sheet2 worksheet:
   a. Adjust the row heights so they match the heights in the Sheet1 worksheet.
   b. Change the month from *January* to *February*.
   c. Change the amount in B4 to *97,655*.
   d. Change the amount in B5 to *39,558*.
   e. Change the amount in B11 to *1,105*.

4. Select both sheet tabs and then insert the following formulas:
   a. Insert a formula in B6 that subtracts the Cost of Sales from the Sales Revenue (*=B4-B5*).
   b. Insert a formula in B16 that sums the amounts in B8 through B15.
   c. Insert a formula in B17 that subtracts the Total Expenses from the Gross Profit (*=B6-B16*).
5. Change the name of the Sheet1 tab to *January* and the name of the Sheet2 tab to *February*.
6. Change the color of the January tab to blue and the color of the February tab to red.
7. Insert a custom footer on both worksheets that prints your name at the left side, the date in the middle, and the file name at the right side.
8. Save, print, and then close **ExcelL1_C5_A2.xlsx**.

Assessment

3 FREEZE AND UNFREEZE WINDOW PANES IN A TEST SCORES WORKBOOK

1. Open **ExcelC05Assessment03.xlsx** and then save the workbook and name it **ExcelL1_C5_A3**.
2. Make cell A1 active and then split the window by clicking the View tab and then clicking the Split button in the Window group. (This causes the window to split into four panes.)
3. Drag both the horizontal and vertical gray lines up and to the left until the horizontal gray line is immediately below the second row and the vertical gray line is immediately to the right of the first column.
4. Freeze the window panes.
5. Add two rows immediately above row 18 and then type the following text in the specified cells:

A18	=	Nauer, Sheryl	A19	=	Nunez, James
B18	=	75	B19	=	98
C18	=	83	C19	=	96
D18	=	85	D19	=	100
E18	=	78	E19	=	90
F18	=	82	F19	=	95
G18	=	80	G19	=	93
H18	=	79	H19	=	88
I18	=	82	I19	=	91
J18	=	92	J19	=	89
K18	=	90	K19	=	100
L18	=	86	L19	=	96
M18	=	84	M19	=	98

6. Insert a formula in cell N3 that averages the percentages in cells B3 through M3 and then copy the formula down to cells N4 through N22.
7. Unfreeze the window panes.
8. Remove the split.
9. Save the worksheet and then print it in landscape orientation.
10. Close **ExcelL1_C5_A3.xlsx**.

4 CREATE, COPY, PASTE, AND FORMAT CELLS IN AN EQUIPMENT USAGE WORKBOOK

1. Create the worksheet shown in Figure 5.10 (change the width of column A to 21.00).
2. Save the workbook and name it **ExcelL1_C5_A4**.
3. With **ExcelL1_C5_A4.xlsx** open, open **ExcelC05Project02.xlsx**.
4. Select and copy the following cells from **ExcelC05Project02.xlsx** to **ExcelL1_C5_A4.xlsx**:
   a. Copy cells A4 through G4 in **ExcelC05Project02.xlsx** and paste them into **ExcelL1_C5_A4.xlsx** beginning with cell A12.
   b. Copy cells A10 through G10 in **ExcelC05Project02.xlsx** and paste them into **ExcelL1_C5_A4.xlsx** beginning with cell A13.
5. With **ExcelL1_C5_A4.xlsx** the active workbook, make cell A1 active and then apply the following formatting:
   a. Change the height of row 1 to 25.50.
   b. Change the font size of the text in cell A1 to 14 points.
   c. Insert Olive Green, Accent 3, Lighter 60% fill color to cell A1.
6. Select cells A2 through G2 and then insert Olive Green, Accent 3, Darker 50% fill color.
7. Select cells B2 through G2 and then change to right alignment, change the text color to white, and turn on italics.
8. Select cells A3 through G3 and then insert Olive Green, Accent 3, Lighter 80% fill color.
9. Select cells A7 through G7 and then insert Olive Green, Accent 3, Lighter 80% fill color.
10. Select cells A11 through G11 and then insert Olive Green, Accent 3, Lighter 80% fill color.
11. Change the orientation to landscape.
12. Print the worksheet centered horizontally and vertically on the page.
13. Save and then close **ExcelL1_C5_A4.xlsx**.
14. Close **ExcelC05Project02.xlsx** without saving the changes.

Figure 5.10 Assessment 4

	A	B	C	D	E	F	G	H
1	EQUIPMENT USAGE REPORT							
2		January	February	March	April	May	June	
3	Machine #12							
4	Total Hours Available	2300	2430	2530	2400	2440	2240	
5	In Use	2040	2105	2320	2180	2050	1995	
6								
7	Machine #25							
8	Total Hours Available	2100	2240	2450	2105	2390	1950	
9	In Use	1800	1935	2110	1750	2215	1645	
10								
11	Machine #30							
12								

Assessment

5   LINK WORKSHEETS IN A SALES WORKBOOK WITH 3-D REFERENCES

1. Open **ExcelC05Assessment05.xlsx** and then save the workbook and name it **ExcelL1_C5_A5**.
2. Change the color of the Sales 2007 tab to purple, the color of the Sales 2008 tab to blue, and the color of the Sales 2009 tab to green.
3. Make the following changes to the workbook:
   a. Make Sales 2007 the active worksheet.
   b. Select columns B, C, and D and then change the width to 16.00.
   c. Insert the heading *Average January Sales 2007-2009* (on multiple lines) in cell B11, centered and bolded.
   d. Insert a formula in cell B12 with a 3-D reference that averages the total in cells B4 through B9 in the Sales 2007, Sales 2008, and Sales 2009 worksheets.
   e. Insert the heading *Average February Sales 2007-2009* (on multiple lines) in cell C11, centered and bolded.
   f. Insert a formula in cell C12 with a 3-D reference that averages the total in cells C4 through C9 in the Sales 2007, Sales 2008, and Sales 2009 worksheets.
   g. Insert the heading *Average March Sales 2007-2009* (on multiple lines) in cell D11, centered and bolded.
   h. Insert a formula in cell D12 with a 3-D reference that averages the total in cells D4 through D9 in the Sales 2007, Sales 2008, and Sales 2009 worksheets.
4. Save the workbook and then print only the Sales 2007 worksheet.
5. Close **ExcelL1_C5_A5.xlsx**.

Assessment

6   LINK DATA BETWEEN A WORD LETTER AND AN EXCEL WORKSHEET

1. Use Excel's Help feature to learn about linking data between programs.
2. After locating and reading the information on linking, open the Word program and then open **WordC05_Letter02.docx**.
3. Save the document and name it **WordExcelL1_C5_A6**.
4. Make Excel the active program and then open **ExcelC05Assessment06.xlsx**.
5. Save the workbook with Save As and name it **ExcelL1_C5_A6**.
6. In column G, insert a formula using the PMT function.
7. Save and then print the worksheet.
8. Select cells A2 through G10 and then copy and link the cells to **WordExcelL1_C5_A6.docx** (between the two paragraphs in the body of the letter).
9. Save, print, and then close **WordExcelL1_C5_A6.docx**.
10. Click the button on the Taskbar representing the Excel workbook **ExcelL1_C5_A6.xlsx** and then change the percentages in cells E3 through E6 to 7.5% and the percentages in cells E7 through E10 to 8.5%.
11. Save, print, and then close **ExcelL1_C5_A6.xlsx**.
12. Make Word the active program and then open **WordExcelL1_C5_A6.docx**.
13. At the message that displays, click Yes.
14. Save, print, and then close **WordExcelL1_C5_A6.docx**.
15. Exit Word.

CASE study
Apply Your Skills

You are an administrator for Gateway Global, an electronics manufacturing corporation. You are gathering information on money spent on supplies and equipment purchases. You have gathered information for the first quarter of the year and decide to create a workbook containing worksheets for monthly information. To do this, create a worksheet that contains the following information:

- Company name is Gateway Global.
- Create the title *January Expenditures*.
- Create the following columns:

Department	Supplies	Equipment	Total
Production	$25,425	$135,500	
Research and Development	$50,000	$125,000	
Technical Support	$14,500	$65,000	
Finance	$5,790	$22,000	
Sales and Marketing	$35,425	$8,525	
Facilities	$6,000	$1,200	
Total			

- Insert a formula in the *Total* column that sums the amounts in the *Supplies* and *Equipment* columns and insert a formula in the *Total* row that sums the Supplies amounts, Equipment amounts, and Total amounts.
- Apply formatting such as fill color, borders, font color, and shading to enhance the visual appeal of the worksheet.

After creating and formatting the worksheet, complete the following:

- Copy the worksheet data to Sheet2 and then to Sheet3.
- Make the following changes to data in Sheet2:
  ○ Change *January Expenditures* to *February Expenditures*.
  ○ Change the Production Department Supplies amount to *$38,550* and the Equipment amount to *$88,500*.
  ○ Change the Technical Support Department Equipment amount to *$44,250*.
  ○ Change the Finance Department Supplies amount to *$7,500*.
- Make the following changes to data in Sheet3:
  ○ Change *January Expenditures* to *March Expenditures*.
  ○ Change the Research and Development Department Supplies amount to *$65,000* and the Equipment amount to *$150,000*.
  ○ Change the Technical Support Department Supplies amount to *$21,750* and the Equipment amount to *$43,525*.
  ○ Change the Facilities Department Equipment amount to *$18,450*.

Create a new worksheet that summarizes the Supplies and Equipment totals for January, February, and March. Apply the same formatting to the worksheet as applied to the other three. Change the tab name for Sheet1 to *Jan. Expenditures*, the tab name for Sheet2 to *Feb. Expenditures*, the tab name for Sheet3 to *Mar. Expenditures*, and the tab name for Sheet4 to *Qtr. Summary*. Change the color of each tab (you determine the colors).

Insert a footer that prints your name at the left side of each worksheet and the current date at the right side of each worksheet. Save the workbook and name it **ExcelL1_C5_CS_P1**. Print all the worksheets in the workbook and then close the workbook.

Part 2

Employees of Gateway Global have formed two intramural co-ed softball teams and you have volunteered to keep statistics for the players. Open **ExcelGGStats.xlsx** and then make the following changes to both worksheets in the workbook:

- Insert a formula that calculates a player's batting average (Hits divided by At Bats).
- Insert a formula that calculates a player's on-base percentage (Walks + Hits divided by At Bats plus Walks). Make sure you insert parentheses in the formula.
- Insert the company name.
- Apply formatting to enhance the visual appeal of the worksheets.
- Horizontally and vertically center the worksheets.
- Insert a footer that prints on both worksheets and prints your name at the left side of the worksheet and the date at the right of the worksheet.

Using Help, learn how to apply conditional formatting to data in a worksheet. Select both worksheets and then apply conditional formatting that inserts red fill and changes text color to dark red for cells in the *Batting Average* column with an average over .400. Save the workbook and name it **ExcelL1_C5_CS_P2**. Print and then close **ExcelL1_C5_CS_P2.xlsx**.

Part 3

Many of the suppliers for Gateway Global are international and use different length, weight, and volume measurements. The purchasing manager has asked you to prepare a conversion chart in Excel that displays conversion tables for length, weight, volume, and temperature. Use the Internet to locate conversion tables for length, weight, and volume. When preparing the workbook, create a worksheet with the following information:

- Include the following length conversions:
  - 1 inch to centimeters
  - 1 foot to centimeters
  - 1 yard to meters
  - 1 mile to kilometers
- Include the following weight conversions:
  - 1 ounce to grams
  - 1 pound to kilograms
  - 1 ton to metric tons
- Include the following volume conversions:
  - 1 fluid ounce to milliliters
  - 1 pint to liters
  - 1 quart to liters
  - 1 gallon to liters

Locate a site on the Internet that provides the formula for converting Fahrenheit temperatures to Celsius temperatures and then create another worksheet in the workbook with the following information:

- Insert Fahrenheit temperatures beginning with zero, continuing to 100, and incrementing by 5 (for example, 0, 5, 10, 15, and so on).
- Insert a formula that converts the Fahrenheit temperature to a Celsius temperature.

Include the company name, Gateway Global, in both worksheets. Apply additional formatting to improve the visual appeal of both worksheets. Rename both sheet names and apply a color to each tab (you determine the names and colors). Save the workbook and name it **ExcelL1_C5_CS_P3**. Print both worksheets centered horizontally and vertically on the page and then close **ExcelL1_C5_CS_P3.xlsx**.

Part 4

Open Microsoft Word and then create a letterhead document that contains the company name *Gateway Global*, the address (you decide the address including street address, city, state, and ZIP code or street address, city, province, and postal code), and the telephone number (you determine the telephone number). Apply formatting to improve the visual display of the letterhead. Save the document and name it **WordGGLtrhd**. Save the document again with Save As and name it **WordL1_C5_CS_P4A**. In Excel, open **ExcelL1_C5_CS_P3.xlsx**. In the first worksheet, copy the cells containing data and then paste them in **WordL1_C5_CS_P4A.docx** using Paste Special. Save, print, and then close **WordL1_C5_CS_P4A.docx**. In Word, open **WordGGLtrd.docx**. Save the document with Save As and name it **WordL1_C5_CS_P4B**. In Excel, make the worksheet active that contains the Fahrenheit conversion information, copy the cells containing data, and then paste them in the Word document using Paste Special. Save, print, and then close **WordL1_C5_CS_P4B.docx**. Close Microsoft Word and then, in Excel, close **ExcelL1_C5_CS_P3.xlsx**.

Maintaining Workbooks

PERFORMANCE OBJECTIVES

Upon successful completion of Chapter 6, you will be able to:

- Create and rename a folder
- Delete workbooks and folders
- Copy and move workbooks within and between folders
- Copy, move, and rename worksheets within a workbook
- Save a workbook in a variety of formats
- Maintain consistent formatting with styles
- Use comments for review and response
- Create financial forms using templates

Tutorial 6.1
Managing Folders and Workbooks
Tutorial 6.2
Advanced Formatting Techniques

Once you have been working with Excel for a period of time you will have accumulated several workbook files. Workbooks should be organized into folders to facilitate fast retrieval of information. Occasionally you should perform file maintenance activities such as copying, moving, renaming, and deleting workbooks to ensure the workbook list in your various folders is manageable. You will learn these file management tasks in this chapter along with creating and applying styles, inserting and printing comments, and using Excel templates to create a workbook.

Note: Before beginning computer projects, copy to your storage medium the Excel2007L1C6 subfolder from the Excel2007L1 folder on the CD that accompanies this textbook and then make Excel2007L1C6 the active folder.

Project ① Manage Workbooks

You will perform a variety of file management tasks including creating and renaming a folder; selecting and then deleting, copying, cutting, pasting, and renaming workbooks; deleting a folder; and opening, printing, and closing a workbook.

Maintaining Workbooks

You can complete many workbook management tasks at the Open and Save As dialog boxes. These tasks can include copying, moving, printing, and renaming workbooks; opening multiple workbooks; and creating and renaming a new folder. Some file maintenance tasks such as creating a folder and deleting files are performed by using buttons on the Open dialog box or Save As dialog box toolbar. Figure 6.1 displays the Open dialog box toolbar buttons.

Figure 6.1 Open Dialog Box Toolbar Buttons

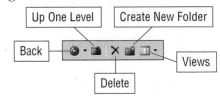

Creating a Folder

Create a Folder
1. Click Office button, *Open*.
2. Click Create New Folder button.
3. Type folder name.
4. Press Enter.

In Excel, you should logically group and store workbooks in folders. For example, you could store all of the workbooks related to one department in one folder with the department name being the folder name. You can create a folder within a folder (called a ***subfolder***). If you create workbooks for a department by individuals, each individual name could have a subfolder within the department folder. The main folder on a disk or drive is called the root folder. You create additional folders as branches of this root folder.

At the Open or Save As dialog boxes, workbook file names display in the list box preceded by a workbook icon and a folder name displays preceded by a folder icon. Create a new folder by clicking the Create New Folder button located on the dialog box toolbar at the Open dialog box or Save As dialog box. At the New Folder dialog box shown in Figure 6.2, type a name for the folder in the *Name* text box, and then click OK or press Enter. The new folder becomes the active folder.

HINT

Change the default folder with the *Default file location* option at the Excel Options dialog box with Save selected.

Create New Folder

Up One Level

If you want to make the previous folder the active folder, click the Up One Level button on the dialog box toolbar. After clicking the Up One Level button, the Back button becomes active. Click this button and the previously active folder becomes active again.

A folder name can contain a maximum of 255 characters. Numbers, spaces, and symbols can be used in the folder name, except those symbols explained in Chapter 1 in the "Saving a Workbook" section.

Figure 6.2 New Folder Dialog Box

Type the new folder name in the *Name* text box.

Project 1a | Creating a Folder

1. Create a folder named *Payroll* on your storage medium. To begin, display the Open dialog box.
2. Double-click the *Excel2007L1C6* folder name to make it the active folder.
3. Click the Create New Folder button (located on the dialog box toolbar).
4. At the New Folder dialog box, type Payroll.
5. Click OK. (The Payroll folder is now the active folder.)

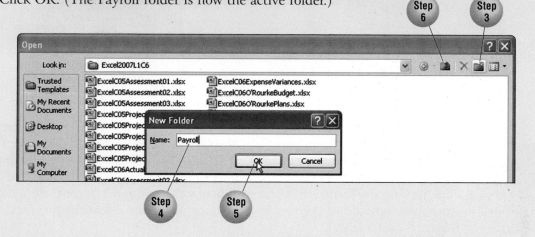

6. Click the Up One Level button on the dialog box toolbar to change back to the Excel2007L1C6 folder.

Renaming a Folder

As you organize your files and folders, you may decide to rename a folder. Rename a folder using the Tools button in the Open dialog box or using a shortcut menu. To rename a folder using the Tools button, display the Open dialog box, click in the list box the folder you want to rename, click the Tools button located in the lower left corner of the dialog box, and then click *Rename* at the drop-down list. This selects the folder name and inserts a border around the name. Type the new name for the folder and then press Enter. To rename a folder using a shortcut menu, display the Open dialog box, right-click the folder name in the list box, and then click *Rename* at the shortcut menu. Type a new name for the folder and then press Enter.

A tip to remember when you are organizing files and folders is to be sure that your system is set up to display all of the files in a particular folder and not just the Excel files, for example. You can display all files in a folder by changing the *Files of type* option at the Open dialog box to *All Files (*.*)*.

QUICK STEPS

Rename a Folder
1. Click Office button, *Open*.
2. Click desired folder.
3. Click Tools button, *Rename*.
4. Type new name.
5. Press Enter.
OR
1. Click Office button, *Open*.
2. Right-click folder name.
3. Click *Rename*.
4. Type new name.
5. Press Enter.

Project 1b **Renaming a Folder**

1. At the Open dialog box, right-click the *Payroll* folder name in the Open dialog box list box.
2. Click *Rename* at the shortcut menu.
3. Type **Finances** and then press Enter.

Step 3

Open

Look in:	Excel2007L1C6
Trusted Templates	Finances
My Recent Documents	ExcelC05Assessment01.xlsx
	ExcelC05Assessment02.xlsx
	ExcelC05Assessment03.xlsx

Selecting Workbooks

You can complete workbook management tasks on one workbook or selected workbooks. To select one workbook, display the Open dialog box, and then click the desired workbook. To select several adjacent workbooks (workbooks that display next to each other), click the first workbook, hold down the Shift key, and then click the last workbook. To select workbooks that are not adjacent, click the first workbook, hold down the Ctrl key, click any other desired workbooks, and then release the Ctrl key.

Deleting Workbooks and Folders

At some point, you may want to delete certain workbooks from your storage medium or any other drive or folder in which you may be working. To delete a workbook, display the Open or Save As dialog box, select the workbook, and then click the Delete button on the dialog box toolbar. At the dialog box asking you to confirm the deletion, click Yes. To delete a workbook using a shortcut menu, display the Open dialog box, right-click the workbook name in the list box, and then click *Delete* at the shortcut menu. Click Yes at the confirmation dialog box.

Deleting to the Recycle Bin

Workbooks deleted from the hard drive are automatically sent to the Windows Recycle Bin. You can easily restore a deleted workbook from the Recycle Bin. To free space on the drive, empty the Recycle Bin on a periodic basis. Restoring a workbook from or emptying the contents of the Recycle Bin is completed at the Windows desktop (not in Excel). To display the Recycle Bin, minimize the Excel window, and then double-click the *Recycle Bin* icon located on the Windows desktop. At the Recycle Bin, you can restore file(s) and empty the Recycle Bin.

Project 1c **Selecting and Deleting Workbooks**

1. At the Open dialog box, open **ExcelC05Project01.xlsx** (located in the Excel2007L1C6 folder).
2. Save the workbook with Save As and name it **ExcelL1_C6_P1**.
3. Close **ExcelL1_C6_P1.xlsx**.

4. Delete **ExcelL1_C6_P1.xlsx** by completing the following steps:
   a. Display the Open dialog box with Excel2007L1C6 the active folder.
   b. Click **ExcelL1_C6_P1.xlsx** to select it.
   c. Click the Delete button on the dialog box toolbar.

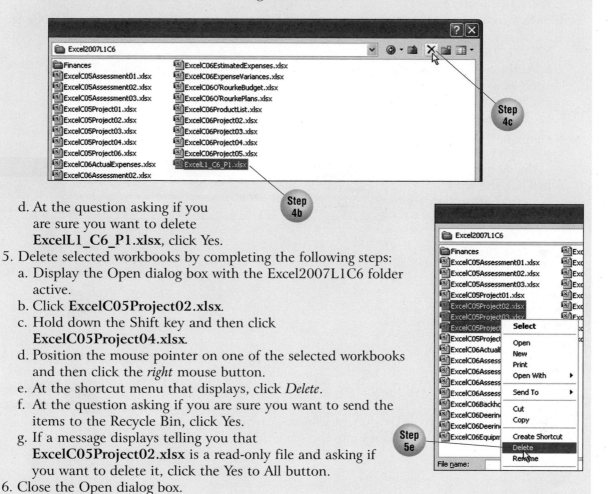

   d. At the question asking if you are sure you want to delete **ExcelL1_C6_P1.xlsx**, click Yes.
5. Delete selected workbooks by completing the following steps:
   a. Display the Open dialog box with the Excel2007L1C6 folder active.
   b. Click **ExcelC05Project02.xlsx**.
   c. Hold down the Shift key and then click **ExcelC05Project04.xlsx**.
   d. Position the mouse pointer on one of the selected workbooks and then click the *right* mouse button.
   e. At the shortcut menu that displays, click *Delete*.
   f. At the question asking if you are sure you want to send the items to the Recycle Bin, click Yes.
   g. If a message displays telling you that **ExcelC05Project02.xlsx** is a read-only file and asking if you want to delete it, click the Yes to All button.
6. Close the Open dialog box.

Copying Workbooks

In previous chapters, you have been opening a workbook from your storage medium and saving it with a new name in the same location. This process makes an exact copy of the workbook, leaving the original on your storage medium. You have been copying workbooks and saving the new workbook in the same folder as the original workbook. You can also copy a workbook into another folder.

Project 1d Saving a Copy of an Open Workbook

1. Open **ExcelC05Assessment01.xlsx**.
2. Save the workbook with Save As and name it **TotalSales**. (Make sure Excel2007L1C6 is the active folder.)
3. Save a copy of the **TotalSales.xlsx** workbook in the Finances folder you created in Project 1a by completing the following steps:
   a. With **TotalSales.xlsx** open, display the Save As dialog box.
   b. At the Save As dialog box, change to the Finances folder. To do this, double-click *Finances* at the beginning of the list box (folders are listed before workbooks).
   c. Click the Save button located in the lower right corner of the dialog box.
4. Close **TotalSales.xlsx**.
5. Change back to the Excel2007L1C6 folder by completing the following steps:
   a. Display the Open dialog box.
   b. Click the Up One Level button located on the dialog box toolbar.
   c. Close the Open dialog box.

Step 5b

Copy a Workbook
1. Click Office button, *Open*.
2. Right-click workbook name.
3. Click *Copy*.
4. Navigate to desired folder.
5. Right-click white area in list box.
6. Click *Paste*.

You can copy a workbook to another folder without opening the workbook first. To do this, use the *Copy* and *Paste* options from a shortcut menu at the Open (or Save As) dialog box. You can also copy a workbook or selected workbooks into the same folder. When you do this, Excel names the workbook(s) "Copy of xxx" (where *xxx* is the current workbook name). You can copy one workbook or selected workbooks into the same folder.

Project 1e Copying a Workbook at the Open Dialog Box

1. Copy **ExcelC05Assessment02.xlsx** to the Finance folder. To begin, display the Open dialog box with the Excel2007L1C6 folder active.
2. Position the arrow pointer on **ExcelC05Assessment02.xlsx**, click the right mouse button, and then click *Copy* at the shortcut menu.
3. Change to the Finance folder by double-clicking *Finances* at the beginning of the list box.
4. Position the arrow pointer in any white area (not on a workbook name) in the list box, click the right mouse button, and then click *Paste* at the shortcut menu.
5. Change back to the Excel2007L1C6 folder by clicking the Up One Level button located on the dialog box toolbar.
6. Close the Open dialog box.

Step 4

Sending Workbooks to a Different Drive or Folder

Copy workbooks to another folder or drive with the *Copy* and *Paste* options from the shortcut menu at the Open or Save As dialog box. With the *Send To* option, you can send a copy of a workbook to another drive or folder. To use this option, position the arrow pointer on the workbook you want copied, click the *right* mouse button, point to *Send To* (this causes a side menu to display), and then click the desired drive or folder.

Cutting and Pasting a Workbook

You can remove a workbook from one folder and insert it in another folder using the *Cut* and *Paste* options from the shortcut menu at the Open dialog box. To do this, display the Open dialog box, position the arrow pointer on the workbook to be removed (cut), click the *right* mouse button, and then click *Cut* at the shortcut menu. Change to the desired folder or drive, position the arrow pointer in a white area in the list box, click the *right* mouse button, and then click *Paste* at the shortcut menu.

Move a Workbook
1. Click Office button, *Open.*
2. Right-click workbook name.
3. Click *Cut.*
4. Navigate to desired folder.
5. Right-click white area in list box.
6. Click *Paste.*

 Cutting and Pasting a Workbook

1. Move a workbook to a different folder. To begin, display the Open dialog box with the Excel2007L1C6 folder active.
2. Position the arrow pointer on **ExcelC05Project06.xlsx**, click the right mouse button, and then click *Cut* at the shortcut menu.
3. Double-click *Finances* to make it the active folder.
4. Position the arrow pointer in the white area in the list box, click the right mouse button, and then click *Paste* at the shortcut menu.
5. If a Confirm File Move dialog box displays asking if you are sure you want to move the file, click Yes. (This dialog box usually does not appear when you cut and paste. Since the files you copied from your student CD-ROM are read-only files, this warning message appears.)
6. Click the Up One Level button to make the Excel2007L1C6 folder the active folder.

Renaming Workbooks

At the Open dialog box, use the *Rename* option from the Tools button drop-down list or the shortcut menu to give a workbook a different name. The *Rename* option changes the name of the workbook and keeps it in the same folder. To use *Rename*, display the Open dialog box, click once on the workbook to be renamed, click the Tools button located in the lower left corner of the dialog box, and then click *Rename*. This causes a thin black border to surround the workbook name and the name to be selected. Type the new name and then press Enter.

You can also rename a workbook by right-clicking the workbook name at the Open dialog box and then clicking *Rename* at the shortcut menu. Type the new name for the workbook and then press the Enter key.

Rename Workbook
1. Click Office button, *Open.*
2. Click desired workbook.
3. Click Tools button, *Rename.*
4. Type new name.
5. Press Enter.
OR
1. Click Office button, *Open.*
2. Right-click workbook name.
3. Click *Rename.*
4. Type new name.
5. Press Enter.

Project 1g Renaming a Workbook

1. Rename a workbook located in the Finances folder. To begin, make sure the Open dialog box displays with Excel2007L1C6 the active folder.
2. Double-click *Finances* to make it the active folder.
3. Click once on **ExcelC05Project06.xlsx** to select it.
4. Click the Tools button that displays in the lower left corner of the dialog box.
5. Click *Rename* at the drop-down list.
6. Type **Analysis.xlsx** and then press the Enter key.
7. If a message displays asking if you are sure you want to change the name of the read-only file, click Yes.
8. Complete steps similar to those in Steps 3 through 6 to rename **ExcelC05Assessment02.xlsx** to *SoftwareTests.xlsx*.
9. Click the Up One Level button.

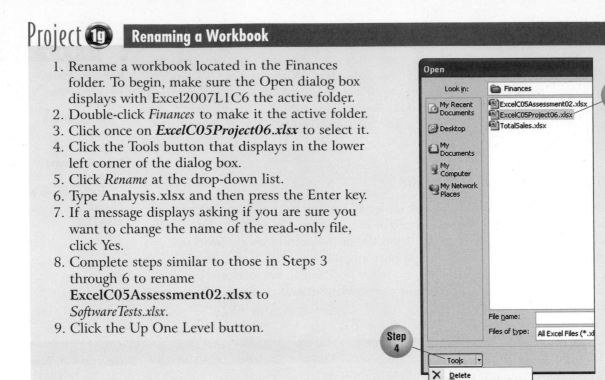

Deleting a Folder and Its Contents

As you learned earlier in this chapter, you can delete a workbook or selected workbooks. In addition to workbooks, you can delete a folder and all of its contents. Delete a folder in the same manner as you delete a workbook.

Project 1h Deleting a Folder and Its Contents

1. Delete the Finances folder and its contents. To begin, make sure the Open dialog box displays with the Excel2007L1C6 folder active.
2. Right-click on the *Finances* folder.
3. Click *Delete* at the shortcut menu.
4. At the Confirm Folder Delete dialog box, click Yes.
5. If the Confirm File Delete dialog box displays, click the Yes to All button.

Printing Workbooks

Up to this point, you have opened a workbook and then printed it. With the *Print* option from the Tools button drop-down list or the *Print* option from the shortcut menu at the Open dialog box, you can print a workbook or several workbooks without opening them.

Project ⑪ Printing Workbooks

1. At the Open dialog box with the Excel2007L1C6 folder active, select *ExcelC05Assessment01.xlsx* and *ExcelC05Assessment02.xlsx*.
2. Click the Tools button located in the lower left corner of the dialog box.
3. Click *Print* at the drop-down list.

Project ② Copy and Move Worksheets into an Equipment Rental Workbook

You will open an equipment rental workbook, open two other workbooks containing equipment rental information, and then copy and move worksheets between the workbooks.

Managing Worksheets

You can move or copy individual worksheets within the same workbook or to another existing workbook. Exercise caution when moving sheets since calculations or charts based on data on a worksheet might become inaccurate if you move the worksheet. To make a duplicate of a worksheet in the same workbook, hold down the Ctrl key and then drag the worksheet tab to the desired position.

Copying a Worksheet to Another Workbook

To copy a worksheet to another existing workbook, open both the source and the destination workbooks. Right-click the sheet tab and then click *Move or Copy* at the shortcut menu. At the Move or Copy dialog box shown in Figure 6.3, select the destination workbook name from the *To book* drop-down list, select the worksheet that you want the copied worksheet placed before in the *Before sheet* list box, click the *Create a copy* check box, and then click OK.

Copy a Worksheet to Another Workbook
1. Right-click desired sheet tab.
2. Click *Move or Copy*.
3. Select desired destination workbook.
4. Select desired worksheet location.
5. Click *Create a copy* check box.
6. Click OK.

Figure 6.3 Move or Copy Dialog Box

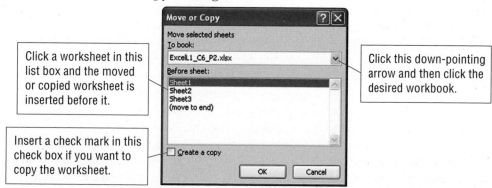

Click a worksheet in this list box and the moved or copied worksheet is inserted before it.

Click this down-pointing arrow and then click the desired workbook.

Insert a check mark in this check box if you want to copy the worksheet.

1. Open **ExcelC06Project02.xlsx** and then save the workbook and name it **ExcelL1_C6_P2**.
2. With **ExcelL1_C6_P2.xlsx** open, open **ExcelC06Equipment.xlsx**.
3. Copy the Front Loader worksheet by completing the following steps:
   a. With **ExcelC06Equipment.xlsx** the active workbook, right-click the Front Loader tab and then click *Move or Copy* at the shortcut menu.
   b. Click the down-pointing arrow next to the *To book* option box and then click *ExcelL1_C6_P2.xlsx* at the drop-down list.
   c. Click *Sheet2* in the *Before sheet* list box.
   d. Click the *Create a copy* check box to insert a check mark.
   e. Click OK. (Excel switches to the **ExcelL1_C6_P2.xlsx** workbook and inserts the copied Front Loader worksheet between Sheet1 and Sheet2.)
4. Complete steps similar to those in Step 3 to copy the Tractor worksheet to the **ExcelL1_C6_P2.xlsx** workbook. (Insert the Tractor worksheet between Front Loader and Sheet2.)
5. Complete steps similar to those in Step 3 to copy the Forklift worksheet to the **ExcelL1_C6_P2.xlsx** workbook. (Insert the Forklift worksheet between Tractor and Sheet2.)
6. Save **ExcelL1_C6_P2.xlsx**.
7. Make **ExcelC06Equipment.xlsx** the active workbook and then close it.

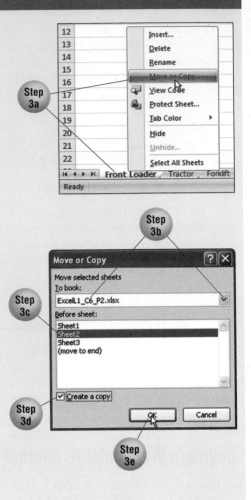

Moving a Worksheet to Another Workbook

To move a worksheet to another existing workbook, open both the source and the destination workbooks. Make active the sheet you want to move in the source workbook, right-click the sheet tab and then click *Move or Copy* at the shortcut menu. At the Move or Copy dialog box shown in Figure 6.3, select the destination workbook name from the *To book* drop-down list, select the worksheet that you want the worksheet placed before in the *Before sheet* list box, and then click OK. If you need to reposition a worksheet tab, drag the tab to the desired position.

Be careful when moving a worksheet to another workbook file. If formulas exist in the workbook that depend on the contents of the cells in the worksheet that is moved, they will no longer calculate properly.

Project 2b **Moving a Worksheet to Another Workbook**

1. With **ExcelL1_C6_P2.xlsx** open, open **ExcelC06Backhoe.xlsx**.
2. Move Sheet1 from **ExcelC06Backhoe.xlsx** to **ExcelL1_C6_P2.xlsx** by completing the following steps:
   a. With **ExcelC06Backhoe.xlsx** the active workbook, right-click the Sheet1 tab and then click *Move or Copy* at the shortcut menu.
   b. Click the down-pointing arrow next to the *To book* option box and then click **ExcelL1_C6_P2.xlsx** at the drop-down list.
   c. Click *Sheet2* in the *Before sheet* list box.
   d. Click OK.

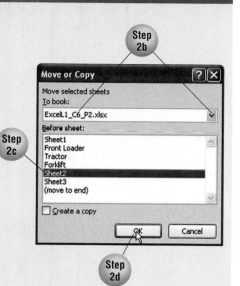

3. Make **ExcelC06Backhoe.xlsx** the active workbook and then close it without saving the changes.
4. With **ExcelL1_C6_P2.xlsx** open, make the following changes:
   a. Delete Sheet2 and Sheet3 tabs. (These worksheets are blank.)
   b. Rename Sheet1 to **Equipment Hours**.
   c. Rename Sheet1 (2) to **Backhoe**.
5. Create a range for the Forklift total hours available by completing the following steps:
   a. Click the Front Loader tab.
   b. Select cells B4 through E4.
   c. Click in the Name box.
   d. Type **FrontLoaderHours**.

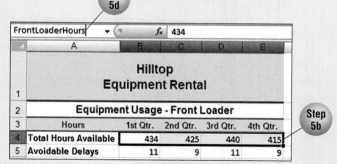

   e. Press Enter.
6. Complete steps similar to those in Step 5 to create the following ranges:
   a. In the Front Loader worksheet, create a range with cells B10 through E10 and name it *FrontLoaderHoursInUse*.
   b. Click the Tractor tab and then create a range with cells B4 through E4 and name it *TractorHours* and create a range with cells B10 through E10 and name it *TractorHoursInUse*.
   c. Click the Forklift tab and then create a range with cells B4 through E4 and name it *ForkliftHours* and create a range with cells B10 through E10 and name it *ForkliftHoursInUse*.
   d. Click the Backhoe tab and then create a range with cells B4 through E4 and name it *BackhoeHours* and create a range with cells B10 through E10 and name it *BackhoeHoursInUse*.

7. Click the EquipmentHours tab to make it the active worksheet and then insert a formula that inserts the total hours for the Front Loader by completing the following steps:
   a. Make cell C4 active.
   b. Type =SUM(Fr.
   c. When you type *Fr* a drop-down list displays with the Front Loader ranges. Double-click *FrontLoaderHours*.
   d. Type) (the closing parenthesis).
   e. Press Enter.

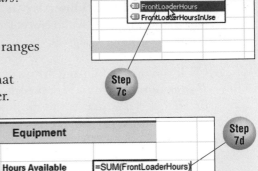

8. Complete steps similar to those in Step 7 to insert ranges in the following cells:
   a. Make cell C5 active and then insert a formula that inserts the total in-use hours for the Front Loader.
   b. Make cell C8 active and then insert a formula that inserts the total hours available for the Tractor.
   c. Make cell C9 active and then insert a formula that inserts the total in-use hours for the Tractor.
   d. Make cell C12 active and then insert a formula that inserts the total hours available for the Forklift.
   e. Make cell C13 active and then insert a formula that inserts the total in-use hours for the Forklift.
   f. Make cell C16 active and then insert a formula that inserts the total hours available for the Backhoe.
   g. Make cell C17 active and then insert a formula that inserts the total in-use hours for the Backhoe.
9. Make the following changes to specific worksheets:
   a. Click the Front Loader tab and then change the number in cell E4 from *415* to *426* and change the number in cell C6 from *6* to *14*.
   b. Click the Forklift tab and then change the number in cells E4 from *415* to *426* and change the number in cell D8 from *4* to *12*.
10. Select all of the worksheet tabs and then create a footer that prints your name at the left side of each worksheet, the page number in the middle, and the current date at the right side of each worksheet.
11. Save, print, and then close **ExcelL1_C6_P2.xlsx**.

Project 3 — Save Workbooks in Various Formats

You will open a workbook and then save it in a previous version of Excel, in text format, and in PDF format.

Saving a Workbook in a Different Format

When you save a workbook, the workbook is automatically saved as an Excel workbook with the *.xlsx* file extension. If you need to share a workbook with someone who is using a different version of Excel, or someone who will open it in an application other than Excel, save the workbook in another format. You can also save an Excel workbook as a Web page and in text format. Save a workbook in a different format with options from the Office button Save As side menu or with the *Save as type* option at the Save As dialog box.

Saving a Workbook in a Previous Version of Excel

If you create workbooks that others will open in a previous version of Excel, consider saving the workbook in the Excel 97-2003 format. If you save a workbook in a previous version, the workbook name displays in the title bar followed by the words *[Compatibility Mode]*. In this mode, some Excel 2007 features may not be available.

You can save a workbook in a previous version with the Office button Save As side menu or with the *Save as type* option at the Save As dialog box. To save using the side menu, click the Office button, point to the *Save As* option, and then click *Excel 97-2003 Workbook* at the side menu as shown in Figure 6.4. At the Save As dialog box, type the name for the workbook, and then click the Save button. Note also that some file formats save the active worksheet and others save the entire workbook. If you want to save a specific worksheet, hide the other worksheets and then save.

QUICK STEPS

Save Workbook in Different Format
1. Click Office button.
2. Point to *Save As*.
3. Click desired format type.
4. Type name for workbook.
5. Click Save button.
OR
1. Click Office button, *Save As*.
2. Type name for workbook.
3. Click down-pointing arrow at right of *Save as type* option box.
4. Click desired type in drop-down list.
5. Click Save button.

Figure 6.4 Save As Side Menu

Click the Excel 97–2003 Workbook option to save a workbook in a previous version of Excel.

If the PDF download is installed on your computer, the PDF or XPS option is available.

1. Open **ExcelC06Project03.xlsx**.
2. Click the Office button, point to the *Save As* option, and then click the *Excel 97-2003 Workbook* option that displays in the side menu.
3. At the Save As dialog box with the *Save as type* option changed to *Excel 97-2003 Workbook (*.xls)*, type ExcelL1_C6_P3_xlsformat in the *File name* text box and then press Enter.

Step 2

Step 3

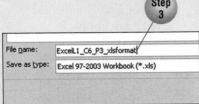

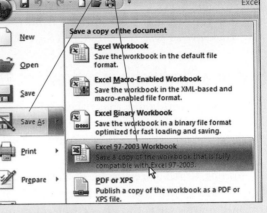

4. At the Compatibility Checker dialog box, click Continue.
5. Close **ExcelL1_C6_P3_xlsformat.xls**.
6. Open **ExcelL1_C6_P3_xlsformat.xls** and then notice that *[Compatibility Mode]* displays after the workbook title at the top of the screen.
7. Close **ExcelL1_C6_P3_xlsformat.xls**.

Saving a Workbook in Text Format

Along with the Save As side menu, you can also save workbooks in different formats with options at the *Save as type* drop-down list at the Save As dialog box. In Project 3b, you will save an Excel worksheet as a text file with tab delimiters.

1. Open **ExcelC06Project03.xlsx**.
2. Click the Office button and then click *Save As*.
3. At the Save As dialog box, type ExcelL1_C6_P3tab in the *File name* text box.
4. Click the down-pointing arrow at the right side of the *Save as type* list box and then click *Text (Tab delimited) (*.txt)* at the drop-down list. (You will need to scroll down the list box to display this option.)

Step 3

Step 4

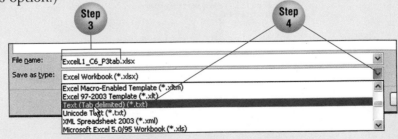

5. Click the Save button.
6. At the message telling you that the selected file type does not support workbooks that contain multiple worksheets, click OK.
7. At the message telling you that the file may contain features that are not compatible with Text (Tab delimited) and asking if you want to keep the workbook in the format, click Yes.
8. Close the workbook. (At the message asking if you want to save the changes, click Yes. At the message asking if you want to keep the workbook in the format, click Yes.)
9. Open Microsoft Word.
10. Display the Open dialog box, change the *Files of type* to *All Files (*.*)* and then open **ExcelL1_C6_P3tab.txt**.
11. Close **ExcelL1_C6_P3tab.txt** and then exit Word.

Saving in PDF Format

The portable document format (PDF) was developed by Adobe Systems and is a format that captures all of the elements of a file as an electronic image. You can view a PDF file on any application on any computer making this format the most widely used for transferring files to other users. A workbook saved in PDF format is printer friendly and most, if not all, of the workbook's original appearance is maintained.

Before saving an Excel workbook in PDF format, you must install an add-in download from the Microsoft Web site. To determine whether or not the download is installed, click the Office button and then point to the *Save As* option. If the add-in is installed, you will see the option *PDF or XPS* in the side menu with the following text below the option: *Publish a copy of the document as a PDF or XPS file*. If the add-in is not downloaded, you will see the option *Find add-ins for other file formats* in the side menu with the following text below the option: *Learn about add-ins to save to other formats such as PDF or XPS*.

If the add-in is not downloaded and you want to download it, click the *Find add-ins for other file formats* option at the side menu. This displays the Excel Help window with information on how to download the add-in. The steps in Project 3c assume that the PDF add-in is downloaded and installed and available on your computer. Before completing Project 3c, check with your instructor.

When you click the *PDF or XPS* option at the Save As side menu, the Save As dialog box displays with *PDF (*.pdf)* specified as the *Save as type* option. At this dialog box, type a name in the *File name* text box and then click the Publish button. By default, the workbook will open in PDF format in Adobe Reader. The Adobe Reader application is designed to view your workbook. You will be able to navigate in the workbook but you will not be able to make any changes to the workbook. After viewing the workbook in Adobe Reader, click the Close button located in the upper right corner of the Adobe Reader window. This closes the workbook and also closed Adobe Reader.

You can open your PDF file in Adobe Reader or in your browser window. To open a PDF workbook in your browser window, click File on the browser Menu bar and then click *Open*. (If the Menu bar is not visible, click the Tools button located in the upper right corner of the window and then click *Menu Bar* at the drop-down list.) At the Open dialog box, browse to the folder containing your PDF workbook and then double-click the workbook. You may need to change the *Files of type* option to *All Files (*.*)*.

1. Open **ExcelC06Project03.xlsx**.
2. Save the workbook in PDF file format by completing the following steps:
   a. Click the Office button and then point to the *Save As* option.
   b. Click *PDF or XPS* in the side menu. (If this option does not display, the PDF add-in download has not been installed.)

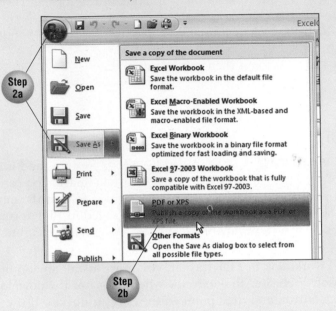

c. At the Save As dialog box with the *Save as type* option set at *PDF (*.pdf)*, click the Publish button.

3. Scroll through the workbook in Adobe Reader.
4. Click the Close button located in the upper right corner of the window to close Adobe Reader.
5. Close **ExcelC06Project03.xlsx**.

Project **4** Create and Apply Styles to a Payroll Workbook

You will open a payroll workbook, define styles and apply styles and then modify the styles. You will also copy the styles to another workbook and then apply the styles in the new workbook.

Formatting with Cell Styles

In Chapter 1 you learned how to apply formatting to cells with the Cell Styles button in the Styles group in the Home tab. A style is a predefined set of formatting attributes such as font, font size, alignment, borders, shading, and so forth. You can apply the styles from the Cell Styles drop-down gallery or create your own style. Using a style to apply formatting has several advantages. A style helps to ensure consistent formatting from one worksheet to another. Once you define all attributes for a particular style, you do not have to redefine them again. If you need to change the formatting, change the style and all cells formatted with that style automatically reflect the change.

Defining a Cell Style

Two basic methods are available for defining your own cell style. You can define a style with formats already applied to a cell or you can display the Style dialog box, click the Format button, and then choose formatting options at the Format Cells dialog box. Styles you create are only available in the workbook in which they are created. To define a style with existing formatting, select the cell or cells containing the desired formatting, click the Cell Styles button in the Styles group in the Home tab, and then click the *New Cell Style* option located toward the bottom of the drop-down gallery. At the Style dialog box, shown in Figure 6.5, type a name for the new style in the *Style name* text box, and then click OK to close the dialog box.

QUICK STEPS

Define a Cell Style with Existing Formatting
1. Select cell containing formatting.
2. Click Cell Styles button.
3. Click *New Cell Style*.
4. Type name for new style.
5. Click OK.

Define a Style
1. Click in a blank cell.
2. Click Cell Styles button.
3. Click *New Cell Style*.
4. Type name for new style.
5. Click Format button.
6. Choose formatting options.
7. Click OK to close Format Cells dialog box.
8. Click OK to close Style dialog box.

HINT
Cell styles are based on the workbook theme.

Cell Styles ▾

Figure 6.5 Style Dialog Box

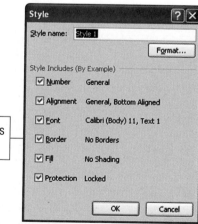

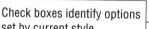
Check boxes identify options set by current style.

Project **4a** | **Defining a Style**

1. Open **ExcelC06Project04.xlsx** and then save the workbook and name it **ExcelL1_C6_P4**.
2. Make Sheet1 the active worksheet and then insert the necessary formulas to calculate gross pay, withholding tax amount, Social Security tax amount, and net pay. *Hint: Refer to Project 5c in Chapter 2 for assistance.*
3. Make Sheet2 the active worksheet and then insert a formula that calculates the amount due.

4. Make Sheet3 the active worksheet and then insert a formula in the *Due Date* column that inserts the purchase date plus the number of days in the *Terms* column. **Hint: Refer to Project 3c in Chapter 2 for assistance.**
5. Define a style named *C06Title* with the formatting in cell A1 by completing the following steps:
   a. Make *Sheet1* active and then make cell A1 active.
   b. Click the Cell Styles button in the Styles group in the Home tab and then click the *New Cell Style* option located toward the bottom of the drop-down gallery.

   c. At the Style dialog box, type **C06Title** in the *Style name* text box.
   d. Click OK.
6. Save **ExcelL1_C6_P4.xlsx**.

QUICK STEPS

Apply a Style
1. Select cells.
2. Click Cell Styles button.
3. Click desired style at drop-down gallery.

Applying a Style

To apply a style, select the cells you want to format, click the Cell Styles button in the Styles group, and then click the desired style at the drop-down gallery. The styles you create display at the top of the drop-down gallery.

Project 4b   Applying a Style

1. With **ExcelL1_C6_P4.xlsx** open, apply the C06Title style to cell A1 by completing the following steps:
   a. Make sure cell A1 is the active cell. (Even though cell A1 is already formatted, the style has not been applied to it. Later, you will modify the style and the style must be applied to the cell for the change to affect it.)
   b. Click the Cell Styles button in the Styles group in the Home tab.
   c. Click the *C06Title* style in the *Custom* section located toward the top of the drop-down gallery.

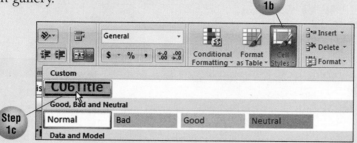

Step 1b

Step 1c

2. Apply the C06Title style to other cells by completing the following steps:
   a. Click the Sheet2 tab.
   b. Make cell A1 active.
   c. Click the Cell Styles button in the Styles group and then click the *C06Title* style at the drop-down gallery. (Notice that the style did not apply the row height formatting. The style applies only cell formatting.)
   d. Click the Sheet3 tab.
   e. Make cell A1 active.
   f. Click the Cell Styles button and then click the *C06Title* style at the drop-down gallery.
   g. Click the Sheet1 tab.
3. Save **ExcelL1_C6_P4.xlsx**.

In addition to defining a style based on cell formatting, you can also define a new style without first applying the formatting. To do this, you would display the Style dialog box, type a name for the new style, and then click the Format button. At the Format Cells dialog box, apply any desired formatting and then click OK to close the dialog box. At the Style dialog box, remove the check mark from any formatting that you do not want included in the style and then click OK to close the Style dialog box.

Project 4c   Defining a Style without First Applying Formatting

1. With **ExcelL1_C6_P4.xlsx** open, define a new style named *C06Subtitle* without first applying the formatting by completing the following steps:
   a. With Sheet1 active, click in any empty cell.
   b. Click the Cell Styles button in the Styles group and then click *New Cell Style* at the drop-down gallery.

c. At the Style dialog box, type **C06Subtitle** in the *Style name* text box.

d. Click the Format button in the Style dialog box.

e. At the Format Cells dialog box, click the Font tab.

f. At the Format Cells dialog box with the Font tab selected, change the font to Candara, the font style to bold, the size to 12, and the color to white.

g. Click the Fill tab.

h. Click the bottom color in the green column as shown at the right.

i. Click the Alignment tab.

j. Change the Horizontal alignment to Center.

k. Click OK to close the Format Cells dialog box.

l. Click OK to close the Style dialog box.

2. Apply the C06Subtitle style by completing the following steps:

a. Make cell A2 active.

b. Click the Cell Styles button and then click the *C06Subtitle* style located toward the top of the drop-down gallery in the *Custom* section.

c. Click the Sheet2 tab.

d. Make cell A2 active.

e. Click the Cell Styles button and then click the *C06Subtitle* style.

f. Click the Sheet3 tab.

g. Make cell A2 active.

h. Click the Cell Styles button and then click the *C06Subtitle* style.

i. Click the Sheet1 tab.

3. Apply the following predesigned cell styles:

a. Select cells A3 through G3.

b. Click the Cell Styles button and then click the *Heading 3* style at the drop-down gallery.

c. Select cells A5 through G5.

d. Click the Cell Styles button and then click the *20% - Accent3* style.

e. Apply the 20% - Accent3 style to cells A7 through G7 and cells A9 through G9.

f. Click the Sheet2 tab.

g. Select cells A3 through F3 and then apply the Heading 3 style.

h. Select cells A5 through F5 and then apply the 20% - Accent3 style.

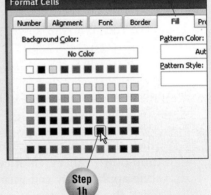

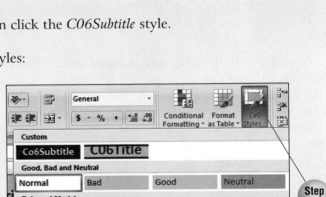

i. Apply the 20% - Accent3 style to every other row of cells (A7 through F7, A9 through F9, and so on, finishing with A17 through F17).
   j. Click the Sheet3 tab.
   k. Select cells A3 through F3 and then apply the Heading 3 style.
   l. Apply the 20% - Accent3 style to A5 through F5, A7 through F7, and A9 through F9.
4. Make Sheet2 active and then change the height of row 1 to 36.00 (48 pixels).
5. Make Sheet3 active and then change the height of row 1 to 36.00 (48 pixels).
6. Make Sheet1 active.
7. Save **ExcelL1_C6_P4.xlsx** and then print only the first worksheet.

Modifying a Style

One of the advantages to formatting with a style is that you can modify the formatting of the style and all cells formatted with that style automatically reflect the change. You can modify a style you create or one of the predesigned styles provided by Word. When you modify a predesigned style, only the style in the current workbook is affected. If you open a blank workbook, the cell styles available are the default styles.

   To modify a style, click the Cell Styles button in the Styles group in the Home tab and then right-click the desired style at the drop-down gallery. At the shortcut menu that displays, click *Modify*. At the Style dialog box, click the Format button. Make the desired formatting changes at the Format Cells dialog box and then click OK. Click OK to close the Style dialog box and any cells formatted with the specific style are automatically updated.

QUICK STEPS

Modify a Style
1. Click Cell Styles button.
2. Right-click desired style at drop-down gallery.
3. Click *Modify*.
4. Click Format button.
5. Make desired formatting changes.
6. Click OK to close Format Cells dialog box.
7. Click OK to close Style dialog box.

Project 4d **Modifying Styles**

1. With **ExcelL1_C6_P4.xlsx** open, modify the C06Title style by completing the following steps:
   a. Click in any empty cell.
   b. Click the Cell Styles button in the Styles group.
   c. At the drop-down gallery, right-click on the *C06Title* style located toward the top of the gallery in the *Custom* section, and then click Modify.
   d. At the Style dialog box, click the Format button.
   e. At the Format Cells dialog box, click the Font tab, and then change the font to Candara.

Step 1b

Step 1c

f. Click the Alignment tab.

g. Click the down-pointing arrow to the right of the *Vertical* option box, and then click *Center* at the drop-down list.

h. Click the Fill tab.

i. Click the light turquoise fill color as shown at the right.

j. Click OK to close the Format Cells dialog box.

k. Click OK to close the Style dialog box.

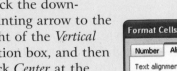

2. Modify the C06Subtitle style by completing the following steps:

a. Click in any empty cell.

b. Click the Cell Styles button in the Styles group.

c. At the drop-down gallery, right-click on the *C06Subtitle* style located toward the top of the gallery in the *Custom* section, and then click *Modify*.

d. At the Style dialog box, click the Format button.

e. At the Format Cells dialog box, click the Font tab, and then change the font to Calibri.

f. Click the Fill tab.

g. Click the dark turquoise fill color as shown at the right.

h. Click OK to close the Format Cells dialog box.

i. Click OK to close the Style dialog box.

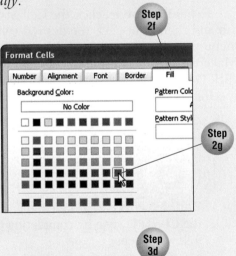

3. Modify the predefined 20% - Accent3 style by completing the following steps:

a. Click the Cell Styles button in the Styles group.

b. At the drop-down gallery, right-click on the *20% - Accent3* style and then click *Modify*.

c. At the Style dialog box, click the Format button.

d. At the Format Cells dialog box, click the Fill tab.

e. Click the light turquoise fill color as shown at the right.

f. Click OK to close the Format Cells dialog box.

g. Click OK to close the Style dialog box.

4. Click each sheet tab and notice the formatting changes made by the modified styles.

5. Change the name of Sheet1 to *Weekly Payroll*, the name of Sheet2 to *Invoices*, and the name of Sheet3 to *Overdue Accounts*.

6. Apply a different color to each of the three worksheet tabs.

7. Save and then print all the worksheets in **ExcelL1_C6_P4.xlsx**.

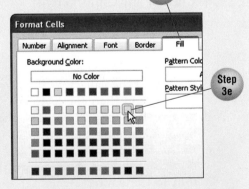

Copying Styles to Another Workbook

Styles you define are saved with the workbook in which they are created. You can, however, copy styles from one workbook to another. To do this, open the workbook containing the styles you want to copy and open the workbook into which you want to copy the styles. Click the Cell Styles button in the Styles group in the Home tab, and then click the *Merge Styles* option located at the bottom of the drop-down gallery. At the Merge Styles dialog box shown in Figure 6.6, double-click the name of the workbook that contains the styles you want to copy, and then click OK.

Figure 6.6 Merge Styles Dialog Box

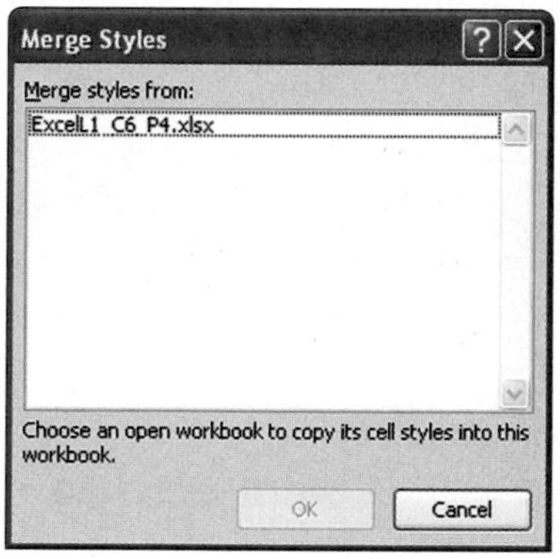

QUICK STEPS

Copy Styles to Another Workbook
1. Open workbook containing desired styles.
2. Click Cell Styles button.
3. Click *Merge Styles* option.
4. Double-click name of workbook that contains styles you want to copy.

Remove a Style
1. Select cells formatted with style you want removed.
2. Click Cell Styles button.
3. Click *Normal* at drop-down gallery.

Delete a Style
1. Click Cell Styles button.
2. Right-click desired style to delete.
3. Click *Delete* at shortcut menu.

Removing a Style

If you apply a style to text and then decide you do not want the formatting applied, return the formatting to Normal, which is the default formatting. To do this, select the cells formatted with the style you want to remove, click the Cell Styles button, and then click *Normal* at the drop-down gallery.

HINT
The Undo command will not reverse the effects of the Merge Styles dialog box.

Deleting a Style

To delete a style, click the Cell Styles button in the Styles group in the Home tab. At the drop-down gallery that displays, right-click the style you want to delete, and then click *Delete* at the shortcut menu. Formatting applied by the deleted style is removed from cells in the workbook.

HINT
You cannot delete the Normal style.

Project 4e Copying and Removing Styles

1. With **ExcelL1_C6_P4.xlsx** open, open **ExcelC06O'RourkePlans.xlsx**.
2. Save the workbook with Save As and name it **ExcelL1_C6_P4b**.

3. Copy the styles in **ExcelL1_C6_P4.xlsx** into **ExcelL1_C6_P4b.xlsx** by completing the following steps:

   a. Click the Cell Styles button in the Styles group in the Home tab.

   b. Click the *Merge Styles* option located toward the bottom of the drop-down gallery.

   c. At the Merge Styles dialog box, double-click **ExcelL1_C6_P4.xlsx** in the *Merge styles from* list box.

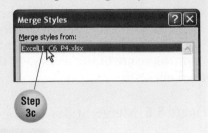

Step 3c

   d. At the message that displays asking if you want to merge styles that have the same names, click Yes.

4. Apply the C06Title style to cell A1 and the C06Subtitle style to cell A2.

5. Increase the height of row 1 to 36.00 (48 pixels).

6. Insert the required formulas in the workbook. *Hint: Refer to Project 3a of Chapter 2 for assistance.*

7. If neccessary, adjust column widths so all text is visible in cells.

8. Save, print, and then close **ExcelL1_C6_P4b.xlsx**.

9. Close **ExcelL1_C6_P4.xlsx**.

Project 5   Insert, Modify, and Print Comments in an Equipment Rental Workbook

You will open an equipment rental workbook and then insert, edit, delete and print comments.

Inserting Comments

QUICK STEPS

Insert a Comment
1. Click in desired cell.
2. Click Review tab.
3. Click New Comment button.
4. Type comment.
OR
1. Right-click desired cell.
2. Click *Insert Comment*.
3. Type comment.

If you want to make comments in a worksheet, or if a reviewer wants to make comments in a worksheet prepared by someone else, insert a comment. A comment is useful for providing specific instructions, identifying critical information, or for multiple individuals reviewing the same worksheet to insert comments. Some employees in a company may be part of a *workgroup*, which is a networked collection of computers sharing files, printers, and other resources. In a workgroup, you may collaborate with coworkers on a specific workbook. Comments provide a method for reviewing the workbook and responding to others in the workgroup.

Inserting a Comment

HINT
You can resize and/or move overlapping comments.

Insert a comment by clicking the Review tab and then clicking the New Comment button in the Comments group. This displays a color shaded box with the user's name inside. Type the desired information or comment in this comment box and then click outside the comment box. A small, red triangle appears in the upper right corner of a cell containing a comment. You can also insert a comment by right-clicking a cell and then clicking *Insert Comment* at the shortcut menu.

New Comment

Displaying a Comment

Hover the mouse over a cell containing a comment and the comment box displays. You can also display comments by right-clicking the cell containing a comment and then clicking *Show/Hide Comments* at the shortcut menu. Turn on the display of all comments by clicking the Show All Comments button in the Comments group in the Review tab. Turn on the display of an individual comment by making the cell active and then clicking the Show/Hide Comment button in the Comments group in the Review tab. Hide the display of an individual comment by clicking the same button. Move to comments in a worksheet by clicking the Next or Previous buttons in the Comments group in the Review tab.

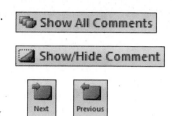

Project 5a — Inserting and Displaying Comments

1. Open **ExcelC06Project05.xlsx**.
2. Save the workbook with Save As and name it **ExcelL1_C6_P5**.
3. Insert a formula in cell H3 that multiplies the rate by the hours and then copy the formula down to cells H4 through H16. (When you copy the formula, click the Auto Fill Options button and then click *Fill Without Formatting* at the drop-down list.)
4. Make cell H17 active and then insert a formula that sums the amounts in cells H3 through H16.
5. Insert a comment by completing the following steps:
   a. Click cell F3 to make it active.
   b. Click the Review tab.
   c. Click the New Comment button in the Comments group.
   d. In the comment box, type Bill Lakeside Trucking for only 7 hours for the backhoe and front loader on May 1.
   e. Click outside the comment box.
6. Insert another comment by completing the following steps:
   a. Click cell C6 to make it active.
   b. Click the New Comment button in the Comments group.
   c. In the comment box, type I think Country Electrical has changed their name to Northwest Electrical.
   d. Click outside the comment box.

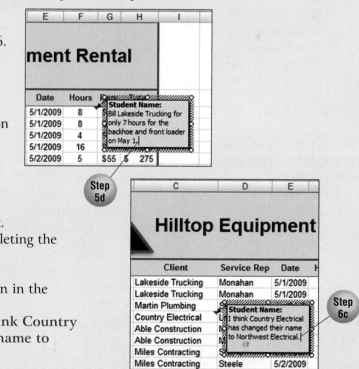

7. Assume that more than one person is reviewing and commenting on this worksheet. Change the user name and then insert additional comments by completing the following steps:

a. Click the Office button and then click the Excel Options button located toward the bottom of the drop-down list.

b. At the Excel Options dialog box make sure *Popular* is selected in the left panel.

c. Select the current name in the *User name* text box (remember the name you are selecting) and then type **Jean Coen.**

d. Click OK to close the dialog box.

e. Click cell D11 to make it active.

f. Click the New Comment button in the Comments group.

g. In the comment box, type **This rental should be credited to Monahan instead of Leuke.**

h. Click outside the comment box.

i. Click cell G11 to make it active.

j. Click the New Comment button in the Comments group.

k. In the comment box, type **The hourly rental for the pressure sprayer is $25.**

l. Click outside the comment box.

8. Complete steps similar to those in Steps 7a through 7d to return the user name back to the original name (the name that displayed before you changed it to *Jean Coen*).

9. Click the Show All Comments button to turn on the display of all comments.

10. Save **ExcelL1_C6_P5.xlsx.**

Step 7b

Step 7c

HINT
Display the document in Print Preview to view how comments will print.

Printing a Comment

By default, comments do not print. If you want comments to print, use the *Comments* option at the Page Setup dialog box with the Sheet tab selected. Display this dialog box by clicking the Page Layout tab, clicking the Page Setup group dialog box launcher, and then clicking the Sheet tab. Click the down-pointing arrow at the right side of the *Comments* option box. At the drop-down list that displays, choose *At end of sheet* to print comments on the page after cell contents, or choose the *As displayed on sheet* option to print the comments in the comment box in the worksheet.

Project 5b Printing Comments

1. With **ExcelL1_C6_P5.xlsx** open, click the Page Layout tab.
2. Click the Orientation button in the Page Setup group and then click *Landscape* at the drop-down list.
3. Click the Page Setup group dialog box launcher.
4. At the Page Setup dialog box, click the Sheet tab.
5. Click the down-pointing arrow at the right side of the *Comments* option box and then click *As displayed on sheet*.
6. Click the Print button that displays toward the bottom of the dialog box and then click OK at the Print dialog box.
7. Turn off the display of comments by clicking the Review tab and then clicking the Show All Comments button.
8. Save **ExcelL1_C6_P5.xlsx**.

Step 4

Step 5

Step 6

Editing a Comment

To edit a comment, click the cell containing the comment and then click the Edit Comment button in the Comments group in the Review tab. (The New Comment button changes to the Edit Comment button when the active cell contains a comment.) You can also edit a comment by right-clicking the cell containing the comment and then clicking *Edit Comment* at the shortcut menu.

Deleting a Comment

Cell comments exist in addition to data in a cell. Deleting data in a cell does not delete the comment. To delete a comment, click the cell containing the comment and then click the Delete button in the Comments group in the Review tab. You can also delete a comment by right-clicking the cell containing the comment and then clicking *Delete Comment* at the shortcut menu.

1. With **ExcelL1_C6_P5.xlsx** open, display comments by completing the following steps:
   a. Click cell A3 to make it the active cell.
   b. Click the Review tab.
   c. Click the Next button in the Comments group.
   d. Read the comment and then click the Next button.
   e. Continue clicking the Next button until a message displays telling you that Microsoft Excel has reached the end of the workbook and asking if you want to continue reviewing from the beginning of the workbook. At this message, click the Cancel button.
   f. Click outside the comment box.

2. Edit a comment by completing the following steps:
   a. Click cell D11 to make it active.
   b. Click the Edit Comment button.
   c. Edit the comment so it displays as *This rental should be credited to Steele instead of Leuke.*

3. Delete a comment by completing the following steps:
   a. Click cell C6 to make it active.
   b. Click the Delete button in the Comments group.

4. Respond to the comments by making the following changes:
   a. Change the contents of F3 from *8* to *7*.
   b. Change the contents of F4 from *8* to *7*.
   c. Change the contents of D11 from *Leuke* to *Steele*.
   d. Change the contents of G11 from *$20* to *$25*.

5. Print the worksheet and the comments by completing the following steps:
   a. Click the Page Layout tab.
   b. Click the Page Setup group dialog box launcher.
   c. At the Page Setup dialog box, click the Sheet tab.
   d. Click the down-pointing arrow at the right side of the *Comments* option and then click *At end of sheet*.
   e. Click the Print button that displays toward the bottom of the dialog box.
   f. At the Print dialog box, click OK. (The worksheet will print on one page and the comments will print on a second page.)

6. Save and then close **ExcelL1_C6_P5.xlsx**.

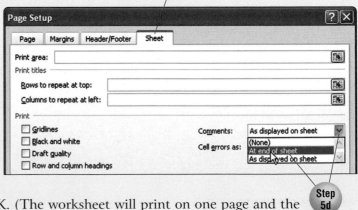

Project 6 · Create a Billing Statement Workbook Using a Template

You will open a Billing Statement template provided by Excel, add data, save it as an Excel workbook, and then print the workbook.

Using Excel Templates

Excel has included a number of *template* worksheet forms formatted for specific uses. For example, Excel has provided template forms for a balance sheet, billing statement, loan amortization, sales invoice, and timecard. To view the templates available, click the Office button and then click *New* at the drop-down list. At the New Workbook dialog box shown in Figure 6.7, click the *Installed Templates* option in the *Templates* section. This displays the installed templates in the middle panel of the dialog box. Note that the first time you download a template, Microsoft checks to determine if you are using a genuine Office product.

QUICK STEPS

Use an Excel Template
1. Click Office button, *New*.
2. Click *Installed Templates* option.
3. Double-click desired template.

Figure 6.7 New Workbook Dialog Box

> Click the *Installed Templates* option to display available templates.

Entering Data in a Template

Templates contain unique areas where information is entered at the keyboard. For example, in the Billing Statement template shown in Figure 6.8, you enter information such as the customer name, address, and telephone number, and also the date, time, description, amount, payment, and balance of items. To enter information in the appropriate location, position the mouse pointer (white plus sign) in the location where you want to type data and then click the left mouse button. After typing the data, click the next location. You can also move the insertion point to another cell using the commands learned in Chapter 1. For example, press the Tab key to make the next cell active, press Shift + Tab to make the previous cell active.

Figure 6.8 Billing Statement Template

Click in a cell and then insert the specified data.

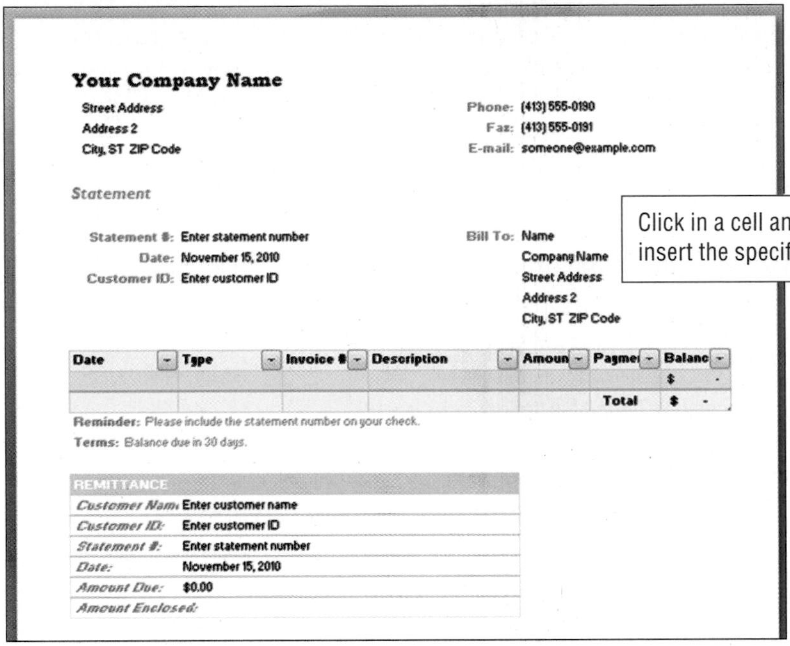

Project ⑥   Preparing a Billing Statement Using a Template

1. Click the Office button and then click *New* at the drop-down list.
2. At the New Workbook dialog box, click the *Installed Templates* option in the *Templates* section.
3. Double-click the *Billing Statement* template in the *Installed Templates* section of the dialog box.

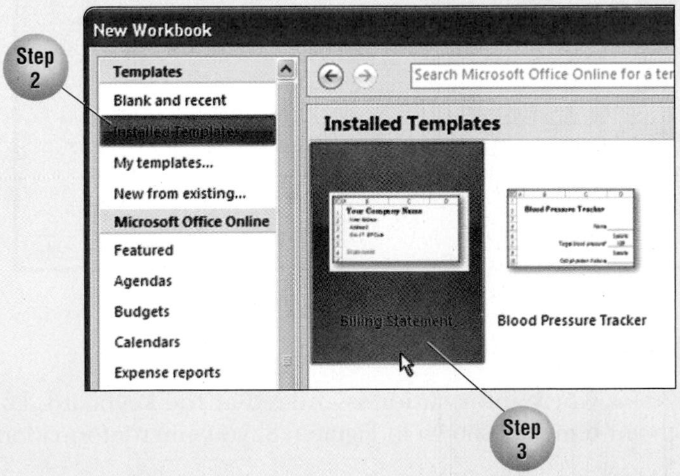

4. With cell B1 active, type **IN-FLOW SYSTEMS**.
5. Click the text *Street Address* (cell B2) and then type **320 Milander Way**.
6. Click in the specified location (cell) and then type the text indicated:

    Address 2 (cell B3) = **P.O. Box 2300**
    City, ST ZIP Code (cell B4) = **Boston, MA 02188**
    Phone (cell F2) = **(617) 555-3900**
    Fax (cell F3) = **(617) 555-3945**
    Statement # (cell C8) = **5432**
    Customer ID (cell C10) = **25-345**
    Name (cell F8) = **Aidan Mackenzie**
    Company Name (cell F9) = **Stanfield Enterprises**
    Street Address (cell F10) = **9921 South 42nd Avenue**
    Address 2 (cell F11) = **P.O. Box 5540**
    City, ST ZIP Code (cell F12) = **Boston, MA 02193**
    Date (cell B15) = (insert current date in numbers as *##/##/####*)
    Type (cell C15) = **System Unit**
    Invoice # (cell D15) = **7452**
    Description (cell E15) = **Calibration Unit**
    Amount (cell F15) = **950**
    Payment (cell G15) = **200**
    Customer Name (cell C21) = **Stanfield Enterprises**
    Amount Enclosed (C26) = **750**

Steps 4–6

IN-FLOW SYSTEMS

320 Milander Way
P.O. Box 2300
Boston, MA 02188

Phone: (617) 555-3900
Fax: (617) 555-3945
E-mail: someone@example.com

Statement

Statement #:	5432		Bill To:	Aidan Mackenzie
Date:	November 15, 2010			Stanfield Enterprises
Customer ID:	25-345			9921 South 42nd Avenue
				P.O. Box 5540
				Boston, MA 02193

Date ▼	Type ▼	Invoice # ▼	Description ▼	Amount ▼	Payment ▼	Balance ▼
11/15/2010	System Unit	7452	Calibration Unit	$ 950.00	$ 200.00	$ 750.00
					Total	$ 750.00

Reminder: Please include the statement number on your check.

Terms: Balance due in 30 days.

REMITTANCE	
Customer Name:	Stanfield Enterprises
Customer ID:	25-345
Statement #:	5432
Date:	November 15, 2010
Amount Due:	$750.00
Amount Enclosed:	$750.00

7. Save the completed invoice and name it **ExcelL1_C6_P6**.
8. Print and then close **ExcelL1_C6_P6.xlsx**.

CHAPTER summary

- Perform file management tasks such as copying, moving, printing, and renaming workbooks and creating a new folder and renaming a folder at the Open or Save As dialog boxes.
- Create a new folder by clicking the Create New Folder button located on the dialog box toolbar at the Open dialog box or Save As dialog box.
- Rename a folder with the *Rename* option from the Tools button drop-down list or with a shortcut menu.
- To select adjacent workbooks in the Open dialog box, click the first workbook, hold down the Shift key, and then click the last workbook. To select nonadjacent workbooks, click the first workbook, hold down the Ctrl key, and then click any desired workbooks.
- To delete a workbook, use the Delete button on the Open or Save As dialog box toolbar, the *Delete* option at the Tools button drop-down list, or with a shortcut menu option.
- Workbooks deleted from the hard drive are automatically sent to the Windows Recycle Bin where they can be restored or permanently deleted.
- Create a copy of an existing workbook by opening the workbook and then using the *Save As* command to assign the workbook a different file name.
- Use the *Copy* and *Paste* options from the shortcut menu at the Open (or Save As) dialog box to copy a workbook from one folder to another folder or drive.
- When you copy a workbook into the same folder from which it originates, Excel names the duplicated workbook(s) "Copy of xxx" (where *xxx* is the original workbook name).
- Use the *Send To* option from the shortcut menu to send a copy of a workbook to another drive or folder.
- Remove a workbook from a folder or drive and insert it in another folder or drive using the *Cut* and *Paste* options from the shortcut menu.
- Use the *Rename* option from the Tools button drop-down list or the shortcut menu to give a workbook a different name.
- Print multiple workbooks by selecting the desired workbooks at the Print dialog box, clicking the Tools button, and then clicking *Print* at the drop-down list.
- To move or copy a worksheet to another existing workbook, open both the source and the destination workbook and then open the Move or Copy dialog box.
- Save a workbook in a different format with options from the Office button Save As side menu or with the *Save as type* option at the Save As dialog box. Click the down-pointing arrow at the right side of the *Save as type* option and a drop-down list displays with the available formats.
- Automate the formatting of cells in a workbook by defining and then applying styles. A style is a predefined set of formatting attributes.
- A style helps to ensure consistent formatting from one worksheet to another. All formatting attributes for a particular style are defined only once. Define a style with formats already applied to a cell or display the Style dialog box, click the Format button, and then choose formatting options at the Format Cells dialog box.

- To apply a style, select the desired cells, click the Cell Styles button in the Styles group in the Home tab, and then click the desired style at the drop-down gallery.

- Modify a style and all cells to which the style is applied automatically reflect the change. To modify a style, click the Cell Styles button in the Styles group in the Home tab, right-click the desired style, and then click *Modify* at the shortcut menu.

- Styles are saved in the workbook in which they are created. Styles can be copied, however, to another workbook. Do this with options at the Merge Styles dialog box.

- Insert comments in a worksheet to provide specific instructions, identify critical information, review a workbook, and respond to others in a workgroup about the workbook.

- Insert, display, edit, and delete comments using buttons in the Comments group in the Review tab.

- By default, comments do not print. To print comments, display the Page Setup dialog box with the Sheet tab selected, and then choose the printing location with the *Comments* option.

- Excel provides preformatted templates for creating forms such as a balance sheet, billing statement, loan amortization, sales invoice, and timecard. Display the available templates by clicking the *Installed Templates* option in the *Templates* section of the New Workbook dialog box.

- Templates contain unique areas where information is entered at the keyboard. These areas vary depending on the template.

COMMANDS review

FEATURE	RIBBON TAB, GROUP	BUTTON, OPTION	OFFICE BUTTON DROP-DOWN LIST	KEYBOARD SHORTCUT
Open dialog box			Open	Ctrl + O
Save As dialog box			Save As	Ctrl + S
Print dialog box			Print	Ctrl + P
Save in PDF format			Save As, PDF or XPS	
Style dialog box	Home, Styles	, New Cell Style		
Merge Styles dialog box	Home, Styles	, Merge Styles		
Insert comment	Review, Comments			Shift + F2
Display all comments	Review, Comments	Show All Comments		
Delete comment	Review, Comments			
Display next comment	Review, Comments			
Display previous comment	Review, Comments			
New Workbook dialog box			New	

CONCEPTS check

Test Your Knowledge

Completion: In the space provided at the right, indicate the correct term, symbol, or command.

1. Perform file management tasks such as copying, moving, or deleting workbooks with options at the Open dialog box or this dialog box.

   SAVE AS

2. Click this button on the Open dialog box toolbar to display the folder that is up a level from the current folder.

   UP ONE LEVEL

3. At the Open dialog box, hold down this key while selecting nonadjacent workbooks.

CTRL

4. Workbooks deleted from the hard drive are automatically sent to this location.

RECYCLE BIN

5. Click the down-pointing arrow at the right side of this option at the Save As dialog box to display a drop-down list of available workbook formats.

SAVE AS TYPE

6. If the PDF format is installed, this option for saving a workbook in PDF file format displays at the Office button Save As side menu.

PDF (or XPS)

7. The Cell Styles button is located in this group in the Home tab.

STYLES GROUP

8. Click the *New Cell Style* option at the Cell Styles button drop-down gallery and this dialog box displays.

STYLE DIALOG BOX

9. A style you create displays in this section of the Cell Styles button drop-down gallery.

CUSTOM

10. Copy styles from one workbook to another with options at this dialog box.

MERGE STYLES

11. This displays in the upper right corner of a cell containing a comment.

RED TRIANGLE

12. The New Comment button is located in the Comments group in this tab.

REVIEW TAB

13. Print comments by choosing the desired printing location with the *Comments* option at the Page Setup dialog box with this tab selected.

SHEET TAB

14. Click this button in the Comments group to display all comments in the worksheet.

SHOW ALL COMMENTS

15. Click this option at the New Workbook dialog box to display available templates.

INSTALLED TEMPLATES

SKILLS check
Demonstrate Your Proficiency

Assessment

1 MANAGE WORKBOOKS

1. Display the Open dialog box with Excel2007L1C6 the active folder.
2. Create a new folder named *O'Rourke* in the Excel2007L1C6 folder.
3. Copy **ExcelC06O'RourkeBudget.xlsx**, **ExcelC06O'RourkePlans.xlsx**, and **ExcelC06Project04.xlsx** to the O'Rourke folder.
4. Display the contents of the O'Rourke folder and then rename **ExcelC06O'RourkeBudget.xlsx** to **EquipmentBudget.xlsx**.
5. Rename **ExcelC06O'RourkePlans.xlsx** to **PurchasePlans.xlsx** in the O'Rourke folder.
6. Change the active folder back to Excel2007L1C6.
7. Delete all of the workbooks in the Excel2007L1C6 folder that begin with *ExcelC05*.
8. Close the Open dialog box.

Assessment

2 MOVE AND COPY WORKSHEETS BETWEEN SALES ANALYSIS WORKBOOKS

1. Open **ExcelC06Assessment02.xlsx**.
2. Save the workbook with Save As and name it **ExcelL1_C6_A2**.
3. Rename Sheet1 to *1st Qtr.*
4. Rename Sheet2 to *Yearly Summary*.
5. Move the Yearly Summary sheet before the 1st Qtr. sheet.
6. Open **ExcelC06DeeringQtrs.xlsx**.
7. Rename Sheet1 to *2nd Qtr.* and then copy it to **ExcelL1_C6_A2.xlsx** (following the 1st Qtr. worksheet).
8. Make **ExcelC06DeeringQtrs.xlsx** active, rename Sheet2 to *3rd Qtr.* and then copy it to **ExcelL1_C6_A2.xlsx** (following the 2nd Qtr. worksheet).
9. Make **ExcelC06DeeringQtrs.xlsx** active and then close it without saving the changes.
10. Open **ExcelC06DeeringFourthQtr.xlsx**.
11. Rename Sheet1 to *4th Qtr.* and then move it to **ExcelL1_C6_A2.xlsx** (following the 3rd Qtr. worksheet).
12. Make **ExcelC06DeeringFourthQtr.xlsx** active and then close it without saving the changes.
13. With **ExcelL1_C6_A2.xlsx** active, make the following changes:
    a. Make 1st Qtr. the active worksheet and then insert a formula to calculate the averages and another to calculate the totals. (Use the Auto Fill Options button to fill without formatting.)
    b. Make 2nd Qtr. the active worksheet and then insert a formula to calculate the averages and another to calculate the totals. (Use the Auto Fill Options button to fill without formatting.)

c. Make 3rd Qtr. the active worksheet and then insert a formula to calculate the averages and another to calculate the totals. (Use the Auto Fill Options button to fill without formatting.)

d. Make 4th Qtr. the active worksheet and then insert a formula to calculate the averages and another to calculate the totals. (Use the Auto Fill Options button to fill without formatting.)

e. Make Yearly Summary the active worksheet and then insert a formula that inserts in cell B4 the average of the amounts in cell E4 for the 1st Qtr., 2nd Qtr., 3rd Qtr., and 4th Qtr. worksheets.

f. Copy the formula in cell B4 down to cells B5 through B9.

g. Make cell B10 active and then insert a formula that calculates the total of cells B4 through B9.

14. Delete the Sheet3 tab.

15. Insert a footer on all worksheets that prints your name at the left, the page number in the middle, and the current date at the right.

16. Horizontally and vertically center the worksheets.

17. Save and then print all of the worksheets in **ExcelL1_C6_A2.xlsx**.

18. Close **ExcelL1_C6_A2.xlsx**.

Assessment

3   DEFINE AND APPLY STYLES TO A PROJECTED EARNINGS WORKBOOK

1. At a blank worksheet, define a style named *C06Heading* that contains the following formatting:
   a. 14-point Cambria bold in dark blue color
   b. Horizontal alignment of Center
   c. Top and bottom border in a dark red color
   d. Light purple fill

2. Define a style named *C06Subheading* that contains the following formatting:
   a. 12-point Cambria bold in dark blue color
   b. Horizontal alignment of Center
   c. Top and bottom border in dark red color
   d. Light purple fill

3. Define a style named *C06Column* that contains the following formatting:
   a. 12-point Cambria in dark blue color
   b. Light purple fill

4. Save the workbook and name it **ExcelL1_C6_A3_Styles**.

5. With **ExcelL1_C6_A3_Styles.xlsx** open, open **ExcelC06Assessment03.xlsx**.

6. Save the workbook with Save As and name it **ExcelL1_C6_A3**.

7. Make cell C6 active and then insert a formula that multiplies the content of cell B6 with the amount in cell B3. (When writing the formula, identify cell B3 as an absolute reference.) Copy the formula down to cells C7 through C17.

8. Copy the styles from **ExcelL1_C6_A3_Styles.xlsx** into **ExcelL1_C6_A3.xlsx**. *Hint: Do this at the Merge Styles dialog box.*

9. Apply the following styles:
   a. Select cells A1 and A2 and then apply the C06Heading style.
   b. Select cells A5 through C5 and then apply the C06Subheading style.
   c. Select cells A6 through A17 and then apply the C06Column style.

10. Save the workbook again and then print **ExcelL1_C6_A3.xlsx**.

11. With **ExcelL1_C6_A3.xlsx** open, modify the following styles:
    a. Modify the C06Heading style so it changes the font color to dark purple (instead of dark blue), changes the vertical alignment to Center, and inserts a top and bottom border in dark purple (instead of dark red).
    b. Modify the C06Subheading style so it changes the font color to dark purple (instead of dark blue) and inserts a top and bottom border in dark purple (instead of dark red).
    c. Modify the C06Column style so it changes the font color to dark purple (instead of dark blue). Leave all of the other formatting attributes.
12. Save the workbook and then print **ExcelL1_C6_A3.xlsx**.
13. Close **ExcelL1_C6_A3.xlsx** and then close **ExcelL1_C6_A3_Styles.xlsx** without saving the changes.

Assessment

4   INSERT, DELETE AND PRINT COMMENTS IN A TRAVEL WORKBOOK

1. Open **ExcelC06Asessment04.xlsx**.
2. Save the workbook with Save As and name it **ExcelL1_C6_A4.xlsx**.
3. Insert the following comments in the specified cells:

    B7   =   **Should we include Sun Valley, Idaho, as a destination?**
    B12   =   **Please include the current exchange rate.**
    G8   =   **What other airlines fly into Aspen, Colorado?**
4. Save **ExcelL1_C6_A4.xlsx**.
5. Turn on the display of all comments.
6. Print the worksheet in landscape orientation with the comments as displayed on the worksheet.
7. Turn off the display of all comments.
8. Delete the comment in cell B12.
9. Print the worksheet again with the comments printed at the end of the worksheet. (The comments will print on a separate page from the worksheet.)
10. Save and then close **ExcelL1_C6_A4.xlsx**.

Assessment

5   APPLY CONDITIONAL FORMATTING TO A SALES WORKBOOK

1. Use Excel Help files to learn more about conditional formatting.
2. Open **ExcelC06Assessment05.xlsx** and then save the workbook and name it **ExcelL1_C6_A5**.
3. Select cells D5 through D19 and then use conditional formatting to display the amounts as data bars.
4. Insert a footer that prints your name, a page number, and the current date.
5. Save, print, and then close **ExcelL1_C6_A5.xlsx**.

CASE study

Apply Your Skills

Part 1

You are the office manager for Leeward Marine and you decide to consolidate into one workbook worksheets containing information on expenses. Copy **ExcelC06EstimatedExpenses.xlsx**, **ExcelC06ActualExpenses.xlsx**, and **ExcelC06ExpenseVariances.xlsx** into one workbook. Apply appropriate formatting to numbers and insert necessary formulas. Include the company name, Leeward Marine, in each worksheet. Create styles and apply the styles to cells in each worksheet to maintain consistent formatting. Rename and recolor the three worksheet tabs (you determine the names and colors). Save the workbook and name it **ExcelC06LeewardExpenses**.

Part 2

As you look at the information in each worksheet in the **ExcelC06LeewardExpenses.xlsx** workbook, you decide that the information should be summarized for easy viewing. Include a new worksheet in the workbook that summarizes each category in Employee Costs, Facilities Costs, and Marketing Costs by estimated costs, actual costs, and expense variances. Insert formulas in the summary worksheet that insert the appropriate totals from each of the three other worksheets. Insert an appropriate header or footer in the workbook. Scale the worksheets so each print on one page. Save, print (all of the worksheets in the workbook), and then close **ExcelC06LeewardExpenses.xlsx**.

Part 3

You are not happy with the current product list form so you decide to look at template forms available at the Microsoft online site. Display the New Workbook dialog box and then download the Product price list template located in the *Lists* category. Open **ExcelC06ProductList.xlsx** and then copy the product information into the Produce price list template. Insert the following company information as required by the template:

Leeward Marine
4500 Shoreline Drive,
Ketchikan, AK 99901
(907) 555-2200
(907) 555-2595 (fax)
www.emcp.com/leewardmarine

Format the product list form with formatting similar to the formatting you applied to the **ExcelC06LeewardExpenses.xlsx** workbook. Save the completed products list form and name it **ExcelC06ProductsList**. Print and then close the workbook.

You need to print a number of copies of the product list and you want the company letterhead to print at the top of the page. You decide to use the letterhead you created in Word and copy the product list information from Excel into the Word letterhead document. To do this, open Word and then open the document named **LeewardMarineLtrhd.docx**. Open **ExcelC06ProductList.xlsx** and then copy the cells containing data and paste them into the Word letterhead document using *Paste Special*. When the product list information is pasted into the Word document, apply blue font color to the data in the cells. Apply any other formatting you think will enhance the cells in the document. Save the Word document with *Save As* and name it **WordC06ProductList**. Print and then close **WordC06ProductList.docx** and then close **ExcelC06ProductList.xlsx**.

Creating a Chart in Excel

PERFORMANCE OBJECTIVES

Upon successful completion of Chapter 7, you will be able to:

- Create a chart with data in an Excel worksheet
- Size, move, and delete charts
- Print a selected chart and print a worksheet containing a chart
- Preview a chart
- Choose a chart style, layout, and formatting
- Change chart location
- Insert, move, size, and delete chart labels, shapes, and pictures

Tutorial 7.1
Creating and Formatting Charts

In the previous Excel chapters, you learned to create data in worksheets. While a worksheet does an adequate job of representing data, you can present some data more visually by charting the data. A chart is sometimes referred to as a *graph* and is a picture of numeric data. In this chapter, you will learn to create and customize charts in Excel.

Note: Before beginning computer projects, copy to your storage medium the Excel2007L1C7 subfolder from the Excel2007L1 folder on the CD that accompanies this textbook and then make Excel2007L1C7 the active folder.

Project 1 Create a Quarterly Sales Column Chart

You will open a workbook containing quarterly sales data and then use the data to create a column chart. You will decrease the size of the chart, move it to a different location in the worksheet and then make changes to sales numbers.

Creating a Chart

In Excel, create a chart with buttons in the Charts group in the Insert tab as shown in Figure 7.1. With buttons in the Charts group you can create a variety of charts such as a column chart, line chart, pie chart, and much more. Excel provides 11

Create a Chart
1. Select cells.
2. Click Insert tab.
3. Click desired chart button.
4. Click desired chart style at drop-down list.

Create Chart as Default Chart Type
1. Select cells.
2. Press Alt + F1.

basic chart types as described in Table 7.1. To create a chart, select cells in a worksheet that you want to chart, click the Insert tab, and then click the desired chart button in the Charts group. At the drop-down gallery that displays, click the desired chart style. You can also create a chart by selecting the desired cells and then pressing Alt + F1. This keyboard shortcut, by default, inserts the data in a 2-D column chart (unless the default chart type has been changed).

Figure 7.1 Chart Group Buttons

These buttons display in the Insert tab and you can use them to create a variety of charts.

Table 7.1 Types of Charts

Chart	Description
Area	An Area chart emphasizes the magnitude of change, rather than time and the rate of change. It also shows the relationship of parts to a whole by displaying the sum of the plotted values.
Bar	A Bar chart shows individual figures at a specific time, or shows variations between components but not in relationship to the whole.
Bubble	A Bubble chart compares sets of three values in a manner similar to a scatter chart, with the third value displayed as the size of the bubble marker.
Column	A Column chart compares separate (noncontinuous) items as they vary over time.
Doughnut	A Doughnut chart shows the relationship of parts of the whole.
Line	A Line chart shows trends and change over time at even intervals. It emphasizes the rate of change over time rather than the magnitude of change.
Pie	A Pie chart shows proportions and relationships of parts to the whole.
Radar	A Radar chart emphasizes differences and amounts of change over time and variations and trends. Each category has its own value axis radiating from the center point. Lines connect all values in the same series.
Stock	A Stock chart shows four values for a stock—open, high, low, and close.
Surface	A Surface chart shows trends in values across two dimensions in a continuous curve.
XY (Scatter)	A Scatter chart either shows the relationships among numeric values in several data series or plots the interception points between x and y values. It shows uneven intervals of data and is commonly used in scientific data.

Sizing, Moving, and Deleting a Chart

When you create a chart, the chart is inserted in the same worksheet as the selected cells. Figure 7.2 displays the worksheet and chart you will create in Project 1a. The chart is inserted in a box which you can size and/or move in the worksheet.

HINT
Hide rows or columns that you do not want to chart.

To size the worksheet, position the mouse pointer on the four dots located in the middle of the border you want to size until the pointer turns into a two-headed arrow, hold down the left mouse button, and then drag to increase or decrease the size of the chart. To increase or decrease the height and width of the chart at the same time, position the mouse pointer on the three dots that display in a chart border corner until the pointer displays as a two-headed arrow, hold down the left mouse button, and then drag to the desired size. To increase or decrease the size of the chart and maintain the proportions of the chart, hold down the Shift key while dragging a chart corner border.

To move the chart, make sure the chart is selected (light turquoise box displays around the chart), position the mouse pointer on a border until it turns into a four-headed arrow, hold down the left mouse button, and then drag to the desired position.

Figure 7.2 Project 1a Chart

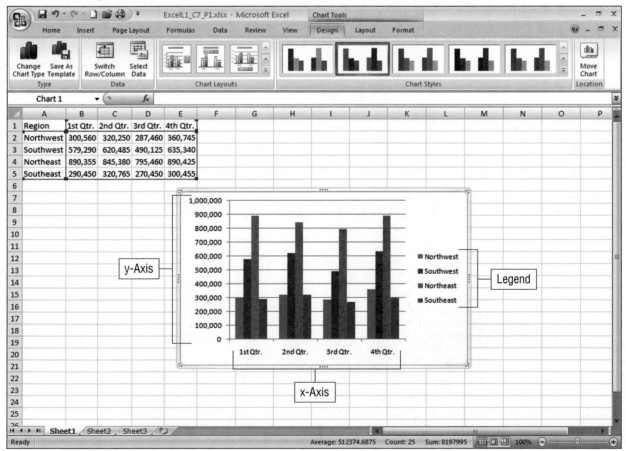

Editing Data

The cells you select to create the chart are linked to the chart. If you need to change data for a chart, edit the data in the desired cell and the corresponding section of the chart is automatically updated.

Project 1a Creating a Chart

1. Open **ExcelC07Project01.xlsx** and then save the workbook and name it **ExcelL1_C7_P1**.
2. Select cells A1 through E5.
3. Press Alt + F1.
4. Slightly increase the size of the chart and maintain the proportions of the chart by completing the following steps:
   a. Position the mouse pointer on the bottom right corner of the chart border until the pointer turns into a two-headed arrow pointing diagonally.
   b. Hold down the Shift key and then hold down the left mouse button.
   c. Drag out approximately one-half inch and then release the mouse button and then the Shift key.

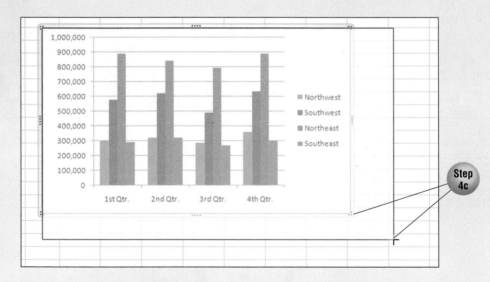

Step 4c

5. Move the chart below the cells containing data by completing the following steps:
   a. Make sure the chart is selected (light turquoise border surrounds the chart).

	A	B	C	D	E	F	G	H	I	J	K
1	Region	1st Qtr.	2nd Qtr.	3rd Qtr.	4th Qtr.						
2	Northwest	300,560	320,250	287,460	360,745						
3	Southwest	579,290	620,485	490,125	635,340						
4	Northeast	890,355	845,380	795,460	890,425						
5	Southeast	290,450	320,765	270,450	300,455						

Step 5c

   b. Position the mouse pointer on the chart border until the pointer turns into a four-headed arrow.

   c. Hold down the left mouse button, drag the chart so it is positioned below the cells containing data, and then release the mouse button.

6. Make the following changes to the specified cells:

   a. Make cell B2 active and then change *300,560* to *421,720*.

   b. Make cell C2 active and then change *320,250* to *433,050*.

   c. Make cell D2 active and then change *287,460* to *397,460*.

   d. Make cell E2 active and then change *360,745* to *451,390*.

7. Save **ExcelL1_C7_P1.xlsx**.

Printing Only the Chart

In a worksheet containing data in cells as well as a chart, you can print only the chart. To do this, click the chart to select it and then display the Print dialog box. At the Print dialog box, *Selected Chart* will automatically be selected in the *Print what* section. Click OK to print only the selected chart.

Previewing a Chart

Preview a chart by clicking the Office button, pointing to the *Print* option, and then clicking *Print Preview*. After previewing the chart, click the Close Preview button, or print the worksheet by clicking the Print button in the Print Preview tab.

Project 1b   Previewing and Printing the Chart

1. With **ExcelL1_C7_P1.xlsx** open, make sure the chart displays.

2. Preview the chart by completing the following steps:

   a. Click the Office button.

   b. Point to the *Print* option.

   c. Click *Print Preview*.

   d. After viewing the chart in Print Preview, click the Close Print Preview button.

3. Print the worksheet by clicking the Quick Print button in the Quick Access toolbar.

4. Save and then close **ExcelL1_C7_P1.xlsx**.

Project 2   Create a Technology Purchases Bar Chart and Column Chart

You will open a workbook containing technology purchases data by department and then create a bar chart with the data. You will then change the chart type, layout, and style and move the chart to a new sheet.

Changing the Chart Design

When you insert a chart in a worksheet, the Chart Tools Design tab displays as shown in Figure 7.3. With options in this tab, you can change the chart type, specify a different layout or style for the chart, and change the location of the chart so it displays in a separate worksheet.

Figure 7.3 Chart Tools Design Tab

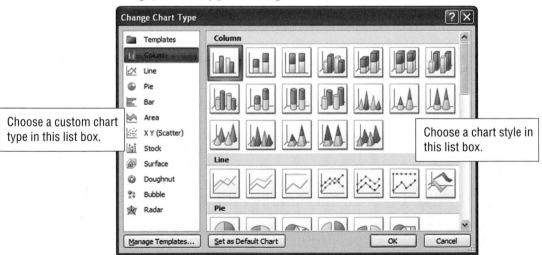

Change Chart Type

Choosing a Custom Chart Style

The chart feature offers a variety of preformatted custom charts and offers varying styles for each chart type. You can choose a chart style with buttons in the Charts group by clicking a chart button and then choosing from the styles offered at the drop-down list. You can also choose a chart style with the Change Chart Type button in the Chart Tools Design tab. Click this button and the Change Chart Type dialog box displays as shown in Figure 7.4. Click the desired chart type in the panel at the left side of the dialog box and then click the desired chart style at the right. If you create a particular chart type on a regular basis, you may want to set that chart type as the default. To do this, click the Set as Default Chart button in the Change Chart Type dialog box.

Figure 7.4 Change Chart Type Dialog Box

Changing the Data Series

A data series is information represented on the chart by bars, lines, columns, pie slices, and so on. When Excel creates a chart, the data in the first column (except the first cell) is used to create the x-axis (the information along the bottom of the chart) and the data in the first row (except the first cell) is used to create the legend. You can switch the data in the axes by clicking the Switch Row/Column button in the Data group in the Chart Tools Design tab. This moves the data on the x-axis to the y-axis and the y-axis data to the x-axis.

Change Chart Data Series
1. Make the chart active.
2. Click Chart Tools Design tab.
3. Click Switch Row/Column button.

Switch Row/Column

Project 2a Creating a Chart and Changing the Design

1. Open **ExcelC07Project02.xlsx** and then save the workbook and name it **ExcelL1_C7_P2**.
2. Create a bar chart by completing the following steps:
   a. Select cells A3 through B9.
   b. Click the Insert tab.
   c. Click the Bar button in the Charts group.
   d. Click the first option from the left in the *Cylinder* section (*Clustered Horizontal Cylinder*).
3. With the chart selected and the Chart Tools Design tab displayed, change the data series by clicking the Switch Row/Column button located in the Data group.

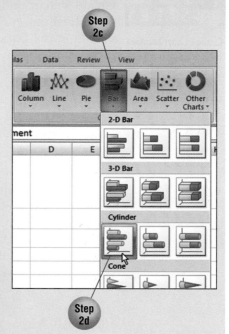

Step 2c

Step 2d

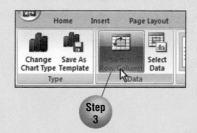

Step 3

4. Change the chart type and style by completing the following steps:
   a. Click the Change Chart Type button located in the Type group.
   b. At the Change Chart Type dialog box, click the *Column* option in the left panel.
   c. Click the *3-D Cylinder* option in the *Column* section (fourth chart style from the left in the second row of the *Column* section).
   d. Click OK to close the Change Chart Type dialog box.
5. Save **ExcelL1_C7_P2.xlsx**.

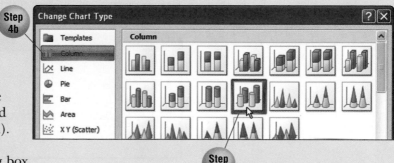

Step 4b

Step 4c

Changing Chart Layout and Style

The Chart Tools Design tab contains options for changing the chart layout and style. The Chart Layouts group in the tab contains preformatted chart layout options. Click the More button (contains an underline and a down-pointing arrow) to display a drop-down list of layout options. Hover the mouse pointer over an option and a ScreenTip displays with the option name. You can also scroll through layout options by clicking the up-pointing arrow or the down-pointing arrow located at the right side of the Chart Layouts group.

Use options in the Chart Styles group to apply a particular style of formatting to a chart. Click the More button located at the right side of the Chart Styles group to display a drop-down list with all the style options or click the up-pointing or down-pointing arrow at the right of the group to scroll through the options.

Changing Chart Location

Change Chart Location
1. Make the chart active.
2. Click Chart Tools Design tab.
3. Click Move Chart button.
4. Click *New Sheet* option.
5. Click OK.

Move Chart

Create a chart and the chart is inserted in the currently open worksheet as an embedded object. You can change the location of a chart with the Move Chart button in the Location group. Click this button and the Move Chart dialog box displays as shown in Figure 7.5. Click the *New sheet* option to move the chart to a new sheet within the workbook. Excel automatically names the sheet *Chart1*. Click the down-pointing arrow at the right side of the *Object in* option box and then click the desired location. The drop-down list will generally display the names of the worksheets within the open workbook. You can use the keyboard shortcut, F11, to create a default chart type (usually a column chart) and Excel automatically inserts the chart in a separate sheet.

If you have moved a chart to a separate sheet, you can move it back to the original sheet or move it to a different sheet within the workbook. To move a chart to a sheet, click the Move Chart button in the Location group in the Chart Tools Design tab. At the Move Chart dialog box, click the down-pointing arrow at the right side of the *Object in* option and then click the desired sheet at the drop-down list. Click OK and the chart is inserted in the specified sheet as an object that you can move, size, and format.

Figure 7.5 Move Chart Dialog Box

Click the *New sheet* option to insert the chart in a separate sheet.

To move the chart to a different sheet, click this down-pointing arrow and then click the desired sheet.

Move Chart

Choose where you want the chart to be placed:

○ New sheet: Chart1

⦿ Object in: Sheet1

OK   Cancel

Deleting a Chart

Delete a chart created in Excel by clicking once in the chart to select it and then pressing the Delete key. If you move a chart to a different worksheet in the workbook and then delete the chart, the chart is deleted but not the worksheet. To delete the chart as well as the worksheet, position the mouse pointer on the Chart1 tab, click the *right* mouse button, and then click *Delete* at the shortcut menu. At the message box telling you that selected sheets will be permanently deleted, click Delete.

Project 2b — Changing Chart Layout, Style, and Location

1. With **ExcelL1_C7_P2.xlsx** open, make sure the Chart Tools Design tab displays. (If it does not, make sure the chart is selected and then click the Chart Tools Design tab.)
2. Change the chart type by completing the following steps:
   a. Click the Change Chart Type button in the Type tab.
   b. Click *3-D Clustered Column* (fourth column style from the left in the top row).
   c. Click OK to close the dialog box.
3. Change the chart layout by clicking the *Layout 1* option in the Chart Layouts group (first option from the left). This layout inserts the words *Chart Title* at the top of the chart.
4. Change the chart style by clicking the More button located at the right side of the Chart Styles group and the clicking *Style 34* (second option from the left in the fifth row).

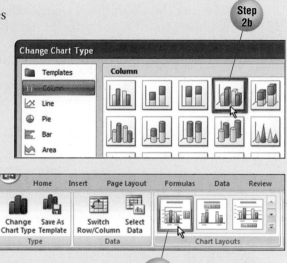

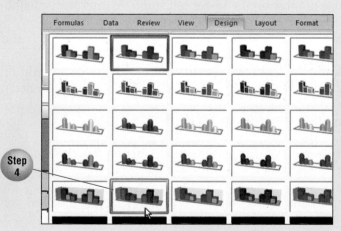

5. Move the chart to a new location by completing the following steps:
   a. Click the Move Chart button in the Location group.
   b. At the Move Chart dialog box, click the *New sheet* option and then click OK. (The chart is inserted in a worksheet named *Chart1*.)
6. Save **ExcelL1_C7_P2.xlsx**.
7. Print the Chart1 worksheet containing the chart.
8. Move the chart from Chart1 to Sheet2 by completing the following steps:
   a. Make sure Chart1 is the active sheet and that the chart is selected (not an element in the chart).
   b. Make sure the Chart Tools Design tab is active.
   c. Click the Move Chart button in the Location group.
   d. At the Move Chart dialog box, click the down-pointing arrow at the right side of the *Object in* option and then click *Sheet2* at the drop-down list.

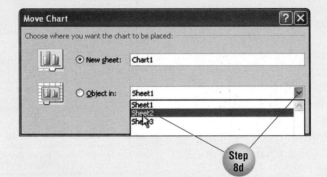

   e. Click OK.
9. Increase the size of the chart and maintain the proportions by completing the following steps:
   a. Click inside the chart but outside any chart elements. (This displays a light turquoise border around the chart.)
   b. Hold down the Shift key.
   c. Position the mouse pointer on the upper left border corner until the pointer turns into a double-headed arrow pointing diagonally.
   d. Hold down the left mouse button, drag left approximately one inch and then release the mouse button and then the Shift key.
   e. Display the worksheet in Print Preview to determine if the chart will print on one page. If the chart does not fit on the page, close Print Preview and then decrease the size of the chart until it fits on one page.
10. Change amounts in Sheet1 by completing the following steps:
    a. Click Sheet1.
    b. Make cell B4 active and then change the number from *$33,500* to *$12,750*.
    c. Make cell B9 active and then change the number from *$19,200* to *$5,600*.
    d. Make cell A2 active.
    e. Click the Sheet2 tab and notice that the chart displays the updated amounts.
11. Print the active worksheet (Sheet2).
12. Save and then close **ExcelL1_C7_P2.xlsx**.

Project 3 Create a Population Comparison Bar Chart

You will open a workbook containing population comparison data for Seattle and Portland and then create a bar chart with the data. You will also add chart labels and shapes and move, size, and delete labels/shapes.

Changing the Chart Layout

Customize the layout of labels in a chart with options in the Chart Tools Layout tab as shown in Figure 7.6. With buttons in this tab, you can change the layout and/or insert additional chart labels. Certain chart labels are automatically inserted in a chart including a chart legend and labels for the x-axis and y-axis. Add chart labels to an existing chart with options in the Labels group in the Chart Tools Layout tab. In addition to chart labels, you can also insert shapes, pictures, and/or clip art and change the layout of 3-D chart labels.

Figure 7.6 Chart Tools Layout Tab

Inserting, Moving, and Deleting Chart Labels

Certain chart labels are automatically inserted in a chart, including a chart legend and labels for the x-axis and y-axis. The legend identifies which data series is represented by which data marker. Insert additional chart labels with options in the Labels group in the Chart Tools Layout tab. For example, click the Chart Title button in the Labels group and a drop-down list displays with options for inserting a chart title in a specific location in the chart.

You can move and/or size a chart label. To move a chart label, click the label to select it and then move the mouse pointer over the border line until the pointer turns into a four-headed arrow. Hold down the left mouse button, drag the label to the desired location, and then release the mouse button. To size a chart label, use the sizing handles that display around the selected label to increase or decrease the size. To delete a chart label, click the label to select it and then press the Delete key. You can also delete a label by right-clicking the label and then clicking *Delete* at the shortcut menu.

1. Open **ExcelC07Project03.xlsx** and then save the workbook and name it **ExcelL1_C7_P3**.
2. Create a Bar chart by completing the following steps:
   a. Select cells A2 through H4.
   b. Click the Insert tab.
   c. Click the Bar button in the Charts group and then click the *Clustered Horizontal Cylinder* option in the *Cylinder* section.
3. Change to a Line chart by completing the following steps:
   a. Click the Change Chart Type button in the Type group.
   b. At the Change Chart Type dialog box, click *Line* located at the left side of the dialog box.
   c. Click the *Line with Markers* option in the *Line* section (fourth option from the left).

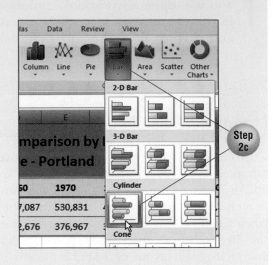

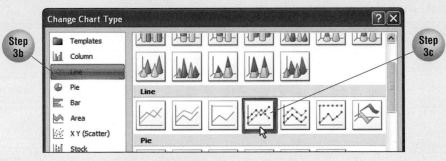

   d. Click OK to close the Change Chart Type dialog box.
4. Click the More button in the Chart Styles group in the Chart Tools Design tab and then click *Style 18* at the drop-down gallery (second option from left in the third row).

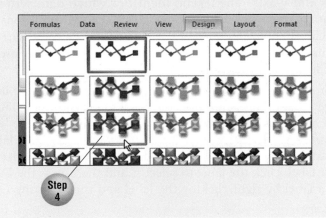

5. Change the layout of the chart by completing the following steps:
   a. Click the Chart Tools Layout tab.
   b. Click the Legend button in the Labels group.
   c. At the drop-down list, click the *Show Legend at Bottom* option.

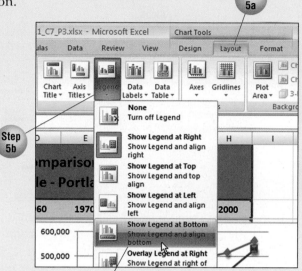

   d. Click the Chart Title button in the Labels group.
   e. At the drop-down list, click the *Above Chart* option.
   f. Select the text *Chart Title* located in the chart title text box and then type **Population Comparison**.
6. Insert an x-axis title by completing the following steps:
   a. Click the Axis Titles button, point to the *Primary Horizontal Axis Title* option at the drop-down list, and then click *Title Below Axis* at the side menu.

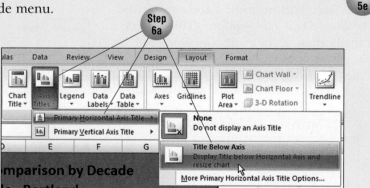

   b. Select the text *Axis Title* located in the title text box and then type **Decades**.

7. Insert a y-axis title by completing the following steps:
   a. Click the Axis Titles button, point to the *Primary Vertical Axis Title* option at the drop-down list, and then click *Rotated Title* at the side menu. (This inserts a rotated title at the left side of the chart containing the text *Axis Title*).

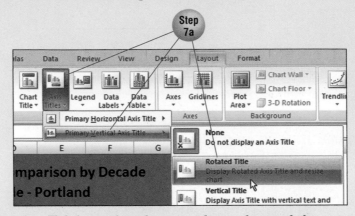

b. Select the text *Axis Title* located in the axis title text box and then type **Total Population**.
8. Click the Gridlines button in the Axes group, point to *Primary Vertical Gridlines*, and then click the *Major & Minor Gridlines* option at the side menu.

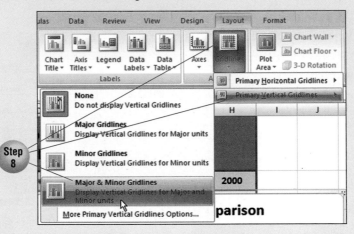

9. Click the Data Table button in the Labels group and then click the *Show Data Table* option. (This inserts cells toward the bottom of the chart containing cell data.)
10. Click the Lines button in the Analysis group and then click *Drop Lines* at the drop-down list.

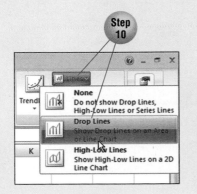

11. Drag the bottom right corner of the chart border to increase the size by approximately one inch.
12. Drag the chart so it is positioned below the data in cells but not overlapping the data.
13. Click the x-axis title (*Decades*) to select the title text box and then drag the box so it is positioned as shown below.

	1940	1950	1960	1970	1980	1990	2000
Seattle	368,302	467,591	557,087	530,831	493,846	516,259	563,374
Portland	305,394	373,628	372,676	376,967	366,383	437,319	529,121

Decades

——Seattle ——Portland

Step 13

14. Print only the selected chart.
15. Delete the horizontal axis title by clicking the axis title *Decades* and then pressing the Delete key.
16. Save **ExcelL1_C7_P3.xlsx**.

Inserting Shapes

The Insert group in the Chart Tools Layout tab contains three buttons with options for inserting shapes or images in a chart. Click the Shapes button in the Insert group and a drop-down list displays with a variety of shape options as shown in Figure 7.7. Click the desired shape at the drop-down list and the mouse pointer turns into a thin, black plus symbol. Drag with this pointer symbol to create the shape in the chart. The shape is inserted in the chart with default formatting. You can change this formatting with options in the Drawing Tools Format tab. This tab contains many of the same options as the Chart Tools Format tab. For example, you can insert a shape, apply a shape or WordArt style, and arrange and size the shape.

Moving, Sizing, and Deleting Shapes

Move, size, and delete shapes in the same manner as moving, sizing, and deleting chart elements. To move a shape, select the shape, position the mouse pointer over the border line until the pointer turns into a four-headed arrow. Hold down the left mouse button, drag the shape to the desired location, and then release the mouse button. To size a shape, select the shape and then use the sizing handles that display around the shape to increase or decrease the size. Delete a selected shape by clicking the Delete key or right-clicking the shape and then clicking *Cut* at the shortcut menu.

QUICK STEPS

Insert Shape
1. Make the chart active.
2. Click Chart Tools Layout tab.
3. Click Shapes button.
4. Click desired shape at drop-down list.
5. Drag pointer symbol to create shape in chart.

Shapes

HINT
Chart elements can be repositioned for easier viewing.

Figure 7.7 Shapes Button Drop-down List

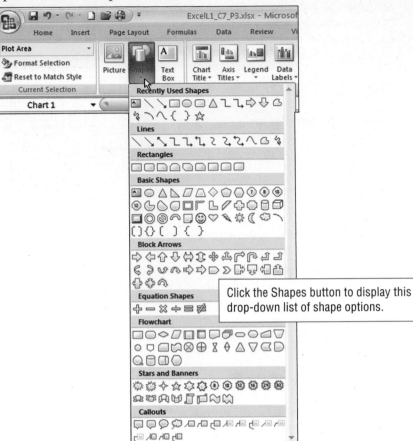

Click the Shapes button to display this drop-down list of shape options.

Project ③b Inserting and Customizing a Shape

1. With **ExcelL1_C7_P3.xlsx** open, make sure the Chart Tools Layout tab displays.
2. Create a shape similar to the shape shown in Figure 7.8. Begin by clicking the Shapes button in the Insert group.
3. Click the *Up Arrow Callout* shape in the *Block Arrows* section (last shape in the second row).
4. Drag in the chart to create the shape.

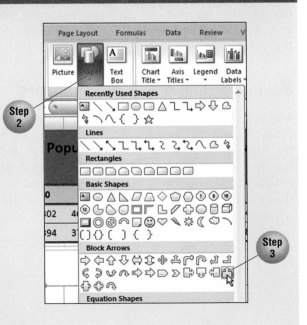

5. Click the More button in the Shapes Styles group (located at the right side of the three shapes) and then click *Subtle Effect - Accent 1* at the drop-down gallery.

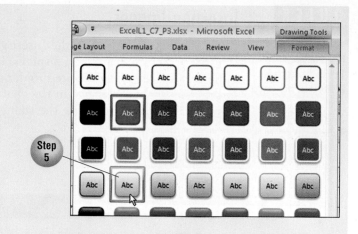

6. With the shape selected, use the sizing handles around the shape to increase and/or decrease the size so it displays as shown in Figure 7.8.

7. Type **Largest Disparity** in the shape box, press Enter, and then type (184,411).

8. Select the text you just typed and then complete the following steps:
   a. Click the Home tab.
   b. Click the Center button in the Alignment group.
   c. Click the Bold button in the Font group.
   d. Click the Font Size button arrow and then click *10*.

9. With the shape selected, drag the shape so it is positioned as shown in Figure 7.8.

10. Save **ExcelL1_C7_P3.xlsx**.

Figure 7.8 Project 3b Chart

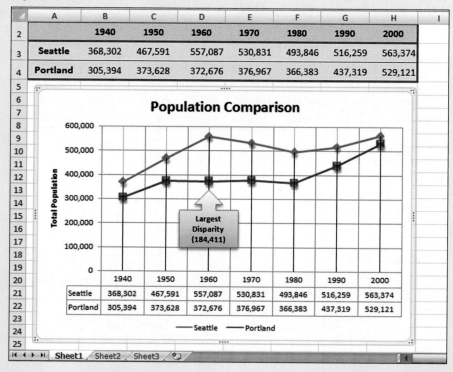

QUICK STEPS

Insert Image
1. Make the chart active.
2. Click Chart Tools Layout tab.
3. Click Picture button.
4. Double-click desired file name.

Inserting Images

Click the Picture button in the Insert group in the Chart Tools Layout tab and the Insert Picture dialog box displays. If you have a picture or image file saved in a folder, navigate to the desired folder and then double-click the file name. This inserts the picture or image in the chart. Drag the picture or image to the desired position in the chart and use the sizing handles to change the size.

Project 3c Inserting a Picture in a Chart

1. With **ExcelL1_C7_P3.xlsx** open, make sure the chart is selected and then click the Chart Tools Layout tab.
2. Insert the company logo by completing the following steps:
   a. Click the Picture button in the Insert group.
   b. At the Insert Picture dialog box, navigate to the Excel2007L1C7 folder on your storage medium and then double-click *WELogo.jpg* in the list box.
3. With the logo image inserted in the chart, use the sizing handles to decrease the size of the image and then move the image so it displays in the upper left corner of the chart area as shown in Figure 7.9.
4. Print only the selected chart.
5. Save and then close **ExcelL1_C7_P3.xlsx**.

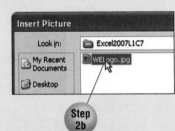

Step 2b

Figure 7.9 Project 3c Chart

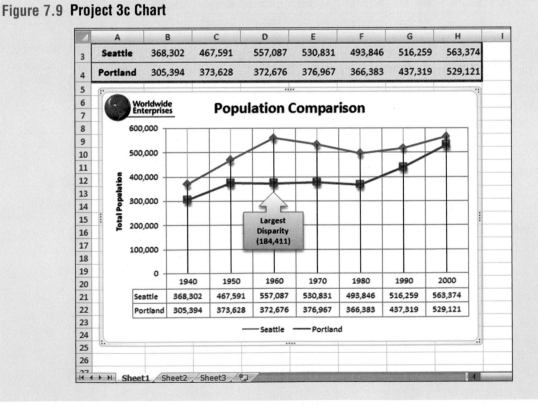

Project 4 Create a Costs Percentage Pie Chart

You will open a workbook containing percentage of costs for company departments and then create a pie chart with the data. You will apply formatting to the chart and then move the chart to a new worksheet.

Changing the Chart Formatting

Customize the format of the chart and chart elements with options in the Chart Tools Format tab as shown in Figure 7.10. With buttons in the Current Selection group you can identify a specific element in the chart and then apply formatting to that element. You can also click the Reset to Match Style button in the Current Selection group to return the formatting of the chart back to the original layout.

Figure 7.10 Chart Tools Format Tab

With options in the Shape Styles group, you can apply formatting styles to specific elements in a chart. Identify the desired element either by clicking the element to select it or by clicking the down-pointing arrow at the right side of the Chart Elements button in the Current Selection group and then clicking the desired element name at the drop-down list. With the chart element specified, apply formatting by clicking a style button in the Shape Styles group. You can also apply a style from a drop-down gallery. Display this gallery by clicking the More button located at the right side of the shape styles. Click the up-pointing or the down-pointing arrow at the right of the shape styles to cycle through the available style options.

HINT
Apply a WordArt style to make numbers stand out.

Chart Elements

1. Open **ExcelC07Project04.xlsx** and then save the workbook and name it **ExcelL1_C7_P4**.
2. Create the pie chart as shown in Figure 7.11 by completing the following steps:
   a. Select cells A3 through B10.
   b. Click the Insert tab.
   c. Click the Pie button in the Charts group and then click the first pie option in the *2-D Pie* section.
3. Click the More button located at the right side of the Chart Styles group.
4. At the drop-down gallery, click the *Style 32* option (last option in the fourth row).

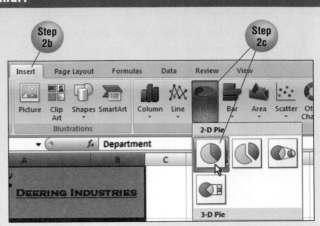

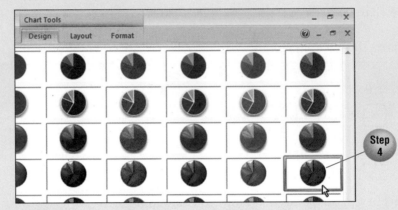

5. Click the Chart Tools Layout tab.
6. Insert data labels by clicking the Data Labels button in the Labels group and then clicking *Outside End* at the drop-down list.
7. Format chart elements by completing the following steps:
   a. Click the Chart Tools Format tab.
   b. Click the down-pointing arrow at the right side of the Chart Elements button in the Current Selection group and then click *Legend* at the drop-down list.
   c. Click the More button in the Shape Styles group and then click the last option in the fourth row (*Subtle Effect - Accent 6*).
   d. Click the down-pointing arrow at the right side of the Chart Elements button in the Current Selection group and then click *Chart Title*.

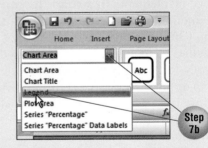

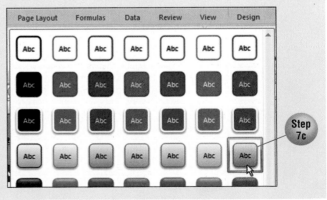

e. Click the More button at the right side of the WordArt styles in the WordArt Styles group and then click the *Gradient Fill - Accent 6, Inner Shadow* (second option from the left in the fourth row).

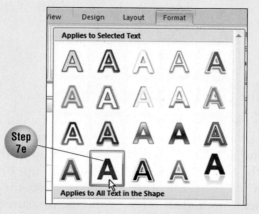

8. Insert the chart in a new sheet by completing the following steps:
   a. With the chart selected, click the Chart Tools Design tab.
   b. Click the Move Chart button in the Location group.
   c. At the Move Chart dialog box, click the *New sheet* option.
   d. Click OK.
9. Print only the worksheet containing the chart.
10. Save and then close **ExcelL1_C7_P4.xlsx**.

Figure 7.11 Project 4

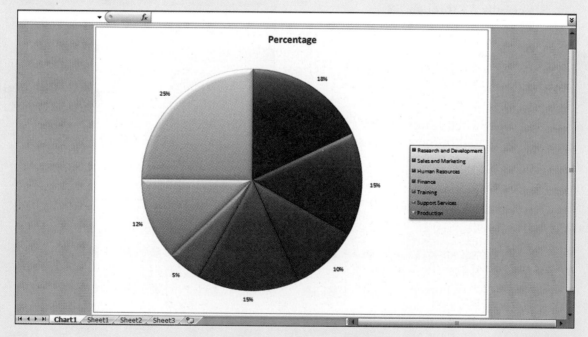

Project ⑤ Create a Regional Sales Column Chart

You will create a column chart using regional sales data, change the layout of the chart, apply formatting, and change the height and width of the chart.

QUICK STEPS

Change Chart Height and/or Width
1. Make the chart active.
2. Click Chart Tools Format tab.
3. Insert desired height and/or width with *Shape Height* and/or *Shape Width* text boxes.

Changing the Chart Height and Width

You can size a chart by selecting the chart and then dragging a sizing handle. You can also size a chart to specific measurements with the *Shape Height* and *Shape Width* measurement boxes in the Size group in the Chart Tools Format tab. Change the height or width by clicking the up- or down-pointing arrows that display at the right side of the button or select the current measurement in the measurement box and then type a specific measurement.

Project ⑤ Changing the Height and Width of a Chart

1. Open **ExcelC07Project05.xlsx**.
2. Save the workbook with Save As and name it **ExcelL1_C7_P5**.
3. Create a Column chart by completing the following steps:
   a. Select cells A3 through B8.
   b. Click the Insert tab.
   c. Click the Column button in the Charts group.
   d. Click the *3-D Clustered Column* option (first option in the *3-D Column* section).
   e. Click the Switch Row/Column button located in the Data group to change the data series.
   f. Click the *Layout 1* option in the Chart Layouts group (first option from the left in the group).
   g. Select the text *Chart Title* and then type **Northeast Regional Sales**.
   h. Click the More button located at the right side of the Chart Styles group and then click *Style 32* at the drop-down gallery (last option in fourth row).

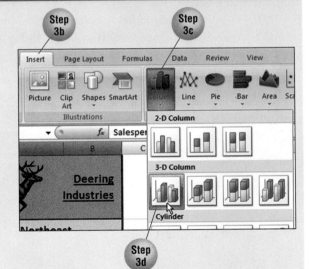

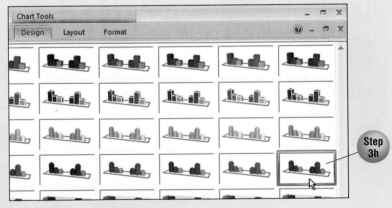

4. Change a series color by completing the following steps:
   a. Click the Chart Tools Format tab.
   b. Click the down-pointing arrow at the right side of the Chart Elements button and then click *Series "Newman, Jared"* at the drop-down list.

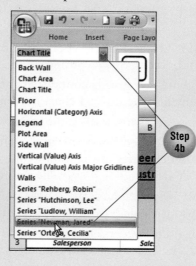

   c. Click the Shape Fill button arrow in the Shape Styles group and then click the dark red color *Red, Accent 2, Darker 25%*.

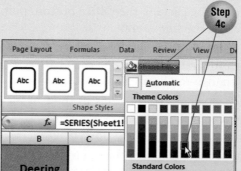

5. Change a series color by completing the following steps:
   a. With the Chart Tools Format tab active, click the down-pointing arrow at the right side of the Chart Elements button and then click *Series "Hutchinson, Lee"* at the drop-down list.
   b. Click the Shape Fill button arrow in the Shape Styles group and then click the dark green color *Olive Green, Accent 3, Darker 25%*.
6. Drag the chart down below the cells containing data.
7. Click the Chart Tools Format tab.
8. Click in the *Shape Height* measurement box in the Size group and then type 3.8.
9. Click the up-pointing arrow at the right side of the *Shape Width* measurement box in the Size group until *5.5* displays in the text box.
10. Print only the chart.
11. Save and then close **ExcelL1_C7_P5.xlsx**.

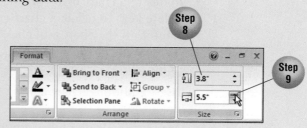

CHAPTER summary

- Create a chart with data in an Excel worksheet. A chart is a visual presentation of data.
- Excel provides 11 basic chart types: Area, Bar, Bubble, Column, Doughnut, Line, Pyramid, Radar, Stock, Surface, and XY (Scatter).
- To create a chart, select cells containing data you want to chart, click the Insert tab, and then click the desired chart button in the Charts group.
- A chart you create is inserted in the same worksheet as the selected cells.
- You can increase or decrease the size of a chart by positioning the mouse pointer on the four dots located in the middle of each border line or the three dots at each corner, and then dragging to the desired size.
- Move a chart by positioning the mouse pointer on the chart border until it turns into a four-headed arrow and then dragging with the mouse.
- Data in cells used to create the chart are linked to the chart. If you change the data in cells, the chart reflects the changes.
- Print by selecting the chart and then displaying the Print dialog box. At the Print dialog box, make sure *Selected Chart* is selected and then click OK.
- Preview a chart by clicking the Office button, pointing to *Print*, and then clicking *Print Preview* at the side menu.
- When you insert a chart in a worksheet, the Chart Tools Design tab is active. Use options in this tab to change the chart type, specify a different layout or style, and change the location of the chart.
- Choose a chart style with buttons in the Charts group in the Insert tab or at the Change Chart Type dialog box. Display this dialog box by clicking the Change Chart Type button in the Type group in the Chart Tools Design tab.
- The Chart Layouts group in the Chart Tools Design tab contains preformatted chart layout options. Use options in the Chart Styles group to apply a particular style of formatting to a chart.
- By default, a chart is inserted in the active worksheet. You can move the chart to a new sheet within the workbook with the *New sheet* option at the Move Chart dialog box. Display this dialog box by clicking the Move Chart button in the Location group in the Chart Tools Design tab.
- To delete a chart in a worksheet, click the chart to select it, and then press the Delete key. To delete a chart created in a separate sheet, position the mouse pointer on the chart tab, click the *right* mouse button, and then click Delete.
- Use options in the Chart Tools Layout tab to change the layout and/or insert additional chart labels, shapes, pictures, or clip art images.
- Insert additional chart labels with options in the Labels group in the Chart Tools Layout tab.
- Use buttons in the Insert group in the Chart Tools Layout tab to insert shapes, pictures, or text boxes.
- To move a chart label, click the label to select it and then drag the label with the mouse. To delete a label, click the label and then press the Delete key.

- Use options in the Chart Tools Format tab to customize the format of the chart and chart elements.
- Change the chart size by dragging the chart sizing handles or by entering a measurement in the *Shape Height* and *Shape Width* measurement boxes in the Size group in the Chart Tools Format tab.

COMMANDS review

FEATURE	RIBBON TAB, GROUP	BUTTON, OPTION	KEYBOARD SHORTCUT
Default chart in worksheet			Alt + F1
Default chart in separate sheet			F11
Change Chart Type dialog box	Chart Tools Design, Type		
Move Chart dialog box	Chart Tools Design, Location		
Shapes button drop-down list	Chart Tools Layout, Insert		
Insert Picture dialog box	Chart Tools Layout, Insert		

CONCEPTS check
Test Your Knowledge

Completion: In the space provided at the right, indicate the correct term, symbol, or command.

1. This is the keyboard shortcut to create a chart with the default chart type.

ALT + F1

2. This type of chart shows proportions and relationships of parts to the whole.

PIE CHART

3. The Charts group contains buttons for creating charts and is located in this tab.

INSERT TAB

4. When you create a chart, the chart is inserted in this location by default.

ACTIVE WORKSHEET

5. Select a chart in a worksheet, display the Print dialog box, and this option is automatically selected in the *Print what* section.

SELECTED CHART

6. When Excel creates a chart, the data in the first row (except the first cell) is used to create this.

LEGEND

7. Click the Picture button in the Chart Tools Layout tab and this dialog box displays.

INSERT PICTURE

8. Click this option at the Move Chart dialog box to move the chart to a separate sheet.

NEW SHEET

9. Use buttons in the Insert group in this tab to insert shapes, pictures, or text boxes.

CHART TOOLS LAYOUT TAB

10. Change the chart size by entering measurements in these text boxes in the Size group in the Chart Tools Format tab.

SHAPE HEIGHT / SHAPE WIDTH

SKILLS check
Demonstrate Your Proficiency

Assessment

1   CREATE A COMPANY SALES COLUMN CHART

1. Open **ExcelC07Assessment01.xlsx** and then save the workbook and name it **ExcelL1_C7_A1**.
2. Select cells A3 through C15 and then create a Column chart with the following specifications:
   a. Choose the *3-D Clustered Column* chart at the Chart button drop-down list.
   b. At the Chart Tools Design tab, click the *Layout 3* option in the Chart Layouts group.
   c. Change the chart style to *Style 26*.
   d. Select the text *Chart Title* and then type **Company Sales**.
   e. Move the location of the chart to a new sheet.
3. Print only the worksheet containing the chart.
4. Save and then close **ExcelL1_C7_A1.xlsx**.

Assessment

2   CREATE QUARTERLY DOMESTIC AND FOREIGN SALES BAR CHART

1. Open **ExcelC07Assessment02.xlsx** and then save the workbook and name it **ExcelL1_C7_A2**.
2. Select cells A3 through E5 and then create a Bar chart with the following specifications:
   a. Click the *Clustered Bar in 3-D* option at the Bar button drop-down list.
   b. At the Chart Tools Design tab choose the *Layout 2* option in the Chart Layouts group.
   c. Choose the *Style 23* option in the Chart Styles group.
   d. Select the text *Chart Title*, type **Quarterly Sales**, and then click in the chart but outside any chart elements.
   e. Display the Chart Tools Layout tab and then insert primary vertical minor gridlines. (Do this with the Gridlines button.)
   f. Display the Chart Tools Format tab and then apply to the chart the *Subtle Effect - Accent 3* option in the Shape Styles group.
   g. Select the *Domestic* series (using the Chart Elements button) and then apply a purple fill (Purple, Accent 4, Darker 25%) using the Shape Fill button in the Shape Styles group.
   h. Select the Foreign series and then apply a dark aqua fill (Aqua, Accent 5, Darker 25%) using the Shape Fill button in the Shape Styles group.
   i. Select the chart title and then apply the *Gradient Fill - Accent 6, Inner Shadow* option with the WordArt Styles button.
   j. Increase the height of the chart to 4 inches and the width to 6 inches.
   k. Move the chart below the cells containing data and make sure the chart fits on the page with the data. (**Hint: Display the worksheet in Print Preview.**)
3. Print only the worksheet.
4. Save and then close **ExcelL1_C7_A2.xlsx**.

Assessment

3 CREATE AND FORMAT A CORPORATE SALES COLUMN CHART

1. Open **ExcelC07Assessment03.xlsx** and then save the workbook and name it **ExcelL1_C7_A3**.
2. Create a column chart and format the chart so it displays as shown in Figure 7.12.
3. Print only the worksheet containing the chart.
4. Save and then close **ExcelL1_C7_A3.xlsx**.

Figure 7.12 Assessment 3

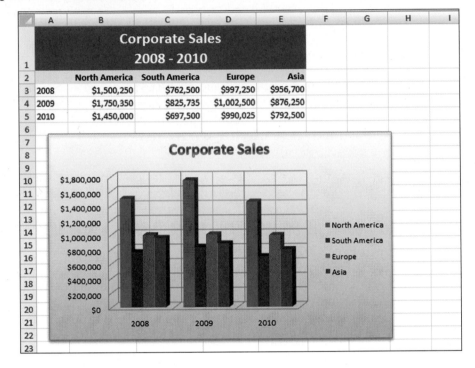

Assessment

4 CREATE A FUNDS ALLOCATIONS PIE CHART

1. At a blank worksheet, create a worksheet with the following data:

   Fund Allocations

Fund	Percentage
Annuities	23%
Stocks	42%
Bonds	15%
Money Market	20%

2. Using the data above, create a pie chart as a separate worksheet with the following specifications:
   a. Create a title for the pie chart.
   b. Add data labels to the chart.
   c. Add any other enhancements that will improve the visual presentation of the data.

3. Save the workbook and name it ExcelL1_C7_A4.
4. Print only the sheet containing the chart.
5. Close ExcelL1_C7_A4.xlsx.

Assessment

5 CREATE AN ACTUAL AND PROJECTED SALES CHART

1. Open ExcelC07Assessment05.xlsx and then save the workbook and name it ExcelL1_C7_A5.
2. Look at the data in the worksheet and then create a chart to represent the data. Add a title to the chart and add any other enhancements to improve the visual display of the chart.
3. Save the workbook and then print the chart.
4. Close ExcelL1_C7_A5.xlsx.

Assessment

6 CREATE AN ATTENDANCE SCATTER CHART

1. Use Excel's Help feature to learn more about chart types and then create a worksheet with the data shown in Figure 7.13. Create a scatter chart from the data in a separate sheet and create an appropriate title for the chart. Use the DATE function to enter the dates in the first column and enter the current year for the date.
2. Save the completed workbook and name it ExcelL1_C7_A6.
3. Print both sheets of the workbook (the sheet containing the data in cells and the sheet containing the chart).
4. Close ExcelL1_C7_A6.xlsx.

Figure 7.13 Assessment 6

HIGHLAND PARK ATTENDANCE

Week	Projected	Actual
July 1	35,000	42,678
July 8	33,000	41,065
July 15	30,000	34,742
July 22	28,000	29,781
July 29	28,000	26,208

CASE study
Apply Your Skills

You are an administrator for Dollar Wise Financial Services and you need to prepare charts indicating home loan and commercial loan amounts for the past year. Use the information below to prepare two charts in Excel. You determine the type and style of chart and the layout and formatting of the chart. Insert a shape in the Commercial Loans chart that contains the text *All-time High* and points to the second quarter amount (*$6,785,250*).

Home Loans
- 1st Qtr. = $2,675,025
- 2nd Qtr. = $3,125,750
- 3rd Qtr. = $1,975,425
- 4th Qtr. = $875,650

Commercial Loans
- 1st Qtr. = $5,750,980
- 2nd Qtr. = $6,785,250
- 3rd Qtr. = $4,890,625
- 4th Qtr. = $2,975,900

Save the workbook containing the two charts and name it **ExcelL1_C7_CS_P1**. Print only the two charts and then close **ExcelL1_C7_CS_P1.xlsx**.

Part
2

You need to present information on the budget for the company. You have the dollar amounts and need to convert the amounts to a percentage of the entire budget. Use the information below to calculate the percentage of the budget for each item and then create a pie chart with the information. You determine the chart style, layout, and formatting.

Total Budget: $6,000,000

Building Costs	=	$720,000
Salaries	=	$2,340,000
Benefits	=	$480,000
Advertising	=	$840,000
Marketing	=	$600,000
Client Expenses	=	$480,000
Equipment	=	$420,000
Supplies	=	$120,000

Save the workbook containing the pie chart and name it **ExcelL1_C7_CS_P2**. Print only the chart and then close **ExcelL1_C7_CS_P2.xlsx**.

One of your clients owns a number of stocks and you like to prepare a daily chart of the stocks' high, low, and close price. Use the Help feature to learn about stock charts and then create a stock chart with the following information (the company stock symbols are fictitious):

	IDE	POE	QRR
High	$23.75	$18.55	$34.30
Low	$18.45	$15.00	$31.70
Close	$19.65	$17.30	$33.50

Save the workbook containing the stock chart and name it **ExcelL1_C7_CS_P3**. Print only the chart and then close **ExcelL1_C7_CS_P3.xlsx**.

You need to prepare information on mortgage rates for a community presentation. You decide to include the information on mortgage rates in a chart for easy viewing. Use the Internet to search for historical data on the national average for mortgage rates. Determine the average mortgage rate for a 30-year FRM (fixed-rate mortgage) for each January and July beginning with the year 2005 and continuing to the current year. Also include the current average rate. Use this information to create the chart. Save the workbook and name it **ExcelL1_C7_CS_P4**. Print only the chart and then close **ExcelL1_C7_CS_P4.xlsx**.

You will be presenting information at an upcoming meeting on the information in the previous challenges for which you created a chart. You decide to include the charts in a PowerPoint presentation so you can display the charts on a screen while presenting. Open PowerPoint and then open the presentation named **ExcelC07Presentation.pptx**. Copy the chart you created in Part 1 to the second slide, copy the chart for Part 2 into the third slide, and then copy the chart for Part 4 into the fourth slide. Increase the size of the charts to better fill the slides. Save the presentation and name it **PPL1_C7_CS_P5**. Print the three slides containing charts. Close **PPL1_C7_CS_P5.pptx**.

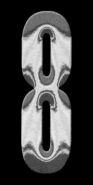

CHAPTER

Adding Visual Interest to Workbooks

PERFORMANCE OBJECTIVES

Upon successful completion of Chapter 8, you will be able to:

- Save a workbook as a Web page
- Create and modify a hyperlink
- Insert symbols and special characters
- Insert, size, move, and format a clip art image
- Draw, format, and copy shapes
- Insert, size, move, and format a picture image
- Insert, format, and type text in a text box
- Insert a picture image as a watermark
- Insert and format SmartArt diagrams
- Insert and format WordArt

excel Chapter 8

Tutorial 8.1
Using Web-Based Features
Tutorial 8.2
Adding Graphic Elements

You can save an Excel workbook as a Web page and then view it in a Web browser. You can also insert hyperlinks in a workbook that connect to a Web site or to another workbook. Microsoft Excel includes a variety of features that you can use to enhance the visual appeal of a workbook. Some methods for adding visual appeal that you will learn in this chapter include inserting and modifying clip art images, shapes, pictures, text boxes, SmartArt, and WordArt.

Note: Before beginning computer projects, copy to your storage medium the Excel2007L1C8 subfolder from the Excel2007L1 folder on the CD that accompanies this textbook and make Excel2007L1C8 the active folder.

Project ① Save a Travel Workbook as a Web Page

You will open a travel destinations workbook and then save the workbook as a single page Web page. You will also create hyperlinks in the Web page that link you to sites on the Internet.

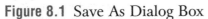
Creating a Web Page

Save Workbook as Single File Web Page
1. Click Office button, *Save As*.
2. Change *Save as type* option to *Single File Web Page (*.mht; *.mhtml)*.
3. Type name in *File name* text box.
4. Click Save button.

You can save an Excel workbook as a Web page and then view it in the default Web browser software. You can also insert hyperlinks in the Web page to jump to other workbooks or sites on the Internet with additional information pertaining to the workbook content.

Saving a Workbook as a Web Page

HINT
Web pages are files containing special formatting codes written in HTML (Hypertext Markup Language).

You can save the entire workbook, a worksheet, or a single item in a worksheet. Save a workbook as a Web page by changing the *Save as type* option at the Save As dialog box. You can save the data in the workbook as a single Web page or as a conventional Web page. If you choose the *Single File Web Page (*.mht; *.mhtml)* option, all data in the workbook such as graphics and other supplemental data is saved in a single Web file. If you choose the *Web Page (*.htm; *.html)* option, Excel creates additional files for supplemental data and saves the files in a subfolder.

When you choose a Web page option at the *Save as type* drop-down list, the Save As dialog box changes as shown in Figure 8.1. At this dialog box, specify which part of the workbook you want published and if you want to add a title to the Web page. Click the Publish button and the Publish as Web Page dialog box appears as shown in Figure 8.2. This dialog box contains advanced options for publishing a Web page.

Figure 8.1 Save As Dialog Box

Type a name for the Web page in this text box.

Click this button to display the Set Page Title dialog box.

Click this button to display the Publish as Web Page dialog box.

Figure 8.2 Publish as Web Page Dialog Box

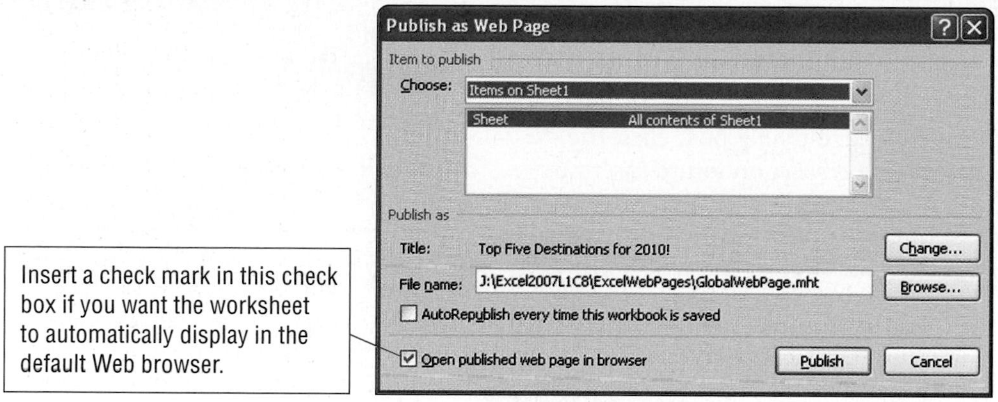

Insert a check mark in this check box if you want the worksheet to automatically display in the default Web browser.

Project ⓵ⓐ Saving a Workbook as a Web Page

1. Create a folder named *ExcelWebPages* within the Excel2007L1C8 folder on your storage medium.
2. Open **ExcelC08Project01.xlsx** and then save the workbook with Save As and name it **ExcelL1_C8_P1**.
3. Click the Office button and then click *Save As*.
4. At the Save As dialog box, double-click *ExcelWebPages* in the list box.
5. Click the down-pointing arrow at the right side of the *Save as type* list box and then click *Single File Web Page (*.mht; *.mhtml)* at the drop-down list.
6. Select the text in the *File name* text box and then type **GlobalWebPage**.
7. Click the Change Title button.

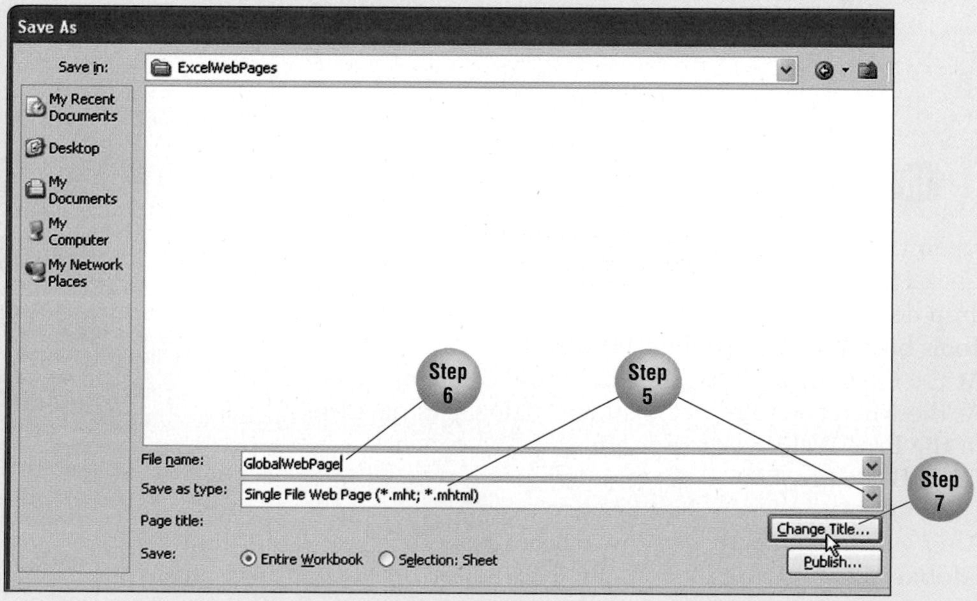

8. At the Set Page Title dialog box, type **Top Five Destinations for 2010!** in the *Page title* text box and then click OK.
9. At the Save As dialog box, click the Publish button.
10. At the Publish as Web Page dialog box, click the *Open published web page in browser* option to insert a check mark.
11. Click the Publish button. (This automatically displays the worksheet in your default Web browser.)

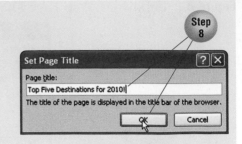

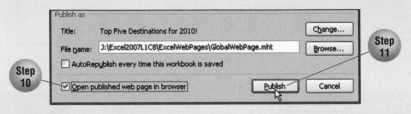

12. After viewing your Web page, close the Web page browser.
13. Save and then close **ExcelL1_C8_P1.xlsx**.

Opening a Workbook in Internet Explorer

Another method for opening a workbook saved as a Web page is to open Internet Explorer, click the File option on the Menu bar, and then click *Open* at the drop-down list. At the Open dialog box, click the Browse button. At the Microsoft Internet Explorer dialog box, navigate to the folder containing the saved Web page and then double-click the Web page file.

Project **1b** ▐ **Opening the Web Page in Internet Explorer**

1. Open Internet Explorer.
2. Click File in the Menu bar and then click *Open* at the drop-down list. (If the Menu bar is not visible, click the Tools button and then click *Menu Bar*.)
3. At the Open dialog box, click the Browse button.
4. At the Microsoft Internet Explorer dialog box, navigate to the ExcelWebPages folder and then double-click **GlobalWebPage.mht**.
5. Click OK at the Open dialog box.
6. After viewing the Web page in Internet Explorer, close **GlobalWebPage.mht**.
7. Close Internet Explorer.

Creating Hyperlinks

A hyperlink is text or an object that you click to go to a different file, an HTML page on the Internet, or an HTML page on an intranet. Create a hyperlink in an Excel worksheet by typing the address of an existing Web page such as *www.emcp.com*. By default, the automatic formatting of hyperlinks is turned on and the Web address is formatted as a hyperlink (text is underlined and the color changes to blue). (You can turn off the automatic formatting of hyperlinks at the AutoCorrect dialog box. Display this dialog box by clicking the Office button, clicking the Excel Options button, and then clicking *Proofing* in the left panel of the Excel Options dialog box. Click the AutoCorrect Options button to display the AutoCorrect dialog box. At this dialog box, click the AutoFormat As You Type tab and then remove the check mark from the *Internet and network paths with hyperlinks* check box.)

You can also create a customized hyperlink by clicking the desired cell in a workbook, clicking the Insert tab, and then clicking the Hyperlink button in the Links group. At the Insert Hyperlink dialog box shown in Figure 8.3, type the file name or Web site address in the *Address* text box and then click OK. You can also use the *Look in* option to browse to the desired folder and file and then double-click the file name. To link to the specified file or Web page, position the mouse pointer (white plus symbol) on the hyperlink until the mouse pointer displays as a hand and then click the left mouse button.

Figure 8.3 Insert Hyperlink Dialog Box

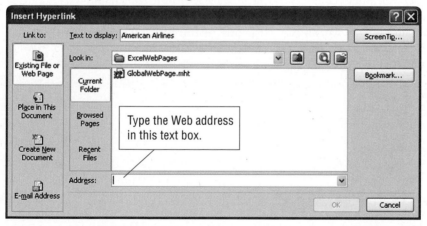

Type the Web address in this text box.

Project 1c   Creating Hyperlinks

1. Display the Open dialog box and then double-click *GlobalWebPage.mht*.
2. Create a hyperlink so that clicking *American Airlines* displays the American Airlines Web page by completing the following steps:
   a. Click cell G10 (this is the cell containing *American Airlines*).
   b. Click the Insert tab.
   c. Click the Hyperlink button in the Links group.

d. At the Insert Hyperlink dialog box, type **www.aa.com** in the *Address* text box. (The *http://* is automatically inserted in the address.)

e. Click OK. (This changes the color of the *American Airlines* text and also adds underlining to the text.)

f. Repeat Steps 2c through 2e in cell G13.

3. Complete steps similar to those in Step 2 to create a hyperlink from *Northwest Airlines* to the URL *www.nwa.com* in cells G11 and G12.

4. Complete steps similar to those in Step 2 to create a hyperlink from *Air Canada* to the URL *www.aircanada.ca* in cell G14.

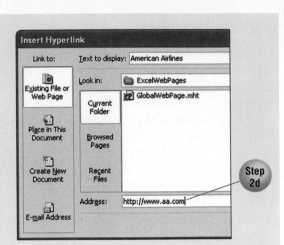

Step 2d

5. Click the Save button on the Quick Access toolbar. At the compatibility dialog box, click Yes.

6. Jump to the hyperlinked sites by completing the following steps:

a. Make sure you are connected to the Internet.

b. Position the mouse pointer on one of the <u>American Airlines</u> hyperlinks until the mouse pointer turns into a hand and then click the left mouse button.

c. When the American Airlines Web page displays, scroll through the page, and then click a hyperlink that interests you.

d. After looking at this next page, click File and then *Exit*.

e. At the **GlobalWebPage.mht** workbook, click the <u>Air Canada</u> hyperlink.

f. At the Air Canada Web page, click the hyperlink to see their site displayed in English.

g. After viewing the Air Canada page, click File and then *Exit*.

h. At the **GlobalWebPage.mht** workbook, click one of the <u>Northwest</u> hyperlinks.

i. At the Northwest Airlines Web page, click a link that interests you.

j. After viewing the Northwest Airlines page, click File and then *Exit*.

7. Change the orientation to landscape.

8. Save **GlobalWebPage.mht** and click Yes at the compatibility dialog box.

9. Print and then close **GlobalWebPage.mht**.

Project ② Insert a Hyperlink in a Company Sales Workbook

You will open a company sales workbook and then create a hyperlink that links you to another Excel workbook.

Edit Hyperlink
1. Right-click hyperlink.
2. Click *Edit Hyperlink*.
3. Make desired changes.
4. Click OK.

Creating a Hyperlink to an Excel Worksheet

In Project 1c, you created hyperlinks from an Excel workbook to sites on the Web. You can also insert hyperlinks in a workbook that link to other Excel workbooks or files in other programs in the Office suite. In Project 2, you will create a hyperlink that displays another Excel workbook.

You can modify or change hyperlink text or the hyperlink destination. To do this, right-click the hyperlink, and then click *Edit Hyperlink*. At the Edit Hyperlink dialog box, make any desired changes and then close the dialog box. The Edit Hyperlink dialog box contains the same options as the Insert Hyperlink dialog box.

HINT

Deactivate a hyperlink by right-clicking the hyperlink and then clicking *Remove Hyperlink* at the shortcut menu.

Project ② Creating and Modifying a Hyperlink to an Excel Worksheet

1. Open **ExcelC08Project02.xlsx**.
2. Save the workbook with Save As and name it **ExcelL1_C8_P2**.
3. Create a hyperlink that will display **ExcelC08Sales.xlsx** by completing the following steps:
   a. Make cell A12 active.
   b. Type **Semiannual Sales** and then press Enter.
   c. Click cell A12 to make it the active cell.
   d. Click the Insert tab.
   e. Click the Hyperlink button in the Links group.
   f. At the Insert Hyperlink dialog box, click the down-pointing arrow at the right side of the *Look in* option and then navigate to the Excel2007L1C8 folder on your storage medium.
   g. Double-click **ExcelC08Sales.xlsx**. (This closes the Insert Hyperlink dialog box and displays the *Semiannual Sales* text as a hyperlink in the workbook.)
4. Display **ExcelC08Sales.xlsx** by clicking the Semiannual Sales hyperlink.
5. Close **ExcelC08Sales.xlsx**.
6. Print **ExcelL1_C8_P2.xlsx**.
7. Modify the hyperlink text in **ExcelL1_C8_P2.xlsx** by completing the following steps:
   a. Position the mouse pointer on the Semiannual Sales hyperlink, click the *right* mouse button, and then click *Edit Hyperlink*.
   b. At the Edit Hyperlink dialog box, select the text *Semiannual Sales* in the *Text to display* text box and then type **Customer Sales Analysis**.
   c. Click OK.
8. Click the Customer Sales Analysis hyperlink.
9. Close **ExcelC08Sales.xlsx**.
10. Save, print, and then close **ExcelL1_C8_P2.xlsx**.

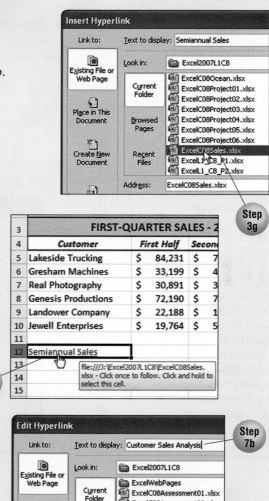

Project ③ Insert a Clip Art Image and Shapes in a Financial Analysis Workbook

You will open a financial analysis workbook and then insert, move, size, and format a clip art image in the workbook. You will also insert an arrow shape, type and format text in the shape, and then copy the shape.

Inserting Symbols and Special Characters

You can use the Symbol button in the Insert tab to insert special symbols in a worksheet. Click the Symbol button in the Text group in the Insert tab and the Symbol dialog box displays as shown in Figure 8.4. At the Symbol dialog box, double-click the desired symbol, and then click Close; or click the desired symbol, click the Insert button, and then click Close. At the Symbol dialog box with the Symbols tab selected, you can change the font with the *Font* option. When you change the font, different symbols display in the dialog box. Click the Special Characters tab at the Symbol dialog box and a list of special characters displays along with keyboard shortcuts to create the special character.

HINT
You can increase and/or decrease the size of the Symbol dialog box by positioning the mouse pointer on the lower right corner until the pointer displays as a two-headed arrow and then dragging with the mouse.

Symbol

Figure 8.4 Symbol Dialog Box with Symbols Tab Selected

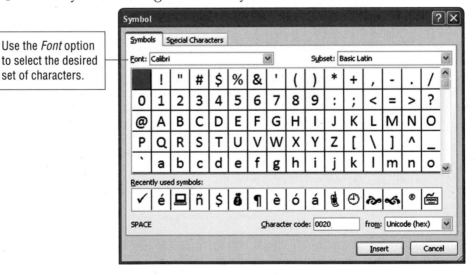

Use the *Font* option to select the desired set of characters.

Project 3a Inserting Symbols and Special Characters

1. Open **ExcelC08Project03.xlsx** and then save the workbook and name it **ExcelL1_C8_P3**.
2. Insert a symbol by completing the following steps:
   a. Double-click cell A2.
   b. Delete the *e* that displays at the end of *Qualite*.
   c. With the insertion point positioned immediately right of the *t* in *Qualit*, click the Insert tab.
   d. Click the Symbol button in the Text group.
   e. At the Symbol dialog box, scroll down the list box and then click the *é* symbol (ninth symbol from the left in the eleventh row).
   f. Click the Insert button and then click the Close button.

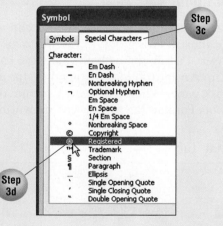

Step 2e

Step 2f

3. Insert a special character by completing the following steps:
   a. With cell A2 selected and in Edit mode, move the insertion point so it is positioned immediately right of *Group*.
   b. Click the Symbol button in the Text group.
   c. At the Symbol dialog box, click the Special Characters tab.
   d. Double-click the ® symbol (tenth option from the top).
   e. Click the Close button.

Step 3c

Step 3d

4. Insert a symbol by completing the following steps:
   a. With cell A2 selected and in Edit mode, move the insertion point so it is positioned immediately left of the *Q* in *Qualité*.
   b. Click the Symbol button in the Text group.
   c. At the Symbol dialog box, click the down-pointing arrow at the right side of the *Font* option box and then click *Wingdings* at the drop-down list. (You will need to scroll down the list to display this option.)
   d. Click the ❖ symbol (seventh option from the left in the sixth row).
   e. Click the Insert button and then click the Close button.

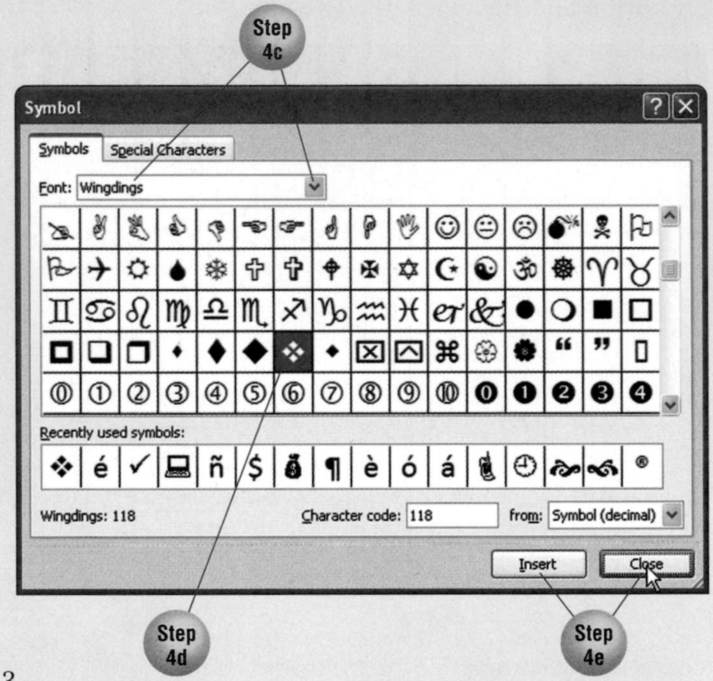

Step
4c

Step
4d

Step
4e

5. Click in cell A3.
6. Save **ExcelL1_C8_P3.xlsx**.

Inserting an Image

You can insert an image such as a picture or clip art in an Excel workbook with buttons in the Illustrations group in the Insert tab. Click the Picture button to display the Insert Picture dialog box where you can specify the desired picture file, or click the Clip Art button and then choose from a variety of images available at the Clip Art task pane. When you insert a picture or a clip art image in a worksheet, the Picture Tools Format Tab displays as shown in Figure 8.5.

Figure 8.5 Picture Tools Format Tab

Customizing and Formatting an Image

With options in the Adjust group in the Picture Tools Format tab you can recolor the picture or clip art image and change the brightness and contrast of the image. You can also reset the picture or clip art back to its original color or change to a different image. Use the Compress Pictures button to compress the size of the image file. Apply predesigned styles with options in the Picture Styles group. Use options in the Arrange group to position the image on the page, specify text wrapping in relation to the image, align the image with other objects in the worksheet, and rotate the image. Use the Crop button in the Size group to remove any unnecessary parts of the image and specify the image size with the *Shape Height* and *Shape Width* measurement boxes.

Sizing and Moving an Image

You can change the size of an image with the *Shape Height* and *Shape Width* measurement boxes in the Size group in the Picture Tools Format tab or with the sizing handles that display around the selected image. To change size with a sizing handle, position the mouse pointer on a sizing handle until the pointer turns into a double-headed arrow and then hold down the left mouse button. Drag the sizing handle in or out to decrease or increase the size of the image and then release the mouse button. Use the middle sizing handles at the left or right side of the image to make the image wider or thinner. Use the middle sizing handles at the top or bottom of the image to make the image taller or shorter. Use the sizing handles at the corners of the image to change both the width and height at the same time. Hold down the Shift key while dragging a sizing handle to maintain the proportions of the image.

Move an image by positioning the mouse pointer on the image border until the pointer displays with a four-headed arrow attached. Hold down the left mouse button, drag the image to the desired position, and then release the mouse button. Rotate the image by positioning the mouse pointer on the green, round rotation handle until the pointer displays as a circular arrow. Hold down the left mouse button, drag in the desired direction, and then release the mouse button.

Inserting a Clip Art Image

Microsoft Office includes a gallery of media images you can insert in a worksheet such as clip art, photographs, and movie images, as well as sound clips. To insert an image in a worksheet, click the Insert tab and then click the Clip Art button in the Illustrations group. This displays the Clip Art task pane at the right side of the screen as shown in Figure 8.6.

Figure 8.6 Clip Art Task Pane

Type in this text box the word or topic for which you are searching.

Use these options to specify where to search and the media types.

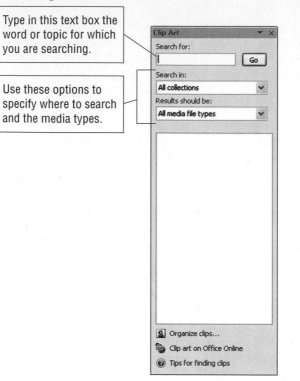

To view all picture, sound, and motion files, make sure the *Search for* text box in the Clip Art task pane does not contain any text and then click the Go button. When the desired image is visible, click the image to insert it in the worksheet. Use buttons in the Picture Tools Format tab shown in Figure 8.5 to format and customize the clip art image.

By default (unless it has been customized), the Clip Art task pane looks for all media images and sound clips found in all locations. You can narrow the search to specific locations and to specific images. The *Search in* option at the Clip Art task pane has a default setting of *All collections*. This can be changed to *My Collections*, *Office Collections*, and *Web Collections*. The *Results should be* option has a default setting of *Selected media file types*. Click the down-pointing arrow at the right side of this option to display media types. To search for a specific media type, remove the check mark before all options at the drop-down list but the desired type. For example, if you are searching only for photograph images, remove the check mark before Clip Art, Movies, and Sound.

If you are searching for specific images, click in the *Search for* text box, type the desired topic, and then click the Go button. For example, if you want to find images related to business, click in the *Search for* text box, type **business**, and then click the Go button. Clip art images related to *business* display in the viewing area of the task pane. If you are connected to the Internet, Word will search for images at the Office Online Web site matching the topic.

Project ③b Inserting an Image

1. With **ExcelL1_C8_P3.xlsx** open, insert a clip art image by completing the following steps:
   a. Click the Insert tab.
   b. Click the Clip Art button in the Illustrations group.
   c. At the Clip Art task pane, click the down-pointing arrow at the right side of the *Results should be* option box and then click the *Photographs*, *Movies*, and *Sounds* check boxes at the drop-down list to remove the check marks. Click in the task pane to remove the drop-down list.

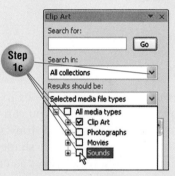

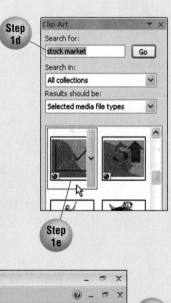

   d. Select any text that displays in the *Search for* text box, type **stock market**, and then press Enter.
   e. Click the image in the list box as shown at the right. (If you are not connected to the Internet and this image is not available, click a similar image.)
   f. Click the down-pointing at the right side of the *Results should be* option box and then click the *Photographs*, *Movies*, and *Sounds* check boxes at the drop-down list to insert check marks.
   g. Close the Clip Art task pane by clicking the Close button (contains an X) located in the upper right corner of the task pane.
2. Size and move the clip art image by completing the following steps:
   a. Click in the *Shape Width* measurement box, type 2.52, and then press Enter.

b. Position the mouse pointer on a border of the clip art image until the mouse pointer displays with a four-headed arrow attached. Hold down the left mouse button, drag the upper left corner of the clip art image so it is positioned in the upper left corner of cell A1, and then release the mouse button.

c. Change the height of the clip art image by positioning the mouse pointer on the bottom middle sizing handle until the mouse pointer displays as a double-headed arrow pointing up and down. Hold down the left mouse button, drag up until the bottom of the clip art image is aligned with the bottom of cell A1, and then release the mouse button.

3. Click outside the clip art image to deselect it.

4. Save **ExcelL1_C8_P3.xlsx**.

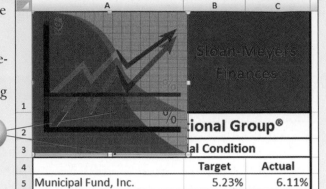

Step 2c

QUICK STEPS

Insert Shape
1. Click Insert tab.
2. Click Shapes button.
3. Click desired shape at drop-down list.
4. Drag in worksheet to create shape.

Inserting a Shape

In Chapter 7, you learned how to insert shapes in a chart. With the Shapes button in the Illustrations group in the Insert tab, you can also insert shapes in a worksheet. Use the Shapes button in the Insert tab to draw shapes in a worksheet including lines, basic shapes, block arrows, flow chart shapes, callouts, stars, and banners. Click a shape and the mouse pointer displays as crosshairs (plus sign). Position the crosshairs where you want the shape to begin, hold down the left mouse button, drag to create the shape, and then release the mouse button. This inserts the shape in the worksheet and also displays the Drawing Tools Format tab shown in Figure 8.7. Use buttons in this tab to change the shape, apply a style to the shape, arrange the shape, and change the size of the shape.

If you choose a shape in the *Lines* section of the drop-down list, the shape you draw is considered a *line drawing*. If you choose an option in the other sections of the drop-down list, the shape you draw is considered an *enclosed object*. When drawing an enclosed object, you can maintain the proportions of the shape by holding down the Shift key while dragging with the mouse to create the shape. You can type text in an enclosed object and then use buttons in the WordArt Styles group to format the text.

Shapes

Figure 8.7 Drawing Tools Format Tab

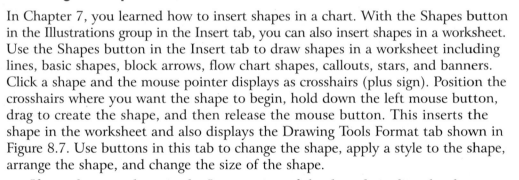

Copying Shapes

If you have drawn or inserted a shape, you may want to copy it to other locations in the worksheet. To copy a shape, select the shape and then click the Copy button in the Clipboard group in the Home tab. Position the insertion point at the location where you want the copied image and then click the Paste button. You can also copy a selected shape by holding down the Ctrl key while dragging the shape to the desired location.

QUICK STEPS

Copy Shape
1. Click in shape to select it.
2. Click Copy button.
3. Position insertion point in desired location.
4. Click Paste button.
OR
1. Click in shape to select.
2. Hold down Ctrl key.
3. Drag shape to desired location.

Project 3c — Drawing Arrow Shapes

1. With **ExcelL1_C8_P3.xlsx** open, create the tallest arrow shown in Figure 8.8 by completing the following steps:
   a. Click the Insert tab.
   b. Click the Shapes button and then click the *Up Arrow* shape (third option from the left in the top row of the *Block Arrows* section).
   c. Position the mouse pointer (displays as a thin, black cross) near the upper left corner of cell D1, hold down the left mouse button, drag down and to the right to create the shape as shown below, and then release the mouse button.

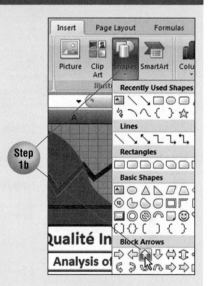

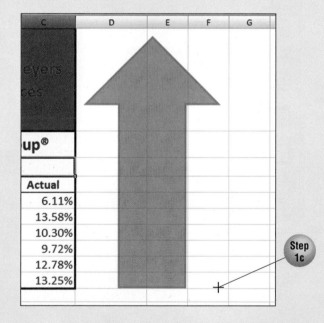

   d. Click in the *Shape Height* measurement box and then type 3.9.
   e. Click in the *Shape Width* measurement box, type 2.2, and then press Enter.

f. If necessary, drag the arrow so it is positioned as shown in Figure 8.8. (To drag the arrow, position the mouse pointer on the border of the selected arrow until the pointer turns into a four-headed arrow, hold down the left mouse button, drag the arrow to the desired position, and then release the mouse button.)

g. Click the More button at the right side of the shapes in the Shape Styles group and then click the *Intense Effect - Accent 1* option (second option from the left in the bottom row).

h. Click the Shape Effects button in the Shape Styles group, point to *Glow*, and then click the last option in the bottom row (*Accent color 6, 18 pt glow*).

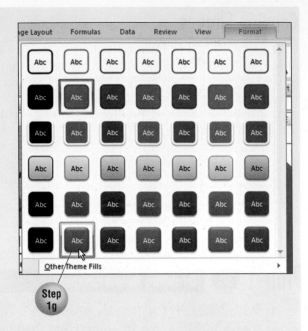

Step 1g

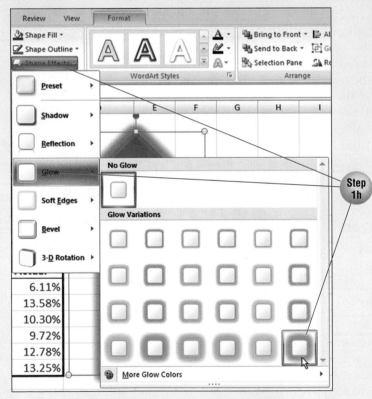

Step 1h

2. Insert text in the arrow shape by completing the following steps:
   a. With the arrow shape selected, type **McGuire Mutual Shares 5.33%**.
   b. Select the text you just typed (*McGuire Mutual Shares 5.33%*).

c. Click the More button at the right side of the styles in the WordArt Styles group and then click the second option from the left in the second row (*Fill - None, Outline - Accent 6, Glow - Accent 6*).

d. Click the Home tab.

e. Click the Top Align button in the Alignment group.

3. With the arrow selected, copy the arrow by completing the following steps:

a. Hold down the Ctrl key.

b. Position the mouse pointer on the arrow border until the pointer displays with a square box and plus symbol attached.

c. Hold down the left mouse button and drag to the right so the outline of the arrow is positioned at the right side of the existing arrow.

d. Release the mouse button and then release the Ctrl key.

4. Format the second arrow by completing the following steps:

a. With the second arrow selected, click the Drawing Tools Format tab.

b. Click in the *Shape Height* measurement box and then type 2.

c. Click in the *Shape Width* measurement box, type 1.7, and then press Enter

d. Select the text *McGuire Mutual Shares 5.33%* and then type **SR Linus Fund 0.22%**.

e. Drag the arrow so it is positioned as shown in Figure 8.8.

5. Change the orientation to landscape. (Make sure the cells containing data and the arrows will print on the same page.)

6. Save, print, and then close **ExcelL1_C8_P3.xlsx**.

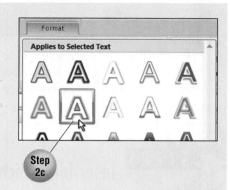

Step 2c

Figure 8.8 Project 3c

	A	B	C	D	E	F	G	H	I
1		Sloan-Meyers Finances %							
2	❖**Qualité International Group**®								
3	Analysis of Financial Condition								
4		Target	Actual						
5	Municipal Fund, Inc.	5.23%	6.11%						
6	McGuire Mutual Shares	8.25%	13.58%						
7	Silverton Growth Fund	10.00%	10.30%						
8	SR Linus Fund	9.50%	9.72%						
9	Regional Power Corporation	11.50%	12.78%						
10	United General Funds	12.00%	13.25%						
11									
12									

Project ④ Insert a Picture and Text Box in a Division Sales Workbook

You will open a division sales workbook and then insert, move, and size a picture. You will also insert a text box and then format the text.

Insert Picture
1. Click Insert tab.
2. Click Picture button.
3. Navigate to desired folder.
4. Double-click desired picture.

Inserting a Picture

To insert a picture in a worksheet, click the Insert tab and then click the Picture button in the Illustrations group. At the Insert Picture dialog box, navigate to the folder containing the desired picture and then double-click the picture. Use buttons in the Picture Tools Format tab to format and customize the picture.

Project ④a Inserting and Customizing a Picture

1. Open **ExcelC08Project04.xlsx** and then save the workbook and name it **ExcelL1_C8_P4**.
2. Make the following changes to the bird clip art image:
   a. Click the bird clip art image to select it.
   b. Click the Picture Tools Format tab.
   c. Click the Rotate button in the Arrange group and then click *Flip Horizontal* at the drop-down list.

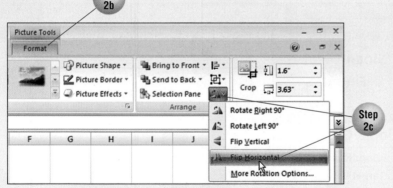

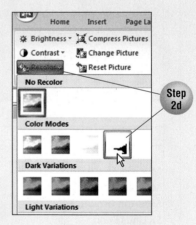

   d. Click the Recolor button in the Adjust group and then click the *Black and White* option in the *Color Modes* section.

e. Click in the *Shape Height* measurement box and
   then type 0.6.

f. Click in the *Shape Width* measurement box, type
   1.3, and then press Enter.

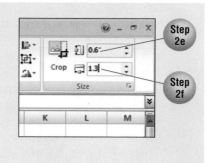

3. Insert and format a picture by completing the
   following steps:

a. Click in cell A1 outside of the bird image.

b. Click the Insert tab.

c. Click the Picture button in the Illustrations group.

d. At the Insert Picture dialog box, navigate to the
   Excel2007L1C8 folder on your storage medium and then
   double-click *Ocean.jpg*.

e. With the picture selected, click the Send to Back button in
   the Arrange group in the Picture Tools Format tab.

f. Use the sizing handles that display around the picture image
   to move and size it so it fills cell A1 as shown in Figure 8.9.

g. Click the bird clip art image and then drag the image so it is
   positioned as shown in Figure 8.9.

4. Save **ExcelL1_C8_P4.xlsx**.

Drawing and Formatting a Text Box

Use the Text Box button in the Insert tab to draw a text box in a worksheet. To
draw a text box, click the Insert tab and then click the Text Box button in the Text
group. This causes the mouse pointer to display as a thin, down-pointing arrow.
Position the arrow in the worksheet and then drag to create the text box. When
a text box is selected, the Drawing Tools Format tab displays with options for
customizing the text box.

    Click a text box to select it and a dashed border and sizing handles display
around the text box. If you want to delete the text box, click the text box border
again to change the dashed border lines to solid border lines and then press the
Delete key.

Project 4b   Inserting and Formatting a Text Box

1. With **ExcelL1_C8_P4.xlsx** open,
   draw a text box by completing the
   following steps:

a. Click the Insert tab.

b. Click the Text Box button in the
   Text group.

c. Drag in cell A1 to draw a text box
   the approximate size and shape
   shown at the right.

2. Format the text box by completing the
   following steps:
   a. Make sure the Drawing Tools Format tab
      is active.
   b. Click the Shape Fill button arrow in the
      Shape Styles group and then click *No Fill*
      at the drop-down gallery.
   c. Click the Shape Outline button arrow in
      the Shape Styles group and then click *No
      Outline* at the drop-down gallery.

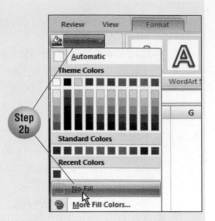

3. Insert text in the text box by completing the
   following steps:
   a. With the text box selected, click the
      Home tab.
   b. Click the Font button arrow and then click *Lucida Calligraphy* at the drop-down gallery.
      (You will need to scroll down the gallery to display this font.)
   c. Click the Font Size button arrow and then click *32* at the drop-down gallery.
   d. Click the Font Color button arrow and then click *White, Background 1* (first option in the
      first row in the *Theme Colors* section).
   e. Type **Seabird Productions**.
4. Move the text box so the text is positioned in cell A1 as shown in Figure 8.9. If necessary,
   move the bird clip art image. (To move the bird image, you may need to move the text box
   so you can select the image. Move the text box back to the desired location after moving
   the bird image.)
5. Save, print, and then close **ExcelL1_C8_P4.xlsx**.

Figure 8.9 Projects 4a and 4b

	A	B	C	D	E
1					
2	**Division**	**1st Half**	**2nd Half**	**Total**	
3	Northeast	$ 934,210	$ 1,002,390	$ 1,936,600	
4	Southeast	$ 745,231	$ 88,732	$ 833,963	
5	Northwest	$ 884,423	$ 745,932	$ 1,630,355	
6	Southwest	$ 342,091	$ 441,293	$ 783,384	
7	European	$ 554,205	$ 441,230	$ 995,435	
8	Asian	$ 779,040	$ 523,490	$ 1,302,530	
9					

Project ⑤ Insert a Watermark in an Equipment Usage Workbook

You will open an equipment usage report workbook and then insert a picture watermark that prints on both pages of the worksheet.

Inserting a Picture as a Watermark

A watermark is a lightened image that displays behind data in a file. You can create a watermark in a Word document but the watermark functionality is not available in Excel. You can, however, insert a picture in a header or footer and then resize and format the picture to display behind each page of the worksheet.

To create a picture watermark in a worksheet, click the Insert tab and then click the Header & Footer button in the Text group. With the worksheet in Print Layout view, click the Picture button in the Header & Footer Elements group in the Header & Footer Tools Design tab. At the Insert Picture dialog box, navigate to the desired folder and then double-click the desired picture. This inserts &[Picture] in the header. Resize and format the picture by clicking the Format Picture button in the Header & Footer Elements group. Use options at the Format Picture dialog box with the Size tab selected to specify the size of the picture and use options in the dialog box with the Picture tab selected to specify brightness and contrast.

QUICK STEPS

Insert Picture as Watermark
1. Click Insert tab.
2. Click Header & Footer button.
3. Click Picture button.
4. Navigate to desired folder.
5. Double-click desired picture.

Project ⑤ | Inserting a Picture as a Watermark

1. Open **ExcelC08Project05.xlsx** and then save the workbook and name it **ExcelL1_C8_P5**.
2. Insert a picture as a watermark by completing the following steps:
   a. Click the Insert tab.
   b. Click the Header & Footer button in the Text group.
   c. Click the Picture button in the Header & Footer Elements group in the Header & Footer Tools Design tab.
   d. At the Insert Picture dialog box, navigate to the Excel2007L1C8 folder on your storage medium and then double-click *Olympics.jpg*.
   e. Click the Format Picture button in the Header & Footer Elements group.
   f. At the Format Picture dialog box with the Size tab selected, click the *Lock aspect ratio* in the *Scale* section to remove the check mark.
   g. Select the current measurement in the *Height* measurement box in the *Size and rotate* section and then type 10.
   h. Select the current measurement in the *Width* measurement box in the *Size and rotate* section and then type 7.5.

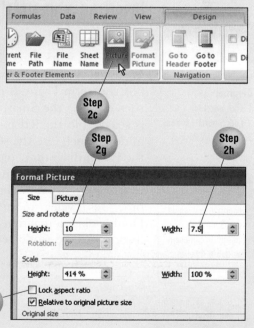

i. Click the Picture tab.
j. At the Format Picture dialog box with the Picture tab selected, select the current percentage number in the *Brightness* option box in the *Image control* section and then type 75.
k. Select the current percentage number in the *Contrast* option box and then type 25.
l. Click OK to close the Format Picture dialog box.
3. Click in the worksheet.
4. Display the worksheet in Print Preview to view how the image will print on page 1 and page 2 and then close Print Preview.
5. Save, print, and then close **ExcelL1_C8_P5.xlsx**. (If you are printing on a laser printer, the text may not print in the worksheet. Check with your instructor before printing this worksheet.)

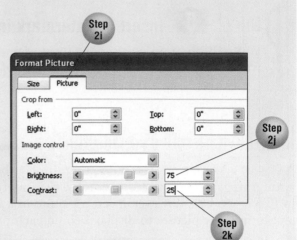

Step 2i

Step 2j

Step 2k

Project 6 Insert and Format Diagrams in a Company Sales Workbook

You will open a workbook that contains two company sales worksheets. You will insert and format a cycle diagram in one worksheet and insert and format a relationship diagram in the other. You will also create and format WordArt text.

Inserting a SmartArt Diagram

QUICK STEPS

Insert SmartArt Diagram
1. Click Insert tab.
2. Click SmartArt button.
3. Double-click desired diagram.

HINT
Generally, you would use a SmartArt diagram to represent text and a chart to represent numbers.

SmartArt

Excel includes the SmartArt feature you can use to insert diagrams and organizational charts in a worksheet. SmartArt offers a variety of predesigned diagrams and organizational charts that are available at the Choose a SmartArt Graphic dialog box shown in Figure 8.10. Display this dialog box by clicking the Insert tab and then clicking the SmartArt button in the Illustrations group. At the dialog box, *All* is selected in the left panel and all available predesigned diagrams display in the middle panel. Use the scroll bar at the right side of the middle panel to scroll down the list of diagram choices. Click a diagram in the middle panel and the name of the diagram displays in the right panel along with a description of the diagram type. SmartArt includes diagrams for presenting a list of data; showing data processes, cycles, and relationships; and presenting data in a matrix or pyramid. Double-click a diagram in the middle panel of the dialog box and the diagram is inserted in the worksheet.

Figure 8.10 Choose a SmartArt Graphic Dialog Box

Double-click the desired SmartArt graphic in this panel.

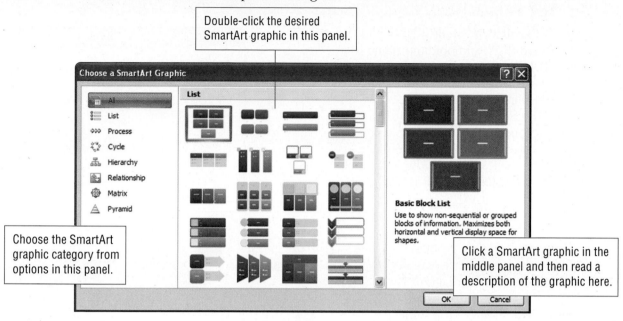

Choose the SmartArt graphic category from options in this panel.

Click a SmartArt graphic in the middle panel and then read a description of the graphic here.

Entering Data in a Diagram

Some diagrams are designed to include text. You can type text in a diagram by selecting the shape and then typing text in the shape or you can display a text pane and then type text in the pane. Display the text pane by clicking the Text Pane button in the Create Graphic group in the SmartArt Tools Design tab. Turn off the display of the pane by clicking the Text Pane button or by clicking the Close button that displays in the upper right corner of the text pane.

Sizing, Moving, and Deleting a Diagram

Increase or decrease the size of a diagram by dragging the diagram border. Increase or decrease the width of the diagram by positioning the mouse pointer on the set of four dots that displays in the middle of the left and right borders until the pointer turns into a left- and right-pointing arrow, hold down the left mouse button and then drag the border to the desired size. Increase or decrease the height of the diagram in a similar manner using the set of four dots that displays in the middle of the top and bottom borders. To increase or decrease both the height and the width of the diagram, drag one of the sets of three dots that displays in each corner of the border.

To move a diagram, select the diagram and then position the mouse pointer on the diagram border until the pointer turns into a four-headed arrow. Hold down the left mouse button, drag the diagram to the desired position, and then release the mouse button. Delete a diagram by selecting the diagram and then pressing the Delete key.

Project 6a Inserting a Diagram in a Worksheet

1. Open **ExcelC08Project06.xlsx** and then save the workbook and name it **ExcelL1_C8_P6**.
2. Create the diagram shown in Figure 8.11. To begin, click the Insert tab.
3. Click the SmartArt button in the Illustrations group.
4. At the Choose a SmartArt Graphic dialog box, click *Cycle* in the left panel.
5. Double-click *Radial Cycle* as shown at the right.
6. If the text pane is not open, click the Text Pane button in the Create Graphic group. (The text pane will display at the left side of the diagram.)
7. With the insertion point positioned after the top bullet in the text pane, type Evergreen Products.
8. Click the *[Text]* box below *Evergreen Products* and then type Seattle.
9. Click the next *[Text]* box and then type Olympia.
10. Click the next *[Text]* box and then type Portland.
11. Click the next *[Text]* box and then type Spokane.
12. Click the Text Pane button to turn off the display of the text pane.
13. Drag the diagram so it is positioned as shown in Figure 8.11. To drag the diagram, position the mouse pointer on the diagram border until the pointer turns into a four-headed arrow. Hold down the left mouse button, drag the diagram to the desired position, and then release the mouse button.
14. Increase or decrease the size of the diagram so it displays as shown in Figure 8.11. Use the sets of dots on the diagram border to drag the border to the desired size.
15. Save **ExcelL1_C8_P6.xlsx**.

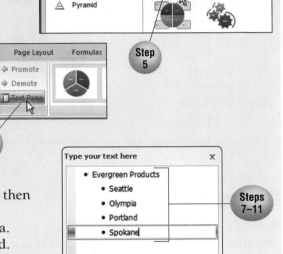

HINT

To restore the SmartArt default layout and color, click the Reset Graphic button in the Reset group in the SmartArt Tools Design tab.

Changing the Diagram Design

When you double-click a diagram at the dialog box, the diagram is inserted in the worksheet and the SmartArt Tools Design tab is active. With options and buttons in this tab, you can add objects, change the diagram layout, apply a style to the diagram, and reset the diagram back to the original formatting.

1. With **ExcelL1_C8_P6.xlsx** open, make sure the SmartArt Tools Design tab is active and the *Spokane* circle shape is selected.
2. Click the Right to Left button in the Create Graphic group. (This switches *Olympia* and *Spokane*.)
3. Click the More button located at the right side of the SmartArt Styles group and then click the *Polished* option at the drop-down list (first option from the left in the top row of the *3-D* section).

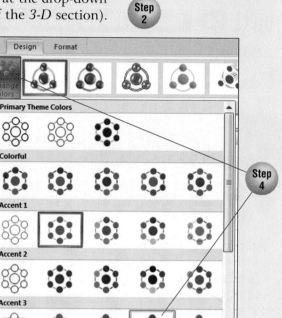

Step 2

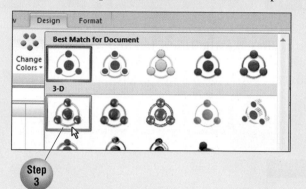

Step 3

4. Click the Change Colors button in the SmartArt Styles group and then click the fourth option from the left in the *Accent 3* section (*Gradient Loop - Accent 3*).
5. Click outside the diagram to deselect it.
6. Change the orientation to landscape. (Make sure the diagram fits on the first page.)
7. Save **ExcelC1_C8_P6.xlsx** and then print the Total Sales worksheet.

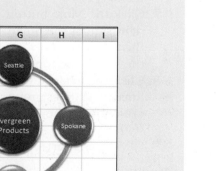

Step 4

Figure 8.11 Projects 6a and 6b

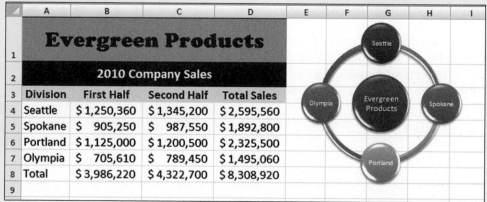

Division	First Half	Second Half	Total Sales
Evergreen Products			
2010 Company Sales			
Seattle	$ 1,250,360	$ 1,345,200	$ 2,595,560
Spokane	$ 905,250	$ 987,550	$ 1,892,800
Portland	$ 1,125,000	$ 1,200,500	$ 2,325,500
Olympia	$ 705,610	$ 789,450	$ 1,495,060
Total	$ 3,986,220	$ 4,322,700	$ 8,308,920

Changing the Diagram Formatting

Click the SmartArt Tools Format tab and options display for formatting a diagram. Use buttons in this tab to insert and customize shapes; apply a shape quick style; customize shapes; insert WordArt quick styles; and specify the position, alignment, rotation, wrapping style, height, and width of the diagram.

Project **6C**   **Changing the Diagram Formatting**

1. With **ExcelL1_C8_P6.xlsx** open, click the Seattle Sales worksheet tab.
2. Create the diagram shown in Figure 8.12. To begin, click the Insert tab and then click the SmartArt button in the Illustrations group.
3. At the Choose a SmartArt Graphic dialog box, click *Relationship* in the left panel and then double-click *Gear* in the middle panel.

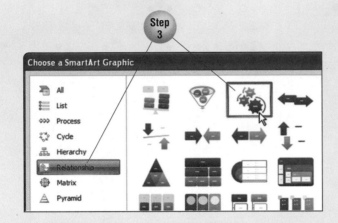

4. Click *[Text]* that appears in the bottom gear and then type **Quality Products**.
5. Click *[Text]* that appears in the left gear and then type **Customized Plans**.
6. Click *[Text]* that appears in the top gear and then type **Exemplary Service**.
7. Click the More button that displays at the right side of the SmartArt Styles group and then click the *Inset* option (second option from the left in the top row of the *3-D* section).
8. Click the Change Colors button in the SmartArt Styles group and then click the third option from the left in the *Accent 3* section (*Gradient Range - Accent 3*).
9. Click the SmartArt Tools Format tab.

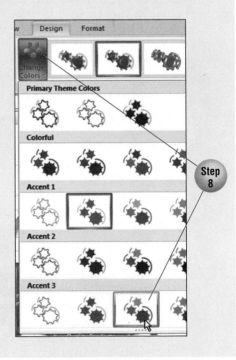

10. Click the Size button located at the right side of the tab.
11. Click in the *Height* text box and then type 3.75.
12. Click in the *Width* text box, type 5.25, and then press Enter.

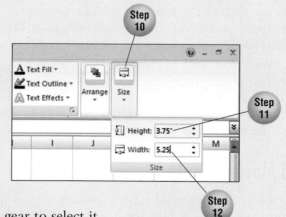

13. Click the bottom gear to select it.
14. Click the Shape Fill button arrow in the Shape Styles group and then click the bottom dark green color (*Olive Green, Accent 3, Darker 50%*) that displays in the *Theme Colors* section.
15. Click the top gear to select it.
16. Click the Shape Fill button arrow and then click the dark green color (*Olive Green, Accent 3, Darker 25%*) that displays in the *Theme Colors* section.
17. Change the orientation to landscape.
18. Move the diagram so it fits on the first page and displays as shown in Figure 8.12.
19. Save **ExcelL1_C8_P6.xlsx** and then print the Seattle Sales worksheet.

Figure 8.12 Project 6c

	Customer	First Half	Second Half	Total Sales
	Evergreen Products			
	2010 Total Sales			
3	**Customer**	**First Half**	**Second Half**	**Total Sales**
4	Harbor Manufacturing	$ 32,500	$ 41,305	$ 73,805
5	Timberlake Designs	$ 10,200	$ 14,230	$ 24,430
6	Cascade Plastics	$ 64,230	$ 50,304	$ 114,534
7	Avalon Clinic	$105,300	$ 105,300	$ 210,600
8	Gravelly Lake Plumbing	$200,500	$ 150,700	$ 351,200
9	Bavarian Productions	$ 45,890	$ 29,405	$ 75,295
10	Stealth Media	$ 5,300	$ 2,950	$ 8,250
11	Robinson Group	$136,492	$ 144,366	$ 280,858
12	Lincoln Services	$ 21,890	$ 18,445	$ 40,335
13	Danmark Contracting	$ 45,750	$ 50,250	$ 96,000
14	Earthway Systems	$ 35,500	$ 28,750	$ 64,250
15			**Total Sales**	$1,339,557

QUICK STEPS

Create WordArt
1. Click Insert tab.
2. Click WordArt button.
3. Click desired WordArt style at drop-down list.
4. Type desired text.

WordArt

Creating WordArt

With the WordArt application, you can distort or modify text to conform to a variety of shapes. This is useful for creating company logos and headings. With WordArt, you can change the font, style, and alignment of text. You can also use different fill patterns and colors, customize border lines, and add shadow and three-dimensional effects.

To insert WordArt in an Excel worksheet, click the Insert tab, click the WordArt button in the Text group, and then click the desired option at the drop-down list. This displays *Your Text Here* inserted in the worksheet in the WordArt option you selected at the gallery. Type the desired text and then use the buttons on the Drawing Tools Format tab to format the WordArt.

HINT

To remove WordArt style from text and retain the text, click the More button in the WordArt Styles group in the Drawing Tools Format tab and then click *Clear WordArt.*

Sizing and Moving WordArt

WordArt text inserted in a worksheet is surrounded by white sizing handles. Use the white sizing handles to change the height and width of the WordArt text. To move WordArt text, position the arrow pointer on the border of the WordArt until the pointer displays with a four-headed arrow attached. Hold down the left mouse button, drag the outline of the WordArt text box to the desired position, and then release the mouse button. When you change the shape of the WordArt text, the WordArt border displays with a purple diamond shape. Use this shape to change the slant of the WordArt text.

Project 6d   Inserting and Formatting WordArt

1. With **ExcelL1_C8_P6.xlsx** open, click the Total Sales worksheet tab.
2. Make cell A1 active and then press the Delete key. (This removes the text from the cell.)
3. Increase the height of row 1 to 136.50.
4. Click the Insert tab.
5. Click the WordArt button in the Text group and then click the last option in the top row (*Fill - Accent 3, Outline - Text 2*).

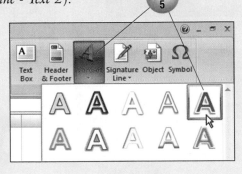

Step 5

6. Type **Evergreen**, press the Enter key, and then type **Products**.
7. Position the mouse pointer on the WordArt border until the pointer displays with a four-headed arrow attached and then drag the WordArt inside cell A1.

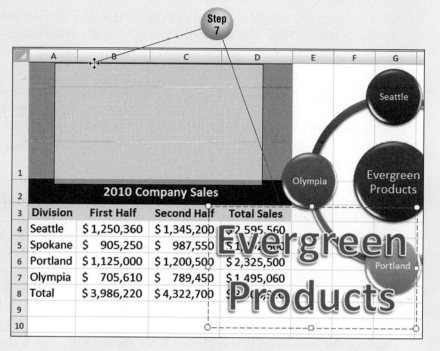

8. Click the Text Fill button arrow in the WordArt Styles group and then click the dark green color (*Olive Green, Accent 3, Darker 25%*).
9. Click the Text Outline button arrow in the WordArt Styles group and then click the dark green color (*Olive Green, Accent 3, Darker 50%*).
10. Resize the chart and position it so it prints on one page with the data.
11. Click the Seattle Sales worksheet tab and then complete steps similar to those in Steps 2 through 10 to insert *Evergreen Products* as WordArt.
12. Save **ExcelL1_C8_P6.xlsx** and then print both worksheets.
13. Close **ExcelL1_C8_P6.xlsx**.

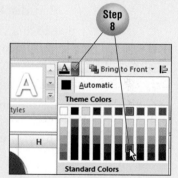

CHAPTER summary

- Save a workbook as a Web page by changing the *Save as type* option at the Save As dialog box to *Single File Web Page (*.mht; *.mhtml)* or *Web Page (*.htm; *.html)*.

- To open a Web page in Internet Explorer, open the browser, click File on the Menu bar, and then click *Open* at the drop-down list.

- To create a hyperlink in a workbook, select the text, click the Insert tab, and then click the Hyperlink button in the Links group. At the Insert Hyperlink dialog box, type the file name or Web site URL in the *Address* text box.

- To modify or edit a hyperlink, right-click the hyperlink and then click *Edit Hyperlink* at the shortcut menu.

- Insert symbols with options at the Symbol dialog box with the Symbols tab or the Special Characters tab selected. Click the Insert tab and then click the Symbol button to display the dialog box.

- With buttons in the Illustrations group in the Insert tab, you can insert a picture, clip art image, shapes, or a SmartArt diagram.

- When you insert a picture or clip art image in a worksheet, the Picture Tools Format tab is active and includes options for adjusting the image, applying preformatted styles, and arranging and sizing the image.

- Change the size of an image with the *Shape Height* and *Shape Width* measurement boxes in the Size group in the Picture Tools Format tab or with the sizing handles that display around the selected image.

- Move an image by positioning the mouse pointer on the image border until the pointer displays with a four-headed arrow attached and then drag the image to the desired location.

- Delete a selected image by pressing the Delete key.

- Rotate an image by positioning the mouse pointer on the green rotation handle until the pointer displays as a circular arrow and then dragging in the desired direction.

- Insert an image in a workbook with options at the Clip Art task pane. Display this task pane by clicking the Insert tab and then clicking the Clip Art button in the Illustrations group.

- With options at the Clip Art task pane, you can narrow the search for images to specific locations and to specific images.

- To draw shapes in a workbook, click the Insert tab, click the Shapes button in the Illustrations group, and then click the desired shape at the drop-down list. Drag in the worksheet to draw the shape. To maintain the proportions of the shape, hold down the Shift key while dragging in the worksheet.

- Copy a shape with the Copy and Paste buttons in the Clipboard group in the Home tab or by holding down the Ctrl key while dragging the shape.

- You can type text in an enclosed drawn object.

- To insert a picture in a worksheet, click the Insert tab and then click the Picture button in the Illustrations group. At the Insert Picture dialog box, navigate to the desired folder and then double-click the file name.

- Draw a text box in a worksheet by clicking the Insert tab, clicking the Text Box button in the Text group and then dragging in the worksheet. Use options at the Drawing Tools Format tab to format and customize the text box.
- A watermark is a lightened image that displays behind data in a file. You can create a picture watermark in a worksheet by inserting a picture in a header or footer and then changing the size and formatting of the picture.
- Insert a SmartArt diagram in a worksheet by clicking the Insert tab, clicking the SmartArt button in the Illustrations group, and then double-clicking the desired diagram at the Choose a SmartArt Graphic dialog box. Customize a diagram with options in the SmartArt Tools Design tab or the SmartArt Tools Format tab.
- Use WordArt to create, distort, modify, and/or conform text to a variety of shapes. Insert WordArt in a worksheet by clicking the Insert tab, clicking the WordArt button in the Text group, and then clicking the desired option at the drop-down list.
- Customize WordArt text with options in the Drawing Tools Format tab.
- Size WordArt using the sizing handles that display around selected WordArt text and move selected WordArt by dragging it to the desired location using the mouse.

COMMANDS review

FEATURE	RIBBON TAB, GROUP	BUTTON	KEYBOARD SHORTCUT
Insert Hyperlink dialog box	Insert, Links		Ctrl + K
Symbol dialog box	Insert, Text		
Clip Art task pane	Insert, Illustrations		
Shapes drop-down list	Insert, Illustrations		
Insert Picture dialog box	Insert, Illustrations		
Text box	Insert, Text		
Choose a SmartArt Graphic dialog box	Insert, Illustrations		
WordArt drop-down list	Insert, Text		

CONCEPTS check

Test Your Knowledge

Completion: In the space provided at the right, indicate the correct term, symbol, or command.

1. Change the *Save as type* option at the Save As dialog box to this to save the open workbook as a single Web page.

   SINGLE FILE WEB PAGE

2. Click the Insert tab and then click the Hyperlink button and this dialog box displays.

   INSERT HYPERLINK DIALOG BOX

3. The Symbol button is located in this tab.

   INSERT TAB

4. The *Font* option is available at the Symbol dialog box with this tab selected.

   SYMBOLS

5. Insert a picture, clip art image, shape, or SmartArt diagram with buttons in this group in the Insert tab.

   ILLUSTRATIONS

6. When you insert a picture or clip art image in a worksheet, this tab is active.

   PICTURE TOOLS FORMAT TAB

7. Maintain the proportions of the image by holding down this key while dragging a sizing handle.

   SHIFT KEY

8. To move an image, position the mouse pointer on the image border until the mouse pointer displays with this attached and then drag the image to the desired location.

   FOUR HEADED ARROW

9. To copy a shape, hold down this key while dragging the shape.

   CTRL

10. When you draw a text box in a worksheet and then release the mouse button, this tab is active.

    DRAWING TOOLS FORMAT TAB

11. This term refers to a lightened image that displays behind data in a file.

    WATERMARK

12. Click the SmartArt button in the Illustrations group in the Insert tab and this dialog box displays.

    SMART ART GRAPHIC DIALOG BOX

SKILLS check

Demonstrate Your Proficiency

Assessment

1 INSERT A TEXT BOX IN AND SAVE A BOOK CLUB WORKBOOK AS A WEB PAGE

1. Display the Open dialog box with Excel2007L1C8 the active folder.
2. Open **ExcelC08Assessment01.xlsx** and then save the workbook and name it **ExcelL1_C8_A1**.
3. Draw a text box at the right side of the Books Galore clip art image with the following specifications:
   a. Change the height to 1.7″ and the width to 2.7″.
   b. Remove the text box outline.
   c. Click the Middle Align button and the Center button in the Alignment group in the Home tab.
   d. Change the font to 32-point Forte and change the font color to blue.
   e. Type **Book of the Month Club News, 2010** in the text box.
4. Change the orientation to landscape.
5. Save and then print **ExcelL1_C8_A1.xlsx**.
6. Save **ExcelL1_C8_A1.xlsx** as a single Web page in the ExcelWebPages folder (you created this folder in Project 8a) on your storage medium and name it **BooksGaloreWebPage**.
7. Open Internet Explorer and then open **BooksGaloreWebPage.mht**.
8. Close Internet Explorer.
9. Print **BooksGaloreWebPage.mht** in landscape orientation.
10. Select E12 and hyperlink it to *www.microsoft.com*.
11. Select E13 and hyperlink it to *www.symantec.com*.
12. Select E14 and hyperlink it to *www.nasa.gov*.
13. Select E15 and hyperlink it to *www.cnn.com*.
14. Make sure you are connected to the Internet and then click the hyperlink to NASA.
15. Jump to a link from the NASA Web page that interests you.
16. Print the page you viewed from NASA and then close the browser application window.
17. Jump to each of the remaining links in the Web page. At each Web page, jump to a link that interests you, print the page, and then close the browser application window.
18. Save (click Yes at the compatibility dialog box) and then close **BooksGaloreWebPage.mht**.

Assessment

2 INSERT A CLIP ART IMAGE AND WORDART IN AN EQUIPMENT PURCHASE WORKBOOK

1. Open **ExcelC08Assessment02.xlsx** and then save the workbook and name it **ExcelL1_C8_A2**.
2. Insert a formula in cell E4 using the PMT function that calculates monthly payments. *Hint: Refer to Chapter 2, Project 3a.*
3. Copy the formula in cell E4 down to cells E5 and E6.
4. Insert a formula in cell F4 that calculates the total amount of the payments. *Hint: Refer to Chapter 2, Project 3a.*
5. Copy the formula in cell F4 down to cells F5 and F6.
6. Insert a formula in cell G4 that calculates to the total amount of interest paid. *Hint: Refer to Chapter 2, Project 3a.*
7. Copy the formula in cell G4 down to cells G5 and G6.
8. Increase the height of row 1 to 75.00.
9. Delete *BAYSIDE TRAVEL* in cell A1.
10. Insert the clip art image shown in Figure 8.13 (search for this clip art by searching only for clip art images [remove check marks from *Photographs*, *Movies*, and *Sound*] and typing **travel** in the *Search for* text box). If this clip art image is not available, choose another image related to travel. (Before closing the Clip Art task pane, reinsert check marks in the *Photographs*, *Movies*, and *Sound* check boxes at the *Results should be* option drop-down list.)
11. Size and move the clip art image so it is positioned as shown in Figure 8.13.
12. Insert the company name as WordArt as shown in Figure 8.13 with the following specifications:
    a. Create the WordArt with the second option from the left in the bottom row of the WordArt drop-down list (*Fill - Accent 6, Warm Matte Bevel*).
    b. Select the WordArt text, click the Text Fill button arrow in the WordArt Styles group, and then click the light blue color (in the *Standard Colors* section) at the drop-down gallery.
13. Change the worksheet orientation to landscape
14. Save, print, and then close **ExcelL1_C8_A2.xlsx**.

Figure 8.13 Assessment 2

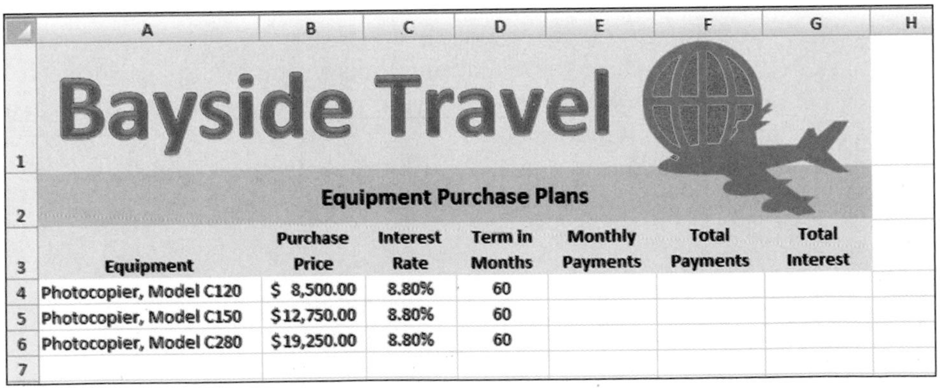

	A	B	C	D	E	F	G	H
1	**Bayside Travel**							
2			Equipment Purchase Plans					
3	Equipment	Purchase Price	Interest Rate	Term in Months	Monthly Payments	Total Payments	Total Interest	
4	Photocopier, Model C120	$ 8,500.00	8.80%	60				
5	Photocopier, Model C150	$12,750.00	8.80%	60				
6	Photocopier, Model C280	$19,250.00	8.80%	60				
7								

Assessment 3

INSERT AND FORMAT SHAPES IN A COMPANY SALES WORKBOOK

1. Open **ExcelC08Assessment03.xlsx** and then save the workbook and name it **ExcelL1_C8_A3**.
2. In cell A1, type **Mountain**, press Alt + Enter, and then type **Systems**.
3. Select *Mountain Systems* and then change the font to 24-point Calibri bold.
4. Change the horizontal alignment of cell A1to left and the vertical alignment to center.
5. Display the Format Cells dialog box with the Alignment tab selected and then change the *Indent* measurement to *1*. ***Hint: Display the Format Cells dialog box by clicking the Alignment group dialog box launcher in the Home tab.***
6. Click outside cell A1.
7. Use the *Isosceles Triangle* shape located in the *Basic Shapes* section of the Shapes drop-down palette to draw a triangle as shown in Figure 8.14.
8. Copy the triangle three times. Add green fill, dark green outline color, and a shadow effect of your choosing to the triangles so they appear in a similar manner to the triangles in Figure 8.14. Position the triangles as shown in the figure.
9. Save, print, and then close **ExcelL1_C8_A3.xlsx**.

Figure 8.14 Assessment 3

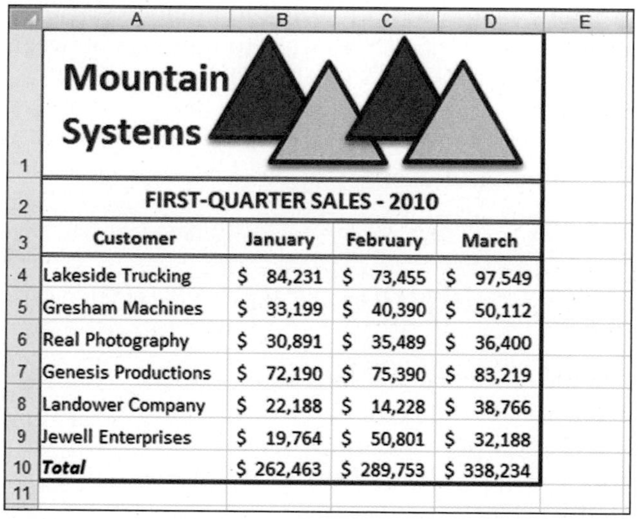

	A	B	C	D	E
1	Mountain Systems				
2	FIRST-QUARTER SALES - 2010				
3	Customer	January	February	March	
4	Lakeside Trucking	$ 84,231	$ 73,455	$ 97,549	
5	Gresham Machines	$ 33,199	$ 40,390	$ 50,112	
6	Real Photography	$ 30,891	$ 35,489	$ 36,400	
7	Genesis Productions	$ 72,190	$ 75,390	$ 83,219	
8	Landower Company	$ 22,188	$ 14,228	$ 38,766	
9	Jewell Enterprises	$ 19,764	$ 50,801	$ 32,188	
10	*Total*	$ 262,463	$ 289,753	$ 338,234	
11					

Assessment 4

INSERT AND FORMAT A SMARTART DIAGRAM IN A SALES WORKBOOK

1. Open **ExcelC08Assessment04.xlsx** and then save the workbook and name it **ExcelL1_C8_A4**.
2. Change the orientation to landscape.
3. Insert a pyramid shape at the right side of the worksheet data using the *Basic Pyramid* SmartArt diagram and insert the following information in the pyramid:
   a. In the bottom shape, type **Red Level**, press Enter, and then type **$25,000 - $49,999**.

b. In the middle shape, type **Blue Level**, press Enter, and then type $50,000 - $99,999.

c. In the top shape, type **Gold Level**, press Enter, and then type **$100,000+**.

d. Change the font size and/or move the text so the text displays in each shape.

e. Change the color of the shapes to match the color level.

f. If necessary, change the color of the text inside the shapes so it is easy to read.

g. Size and/or move the diagram so it displays attractively at the right side of the worksheet data. (Make sure the entire diagram will print on the same page as the worksheet data.)

4. Save, print, and then close **ExcelL1_C8_A4.xlsx**.

Assessment

5 APPLY CONDITIONAL FORMATTING TO CELLS IN A SALES WORKBOOK

1. Using the Help feature, learn about applying conditional formatting to numbers in cells that match a specific range.

2. Open **ExcelL1_C8_A4.xlsx** and then save the workbook and name it **ExcelL1_C8_A5**.

3. Using the conditional formatting feature, apply the following formatting to amounts in the *Total* column:

a. Apply red color formatting to numbers between $25,000 and $49,999.

b. Apply blue color formatting to numbers between $50,000 and $99,999.

c. Apply gold color formatting to numbers between $100,000 and $500,000.

4. Save, print, and then close **ExcelL1_C8_A5.xlsx**.

CASE study
Apply Your Skills

Part 1

You are the office manager for Ocean Truck Sales and are responsible for maintaining a spreadsheet of the truck and SUV inventory. Open **ExcelC08Ocean.xlsx** and then save the workbook and name it **ExcelL1_C8_CS_P1**. Apply formatting to improve the appearance of the worksheet and insert at least one clip art image (related to "truck" or "ocean"). Save **ExcelL1_C8_CS_P1.xlsx** and then print the worksheet.

Part 2

You have been asked to save the inventory worksheet as a Web page for viewing online and also to insert hyperlinks to various sites. With **ExcelL1_C8_CS_P1.xlsx** open, locate at least one financial institution in your area that will finance an automobile and then insert in the worksheet a hyperlink to that site. Locate another site that provides information on book value of a used automobile and then insert in the worksheet a hyperlink to that site. Save the workbook as a single Web page with the name **ExcelC08OceanWebPage**. Open your Internet browser and then open the Web page. Click each hyperlink to make sure it takes you to the proper Web site. Close your Internet browser and then close **ExcelC08OceanWebPage.mht**.

Part 3

Open **ExcelL1_C8_CS_P1.xlsx** and then save it with Save As and name it **ExcelL1_C8_CS_P3**. You make the inventory workbook available to each salesperson at the beginning of the week. For easier viewing, you decide to divide the workbook into two worksheets with one worksheet containing all Ford vehicles and the other worksheet containing all Chevrolet vehicles. Rename the worksheet tabs to reflect the contents. Sort each worksheet by price from the most expensive to the least expensive. The owner offers incentives each week to help motivate the sales force. Insert in the first worksheet a SmartArt diagram of your choosing that contains the following information:

> Small-sized truck = $100
> 2WD Regular Cab = $75
> SUV 4x4 = $50

Copy the diagram in the first worksheet and then paste it into the second worksheet. Change the orientation to landscape and then save, print, and close **ExcelL1_C8_CS_P3.xlsx**.

Part 4

As part of your weekly duties, you need to post the incentive diagram in various locations throughout the company. You decide to insert the diagram in PowerPoint for easy printing. Open **ExcelL1_C8_CS_P3.xlsx** and then open PowerPoint. Change the slide layout in PowerPoint to Blank. Copy the diagram in the first worksheet and paste it into the PowerPoint blank slide. Increase and/or move the diagram so it better fills the slide. Print the slide and then close PowerPoint without saving the presentation. Close **ExcelL1_C8_CS_P3.xlsx**.

ASSESSING proficiency

In this unit, you have learned how to work with multiple windows; move, copy, link, and paste data between workbooks and applications; create and customize charts with data in a worksheet; save a workbook as a Web page; insert hyperlinks; and insert and customize pictures, clip art images, shapes, SmartArt diagrams, and WordArt.

Note: Before beginning computer assessments, copy to your storage medium the Excel2007L1U2 subfolder from the Excel2007L1 folder on the CD that accompanies this textbook and then make Excel2007L1U2 the active folder.

Assessment 1 Copy and Paste Data and Insert WordArt in a Training Scores Workbook

1. Open **ExcelU02Assessment01.xlsx** and then save the workbook and name it **ExcelL1_U2_A1**.
2. Delete row 15 (the row for *Kwieciak, Kathleen*).
3. Insert a formula in cell D4 that averages the percentages in cells B4 and C4.
4. Copy the formula in cell D4 down to cells D5 through D20.
5. Make cell A22 active, turn on bold, and then type **Highest Averages**.
6. Display the Clipboard task pane and make sure it is empty.
7. Select and then copy each of the following rows (individually): row 7, 10, 14, 16, and 18.
8. Make cell A23 active and then paste row 14 (the row for *Jewett, Troy*).
9. Make cell A24 active and then paste row 7 (the row for *Cumpston, Kurt*).
10. Make cell A25 active and then paste row 10 (the row for *Fisher-Edwards, Theresa*).
11. Make cell A26 active and then paste row 16 (the row for *Mathias, Caleb*).
12. Make cell A27 active and then paste row 18 (the row for *Nyegaard, Curtis*).
13. Click the Clear All button in the Clipboard task pane and then close the task pane.
14. Insert in cell A1 the text *Roseland* as WordArt. Format the WordArt text to add visual appeal to the worksheet.
15. Save, print, and then close **ExcelL1_U2_A1.xlsx**.

Assessment 2 Manage Multiple Worksheets in a Projected Earnings Workbook

1. Open **ExcelU02Assessment02.xlsx** and then save the workbook and name it **ExcelL1_U2_A2**.
2. Delete *Roseland* in cell A1. Open **ExcelL1_U2_A1.xlsx** and then copy the *Roseland* WordArt text and paste it into cell A1 in **ExcelL1_U2_A2.xlsx**. If necessary, increase the height of row 1 to accommodate the WordArt text.
3. Notice the fill color in cells in **ExcelL1_U2_A1.xlsx** and then apply the same fill color to cells of data in **ExcelL1_U2_A2.xlsx**. Close **ExcelL1_U2_A1.xlsx**.
4. Select cells A1 through C11 and then copy and paste the cells to Sheet2 keeping the source column widths.
5. With Sheet2 displayed, make the following changes:
   a. Increase the height of row 1 to accommodate the WordArt text.
   b. Delete the contents of cell B2.
   c. Change the contents of the following cells:
   > A6: Change *January* to *July*
   > A7: Change *February* to *August*
   > A8: Change *March* to *September*
   > A9: Change *April* to *October*
   > A10: Change *May* to *November*
   > A11: Change *June* to *December*
   > B6: Change *8.30%* to *8.10%*
   > B8: Change *9.30%* to *8.70%*
6. Make Sheet1 active and then copy cell B2 and paste link it to cell B2 in Sheet2.
7. Rename Sheet1 to *First Half* and rename Sheet2 to *Second Half*.
8. Make the First Half worksheet active and then determine the effect on projected monthly earnings if the projected yearly income is increased by 10% by changing the number in cell B2 to *$1,480,380*.
9. Save the workbook (two worksheets) again and then print both worksheets of the workbook so they are horizontally and vertically centered on each page.
10. Determine the effect on projected monthly earnings if the projected yearly income is increased by 20% by changing the number in cell B2 to *$1,614,960*.
11. Save the workbook again and then print both worksheets of the workbook so they are horizontally and vertically centered on each page.
12. Close **ExcelL1_U2_A2.xlsx**.

Assessment 3 Create Charts in Worksheets in a Sales Totals Workbook

1. Open **ExcelU02Assessment03** and then save the workbook and name it **ExcelL1_U2_A3**.
2. Insert the heading **Average Sales 2008-2010** (on multiple lines) in cell A13. ⟨ALT ENTER⟩
3. Insert a formula in cell B13 with a 3-D reference that averages the total in cells B4 through B11 in Sheet1, Sheet2, and Sheet3.
4. Insert a formula in cell C13 with a 3-D reference that averages the total in cells C4 through C11 in Sheet1, Sheet2, and Sheet3.
5. Rename Sheet1 to *2008 Sales*, rename Sheet2 to *2009 Sales*, and rename Sheet3 to *2010 Sales*.
6. Make the 2008 Sales worksheet active, select cells A3 through C11 and create a column chart. Click the Switch Row/Column button at the Chart Tools Design tab. Apply formatting to increase the visual appeal of the chart. Drag the chart below the worksheet data. (Make sure the chart fits on the page.)

7. Make the 2009 Sales worksheet active and then create the same type of chart you created in Step 6.
8. Make the 2010 Sales worksheet active and then create the same type of chart you created in Step 6.
9. Save the workbook and then print the entire workbook.
10. Close **ExcelL1_U2_A3.xlsx**.

Assessment 4 Create and Format a Line Chart

1. Type the following information in a worksheet:

Country	Total Sales
Denmark	$85,345
Finland	$71,450
Norway	$135,230
Sweden	$118,895

2. Using the data just entered in the worksheet, create a line chart with the following specifications:
   a. Apply a chart style of your choosing.
   b. Insert major and minor primary vertical gridlines.
   c. Insert drop lines. (Do this with the Lines button in the Analysis group in the Chart Tools Layout tab.)
   d. Apply any other formatting to improve the visual appeal of the chart.
   e. Move the chart to a new sheet.
3. Save the workbook and name it **ExcelL1_U2_A4**.
4. Print only the sheet containing the chart.
5. Change the line chart to a bar chart of your choosing.
6. Save the workbook and then print only the sheet containing the chart.
7. Close **ExcelL1_U2_A4.xlsx**.

Assessment 5 Create and Format a Pie Chart

1. Open **ExcelU02Assessment05.xlsx** and then save the workbook and name it **ExcelL1_U2_A5**.
2. Create a pie chart as a separate sheet with the data in cells A3 through B10. You determine the type of pie. Include an appropriate title for the chart and include percentage labels.
3. Print only the sheet containing the chart.
4. Save and then close **ExcelL1_U2_A5.xlsx**.

Assessment 6 Insert a Text Box in and Save a Travel Workbook as a Web Page

1. Open **ExcelU02Assessment06.xlsx** and then save the workbook and name it **ExcelL1_U2_A6**.
2. Insert a text box in the workbook with the following specifications:
   a. Draw the text box at the right side of the clip art image.
   b. Remove the fill in the text box and the outline around the text box.
   c. Type Call 1-888-555-1288 for last-minute vacation specials!
   d. Select the text and then change the font to 20-point Bradley Hand ITC in blue color and turn on bold.
   e. Size and position the text box so it appears visually balanced with the travel clip art image.
3. Make sure you are connected to the Internet and then search for sites that might be of interest to tourists for each of the cities in the worksheet. Write down the URL for the best Web page you find for each city.

URL- UNIFORM RESOURCE LOCATOR
ie: www.
http.

4. Create a hyperlink for each city to jump to the URL you wrote down in Step 3. (Select the hyperlink text in each cell and change the font size to 18 points.)
5. Save **ExcelL1_U2_A6.xlsx** and then print the worksheet.
6. Create a new folder named TravelWebPages in the Excel2007L1U2 folder.
7. Save **ExcelL1_U2_A6.xlsx** as a single file Web page in the TravelWebPages folder with the following specifications:
   a. Name the Web page **TravelAdvantageWebPage**.
   b. Change the title to *Winter Getaway Destinations!*
8. Open Internet Explorer and then open **TravelAdvantageWebPage.mht**.
9. Test the hyperlinks to make sure you entered the URLs correctly by clicking each hyperlink and then closing the Web browser.
10. Close **TravelAdvantageWebPage.mht** and then close Internet Explorer.
11. Save and then close **ExcelL1_U2_A6.xlsx**.

Assessment 7 Insert Clip Art Image and Smart Diagram in a Projected Quotas Workbook

1. Open **ExcelU02Assessment07.xlsx** and then save the workbook and name it **ExcelL1_U2_A7**.
2. Insert a formula in cell C3 using an absolute reference to determine the projected quotas at 10% of the current quotas.
3. Copy the formula in cell C3 down to cells C4 through C12.
4. Insert a clip art image in row 1 related to money. You determine the size and position of the clip art image. If necessary, increase the height of the row.
5. Apply the following conditional formatting to the values in cells C3 through C12:
   Apply green color to values from $50,000 to $99,999.
   Apply blue color to values from $100,000 to $149,999.
   Apply red color to values from $150,000 to $200,000.
6. Insert a SmartArt diagram at the right side of the chart that contains three shapes. Insert the quota ranges in the shapes as identified in Step 5 and apply color fill to match the conditional formatting. (For example, type $50,000 to $99,999 in a shape and then apply green fill color to the shape.)
7. Change the orientation to landscape and make sure the diagram fits on the page.
8. Save, print, and then close **ExcelL1_U2_A7.xlsx**.

Assessment 8 Insert Symbol, Clip Art, and Comments in a Sales Workbook

1. Open **ExcelU02Assessment08.xlsx** and then save the workbook and name it **ExcelL1_U2_A8**.
2. Delete the text *Landower Company* and then type **Económico** in the cell. (Use the Symbol dialog box to insert *ó*.)
3. Insert a new row at the beginning of the worksheet.
4. Select and then merge cells A1 through D1.
5. Increase the height of row 1 to approximately 100.50.
6. Insert the text *Custom Interiors* as WordArt in cell A1. You determine the formatting of the WordArt. Move and size the WordArt so it fits in cell A1.
7. Insert the following comments in the specified cells:
   D4 = Increase amount to $100,000.
   A5 = Change the name to Gresham Technology.
   A9 = Decrease amounts for this company by 5%.

8. Turn on the display of all comments.
9. Print the worksheet with the comments as displayed on the worksheet.
10. Turn off the display of all comments.
11. Delete the comment in A5.
12. Print the worksheet again with the comments printed at the end of the worksheet. (The comments will print on a separate page from the worksheet.)
13. Save and then close **ExcelL1_U2_A8.xlsx**.

Assessment 9 Insert and Format a Shape in a Budget Workbook

1. Open **ExcelU02Assessment09.xlsx** and then save the workbook and name it **ExcelL1_U2_A9**.
2. Make the following changes to the worksheet so it displays as shown in Figure U2.1:
   a. Select and then merge cells A1 through D1.
   b. Add fill to the cells as shown in Figure U2.1.
   c. Increase the height of row 1 to the approximate size shown in Figure U2.1.
   d. Insert the text **SOLAR ENTERPRISES** in cell A1 set in 20-point Calibri bold, center and middle aligned, and set in aqua (Aqua, Accent 5, Darker 25%).
   e. Insert the sun shape (located in the *Basic Shapes* section of the Shapes button drop-down list). Apply orange shape fill and change the shape outline to aqua (Aqua, Accent 5, Darker 25%)
3. Save, print, and then close **ExcelL1_U2_A9.xlsx**.

Figure U2.1 Assessment 9

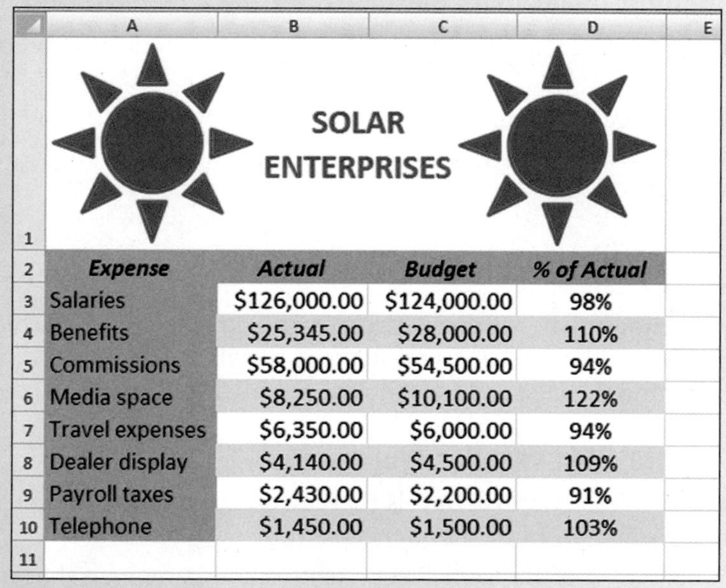

	Expense	Actual	Budget	% of Actual
3	Salaries	$126,000.00	$124,000.00	98%
4	Benefits	$25,345.00	$28,000.00	110%
5	Commissions	$58,000.00	$54,500.00	94%
6	Media space	$8,250.00	$10,100.00	122%
7	Travel expenses	$6,350.00	$6,000.00	94%
8	Dealer display	$4,140.00	$4,500.00	109%
9	Payroll taxes	$2,430.00	$2,200.00	91%
10	Telephone	$1,450.00	$1,500.00	103%

WRITING activities

The following activities give you the opportunity to practice your writing skills along with demonstrating an understanding of some of the important Excel features you have mastered in this unit. Use correct grammar, appropriate word choices, and clear sentence constructions.

Activity 1 Prepare a Projected Budget

You are the accounting assistant in the financial department of McCormack Funds and you have been asked to prepare a yearly proposed department budget. The total amount for the department is $1,450,000. You are given the percentages for the proposed budget items, which are: Salaries, 45%; Benefits, 12%; Training, 14%; Administrative Costs, 10%; Equipment, 11%; and Supplies, 8%. Create a worksheet with this information that shows the projected yearly budget, the budget items in the department, the percentage of the budget, and the amount for each item. After the worksheet is completed, save the workbook and name it **ExcelL1_U2_Act01**. Print and then close the workbook.

Optional: Using Word 2007, write a memo to the McCormack Funds Finance Department explaining that the proposed annual department budget is attached for their review. Comments and suggestions are to be sent to you within one week. Save the file and name it **ExcelL1_U2_Act01_Memo**. Print and then close the file.

Activity 2 Create a Travel Tours Bar Chart

Prepare a worksheet in Excel for Carefree Travels that includes the following information:

Scandinavian Tours

Country	Tours Booked
Norway	52
Sweden	62
Finland	29
Denmark	38

Use the information in the worksheet to create and format a bar chart as a separate sheet. Save the workbook and name it **ExcelL1_U2_Act02**. Print only the sheet containing the chart and then close **ExcelL1_U2_Act02.xlsx**.

Activity 3 Prepare a Ski Vacation Worksheet

Prepare a worksheet for Carefree Travels that advertises a snow skiing trip. Include the following information in the announcement:

- At the beginning of the worksheet, create a company logo that includes the company name *Carefree Travels* and a clip art image related to travel.
- Include the heading *Whistler Ski Vacation Package* in the worksheet.
- Include the following below the heading:
  - Round-trip air transportation: $395
  - Seven nights' hotel accommodations: $1,550
  - Four all-day ski passes: $425

○ Compact rental car with unlimited mileage: $250
○ Total price of the ski package: (calculate the total price)
• Include the following information somewhere in the worksheet:
○ Book your vacation today at special discount prices.
○ Two-for-one discount at many of the local ski resorts.

Save the workbook and name it **ExcelL1_U2_Act03**. Print and then close **ExcelL1_U2_Act03.xlsx**.

Find Information on Excel Books and Present the Data in a Worksheet

Locate two companies on the Internet that sell new books. At the first new book company site, locate three books on Microsoft Excel. Record the title, author, and price for each book. At the second new book company site, locate the same three books and record the prices. Create an Excel worksheet that includes the following information:

• Name of each new book company
• Title and author of the three books
• Prices for each book from the two book company sites

Create a hyperlink for each book company to the URL on the Internet. Then save the completed workbook and name it **ExcelL1_U2_InternetResearch**. Print and then close the workbook.

Create a Customized Time Card for a Landscaping Company

You are the manager of a landscaping company and are responsible for employee time cards. Locate the time card template that is available with *Installed Templates* selected in the New Workbook dialog box. Use the template to create a customized time card for your company. With the template open, delete the Company Name that displays in the middle header pane. Insert additional blank rows to increase the spacing above the Employee row. Insert a clip art image related to landscaping or gardening and position and size it attractively in the form. Include a text box with the text Lawn and Landscaping Specialists inside the box. Format, size, and position the text attractively in the form. Fill in the form for the current week with the following employee information:

Employee = Jonathan Holder
Address = 12332 South 152nd Street, Baton Rouge, LA 70804
Manager = (Your name)
Employee phone = (225) 555-3092
Employee e-mail = None

Regular hours = 8 hours for Monday, Tuesday, Wednesday, and Thursday
Overtime = 2 hours on Wednesday
Sick hours = None
Vacation = 8 hours on Friday
Rate per hour = $20.00
Overtime pay = $30.00

Save the completed form and name it **ExcelL1_U2_JobStudy**. Print and then close **ExcelL1_U2_JobStudy.xlsx**.

INDEX

workbooks, 199, 200, 203–204
workbooks at Open dialog box, 204
workbooks to another folder or drive, 205
worksheets, 167
worksheets between programs, 185–186
worksheets into Word documents, 186–187
worksheets to another workbook, 207–208
Copy option: at Open or Save As dialog box, 204, 205, 230
COUNT function, 48, 60
Create Graphic group, 293
Create New Folder button, 200, 230
Crop button, 281
Cube function category: in Excel, 43, 45
Currency category: at Format Cells dialog box, 86
Currency formatting: applying to numbers, 82
Current Selection group, 257
Custom category: at Format Cells dialog box, 86
Customize Quick Access Toolbar button, 14, 18
Customizing. *See also* Formatting
clip art images, 282
diagrams, 301
Help feature, 29, 31
hyperlinks, 275
images, 281
layout of chart labels, 249
margins, 110
pictures, 288–289
print jobs, 124, 139
shapes, 254–255, 296
text boxes, 289
WordArt, 301
Custom sort: completing, 132–133
Cut button, 158, 159, 188, 190
Cutting: workbooks, 205

D

Data. *See also* Cells
aligning and indenting in cells, 87–90
clearing in cells, 74
editing in cell, 12–13
editing in charts, 242, 262
entering in cells, 10–11, 30
entering in diagrams, 293
entering in templates, 227–228
filtering, 134–136, 141
finding and replacing in worksheets, 127–129
finding average of, 30

inserting in cells, with AutoComplete, 16
inserting in cells, with fill handle, 16–17, 18
linking between worksheets, 182–184
moving, copying, and pasting, 181, 188, 189
moving within and between workbooks, 157–190
rotating in cells, 88–90
scaling in worksheets, 117–118
selecting within cells, 23
sorting, 132–134, 141
sorting in two columns, 134
sorting more than one column, 134
Database function category: in Excel, 43, 45
Data group, 245
Data series: changing, 245
Data Table button, 252
Date and time functions: writing formulas with, 51–52
Date category: at Format Cells dialog box, 86
DATE function, 51, 60
using, 52
Date serial numbers: calculating, 51, 60
Date & Time button, 51
Date & Time function category: in Excel, 43, 45
Decimal places: number formatting and, 83
Decrease Decimal button, 83, 99, 101
Decrease Font Size button, 75, 100
Decrease Indent button, 101
Defined Names group, 175
Define Name button, 175
Degrees text box: in Format Cells dialog box, 88
Delete button, 74, 99, 100, 230
Delete dialog box, 74
Delete key, 12, 247, 262, 289, 293, 300
Deleting
cells, 74, 99, 100
chart labels, 249
charts, 241, 247, 262
columns, 74, 100
comments, 225–226, 230, 232
diagrams, 293
folder and its contents, 206
folders, 202
rows, 74, 100
shapes in charts, 253
styles, 221
text boxes, 289

workbooks, 199, 202–203, 230
workbooks to Recycle Bin, 202
Dependent worksheets, 183, 189
Design: worksheets, 137
Destination formatting, 188
Destination program, 185, 186, 189
Destination themes, 188
Destination worksheets, 189
Diagrams. *See also* Charts
changing formatting of, 296–297
customizing, 301
data entered in, 293
designs, changing, 294–295
inserting in worksheets, 294
predesigned, 292
sizing, moving, and deleting, 293
Dialog boxes
getting help in, 28
Help buttons in, 31
Discounts/discount amounts: writing IF statements for identification of, 55
Division operator (/): formulas written with, 38, 60
Dollar sign ($)
before column and/or row cell references in formulas, 56, 60
formatting numbers and, 82
Doughnut charts, 239, 262
Down time: writing formulas by pointing, for calculating percentage of, 42
Draft quality option: at Page Setup dialog box with Sheet tab selected, 119
Drawing
shapes, 284, 285–287, 300
text boxes, 289
Drawing Tools Format tab, 253, 284, 289, 298, 301
Drives: different, sending workbooks to, 205
Dynamic links, 182

E

Edit Comment button, 225
Edit Hyperlink dialog box, 277
Editing
cells, 174
comments, 225–226, 230
data in cells, 12–13
data in charts, 242
formulas, 53
hyperlink text, 277, 300
Editing group, 10, 19, 30, 37, 39, 45, 60, 74, 97, 99, 127, 128, 132, 134

formatting, 126–127
formulas inserted in, 19, 37
functions inserted in, 43
headers/footers inserted in, 121–123
hiding in workbooks, 169
hiding/unhiding, 170, 188, 190
hyperlinks created in/to, 275, 276–277
inserting, 164–166, 188
inserting pictures in, 288–289
linking cells between, 183–184
linking data between, 182–184
linking those with 3-D reference, 184–185, 189
managing, 167, 188, 207–210
maximum and minimum values found in, 47–48
moving to another workbook, 208–210, 230
multiple, creating workbooks with, 158
multiple, formatting, 169–170, 188
multiple, printing workbooks with, 171
open, copying selected cells from one to another, 182
page breaks inserted into/removed from, 114, 115–116
page size changes for, 113

pictures inserted in, 300
picture watermarks created in, 291
planning and creating, 137–138, 139
previewing, 79, 99
printing specific areas of, 120–121
printing specific cells in, 125
removing splits from, 172, 188–189
rows deleted and cleared in, 74–75
saving as Web pages, 272
scaling data in, 117–118
shapes inserted in, 284
SmartArt diagrams inserted in, 292, 301
sorting data in, 132–134
source, 183, 189
spelling checking in, 125, 126–127, 139
splitting into windows, 171–174
symbols inserted in, 278, 300
text boxes drawn in, 289, 301
WordArt inserted in, 298
Worksheet tabs
color applied to, 167
selecting, moving, renaming, and changing color of, 167
Wrap Text button, 76, 101

Wrap text option: in Format Cells dialog box, 88

X

x-axis
changing data series in chart and, 245
chart labels for, 249
inserting, 251
.xlsx file extension: workbooks saved as Excel workbooks with, 211
XY (scatter) charts, 239, 262

Y

y-axis
changing data series in chart and, 245
chart labels for, 249
inserting, 252

Z

Zoom In button, 80
Zooming: in on worksheets in Print Preview, 79, 80
Zoom In option, 79
Zoom Out button, 80
Zoom setting: changing, 80
Zoom slider bar, 79, 80, 99